Southern Literary Studies
Fred Hobson, Editor

Peter Taylor

Peter Taylor

A Writer's Life

HUBERT H. McALEXANDER

 Louisiana State University Press   *Baton Rouge*

Designer: Barbara Neely Bourgoyne
Typeface: Minion
Typesetter: Coghill Composition, Inc.
Printer and binder: Thomson-Shore, Inc.

Library of Congress Cataloging-in-Publication Data

McAlexander, Hubert Horton.
      Peter Taylor : a writer's life / Hubert H. McAlexander.
         p.   cm. — (Southern literary studies)
      Includes bibliographical references (p.) and index.
      ISBN 0-8071-2706-X (cloth : alk. paper)
      1. Taylor, Peter Hillsman, 1917–   2. Authors, American—20th century—Biography.   3.
College teachers—United States—Biography.   4. Southern States—Intellectual life—1865–
I. Title.   II. Series.

      PS3539.A9633 Z77   2001
      813′.54—dc21
      [B]   2001029027

for Patricia Jewell McAlexander

Contents

Illustrations

Peter Taylor and Robert Lowell

John Crowe Ransom

Peter Taylor in Key West in the 1970s

Peter Taylor toasting Henderson Hayward

Preface

A central figure in the history of the American short story in the twentieth century, Peter Taylor remained secure enough in his talent, independent enough in spirit, and devoted to his craft in such measure that, despite the lack of a large audience and in the face of changing literary fashions, he persevered in developing the complex, subtle, carefully crafted stories bearing the mark of his distinctive vision. He virtually established what is now called the dysfunctional family as a major subject in American fiction. Exploring the sorts of self-deception to which we are prone, he became master of the false epiphany. All this he achieved in works of fiction with quiet surfaces in which, as John Casey has noted, all the fireworks lie underneath.

For most of his writing career of nearly sixty years, he had to content himself with the respect and admiration of fellow artists, rather than great successes in the marketplace. In 1948, Robert Penn Warren hailed his first collection as the work of "a very gifted young writer." Twenty-one years later, Joyce Carol Oates acclaimed *The Collected Stories of Peter Taylor* as "one of the major books of our literature." Writing in *Harper's* in 1986, Madison Smartt Bell called Peter Taylor "arguably the best American short story writer of all time." Shortly before, Anne Tyler, after ranking Taylor "the undisputed master of the short story form," placed herself among a large body of writers "who have practically memorized all he has produced."

Peter Taylor lived a rich, full life—one that enhanced the lives that he touched. Possessed of an insatiable social appetite, he was warm and winning, a devoted friend. Over his span of seventy-seven years, he formed close bonds in three literary generations. His mentors included Allen Tate, John Crowe Ransom, Robert Penn Warren, and Cleanth Brooks; and both Caroline Gordon and Katherine Anne Porter also became his friends. In his own generation, in addition to his wife, the poet Eleanor Ross Taylor, he sustained deep, lifelong relationships with Robert Lowell, Jean Stafford, and Randall Jarrell. He also knew well Adrienne Rich, Richard Wilbur, Eudora Welty, Elizabeth Bishop, James Dickey, James Merrill, Donald Justice, William Maxwell, and Robert and Sally Fitzgerald. His era was the first in which most writers earned a living in the academic world, and Peter Taylor became a model of the writer-teacher. In his later years, after the premature deaths of many intimates, he would say that his best friends were now his students. Among these were John Casey and the expatriate novelist James Thackara. His circle of younger friends included other writers as well: Ann Beattie, James Alan McPherson, Richard Howard, Alison Lurie, Alan Williamson, Fred Chappell. Peter Taylor was never far from the matrix of literary life in his time.

His generation was perhaps the most self-destructive literary generation in American history. While his friends were having breakdowns, drinking themselves to death, divorcing again and again, walking into the path of oncoming cars, Peter Taylor remained married to the same person for fifty-one years and lived an ostensibly conventional life. It was an amazing balancing act. No one can read Taylor's work without realizing his acute knowledge of the inward dangers to which humankind is subject. He spent a lifetime exploring those dangers in his fiction. But he managed to keep those inner horrors at bay in his own life as he charted the tensions between the demands of the psyche and those of the social order.

He was foremost a writer, and he would admit his great good luck in the literary life. He had gravitated in his youth to important writers who offered instruction and support. He had found a group of peers who stimulated and sustained each other through the years. He had been published early and always had the praise of those who counted most. Finally, after many years, when he most needed it psychologically, he won wider public recognition: the

Gold Medal for the Short Story from the American Academy and Institute of Arts and Letters, the Pulitzer Prize, and the Ritz-Hemingway Prize—the last two awards for a novel, a form he had resisted for years. But, for almost a decade toward the end, he was beset by pain and illness, and only then did he prove the strength of his dedication to his art.

Acknowledgments

For this biography my greatest debt is to Eleanor Ross Taylor, who allowed me access to the Taylor papers in her possession and encouraged me during the long process of research and composition. Characteristically she has respected my readings of various situations, works, and people, even when these opinions differ from her own. Next I wish to thank Barbara Thompson Davis and J. William Broadway, who made available important documents and the tapes of their extensive and invaluable interviews with Peter Taylor.

I am also indebted to the host of people who talked with me about my subject. I have acknowledged all of them in the notes, but a few I must mention here also. Mettie Taylor Dobson freely shared memories of her family and of her brother's childhood, as did Katherine Baird Taylor and Ross Taylor of the last half of their father's life. The living members of The Entity—Bruce and Gertrude Smith Fulton and Thomas E. Mitchell—brought to life for me their Memphis social scene of the 1930s. Their memories were supplemented by those of Felder Heflin; Tom and Sarah Booth White, who also lent me Peter Taylor's letters to them; Virginia Jett McCallum; the late Annie Rose Wallace Buchman; Mary Jane Peeples Ray; and Katherine Farnsworth Cavender.

Much of my understanding of the Kenyon years is due to extended conversations with John Thompson. I wish to thank Mary Jarrell and Elizabeth Hardwick for their cooperation; it was crucial in my attempt to assess the central roles of Robert Lowell and Randall Jarrell in Peter Taylor's life. Many of Peter Taylor's colleagues at various colleges and universities offered important insights and facts, and his students—in particular, Lawrence Reynolds, James Thackara, Stephen Goodwin, Anne Hobson Freeman, Robert Wilson, David Lynn, Daniel O'Neill, and Brian Griffin—provided vivid portraits. From their varied perspectives, the late Robie Macauley, William Alfred, Richard Wilbur, Fred Chappell, Jane Barnes, Richard Howard, Alan Williamson, John Casey, Alison Lurie, Wyatt Prunty, and Mark Trainer proved especially stimulating and helpful sources.

The largest collection of Peter Taylor papers is housed at Vanderbilt University, where the staff was exceptionally accommodating during my years of work there. The same was true at the University of Virginia, which has another large holding. Stuart Wright, whose *Peter Taylor: A Descriptive Bibliography, 1934–1987* has been invaluable, generously opened his private collection to me. I am also grateful for the cooperation of libraries housing the papers of those figures so important in Peter Taylor's life: Harvard University and University of Texas (the papers of Robert Lowell and Elizabeth Hardwick); Yale University (the papers of Robert Penn Warren); Princeton University (the papers of Allen Tate and Caroline Gordon); University of Colorado at Boulder, where I owe particular gratitude to Kris McCusker (the papers of Jean Stafford); the Berg Collection at the New York Public Library (papers of Randall Jarrell)—as well as to libraries at the University of Memphis, Washington University, and the University of Michigan and to the interlibrary loan office at the University of Georgia. Another significant debt I am happy to acknowledge is to the Rare Books and Manuscripts Division of the New York Public Library, which houses both the *New Yorker* Records and the files of Farrar, Straus and Giroux. Judith Jones, Peter Taylor's last editor at Alfred A. Knopf, was as generous and helpful as she had been to him, especially in allowing me access to the Knopf files.

Closer to home I wish to thank two colleagues: Frances Nicol Teague, both for aid in research and for sound advice, and Hugh Ruppersburg for nudging me into action at the beginning of the project and for continued encouragement and backing over the six years. Bradley Edwards served as my research assistant during the most important period of research and then gave intelligent editorial advice in the final stages of the book. My wife Pat never flagged in her support and enthusiasm for the project. As always, she was in addition a wise editor. I am also grateful for the financial assistance of the Department of English at the University of Georgia (under the headship of Anne Williams), as well as of the university's Humanities Center and Senior Faculty Research Grant program. Finally, at LSU Press, I was fortunate to fall into the hands of a particularly sympathetic editor, John Easterly.

Peter Taylor

1

The Taylors ··

"A wedding of wide social interest throughout the state," the Nashville *Tennessean* called the marriage in Washington on January 8, 1908, of Miss Katherine Baird Taylor, daughter of Tennessee Senator Robert Love Taylor, to Matthew Hillsman Taylor, a promising young lawyer of Trenton. Nine years later to the day, the union would produce their fourth child and second son. Named after his father, but always called "Pete," the son would take the name Peter Taylor only years later. In retrospect it seems that the union provided the perfect background for a writer, tying him so closely to the matrix of a culture, the "long green hinterland that is Tennessee," as he spoke of it. A perfect background, of course, if one had the sensibility and the talent to know how to use it.[1]

Both Katherine and Hillsman were great talkers, great storytellers, reciting the stories and legends of Tennessee, usually from the perspective of family. This union of Taylors, one from the eastern mountain region, the other from the western cotton country, encompassed the state and led back to its earliest days. The two Taylor families were no kin, the eastern one of Virginia extraction, and the western one of Carolina origin.

When Peter Taylor would speak of "the Taylors," as when he noted that "the Taylors were always careful to marry above themselves," he was nearly always speaking of his mother's family. They were clearly the more prominent, their history the more fabulous. The first recorded of these Taylors was one Isaac, a lowland Scot who paused in northern Ireland before emigrating to America and settling in the Valley of Virginia about 1740. In the early years of the American Revolution, his son Andrew sold the family farm in Rockbridge County and moved beyond the fringes of civilization to a settlement on the Watauga River in the territory disputed between the colonies of Virginia and North Carolina soon to become Tennessee. Thus the Taylors were present at the very dawn of Tennessee history. It was a son in the third American generation, however, who first gave luster to the name in the region: General Nathaniel Taylor (1771–1816). Sent back to Lexington, Virginia, for his education, there he married a daughter of the Patton family. He returned home to distinguish himself in a land now honeycombed with Taylor half-brothers, uncles, and cousins. In 1796, the first General Assembly of Tennessee appointed Nathaniel Taylor gentleman justice of the new county of Carter. He was subsequently chosen high sheriff, served in both houses of the assembly, and was named brigadier general under Andrew Jackson in the War of 1812. His brigade being stationed at Mobile, General Taylor unfortunately had no part in Jackson's great victory in New Orleans on January 8, 1815, an anniversary celebrated well into the twentieth century as "Jackson Day"—and significant to Peter Taylor as the date of his own birth and of his parents' marriage.[2]

The general's "family and social connections were rapidly increasing and all were ready to back him in any aspiration for preferment," noted his biographer. "Cut off at the age of forty-five, with many years reasonably in expectancy, and with a worthy record already to his credit, one wonders whether, had his been the normal span of life, the first Governor Taylor of Tennessee would have been Nathaniel."[3]

The general's son James Patton Taylor (1794–1833) died even younger, and though he was a lawyer who served as district attorney, his major contribution to the family was his marriage into one of the most distinguished of Tennessee families. In 1816, he married Mary Cocke Carter. Her grandfather, Colonel John Carter, was a leader of the Watauga Association, chairman of the committee that in 1772 drafted the first written laws west of the Allegheny Mountains, and Secretary of the State of Franklin (1784–1789), the ill-fated attempt led by John Sevier and Carter to secede from the Colony of North Carolina. This

John Carter, about whom almost nothing is known before his appearance on the Watauga, is reputed to have been of the family of Robert "King" Carter, the Virginia dynast. John, who left the largest estate west of the mountains at his death in 1781, did give a son the name Landon, one used recurrently in that Virginia dynasty. General Landon Carter (1760–1800), a soldier of the Revolution educated at Liberty Hall in North Carolina, served the State of Franklin as member of the Council, secretary of state, and Speaker of the Senate. In 1796, he was a delegate to the convention that framed the Constitution of the State of Tennessee. At the time of statehood, Carter County was named in his honor, and the county seat, Elizabethton, in honor of his wife, Elizabeth Maclin, member of another distinguished founding family, one of whom was Tennessee's first secretary of state. General and Mrs. Carter lived in the Carter Mansion in Elizabethton (built in 1772 by his father), a plain frontier dwelling on the exterior with fine woodwork in the Virginia manner within. In a strange turn, at the time of his son's marriage into the Carter family, General Nathaniel Taylor built his own mansion near Elizabethton and named it Sabine Hill, apparently after Sabine Hall, the estate of the distinguished Revolutionary figure Landon Carter of Virginia.[4]

All of this early family history Peter Taylor knew as legend, some of it quite hazy. Though he was aware of his descent from General Landon Carter and relished telling that the general often signed himself "Landon Carter of Tennessee," he never knew just how he was descended. That was the stuff of dry genealogy. But beginning with the son of the Taylor-Carter union, the Reverend Nathaniel Greene Taylor (1819–1887), family stories and all the intricate family connections had been transmitted in full detail. This was the visitable past for him.

Nathaniel Greene Taylor, a Princeton graduate of 1840, followed the family pattern of marrying well, choosing for his wife Emmaline Haynes—the daughter of David Haynes, described by a biographer as a "plain, unlettered farmer," who amassed so much wealth that he came to be called "King David." The King's wife was Rhoda Taylor, a close relation of General Nathaniel Taylor. Emmaline Haynes' brother, who bore the name of a valued friend, Landon Carter, was Speaker of the Tennessee Senate, an elector for Breckinridge in the 1860 election, and a Confederate senator from Tennessee. Always in political opposition to Senator Haynes was the Reverend Nathaniel Greene Taylor, first a Presbyterian (the dominant religion of this frontier elite), then a Methodist minister, but also a merchant, lawyer, member of Congress both before and

after the Civil War, and commissioner of Indian affairs under President Andrew Johnson.[5]

This would have been a storied enough past for any family, but it was to
serve often merely as background for the most celebrated of all the family
figures, the best-known scion of this enmeshed group of Taylors, Carters, and
Hayneses, fourth of the nine children of the Reverend Nathaniel Taylor and
Emma Haynes, and Peter Taylor's grandfather—Governor and Senator Robert
Love Taylor of Tennessee."Our Bob," as he was known from the time of his
1878 election to Congress as a Democrat in an old Whig-Republican district,
was poetic, expansive, generous, magnetic. At his death, the *New York Times*
commented that "probably he was the only man who ever held high office
and had uninterrupted political success for no other reason and with no other
excuse than that people loved him."[6] The statement, while oversimplifying his
career and minimizing his accomplishments, obviously captures an essential
truth. The favorite of his family and the pet of his parents, he had no real taste
for the law in which he was trained. As his brothers admitted, he was "totally
unfitted for the practical [and] everyday."[7] In and out of politics all his adult
life, he was also at various times a government pension agent, an editor, and
a star of the lyceum circuit.

Bob Taylor and indeed the entire Taylor family gained national attention
in the 1886 campaign for the Tennessee governorship, in which Bob, as a
Democrat, ran against his older brother Alf, a Republican. The products of a
musical family circle, the brothers took their fiddles on the campaign trail.
They traveled together across the state debating each other, afterward often
sleeping in the same bed. Their father, though he did not actively campaign,
was also on the ballot as candidate of the Prohibition ticket. Called "The War of
the Roses," the race was covered by every important newspaper in the country,
some featuring a lithograph with portraits of the parents, the nine children,
and Senator Landon C. Haynes, as well as sketches of the old homestead and
scenes of the Watauga Valley.[8]

The family had entered American folklore. Bob won the race and served
three non-consecutive terms as governor (Alf finally held the office in the
1920s when he was in his seventies). Despite their political opposition, the two
brothers were close. Bob was much the more worldly, but he always came to
Alf in his times of trouble, whether affairs of the heart or his frequent financial
difficulties. Very attractive to women, Bob was married three times. First, he
married Sally Baird, of a prominent Asheville, North Carolina, family. It was

both a wise marriage and a love match, and she was the mother of his five children. After her death, he made an unwise brief match with the daughter of an Alabama governor, and finally in later middle age he entered into a safe, unromantic union with Miss Mamie Love St. John, member of a family that the Taylors claimed as cousins.[9]

Money was frequently a pressing problem both because of Bob's extreme generosity and his utter lack of pecuniary sense. In Alf's view, Bob's special genius was as an actor, and at Alf's urging, when Bob was almost bankrupt after his second term as governor, he took to the lecture circuit, becoming a phenomenal success with his lecture "The Fiddle and Bow." After Alf's own third term in Congress (from the old Taylor district, which both the Reverend Nathaniel Taylor and Bob had represented), Alf joined Bob on the circuit in 1895. Fiddling, singing, and giving a joint lecture named "Yankee Doodle and Dixie," the brothers took in $40,000 in seven months.[10]

Still to come for Bob was a third term as governor of Tennessee and finally his dream, election to the United States Senate in 1907. In the five years before his death, he came to be known as the most popular man in the Senate. The other senators would watch for his entrance to the chamber and gather to listen to his stories. Though a Democrat, he was a favorite of President William Howard Taft and a member of the president's inner circle. At the senator's death, his body was taken in a special railroad car, first to Nashville, where the body lay in state at the capitol, then in a circling route to Knoxville for burial. Thousands thronged the stations along the way as well as the capitol and the cemetery at Knoxville. The cortege became legendary.[11]

Senator Taylor hovered over Peter Taylor's childhood, a benevolent ghost, and Peter Taylor's last completed work, *In the Tennessee Country*, had its beginnings with that legendary funeral train. Senator Taylor was kept vividly alive by the many stories of his daughter Katherine, Peter Taylor's mother. Petite Kate was even more naturally musical than her father and from an early age entertained family and friends by dancing and singing and playing a variety of instruments, including the piano and the banjo. Having lost her mother early in life, she was reared "up on Chucky" (the Nolichucky River region in East Tennessee) by her Aunt Jenny, Mrs. Alf Taylor; in Greensboro, North Carolina, by Baird relatives; and in her father's household at various places in Tennessee—Johnson City, Knoxville, Chattanooga, and recurrently Nashville—under the two stepmothers. She could play the banjo and perform mountain dances, but she had graduated from one of the most fashionable finishing schools in that part of the South, Belmont College in Nashville. She had a wonderful clear voice, almost that of an actress, and as her son later acknowledged, she was "the best teller of tales I know."[12]

This charming young woman was introduced to her future husband by his Aunt Katty, an intimate of the senator and his last wife. Matthew Hillsman Taylor was already a young man of great promise. Known widely as Red Taylor, star football player first at the University of Tennessee and then at Vanderbilt University, the big, strapping, and bright Hillsman had gone on for a law degree. Afterward he returned to Trenton, the little West Tennessee town of origin, to practice in his father's law firm. At the time of his marriage, at the age of twenty-four, he became the youngest Speaker of the Tennessee House of Representatives in history.[13]

Trenton was a place of a little over two thousand people, county seat of Gibson County, which lay in the center of the West Tennessee cotton country. A point of special pride for Hillsman was the courthouse, "a moorish looking edifice," as Peter Taylor described it, "with four steep-roofed turrets, a clocktower and dome, with high porches and various orders of red and yellow brick." A hideous structure to Peter Taylor, but beautiful to Hillsman because *his* father, Colonel Robert Zachary Taylor, had been the major force behind pulling down the old Georgian courthouse of the 1840s and erecting the moorish pile.[14] The square surrounding the structure was ringed with two-story buildings, one containing the Taylor law office; and running southward for upwards of a mile were the three major streets—High, College, and Church. Trenton was a pleasant, prosperous town, with comfortable, substantial clapboard houses—a few of them antebellum, most Victorian or turn of the century—lining the three long streets, which were shaded by maples and elms.

The first seven years of their marriage the Hillsman Taylors lived far out College Street at the edge of town in his father's house, a huge three-story structure of gables and encircling porches built for Colonel Taylor in the 1880s, every stick of wood in it, the family boasted, being oak. Hillsman's relationship with his father was a complicated one, a mixture of love, respect, and fear. He had brooked Colonel Taylor's wrath when he left the University of Tennessee to go to Vanderbilt, and he had been one of several young men expelled from the Baptist Church, of which R. Z. Taylor was a pillar, for drinking, dancing, and card playing. But he was the most talented of the colonel's three sons, and Hillsman felt a strong obligation to come back to his father's law firm, no matter what his own preferences were. His marriage was a great source of pleasure to his parents; Katherine was like another daughter. She would later say that the years in Trenton were the happiest of her life. For the girl who had moved over and over again and been in the care of various relatives, Trenton meant stability, and it offered all the warmth of a small town and a close family.[15]

These West Tennessee Taylors were Marylanders who had come to the state by way of the Carolinas. A staunch Baptist, despite an old Catholic strain in his mother's family, Kenelm Taylor had emigrated to Tennessee in 1822, and his son Basil Manly Taylor (1811–1886) had later settled in Gibson County. Basil Manly was the father of eleven children. Nearly all had remained near Trenton, so by the early years of the twentieth century, Taylors abounded in Gibson County, of all classes and conditions.[16]

Robert Zachary Taylor was the most distinguished of the eleven children, his biography and photograph occupying a prominent place in the illustrated history of Gibson County published in 1901. A lawyer, he also had farming and business interests and was active in politics. He had enlisted in the Confederate Army when just a boy, serving as a private under Nathan Bedford Forrest. But, a consistent delegate to Confederate reunions, he had eventually been "promoted" there to colonel.[17]

Two of the colonel's siblings also loomed large in the extended family, Annie and Katrina, or Katty. Neither had children. Annie had married Lemuel Tyree, Confederate soldier under Forrest, Princeton graduate, lawyer, county judge, and mayor of Trenton. The Tyrees lived in a big brick house just off the square on High Street, from which Aunt Annie could keep an eye on everything. Tall like many of the Taylors, Annie was also sweet-natured and down to earth, the opposite of Aunt Katty, who was a personage long remembered in Trenton. Her husband, Samuel Beverly Williamson, an intimate of Governor Taylor, had benefited from the governor's patronage. Upon Williamson's death, Aunt Katty moved to Washington to be near the Taylors, taking a small apartment at Stoneleigh Court, where they lived. She maintained this fashionable address for decades, returning to Trenton at the end of the Washington season to live off relatives for several months, replying to all inquiries, "No definite place of abode. Just visiting around." When in Trenton she could be seen daily walking the mile out to the cemetery, where she held conversations with her husband, a manifestation of her dabbling in spiritualism while in Washington. Reared a Taylor Baptist, she had also become there a convert to Catholicism. It was she who had introduced Hillsman to Katherine Taylor.[18]

This was the older generation of the family that Katherine had married into. In addition, living in Trenton were Hillsman's two sisters and two brothers. The young bride was immediately taken into the bosom of the town. She joined her husband's church, the Methodist, where she played the organ. She was in the ladies bridge club of four tables, and the Hillsman Taylors were in a young couples' dinner club. After the first year and a half of marriage, she was also kept busy with her growing family. The first child, Sally Baird, was born in October of 1910; next came Mettie Ivie, named for Hillsman's mother, in the summer of 1912. After the birth in the spring of 1915 of the first son, Robert Love, named for the governor and senator, the family moved from Colonel Taylor's house to a place of their own, one of a pair of Queen Anne cottages on High Street. There was born on January 8, 1917, Matthew Hillsman Taylor, Jr. A sickly baby, as his grandfather "Our Bob" had been, he received much doting attention, not only from his nurse and his family, but from the next-door neighbor Mrs. John Wade. In good-natured mockery of Mrs. Wade's baby talking to the "pete" (i.e., sweet) child, the family began calling the baby "Pete," and the name stuck.[19]

In the early 1980s, when Barbara Thompson asked Peter Taylor about his first memories, he mentioned two. "Standing on the lawn of the house at Trenton and seeing a wild sunset, reds, a red-brick sunset," he said, "a thing which both exhilarated and terrified me, being out there alone. And another early memory—I was alone again, I played alone a lot, although I had [a brother] and sisters around—was of seeing the first airplane that I'd ever seen. A little one. They never landed near Trenton. Seeing that tiny plane up in the sky, knowing a man was in it, made me feel very lonely."[20] This is a revealing statement from a man who as an adult was compulsively social.

Mettie, the sister who mothered him a great deal in his early years, remembers Pete as a shy child, who spent much time with an imaginary playmate, with whom he would have conversations. Peter Taylor's story "Demons" captures some sense of this imaginative childhood world so different from that of adults. Little Pete was also, in Mettie's view, a "big scaredy-cat," the older children having only to point to a dark corner and say menacingly, "What's that?" to elicit his screams. Mettie played upon his fears, and he was so sensitive that her pretense of choking herself always upset him badly.[21]

Such intensity of attachment was even stronger in the case of his mother. At the time that the young man Peter Taylor learned that his wife was pregnant for the first time, he sent to a close friend a series of disconnected memories of his own life. Among them was the vivid recollection of his mother's having to go to a nearby town on some errand and of his running after her Ford sedan halfway to the edge of town crying, "I'll never see you again!" Another incident that he mentioned often was a time that he had fallen off his bicycle and hurt himself but did not cry until he saw his mother watching from a window. "I was a Mama's boy," he admitted to Barbara Thompson. But in his view, his mother "rejected my adoration to some extent. . . . She was very affectionate but she did not pay me any more attention than she did the other children." Then he went on to put the whole situation in decidedly Freudian terms: "If she had not been that way I think she might have ruined my life, because that is often the fate of little boys who adore their mothers. If the mother responds, it's a love affair for life. But my mother wouldn't have it so. She was much too interested in my father. He was the only man in her life. At an early age I had to look around for someone else." The conflicted feelings about his mother, however, were not actually so easily resolved.[22]

Despite such submerged conflicts, Peter Taylor's childhood was generally a happy one, characterized by the sense of security and safety enjoyed by the privileged in an American small town in the early years of the century. Automobiles had come to Trenton about 1910, but buggies, figures on horseback, and wagons drawn by mules still dominated the scene. Children had virtually the run of the town, and Pete had all the toys and pets that he desired. A neighbor recalled Bob and Pete as long-legged young boys who "with their Shetland pony and cowboy paraphernalia kept things in a lively stir."[23]

Shortly after Hillsman Taylor's marriage, however, a shocking incident had occurred that revealed forces beneath the peaceful, privileged social surface. In October of 1908, when Hillsman's father Colonel Taylor was sixty-two, the colonel was kidnapped and barely escaped death. For more than a year, a group of outlaws called the Night Riders had carried on a reign of terror in the extreme western counties along the Tennessee-Kentucky border. The unchecked lawlessness culminated in the kidnapping of Colonel Taylor and his law partner Captain Quentin Rankin from the Walnut Log Hotel in Samburg on the edge of Reelfoot Lake. As the hooded men were setting about to hang Captain Rankin, Colonel Taylor dived into the black waters of the lake and escaped his captors. The governor called out the militia, and a posse was organized that eventually arrested the men responsible and found Colonel Taylor, half-dead after wandering for days in the swampy woods. The Night Rider incident assumed a central place in Taylor annals. A haunting reminder for the grandchildren was Captain Rankin's clothing kept always on the top of their grand-father's wardrobe.[24]

Peter Taylor's grandmother died almost a year before his birth, and Colonel Taylor sold the huge house on the outskirts of Trenton and bought a place on High Street, where he lived with his youngest daughter Bess (now Mrs. Marc Anthony) and her family. Colonel Taylor was an imposing, courtly, masterful figure during the child's first years, suggesting in appearance Robert E. Lee incarnate. Still active in old age, he continued to practice law until the last few months of his life. At his death on June 3, 1922, he was greatly mourned, his funeral being one of the largest in the history of the town. Hillsman Taylor was devastated; young Pete would always remember his tears. But Hillsman was also, as he gradually realized, now free to chart the course of his future.[25]

A political career had long been one of his options. After serving as Speaker of the Tennessee House of Representatives, he was in 1915 elected attorney general of the Thirteenth Judicial District, and in 1921 a meeting of two hun-dred West Tennessee leaders had urged him to become a candidate for gover-nor. Offers from various prestigious Tennessee law firms had also come his way. In the end, he chose the opportunity offered by Rogers Caldwell of Nash-ville, soon to be known as the greatest financier in the South: he would attach himself to Caldwell's enterprises as a corporation lawyer.[26]

In September of 1923, Pete had spent only a few weeks in the first grade before a neighbor and fellow member of the Methodist church reported to the school board that he was under age—an instance of the kind of meddle-someness that also characterizes small towns. So there was less uprooting for the child than there might have been when Hillsman made his decision in 1924 to leave Trenton. He had moved his family three times already within Trenton, but this was the first of the historic treks that the Taylors were to set out upon. They were to take a furnished house near Nashville for the summer, until a permanent place became available in the fall, so the Trenton household was left intact. Still the entourage that left the College Street house on a June morning in 1924 was impressive. First came Hillsman's new Nash touring car, parents in the front seat and the four children taking turns occupying the back seat and the two little jump seats. Following the Nash was Katherine's two-door Ford sedan with two servants, Horace and Maud; a brown and white setter named Joe; a black and brown feist called Black Puppy; a cat named Kitten; and Katherine's canary. As the caravan pulled away from the College Street house, with its gingerbread porches and iron fence, the children begged their mother to take one last look. Through her tears she said, "No, if I looked back I might turn to a pillar of salt." She was still crying as they drove through the courthouse square and across the Forked Deer River on the edge of Trenton. She would always retain fond memories of the years in Trenton, yet as Peter Taylor later wrote, "She was ever forward looking and ever enthusiastic about any new turn life seemed to be taking." The Taylors were about to enter a different sphere, and this leaving behind of the small-town South to engage the larger world would be a crucial factor in shaping the kind of writer that Katherine Taylor's youngest child would become.[27]

2

Nashville and St. Louis ···

Like most of the country in 1924, Nashville was enjoying a boom period. The city's prosperity was directly linked to its emergence as a regional investment center, and the man most responsible was Rogers Caldwell. Leaving his wealthy father's insurance agency in 1917, he had founded Caldwell and Company, a municipal bond house that with bewildering speed acquired real estate, banks, insurance companies, industrial firms, newspapers, and a whole spectrum of other businesses—its assets eventually reaching $233 million.[1]

Six years younger than Hillsman Taylor, Caldwell had admired Red since his football days at Vanderbilt and had vigorously recruited him for Caldwell and Company. The position was of course a plum for the thirty-eight-year-old country lawyer. Hillsman would be moving in the top ranks of the Nashville legal and financial world, and his family in the highest social circles. Caldwell had even arranged that the Taylors live near his estate, Oak Hill, a few miles south of the city down the Franklin Pike in a fashionable country neighborhood. Because the Claiborne place on Hogan Lane, which the Taylors were to rent, would not be available until fall, they were to stay through the summer in a famous Tennessee house, Traveller's Rest, built by John Overton, law partner and business associate of Andrew Jackson. The Taylors were obviously to be taken in by the old Nashville of tradition and history and the new city of money and promise.

The journey from Trenton to Nashville was memorable. Twelve hours after leaving Trenton, the family still had not reached Nashville, a distance of 150 miles. On Nine Mile Hill, nine miles west of the city, the caravan had its ninth flat tire of the day. It was nearly midnight when the Taylors arrived at Colonel Dickinson's darkened house off Franklin Pike, where they were to get the key to Traveller's Rest. Suddenly lights were being turned on, and soon the Dickinsons and their servants, all in their nightclothes, were rushing from the house, insisting that the Taylors come in to be fed and to spend the night. "It was as though we had been travellers in the wilderness a hundred years back and were being welcomed at the isolated cabin of a pioneer family," Peter Taylor wrote sixty years afterward. "What a glorious beginning our welcome to Nashville was."[2]

The next morning the Taylors moved over to Traveller's Rest. Still owned by Overton descendants in the Williams family, the house begun in 1799 had been added to a number of times up through the late nineteenth century. It was a structure of several levels, many rooms and passageways, filled with all sorts of interesting things. Both the house and the rocky but verdant countryside captured the imagination of the young boy. At the end of the summer, the Williamses returned from their mountain house, and the Taylors moved into the Claiborne place on a hilltop two miles away, a story-and-a-half frame structure that the children called the "House of Seven Gables."[3]

"I never became accustomed to the romance of the new terrain," Peter Taylor recalled to his college friend Robie Macauley, "never failed to be excited by the sight of a little spring spurting out of a hillside and pouring down over mauve-tinted rocks to the neat creek bed in the valley." And then he recorded an experience he could never forget:

> My sister and I used to play beside the little creek and on the hillside behind our house, building scores of tiny cities of stones and pieces of broken bricks all connected by roads that crossed and recrossed the stream. Sometimes when my sister would go to the house to fetch some toy or perhaps to the back of the milkhouse to dig up a prize piece of moss for grass in the park of a new city, I would survey all of our work from my favorite limb of the chestnut tree with a seriousness that I never showed even my sister who was nearer to me than anyone in the world. Perched there once . . . , I felt certain that as [my grandfather]

took his last look backward in his ascension to heaven the whole of his beloved
state of Tennessee must have appeared just so to him.

Others, of course unaware of the child's intense secret visions, still remembered even seventy years later not only those roads and parks and cities in the
creek bed, but also the child's imagination and powers of description.[4]

Another quality already marked in the boy was a pervasive historical consciousness. "I don't believe any child was ever more conscious and curious
about his own background than I was," Peter Taylor later told Robert Penn
Warren. "Nashville in my eyes was a great, 'historic' city; and nothing excited
my imagination more than to learn that some building or other had been
'standing' in 1860."[5]

Shortly after the move to the "House of Seven Gables" on Hogan Lane, the
family established the pattern that was to characterize their lives in Nashville.
Hillsman and Katherine had been taken into the horsey set to which the Caldwells belonged. Sally and Mettie, now fourteen and twelve, were enrolled in
the preparatory department of Ward-Belmont College, the institution formed
by the merger of Nashville's two fashionable academies for young ladies,
Ward's Seminary and Belmont College. Bob, now ten, and Pete, seven, were
sent to Robertson Academy, an elementary school founded in 1806 south of
Nashville, now a public school, but one with an endowment. Hillsman and
the girls commuted every day to Nashville, either by car or by the train that
ran alongside Franklin Pike, the Interurban. Like most of the students, Bob
and, after the first year, Pete rode their ponies to school.[6]

Unlike Bob, Pete hated riding the pony, and this became a serious source
of contention between father and son. The West Tennessee Taylors had always
been good riders and fanciers of fine horses. Bob fit the pattern. Hillsman had
even once discovered Bob and Mettie on the tennis court jumping their horses
over the net. But Pete never liked riding. Pete's mount, not actually a pony,
but a "hard-mouthed little horse" ironically named Red, was mean and willful,
often balking. The only way that Pete could be sure that Red would actually
take him all the way to school was to ride with Bob, Red following Bob's horse.
Hillsman required that each boy saddle his own mount every morning. Never
good with his very large hands, Pete was clumsy and slow, and Bob delighted
in saddling up quickly and leaving his younger brother behind. Again and
again, Pete was unable to get Red past the gate of the small estate. During
Hillsman's subsequent lectures to Pete on horsemanship, the boy would just
stare off into space, miserable with the whole situation.[7]

His mother was sympathetic, and the roles of his parents and their relation to their youngest child were fixed in Peter's mind as much by the situation with the horse as by anything in his childhood. Terrified of horses, Katherine never rode. Probably she did say to Pete, "They're stupid beasts. . . . They're not like dogs. They hate us all," the words that Peter Taylor gives to Phillip Carver's mother in *A Summons to Memphis*. But significantly, when Peter Taylor came to write of the incident in this late novel, he revised the past, making it the way he must have wished at the time it could be. The novel has the mother see the boy's dilemma, get into her riding clothes, and ride alongside him the two miles until they reach the lane leading to Robertson Academy. There she leaves him, and he rides alone triumphantly to the schoolhouse. How he must have wished that she could be his savior, an effective foil to the rigidity of his father. But sympathetic as she might often be, she was never able to fill that role, and her son who loved her so deeply could never quite forgive her for it.[8]

The family's time in Nashville was marked by a growing intimacy with the Caldwells. Childless, Rogers Caldwell and his wife doted on the Taylor children. Katherine, who was never completely comfortable in the Nashville horsey set (not only because she feared horses, but because she considered that social group fast), was friendly enough with Margaret Caldwell, a splendid horsewoman, but she developed a deep attachment to Margaret's mother, Mrs. Trousdale, who was included in all social activities. The closest bond, however, was that between Hillsman and the young financier, who spent much time after business hours in each other's company, riding or foxhunting or just in easy, relaxed, far-ranging conversation. The growing friendship added to Caldwell's great confidence in Hillsman's abilities, and soon Red Taylor was put in charge of Cotton States Insurance Company.[9]

In January of 1926, Caldwell and Company purchased for $14 million the Missouri State Life Insurance Company based in St. Louis, an event that had a profound effect on the lives of all the Taylor family. Soon after the acquisition Caldwell determined that Hillsman was the person to oversee his interests in Missouri, so a little over two years after the move from Trenton, the Taylors set out on another of their historic treks. "We left behind not a sheet of paper or a picture or a single stick of Mother's heavy, mid-Victorian furniture," Peter Taylor noted. "Every keepsake in the attic, every old toy any of us children had ever had, every coal scuttle or garden tool in the cellar went with us." Behind the moving vans came, as had now become the custom, two automobiles, a new Packard and a Buick sedan, in which rode the family, the servants, and the pets.[10]

Hillsman may well have known at the time Caldwell's plans for his friend, for within six months after the move to St. Louis, Hillsman was made president of Missouri State Life. From country attorney, to corporation lawyer, to the executive head of an important company in a major American city—his rise had been amazingly swift. The Taylors had moved among the rich and fashionable in Nashville, but Nashville was a provincial place in comparison with St. Louis, which at the turn of the century had already boasted over a hundred millionaires.[11]

In St. Louis, the Taylors were fashionably quartered in Lenox Place, and the children sent to the schools favored by the exclusive West End—Sally and Mettie to Mary Institute, founded by T. S. Eliot's grandfather in 1859 (until after much homesickness and pleading they were allowed to return to Ward-Belmont), and Bob and Pete to Miss Rossman's School.[12] Hillsman and Katherine were an attractive couple, and in addition to Hillsman's importance in the financial world, she was the daughter of a former United States senator. There was every reason for them to be taken into society.

Katherine entered gladly the St. Louis social whirl. Of foremost concern now was the fact that the two Taylor daughters must soon be introduced to society. Though the Taylors possessed no long St. Louis lineage, the issue of family could easily be met. Still, there were rather clear steps leading toward a debut and presentation as a Maid of Honor at the Veiled Prophet's Ball, a St. Louis institution going back to 1878. Though other schools were acceptable avenues, Mary Institute was the preeminent preparatory school for future debutantes. Next came college at Vassar or Bryn Mawr, or much more commonly a year or two at Miss Porter's School in Farmington, Connecticut, Miss Wright's School at Bryn Mawr, Pennsylvania, or Miss Finch's School in New York. Summers were often spent at family cottages at Charlevoix or Harbor Beach, Michigan; Lake George, New York; or North Haven, Maine. And virtually de rigueur was a European tour under the care of certain fashionable chaperones.[13]

The perfect setting for the future debutantes was ensured when in 1929, on the eve of the Great Depression, Missouri State Life took possession of a great St. Louis mansion at 5 Washington Terrace, and Hillsman chose to make it his residence. A private street laid out with a center parkway, Washington Terrace is entered through a clock-tower gatehouse that remains a major city landmark. Built in 1902, No. 5 is considered by architectural historians "the most impressive of the Beaux Arts palaces on any St. Louis street." Rising three stories above a basement, the house had an elaborately detailed interior, the mahogany paneling being especially fine. The third floor contained a ball-room, and the insurance company had gained title to both the house and its furnishings, many of them French and Italian antiques.[14] In Washington Terrace, the family began to live on a scale beyond anything they had ever known.

The Taylors, however, made a point of retaining close Tennessee ties, the most striking evidence being their servants, whom Hillsman always imported from Trenton. Peter Taylor later claimed that at one time in St. Louis, his father had five African Americans from the Tennessee town in his employ. It is clear that for a period Hillsman did have three Trenton servants—the butler B. M. Taylor (named for Hillsman's own grandfather), who attired in a white coat answered the door, served at the table, and cleaned the first floor, and a married couple, Irby and Lucille Rogers, who were chauffeur and cook.[15]

The Taylors also belonged to the Tennessee Society of St. Louis, which every January 8 had a Jackson Day celebration. One of the unforgettable experiences of Peter Taylor's St. Louis years was Great-uncle Alf Taylor's coming to give the Jackson Day address. Governor of Tennessee in the early 1920s when he was in his seventies, this older brother of Peter's maternal grandfather talked of his family's time in Washington after the Civil War when his father was serving in the Andrew Johnson administration as commissioner of Indian af-fairs. The Jackson Day celebration formed the background against which Peter Taylor set his first full-length play, *Tennessee Day in St. Louis,* and some of Uncle Alf's stories he found use for in his last completed work, *In the Tennessee Country.* As a boy listening to Uncle Alf, he felt eerily that he had heard the past speak.[16]

In addition to such reminders of his Tennessee background, there were also frequent trips back to the home state. The Taylors nearly always went to Trenton for holidays, and they made summer visits to the Caldwells at their new mansion, Brentwood Hall, inspired by Andrew Jackson's Hermitage and built on the next hill from the "House of Seven Gables." During these visits Pete would spend some of the time with the Williams children at Traveller's Rest, making it seem in later years that he had lived there longer than he actu-ally had. There were also trips to his mother's beloved East Tennessee. On one of these, his parents took him to see Samuel Cole Williams, the distinguished Tennessee historian living in Johnson City. There in Williams' library,

modeled after Sir Walter Scott's at Abbotsford, the old man presented the child
with a copy of his *The Lost State of Franklin*. Again, the boy had touched the
distant past.[17]

Of equal importance were the long stretches of summer that he spent in
Trenton. Customarily, the girls accompanied their parents on vacations (one
being a trip to California in a private railroad car), while Bob was sent to camp
and Pete left in the care of Aunt Bess in Trenton. Now, more than when he
was a small child living there, he developed his strong sense of the Southern
small town and his family's relation to it.[18]

Tall, raw-boned, often severe, and endowed with a biting wit, Bess was not
a favorite of Katherine's. Pete well remembered the day in 1922 when Bess
had knelt beside his mother's chair begging her forgiveness for working against
Uncle Alf in the governor's race, and his so often soft and yielding mother
saying, "Some things can never be forgiven." Less personally, Katherine could
not understand why a woman would involve herself in politics, and she
watched aghast over the years as Bess became a power in the West Tennessee
Democratic Party. There were in addition other breaches of trust experienced
years before, when the young bride had first come to Trenton. But Bess wor-
shipped her brother Hillsman, and she was fond of her nephew. Peter Taylor
remembered her as the first person to treat him ironically. Strict like Hillsman,
Bess had the boy performing unaccustomed chores like pulling grass from the
brick sidewalk along High Street, and she made equally unaccustomed rules,
like the requirement that he eat his butter beans before he could have any of
the chocolate pie over on the sideboard. The family genealogist, Bess insisted
that the Taylors had originally been Taliaferros—as Peter Taylor later realized,
she wanted no one to think that the family had originally made clothes.[19] While
her husband, Marc Anthony, worked as a salesman in Memphis for her
wealthy brother-in-law, Bess remained in Trenton with her two children, both
older than Pete, and lived in her father's house on High Street. Serving as cook
was Easter Sellers, called Mammy, the strong-willed old black woman who
had nursed Hillsman and his siblings and later Hillsman's own children and
who had run Pete's grandfather's household with an iron hand. Hillsman had
bought Mammy her own house, and she was a familiar figure on the streets
of Trenton driving a wagon filled with buckets of slop that she collected to
feed her pigs. She would talk often with Pete about his father's childhood and
about how things used to be. Her stories, her great age (she said that she had

been "a girl up at the Big House when Freedom came") and her longtime association with the family influenced the boy's sense of continuity.[20]

In the summers, Great-aunt Katty was down from Washington, spending much of the time with her sister Mrs. Tyree, and Pete had opportunity to observe her imperious ways. On First Monday, the big trading day when virtually the whole county came to the courthouse town to buy and sell everything from pocket knives to mules, Aunt Katty was kept busy shooing away the country people who tried to tether their livestock to the iron fence surrounding Aunt Annie's house off the square. Of no importance was the fact that Aunt Annie did not mind their doing it in the least. But the recurrent memory of Trenton summers for Peter Taylor was spending the night out on the second-floor sleeping porch at the High Street house and hearing in the early morning, through his sleep, the sound of the horses coming into town. What a world away from St. Louis that all was.[21]

St. Louis for the boy was not only automobiles and trolley cars, tall office buildings and great mansions, but all the nurturing institutions of the privileged, as well as social glamour, represented most vividly to him by the Veiled Prophet's Ball. The first of the institutions to which he was exposed was Miss Rossman's School. He loved it, and he adored Miss Rossman. Though considered very strict, the spinster with her pince-nez, her clipped, precise speech, and her sensible shoes, responded warmly to the boy. Though she could never understand why he did not excel in mathematics, which was her major interest, she appreciated his talents and was proud when he won the sixth-grade literary prize for an essay on his paternal grandfather Taylor and the Night Riders.[22]

After graduating from Miss Rossman's, Pete was enrolled at Country Day, the leading St. Louis school for boys. Here too he was generally happy, though the school's athletic program became the bane of his existence, especially when in the seventh grade he was forced to play on the basketball team because he was the tallest boy in the class. But he was becoming more outgoing, and a classmate remembers him as getting along well with everyone. Among the closest of his friends were Andy Gunter, who shared Pete's dislike of sports; Andy's younger brother John; Ashley Gray; and Thomas Kirkpatrick. These boys were recruited for the plays that Pete began staging in the third-floor ballroom of the Washington Terrace house. Inspired by Mardi Gras costumes in the Gunter attic, Pete wrote a series of plays about a character whom he named Count Philip de Reservoir. Admission was charged, and all the neighborhood children came to see the performances.[23]

If the sixth-grade essay and the Count de Reservoir plays were early manifestations of his literary bent, then another event in the Washington Terrace
ballroom was equally indicative of another side of his nature, his attraction
to society. Jack Shinkle, a schoolmate whose grandfather had founded one of
the world's largest shoe companies and who was drawn to Pete because he
was so very different from the usual St. Louis midwestern boy, was "staggered"
when at age twelve he received an invitation to a tea dance Pete was hosting.
Having watched as his sisters went off on their rounds of social engagements,
Pete thought the ballroom demanded such an occasion, and finally his mother
let him have his way. Irby, the chauffeur, was a wonderful natural musician,
and though he played the piano by ear, Pete had Lucille turning pages of sheet
music as Irby played. His mother forbade his sisters' going upstairs and mar-
ring the boy's pleasure. But they peeked out the windows to see the little girls
sweep up the walk in their long dresses. Pete's date was Susie Thompson,
whom he had a crush on at the time and for years to follow.[24]

Mettie and Sally said that Pete could talk Katherine into anything. That
may have been so, but Pete felt also a distance between his mother and himself
that he could never bridge. The relationship is perhaps best exemplified by a
story that he told over and over in later life. More than once he heard people
say to his mother, "Oh, he's your favorite." To this she would always reply,
"Well, if he is, it's because I'm his favorite." In addition to such calculated
distancing, in the St. Louis years Katherine was always preoccupied with the
family's social life. More and more Pete turned to the servants, Lucille and
B.M., as the confidants to whom he could pour out his dreams and anxieties.
He was never to forget the roles that they played in his emotional life.[25]

Pete's St. Louis friends saw the Taylor family group in terms that were confirmed by many later intimates. Pete and Bob, who were not close, seemed
almost opposites in temperament, Pete's schoolmates finding Bob assertive
and prone to pontificating. The girls, who of course were several years older,
were both attractive and outgoing. Sally, a honey blonde, seemed a counterpart
of Pete in personality, but it was the dark-haired and blue-eyed Mettie to
whom the younger boy was closer. Katherine, with her sparkling eyes and
ready laugh, charmed all Pete's friends. Hillsman lacked her sense of fun. Mettie and Pete, in fact, thought him totally lacking a real sense of humor, and
would wonder together just why he laughed at the things he did laugh at.
Though Pete's friends found Hillsman perfectly polite, he was obviously not
much interested in them. During this time Hillsman was, indeed, growing

increasingly remote. Because he had not wanted his children to fear him as he had his own father, he had never punished the children himself, and Katherine had had to do what switching was done when the children were little. Still he was strict. He was a formidable man, and he did create scenes. He could never accept the fact that Pete, who was a big boy, would not play football. For several years that was an ongoing controversy. He could reduce his daughters to tears over matters like the lengths of their dresses. And Pete, who was particularly sensitive to seeing his mother upset, greatly resented those times that Hillsman would blow up at her and then storm out of the house.[26]

There were reasons behind Hillsman's behavior that he kept from his family. Things were not going well for the Caldwell empire. Business historians now agree that many of Rogers Caldwell's troubles were due as much to his alliance with the Tennessee political figure Luke Lea as to the 1929 stock market crash. Through Lea's influence and because of Lea's aspirations, Caldwell and Company became embroiled in political controversy and entangled in political corruption. So bitter did feeling grow toward Caldwell that, as his obituary noted, "he was personally blamed for the Great Depression in Tennessee." At first, however, it seemed to many that Caldwell himself was weathering the storm, especially when in May of 1930 Caldwell and Company merged with another giant, BancoKentucky. But throughout 1930, Caldwell was madly scrambling for cash and transferring assets among his various holdings, often unbeknownst to the directors of the affected companies. In 1929, Hillsman was personally indebted to Caldwell and Company for $130,000, and in addition to concern about his own finances, he was deeply worried about Missouri State Life and all of the people depending upon the company. In 1930, he summoned his brother Don from Nashville and put him in charge of the real estate and farm loan division to rearrange payments for farmers so that they would not lose their land.[27]

But Hillsman kept his deep concerns to himself, and the Taylors, like much of St. Louis society, continued to live as though there had been no crash. Sally and Mettie spent the 1929–30 school year at Miss Finch's in New York and, more remarkably considering the times, the following summer they toured Europe under the chaperonage of Mrs. Atwell T. Lincoln. Formerly a Miss Porter from Nashville, Mrs. Lincoln lent just the proper cachet and in her person represented just the right blend of past and present, of Tennessee and St. Louis. On October 9, 1930, Sally and thirty-five other debutantes were presented to society as Maids of Honor to the Queen at the fifty-first Veiled

Prophet's Ball. Preceded by an elaborate parade featuring several bands and nineteen floats illuminated by fifteen thousand electric bulbs, the ball was held in the St. Louis Coliseum before a crowd of seven thousand people. After hours of pageantry, to the strains of the March from *Aida* the ever mysterious Veiled Prophet appeared to select his queen, place upon her brow the crown of seventy-one diamonds, and begin the dancing. Hours later, the evening ended with the queen's supper at the Jefferson Hotel, attended by fifteen hundred. How glamorous this all seemed to the creator of Count de Reservoir, and what tales he would spin about it for years to come.[28]

In the midst of all the revelry of the following debutante season, on November 14, 1930, Caldwell and Company announced its insolvency and went into receivership. In the following two weeks, 120 affected banks in seven states closed, and in April of 1931 Rogers Caldwell was indicted by the commonwealth of Kentucky for fraud in connection with the BancoKentucky merger. During the summer the market price of Missouri State Life stock began to fall, and by autumn a struggle ensued for control of the company.[29]

Despite everything, plans went forward for Mettie's debut, and on October 7, 1931, she was presented at the Veiled Prophet's Ball. All the while, a movement was growing to oust Hillsman from the presidency of the insurance company. Now his only hope was for Rogers Caldwell himself to appear before the board of directors to explain that Hillsman had known nothing of Caldwell's mortgaging Missouri State assets and transferring the funds to other holdings. Caldwell promised that he would come. On a gloomy November day, Pete became aware for the first time that something was wrong. Standing at the top of the stair, he overheard his parents speaking in the hall below, their tones conveying more to the fourteen-year-old boy than the words they uttered.[30]

Despite his promise, Rogers Caldwell betrayed Hillsman. Not only had he secretly mortgaged the company's assets, but he also never came to St. Louis to support his friend. On December 1, Hillsman announced his resignation. Back at home, he forbade that the name Rogers Caldwell be uttered under his roof ever again.[31]

Hillsman's whole life had been one success after another. Now at the age of forty-seven, he was ruined, and though his name was never linked with the financial scandal of Caldwell and Company, he felt that he was dishonored. On the first day of 1932, the Taylors moved from Washington Terrace to an apartment on Waterman Avenue. Shortly afterward, the furnishings of the mansion were sold at public auction, and within a few years the structure was razed, leaving only a great crater where the basement had been.[32]

As deeply as the experience scarred Hillsman Taylor, equally did it mark his younger son. Toward the end of his life Peter Taylor surprised a friend by an apparently random remark justifying a part of his nature: "After all, if I had not been attracted to the beautiful people, I would not have had my subject." That was true; a part of him loved society and was drawn to the rich and fashionable. But another part realized acutely the fragility of any social order and the price one paid for living within such a structure. As with F. Scott Fitzgerald, it was the two sides that made the writer Peter Taylor.[33]

3

Memphis

All through the spring of 1932, Hillsman Taylor pondered his future. He had put out all sorts of feelers, but nothing had materialized. In the summer he and Katherine went down alone to Trenton for a few weeks. Later Katherine was to tell her younger son that there were moments when in his despair Hillsman considered forgetting the larger world where he had cut such a figure and going back home to practice in the old law office. But something in him could not make such a retreat, and finally he was offered a position in a Memphis law firm.[1]

Now came the greatest of the family uprootings. Again there was a caravan; again nothing was left behind. But while the previous journeys had been based on successes and directed toward an even more glorious future, this one was marked by defeat and regret. The Taylors arrived in Memphis in October. The city was a place where Hillsman and Katherine did have ties. Hillsman's oldest sister, Annie, was the wife of a wealthy Memphis businessman, and Katherine had a number of friends there from her Nashville schooldays. It was very important to both Taylors to keep up appearances. Hillsman quickly became a member of the Memphis Country Club, a primary mark of social status, and the Taylors were listed soon afterward in the first city social register. Hillsman had rented a large house with a fashionable address, 79 Morningside Park. A twenties structure, it was entered through a foyer, floored with black and white marble, and dominated by a grand sweeping spiral stair with an iron balustrade. This entry opened onto a long living room, twenty by forty feet, with Palladian windows to the floor. Appearances were indeed being maintained, but there were no spare funds, not even pocket money for wife and children.[2]

Pete entered school over a month late, and it was a bewildering experience. After all the years of private schools, he was sent to the largest public school in the city, Central High. Hillsman was delighted to find that the principal was the man who had been head of his old school at Trenton, but that was little help to the tall, gawky fifteen-year-old amid two thousand strangers. Pete was, however, naturally gregarious, and by Christmas he was making friends. Through the agency of his mother, he was invited to his first dance in Memphis, at the home of Josephine Tully, where he met the young society crowd, which included most of the girls that he would date during high school.[3]

By the end of this, his sophomore year, he had also met Felder Heflin, whom he would always speak of in later years as his oldest friend. Felder's father and Hillsman were business acquaintances, and the couples were social friends at the country club. Felder's earliest memories of the Taylor sons were at the Christmas dances, where "they were wearing tab collars [apparently a St. Louis fashion] and dancing with all the girls as if they'd been in Memphis forever." Felder's outrage at such cheek gradually subsided, and by summer a friendship had begun.[4]

Such a bond was particularly welcomed because, adding to the general disorientation of the fall, on January 8, 1933, Mettie became engaged to her St. Louis sweetheart, Duncan Dobson. Pete was devastated at losing the sister who had been so close. "Well, I guess you won't have time for me anymore," he burst out on hearing the news. So wrenching and primal an emotional experience was it for him that he would draw upon it in creating the teenaged boy in his first play. On April 18, Mettie came down the grand stair to be married in a rather simple home wedding, which the Memphis paper still called "a brilliant affair of late afternoon." One of the close relationships of Pete's life had ended.[5]

There were tensions in the family circle as well. In the late spring, Bob came home to Memphis after graduating from St. Louis Country Day School. He and Hillsman had a "big blow-up" over Bob's choice of colleges, fueled no doubt by both Bob's arrogance over possibilities and his father's money worries. The result was Bob's decision not to go to college, but to get a job and move out of the house. The brothers too were not getting along well. For years the bond between them had been tenuous at best, and Bob's return to Memphis served now to remind Pete of certain of his own inadequacies. Bob had always had a steady girl, and the girls thought him much better looking than Pete. People would remark that Bob resembled Douglas Fairbanks, Jr. In contrast, Pete had overheard a girl say, "Pete's ugly as sin, but he's a good ole boy." The younger brother brooded over the comparison.[6]

In June, the lease on the Morningside house was up, and the Taylors moved again. This time the move was just a few blocks, to 1583 Peabody, a good Memphis street lined with some mansions and many substantial bourgeois structures. It was one of the latter that Hillsman had rented, two stories with basement and attic, a blocky porte cochere at the side, and a two-story building at the back, a garage with servants quarters above—all built of ugly wire-cut burgundy-colored brick. By this time, Katherine had come into possession of mid-nineteenth-century portraits of her grandparents, so large that each filled a space almost from floor to ceiling. Friends remembered with what pride Pete pointed out the paintings; the same friends also remembered how often the family referred to their grand days in St. Louis.[7]

Despite the various disruptions, the fall of 1933 was a better time for Pete. He was no longer a new boy at Central. His friend Felder, one year his senior, was editor of the school paper, the *Warrior,* and he appointed Pete one of the paper's five reporters. The two would walk home from school together, and Felder would stop at Pete's house for long, serious adolescent talks, "solving the problems of the world." Within a month Pete was mentioned in the paper's gossip column for the first time, in this cryptic sentence: "Pete Taylor and David Heur complain that Ann Williford won't pay her debts." At Thanksgiving, his name appeared again, with this telling note: "Pete Taylor's tired of being 'a swell friend' to girls, especially since Peggy Jones has fallen for his brother instead of him." Pete, however, had now met the girl who would figure significantly in his life over the next few years: Virginia Jett, to whom Felder had introduced him.[8]

The Jetts, like many Memphis families in the Great Depression, had fallen on hard times. Before his death, Virginia's father, an important figure in Memphis real estate, had met financial ruin. Having lost their fine house in Hein Park, the Jetts had been forced to move to a smaller place in a run-down neighborhood, where the aristocratic but penniless widow was rearing her four children. All was gone except pride and remnants of social standing. At seventeen, Virginia Jett was a "willowy Katharine Hepburn sort of beauty" with great artistic talent. Pete was immediately smitten, but she was, after all, one of Felder's crushes. That Christmas Eve, Felder and Virginia and Pete and Elizabeth Farnsworth went joyriding in Hillsman's embarrassingly grand green and black Packard limousine with glass partition between driver and passengers. Hillsman took a great deal of kidding about the car. To the remark, "That's a mighty fine car for these hard times," he would simply reply, "What can I do with it? I can't sell it. Might as well keep it." He kept it, but could not always afford to run it, and he rarely gave Pete any money. The four young people looked back to the evening as an hilarious Depression experience. The car ran out of gas, and the four pushed it to a filling station at the corner of Poplar and McLean and scraped together enough change to buy gas and get the group back to their homes.[9]

That fall still another change came in the Taylor family, eventually an important one for Pete. On October 14, 1933, Sally Taylor was married in the Peabody house, with only the immediate families present, to the young attorney Millsaps Fitzhugh. Hillsman had at first opposed the match. Millsaps was a member of a prominent family of great wealth, a successful lawyer, and already well known in the Democratic Party—but he had been through a lurid divorce from a dancer that had been spread over the newspapers, and he had custody of a four-year-old daughter. Sally was the most popular member of the family and the one who could best handle her father. After some bitter confrontations, she prevailed. Sally and Millsaps were both outgoing, worldly, intelligent, and well-read. Sally would play an increasingly important part in her brother's life; it was Millsaps who would soon introduce Pete to Tolstoy; and the child, Louise, came to seem almost like a little sister.[10]

Pete had made the honor roll at the end of his sophomore year, and in the fall he was very much enjoying several of the intellectual spinster teachers at Central—Miss Elizabeth Clinton, his first English teacher there; Miss Vermonta Wilson, whose schoolroom was decorated with a bust of Shakespeare and a framed rendering of his epitaph; and particularly Miss Rebecca Young, the Latin teacher. He was especially sensitive to the role these guardians of culture played in his life and in that of the community. That spring Katharine Cornell came to Memphis in *The Barretts of Wimpole Street,* and the *Warrior* of April 25 featured the first piece identified as by Pete Taylor, billed as an interview with the actress. An ironic treatment of his seeking an autograph

and being asked to hold the dog portraying Flush in the play while Miss Cornell
was signing, it is typical of the often detached and humorous way that he would
present himself all his life. He had by now also begun to dabble in another of
the arts. Always fond of doodling and sketching, Pete began attending the
Saturday School, a free art school run by the Memphis Academy of Art. This
was an interest that he shared not only with Virginia Jett, but also with a friend
Pete had met when he saw the boy sketching by the pool at the country club.
Bruce Fulton was the younger of two sons of a wealthy Memphis cotton man
and his wife, who were members of a very fast Memphis set. A neglected child,
Bruce was a golden boy, blond and terrifically handsome, and a totally free
spirit. He was like a character from a novel.[11]

By the end of his junior year, Pete had created his high school persona. He
had not chosen the route of the popular high school fraternities. He was a bit
aloof and wry. When a *Warrior* columnist asked students their favorite radio
show and "gastronomic weakness," his reply was "Kate Smith and caviar."
His photograph in the senior yearbook with accompanying caption, "Don't
be ludicrous," projects his image as a dandy and a sophisticate. But there was
always his wonderful sense of humor to undercut it all, just as his snobbery,
his desire to be in just the right set, was undercut by his warmth and his interest
in all sorts of people, no matter what their social niche.[12]

In the fall of his senior year, Pete was named assistant editor of the *Warrior*.
That year he consistently made the honor roll and was the star member of the
new writing class begun by Miss Vermonta Wilson. In January he was named
editor of the paper. He contributed regularly a satirical column, "Lord Chat-
terfill'd's Letters to His Son," as well as writing the editorial page. At his graduation in May of 1935, he was awarded the $2,000 scholarship to Columbia
University given each year to a Central High graduate. It surprised Pete when
his father objected to his going to Columbia, but he was sure that Hillsman
would relent, and there were other matters to focus upon. Pete had arranged
for free passage to Europe through a friend, Jimmy Smithwick, whose father
was in the cotton business and who had gone over under the same arrangement
once before on a merchant ship loaded with cotton. Leaving a bon voyage
party the night of May 28, after midnight Pete boarded the Illinois Central's
crack train the *Panama Limited* for the port city.[13]

"When you are hungry, any old wet cracker tastes fairly good," Pete began
his travel diary. "My eyes must have been hungry," he continued, for he had
waked at five o'clock and begun devouring the sights from the window. Jimmy

Smithwick, who had gone down ahead of Pete, met him at the station in New Orleans. When they went to the ship, they were astounded to learn that no longer would the line offer free passage—the boys would have to work their way scrubbing decks. They were thrown into a quandary. "Decided not to go to Europe," Pete wrote. "Then to go. Then not. Then to. Then not etc until eight o'clock. We, at that time, forgot our troubles and went over to the Monteleon Hotel, climbed up the fire escape, and looked in on Huey Long's antics while broadcasting." The next morning they determined to go. The ship sailed at five that afternoon.[14]

The diary provides an interesting glimpse of the young Pete Taylor. It reveals an intelligent, curious, social being, still very much a kid. "We sleep aft with the sailors," he wrote after his first night at sea. "Jimmy and I took bunks one above the other. I work in the sailor's mess room: Jimmy up forward. I was disappointed at first, but later glad because Carl, the head of it, is a swell guy and so are the sailors. I wait on the tables, clean the rooms. Am tired at night." The work got harder, and he was beset by homesickness: "Wish I could quit thinking about home so much. . . . How I should like to see Mother." But he could lose himself in high-minded discussions: "I argued with Jimmy all afternoon over whether or not we should join England politically as well as economically in trying to promote world accord." After more than two weeks, they saw land, the southern coast of Ireland. The ship docked at Liverpool at midnight, June 19.

By the next morning the boys were in London, where the first day, they went to the Victoria and Albert Museum, Natural History and Science Museum, Buckingham Palace, Westminster Abbey, and the Houses of Parliament, capped by a visit to the Craven Hotel Bar, where Pete noted that he had a martini (evidently his first). The pace did not slow much during the next nine days. One morning while Jimmy was transacting some business, Pete went on his own literary tour: "I to Temple Church which was built, in part, in 1185. Many crusaders are buried there. Samuel Johnson & Oliver Goldsmith frequented it. Then I went into Dr. Johnson's house. It is a beautiful 18th century house. There are two rooms on each of the three flours. All of these are paneled. On the fourth floor is Johnson's attic in which he wrote his dictionary. I looked up 'Oats' in an original edition there." The days that followed were equally full.

On the morning of June 28, the boys received a call telling them that the ship was leaving Liverpool the next day. After a series of misadventures, they made the sailing, but only because the ship had been delayed several hours. We "now are on our way to the good old U.S.A.," Pete wrote that night. The trip home was much better than the voyage over. The weather was beautiful, the seas calm, and the moon shining in the night sky. The work was hard, but Pete found time to read H. G. Wells and to sketch a portrait of Carl the head cook, and he loved the evenings on deck talking long hours with the other "work-a-ways" and the crew members. On July 14, the ship passed the Bahama Islands: "We went close enough to see the beautiful palm trees and thatch huts," he noted. "The islands, with the white sand beaches and green foliage, look like the islands you dream about running away to." Five days later, the ship docked in Galveston, and the boys boarded a train for home.

Memphis was sweltering. After a few days of being welcomed back home, Pete broached the subject of Columbia. Hillsman was still opposed, but Katherine and Pete both still thought he would relent. The hot weeks wore on. At the beginning of September, Katherine, who had been buying Pete clothes for college, began packing his wardrobe trunk. For the last week before the intended departure for New York, he and his father did not speak to each other. Then the day came when Pete had to know. Hillsman exploded as he repeated his position. He would send Pete to his old school, Vanderbilt, but he could not afford Columbia and New York, even with the $500-a-year scholarship. To the end of his days, rather perversely, the younger son saw no parallel between this great row and the earlier scene between his father and Bob. In Pete's mind, his father sensed that this was a choice between the artistic life (however presently undefined) and his son's following in his footsteps and preparing to study law. Hillsman's opposition was the culmination of all the times he had opposed Pete's expressing his nature and tried to shape his son in his own image. The son never forgave the father, and, surprisingly, at eighteen this usually affable and certainly callow young man found the strength within himself to stand up to his formidable patriarch. He would not become a lawyer; he would not go to college. The Central High *Warrior* of September 19 reported that the Columbia scholarship given by the school "may not be used, since the holder has not definitely decided what he will do this year."[15]

What was he to do? Millsaps and Sally, who were his supporters, came to his rescue. Through their neighbor Frank Allgren, editor of the *Memphis Commercial Appeal,* they arranged a job at the paper. Pete was primarily an errand boy, but it was a job. It provided him a view of a different kind of life.

But he realized rather quickly that this was not what he wanted, and often he was angry and confused.[16]

By Christmas, Pete had become aware of opportunities right there in Memphis that he should take advantage of. A number of his former classmates were enrolled at Southwestern College, a small, solid, and rather fashionable liberal arts school out near Overton Park. These friends talked frequently about Sam Monk, an odd but enthralling English professor, and the newspapers noted the literary successes of a young lecturer named Allen Tate. Pete decided to enroll as a special student second semester and take a course from each.

Sam Monk was excellent, but very demanding, and Pete received a C in English literature because he did not work hard enough. He was spending all his time on Tate's freshman composition course. Years later, when asked who among the famous writers he had had as teachers was the best, Peter Taylor replied immediately, "Tate. He made literature and ideas seem more important than anything else in the world, and you wanted to put everything aside and follow him."[17]

Tate was thirty-five, a slight man with an enormous head, a protruding forehead, and a courtly manner. Always nattily dressed, he was voluble, dramatic, and magnetic. As a student at Vanderbilt in 1921, studying under John Crowe Ransom and Donald Davidson, he was the first undergraduate to be included in the group of poets who came to be called The Fugitives. Eventually Tate brought into the group the fourth member to gain a wide reputation, an even younger student, Robert Penn Warren. These four would play leading roles in that literary phenomenon called the Southern Renaissance. By the late 1920s, this group within a group was moving beyond poetry and literary criticism into social criticism. The result, to which all four contributed, was *I'll Take My Stand: The South and the Agrarian Tradition by Twelve Southerners* (published in 1930), an attack upon industrial capitalism and a defense of the Southern Agrarian tradition.

Knowing of Tate's Agrarian sympathies, Pete closed his first theme by quoting his grandfather Robert Love Taylor: "Speak not to me of the New South; there is only the Old South, risen, with the prints of the nails in her hands." The paper received an A-plus. Tate later recalled, "I found I could not teach him anything so I asked him to leave the class after about two weeks. The simple truth is that he did not need to know anything I could teach him. He had a perfection of style at the age of 18 that I envied." The compliment apparently was not a fulsome one. Something had happened to Pete Taylor. Tate had inspired him to tap resources that the young boy who kept the travel diary never realized that he possessed. Later commenting on Tate's influence on young writers, Peter Taylor wrote, "He gave all of us what was the most significant thing in the world for us at the time. He inspired us with ideas concerning the importance of becoming a writer. Along with his other great talents, he had a talent for doing just that. One never again doubted what one's calling was."[18]

Tate invited his student to dinner, and for the first time the boy found himself among literary people. Tate had already distinguished himself as a poet, critic, and biographer, and would come to be considered one of the preeminent literary men of his time. His wife, Caroline Gordon, was working furiously to complete her third novel. Caroline was nothing like what Pete had expected a professor's wife to be. "She was plump then and didn't fix herself up," he recalled, "but she was full of laughter and fierce." The Tates had lived among the literati of Greenwich Village in its great days in the twenties; they had known Gertrude Stein's circle in Paris. To both of them, writing was as important as breathing, and they gave of themselves freely to young writers. Pete was intoxicated.[19]

Shortly afterward Tate suggested that Pete leave the composition class and that the two of them read Chaucer together, instead. Peter Taylor later recalled that "we read it while sitting out under the trees on the campus and leered at the coeds who passed by." In the summer the boy took both courses that Tate was teaching, one in modern literature and the other in creative writing. In the first, Tate introduced him to the work of Henry James; in the second, Pete wrote his first two short stories.[20]

Peter Taylor revealed in a late interview that the first novel he read that suggested what he might do in fiction with his own experience was Margaret Ayer Barnes' *Within This Present* (1933). Inspired by the example of Edith Wharton, Barnes' exploration of upper-middle-class life in Chicago "touched on what I had seen." Additionally, her treatment of the place of women in that social order must have resonated for a young man who would make that one of his major themes. But interestingly enough, the stories that he wrote for Tate's class, probably as a result of Tate's Agrarian interests, are set in a small town based upon Trenton.[21]

The first, "The Party," is a strikingly muted piece. It is concerned with a supper party given by a young couple who have remained in the country, on a family farm outside the little courthouse town where they grew up. The guests are a group of old friends who have moved to cities. The story, which abounds with names connected with the Taylor family, shows a good ear for speech, but there are too many undifferentiated characters and little dramatic focus until the last scene. That scene, while not completely successful, displays elements that came to be Taylor hallmarks. Only after the guests have gone, do we discover that the husband has insisted on the party in order to gauge his beautiful wife's satisfaction with the life they are living. Upon her judging their guests "a little shallow . . . like little children," he surprisingly responds, "And you'd like to be that free and that happy?" "Yes, I think I might," she says. But he never receives a reply to his next question, "Will it be easier or harder after tonight?" Has the wind blowing a loose shutter against the house caused her not to hear? She says good night, and when he climbs into bed, she is already asleep. Has the husband projected his own dissatisfaction upon his wife? Is the wife unwilling to let him do that, or is she simply unwilling to let him know her? Will he ever know her or himself?[22]

Taylor is exploring an Agrarian manner of living of the kind advocated by Tate and his associates, but once taking this kind of life as setting or subject, he resists Agrarian influence. Though he might espouse Agrarian ideals in his conversation (and later in letters), in his fiction he was driven not by ideals but by exploring life as he found it. Here he probes the issues of perception, communication, love, and freedom that would engage him throughout his career. In "The Party," he shows himself as independent in resisting Tate's social ideas as in resisting his father's goals.

The other story, "The Lady Is Civilized," is more ambitious and complex. Here Taylor attempts to create mood and to convey a sense of psychic isolation through landscape and weather in a tale of bitterly ironic inversion. The "civilized" adultery committed by Beatrice Gray in order to gain an inheritance is counterpointed by a crime of passion committed by Mrs. Gray's African American maid, Sana—the brutal slaughter and dismembering of her husband. When Ernest Gray, Beatrice's embittered lawyer husband, agrees to defend Sana, Beatrice must pretend that she does not see his defense as a judgment upon his wife: a dramatic statement of his greater sympathy for an act generated by the heat of passion rather than by cold, selfish calculation. It would be years before Taylor would again treat a situation of such violence, but he would return much sooner to characters who refuse to see themselves in the members of another race. While again not a mature work, the story does display some power, and it is a remarkable effort by a nineteen-year-old.[23]

The heady six months at Southwestern were marred only by the fact that the Tates had decided to leave Memphis and teaching at the end of the summer term. But Tate was sending Pete's stories off to Robert Penn Warren at the *Southern Review,* and in an ironic turn of events, he had counseled his student to go to Vanderbilt and study under John Crowe Ransom and Donald Davidson. Hillsman was delighted that his son now wanted to go to his old school, and as for John Ransom, why, Hillsman remembered when Ransom arrived at Vanderbilt wearing knee breeches. In the fall, Pete set out for Nashville "with parental blessings—and parental money." Before he left, at home one day alone, a man compiling the new city directory had rung the bell. When the new volume appeared, included in the household at 1583 Peabody was Hillsman Taylor, Jr., "writer."[24]

4

Vanderbilt and the Return Home ··

Though no one knew at the time, in the fall of 1936 Vanderbilt was nearing the end of its great literary era. It was still the center of the Fugitive-Agrarian group, and though Tate, Warren, and Andrew Lytle had left Nashville, they were drawn back frequently for visits. But only Ransom and Davidson were now in residence and on the faculty. Fifty years after he entered Vanderbilt, Peter Taylor recalled registering at University Hall. He had gone up to an English department table and told Donald Davidson that he came with a recommendation from Allen Tate. Davidson then led him to John Crowe Ransom, who was registering students at another table. Taylor reminisced, "I can hear his voice now as clear as clear. It was *that* important to me, that I should remember it now as clear as ever: 'John, here's a boy Allen has sent us from Memphis.' " "That's how it was in those days," Taylor wrote, "the small, old world we knew then in Tennessee."[1]

Once again, in his own country the young man had found a mentor. Ransom was quite different from his flamboyant old student Allen Tate. In dress and manner he reminded Pete of a Methodist preacher (and he did come from a long line of them). Allen Tate has written of their differences that, as opposed to himself, Ransom had "perfect self-control," his language "always moderate and urbane." Ransom was not the dynamic teacher that Tate was; he in fact prided himself on not being "evangelical." But Taylor responded to his different style and took English courses under him every term. Those courses were a highlight in a complicated year.[2]

Another source of pleasure was Pete's living arrangement. With a quintessential Peter Taylor touch, he had chosen to live not in a dormitory, but to take a room in the home of a Nashville society matron whose husband had just died. Full of wonderful Nashville stories, the charming Nell Falls Handly lived in an immense three-story Second Empire house with Honduras mahogany paneling, marble mantels, ornate mirrors, and a long dining table seating twenty-four. The table must have suggested the best way to support herself in the midst of the Great Depression. She could board (and house) Vanderbilt students. The only trouble was that whenever she got ahead financially, she would treat the boys to extra desserts and special dishes and thus spend all the extra income.[3]

Mrs. Handly had two sons—Joe, about Pete's age, and Avery, four years older. Plump, exuberant, and outrageous, Avery became another of the artists that Pete counted among his friends. All of Nashville knew of Avery's antics. When just a boy, he had screamed to a passer-by who made fun of him as he stood crying on the front porch, "What would you do if you had been beaten with a red-hot poker!" He had already graduated from Vanderbilt, where he fell under the influence of the Agrarians. Among other antics, he had composed an Agrarian opera, "John Ransom's Cow." Avery was now studying art in Nashville, and he would later go to Kansas City for study under Thomas Hart Benton.[4]

When the boy transferring from Southwestern registered at Vanderbilt, he had presented himself as Peter Hillsman Taylor, one of the names that he had used to sign his stories. But he was still "Pete" to Felder Heflin and other Memphis friends, and he was even called "Himmie" by some boys who remembered him from his Nashville childhood. He was seeing some of them frequently now, for in exchange for his father's financial support, he had agreed both to take a pre-law course and to participate in fraternity rush. Hillsman had been a Kappa Alpha, and the Nashville boys were Phi Delta Thetas. When the time for pledging came, a telegram arrived from Memphis: "Don't care which one you choose. Just choose one." To Felder's surprise and relief, Pete joined his bunch, Sigma Alpha Epsilon.[5]

Pete had now to balance fraternity life—the meetings, football weekends, and dates with sorority girls—with a difficult academic schedule, which included math, always his weak subject. He had a few dates with Jane Bagley, a Nashville Tri-Delta, whose sister was a friend of Sally's. "He was lanky and skinny with a bad cross-bite," but "game for anything," she described him, "the most unusual, interesting person." In her view, he was an observer, and she, a doer. "After all," she quipped commenting on her subsequent life, "later I 'did divorces.' " For the Sigma Alpha Epsilon formal, Felder had invited Virginia Jett, so Pete asked his first crush, Susie Thompson of St. Louis, who was now reigning Queen of the Veiled Prophet's Ball. Susie, whom Pete had kept in touch with, was the ultimate trophy date.[6]

Things were not so sparkling for Pete, however, in the Vanderbilt classrooms. His grades for the first term were mediocre. He failed college algebra, and his only A was in the English course under Ransom. But literarily, Vanderbilt *was* exciting. Two brilliant graduate students dominated the student scene. The first was an eccentric Mississippian, George Marion O'Donnell, an Agrarian disciple, short, a chain-smoker with a high voice, and rather like Auden in build and movement. He and his group met at night at Melfi's, a beer joint. In opposition was Randall Jarrell, in the words of John Crowe Ransom, the enfant terrible of Vanderbilt. Since his freshman year at the school, the prodigy had bowled his English professors over with his intellect and talent, dominated their classes, and intimidated the other students. Jarrell, who in contrast to O'Donnell was utterly without vices, spurned Agrarian ideas from a Marxist-Freudian position. To Robert Lowell, in those early days Randall had the "harsh luminosity of Shelley"; he was "unsettlingly brilliant, precocious, knowing, naive, and vexing." He held court outside the student union building, where his would-be disciples met to play touch football. How Pete Taylor must have hated the football, but he went nonetheless. "It was Randall's talk we wanted of course, and his talk on the sidelines and even while the game was in progress was electrifying," he wrote. "It was there that I first heard anyone analyze a Chekhov story. I have never since heard anything to equal it." In addition to the stimulation of Ransom and Jarrell, Allen Tate was living nearby that year and would frequently come to town for a day or so. There was one particularly memorable evening spent at a faculty apartment near the campus when Tate and Jarrell argued over Dante.[7]

By spring, Peter Taylor was having some literary success. The *Southern Review* had rejected the two stories written for Allen Tate's class, the editors finding "The Lady Is Civilized" the more promising of the two, but rejecting it

finally because of its "rather too obvious irony." But a literary magazine starting in Oxford, Mississippi, named *River,* took both stories. The first issue,
March 1937, featured a critical article by George Marion O'Donnell, and
stories by Peter Taylor and a young woman named Eudora Welty. The second
and final issue, that of April 1937, carried the second Taylor story.[8]

The elation of seeing his name in print, once as Peter Taylor and once as
Peter Hillsman Taylor, was dampened by events on the Vanderbilt campus.
Kenyon College in Gambier, Ohio, had made John Crowe Ransom an attractive offer, and the powers at Vanderbilt seemed to be making no serious effort
to keep Ransom from accepting it. A spirited campaign was launched by Ransom supporters, spearheaded by Allen Tate, that included contacting important alumni and those distinguished in the American literary establishment,
as well as writing letters to the Nashville papers. Randall Jarrell led a delegation
of students, which included Pete, to the office of Chancellor James Kirkland
to present him with a petition signed by three hundred of the student body.
But these efforts were to no avail. Shortly before the end of term, Ransom
announced his decision to leave Vanderbilt.[9]

Randall Jarrell and other students were following Ransom to Ohio, but
Hillsman was not receptive to the idea of Pete's doing that. In his view, the
year at Vanderbilt had been a dismal failure. In the spring trimester, Pete made
three F's—in botany, trigonometry, and gym—and was placed on probation.
Hillsman ordered his son home. Peter Taylor later said that failing the math
courses at Vanderbilt convinced his father that his younger son would never
be a lawyer. But Hillsman still could not countenance the idea that his son
would be an artist. Upon returning home, Pete was immediately enrolled again
at Southwestern. He took two English courses, one under Sam Monk, and
made A's in both. If this was an effort to redeem himself in his father's eyes,
it was not successful.[10]

Living at home again, Pete reencountered the old rhythms and the old tensions. One familiar pattern was the frequent visits by kin and connections.
"The Taylors have always visited their relations," noted one of the East Tennessee family with peculiar satisfaction. Of course the West Tennessee family did
too, and there were numerous sojourns by Trenton connections as well. For
Peter Taylor, exposed now so fully to Agrarian ideas, these visitors provided
glimpses of the old culture that people like his parents had left behind to engage
modern life in Southern cities. One oft-told family tale was of a visit that Uncle
Alf Taylor and his wife had paid to St. Louis. Accustomed to getting up at the

crack of dawn, the old couple had paced the porch for hours until Hillsman and Katherine woke and were ready for breakfast. Another memorable figure and representative of an earlier time and way of life was Mrs. Latta Biggs Jetton, or Miss Latta, as she was called in the Southern way, the grand dame of Trenton.[11]

Such visits would have various fictional uses in later years, but the visitors also registered their own impressions of the Hillsman Taylor household. The young bride of Uncle Alf's lawyer son came to Memphis that summer with her husband for the Tennessee Bar convention. She left charmed by Katherine's many stories, and impressed with what a good-looking couple the Hillsman Taylors were, and with the grand-style dinner at the Peabody house, served by a butler in a white coat. The most engaging family member was Sally Taylor Fitzhugh. Petite, pretty, and witty, when told at a bar convention party that it was time to go, she protested, "Oh, but I haven't had any fun yet!" Pete was little in evidence.[12]

Aunt Louise St. John Taylor, the second wife of Katherine's youngest brother, actually stayed in the house on Peabody that summer. A Goucher graduate and a great reader, she was particularly fond of Pete and more inclined to seek him out. He had fixed up the servant's quarters over the garage, and sitting in the yard, she could hear his typewriter clattering away. Hillsman hated the very sound. The boy needed to be making some money or preparing himself to make some. In all things, Hillsman had his views, and he expected others to submit to them. Katherine was sympathetic to her son, but she also tried to please her husband and keep everything running smoothly.[13]

Despite the ongoing conflict with his father, Pete did find compensations in his return to Memphis. One was the opportunity to see more of Virginia Jett. When he was at Southwestern a year earlier, Virginia had chosen him to be her escort for the Cotton Carnival, in which she was a lady-in-waiting. The bond between them, she would later recall, was simply friendship and their shared aspirations as artists. But while at Vanderbilt, Pete had told his friend Tom White that he and Virginia were in love. When Pete returned to Memphis, Virginia was still taking classes at the art academy under George and Henrietta Amiard Oberteuffer, both nationally known artists. She was also working at Lowenstein's Department Store on Main Street and painting children's portraits in order to save enough money to study in New York. Pete made a booklet for her entitled "Ephemeral Doggerel," satirical verses with illustrations. He presented it with an accompanying note: "I want you to know that it took

longer to make this cover and do these drawings than to write these poems."
The two would go on long walks, and he would recite poetry to her, returning
often to the lines

> Remember that day in Versailles,
> You were just as the old monk said of you,
> The child of the wind and the sky,
> With the soul of a butterfly.

Both, however, still continued to date various other people. Pete would often
take out Virginia's friend Elizabeth Farnsworth, another ethereal beauty and
the only Memphis girl to gain the ultimate honor at Vassar, selection for Daisy
Chain. Farnsworth was an old Memphis name, with a kind of glamour
attached to it. The Farnsworth parents were cultivated people who had a lovely
home with a good library and a beautiful walled garden. Pete enjoyed the
ambiance. When Elizabeth was not available, he would sometimes take out
her younger sister, Katherine, who was called Ki. "Liz was the nice one, and
I was the bad one. But Pete and I had more fun," Ki later commented. She
found Pete the "funniest looking fellow." The sides of his face didn't seem to
match, but he had "the most delightful laugh."[14]

When Pete came back from Vanderbilt, he also renewed ties with a group
forming even before he left, whose bonds were firmly fixed that fall at Southwestern. Handsome, outrageous Bruce Fulton, who had attended several high
schools but had graduated from none, entered Southwestern as a special student. His friend Tommy Mitchell, beginning his junior year, was enrolled for
one last term before he transferred to Southern Methodist University in Dallas.
Tommy had introduced Bruce to Gertrude Smith, now finishing her senior
year, and by the summer of 1937, the two were seriously involved. Gertrude
had brought into the group her neighbor and classmate Mimi Bennett, who
had moved to Memphis the year before from the Pacific Northwest. Pete found
them all congenial, attractive, and more fun than anyone else. He dubbed the
five of them "The Entity." They became inseparable.[15]

Most were in the Memphis Country Club, but they looked askance at the
fraternity and sorority scene and Memphis standards of propriety. They were
the Memphis bohemian set. Tommy was almost as handsome as Bruce, but
tall and dark. Like Bruce, he sketched and painted, and would later receive a
fine arts degree from Southern Methodist. Gertrude and Mimi lacked the boys'

Hollywood good looks, but both had plenty of charm and wonderful senses of humor. Mimi possessed a graceful manner and a beautiful speaking voice, and Gertrude, though she hardly acknowledged it to herself, was highly intelligent. In the beginning often no one had a date; the five just went out together. Then Tommy and Pete were both dating Mimi, but Pete lost out when he went to Vanderbilt. Gertrude recorded in her 1936 diary: "The five of us drank a whole pint of Old American bourbon, which we bought for a dollar." Later they could drink more, and they did, especially at the frequent "Gin Picnics" at Riverside Park. Avery Handly stopped over in the late summer of 1937. Pete brought him along, and Avery performed an entire opera, taking all parts including those of several musical instruments. To another picnic Pete invited his two very tall, rather loud, but very popular twin cousins from Trenton, the Haynes girls. Emulating his mother, who had a vast repertoire of poems, Pete was always ready to recite poetry to the group, a favorite being the melodramatic nineteenth-century piece "Lasca," which he claimed that he had written.[16]

While Pete was at Vanderbilt, Bruce's father had married, as his second wife, Dudley Hewett, a talented portrait painter just a few years older than his sons. Since Dudley's studio on the fifth floor of the Messick Building at the corner of Second and Union was used only during the day, Bruce appropriated it for nighttime parties. Much of the revelry went on in the elevator, where the bar was set up, and Bruce invited all sorts of people. Jimmy Smithwick, who had accompanied Pete to Europe, was often on hand, and a rather unusual girl enrolled at Southwestern that year, artistic and independent, a pianist. She went out with a number of boys, and on one occasion a close friend of Pete's slept with her. Peter Taylor would draw on his memories of her many years later when he was writing "The Old Forest."[17]

The Entity also discovered their own special places. One was the Stockyards Cafe on the riverfront, a dive filled with rough, drunken people. But the spot that they eventually made somewhat fashionable was The Jungle at Proctor, Arkansas. Across from the bluffs of Memphis, the flatlands of Arkansas sprawl in the distance, and like many places across the river from cities, West Memphis, Arkansas, and environs offered forbidden pleasures and experiences. The Jungle was a roughly constructed wooden building with a big central dance floor surrounded by alcoves that could be closed off with curtains. No one ever told a parent that the plan for the evening was a trip across the river, but The Entity went frequently enough to become favorites with the proprietors,

Ma and Pa Jungle, as they were dubbed. Pa was a mute, and Ma, short and obese with a black dutch bob, really ran the place. One night during a police raid, Ma hustled The Entity into the ladies' room and locked the door. When the place burned a few years later, Ma and Pa died in the fire, and only then was it learned that they had a daughter, safe at St. Mary's Episcopal School for Girls in Memphis. The situation provided an irony not lost on Peter Taylor.[18]

Felder Heflin very much disapproved of Pete's bohemian period, and Pete, loving the drama, would play up his dual lives as represented by Felder and Bruce. There were other friends who belonged to neither camp. Annie Rose Wallace and Les Buchman, who would marry within a year, were two, and Tom White. Though Pete had not known him well, Tom had been a classmate at Central, one interested in everything that Pete was not—fraternities and sports. Tom lived near the Taylors, and when Pete was first at Southwestern, he had begun riding to school with Tom. Now back at Southwestern, he accompanied Tom to a couple of Sigma Alpha Epsilon meetings, and the two became friends. For Peter Taylor, Tom White would come to be a representative figure, to stand somehow for "my crowd."[19]

These experiences and these figures would resonate in Peter Taylor's later fiction. But at the moment he was having trouble writing. Superstitiously, he felt, at first, that he could compose only on the arm of the porch swing at the Peabody house, where he had written those first stories for Allen Tate's class. But the old location did not work the old magic. In later years, he came to understand his problem. He explained to Barbara Thompson:

> You have to have two things when you begin to write. You have to have some instinct for writing stories—you may write your first stories just from that, entirely—but you also have to have some ability to learn how you did it and how it's done: how to improve upon it.
>
> I so often see young writers who do what I did, which is to write two or three stories that were quite good, and then for several years not be able to write a decent story because I was so self-conscious about it, afraid that I'd make some awful mistake with what I was doing and discovering and learning. That's when I think it is helpful to have an older writer to talk to about your work.

But there was now no older writer around that he could talk to.[20]

So Pete enjoyed The Entity and his other friends and dutifully went to his classes at Southwestern, finishing the term with a lackluster record, even making a B − and a C − in his two English classes. On New Year's Eve, The Entity sneaked away from a debutante party and headed for The Jungle in Mrs. Bennett's big sedan. On the way home, the car left the road and ended up stuck in a muddy field. As Mimi and Gertrude dragged their long black velvet evening dresses through the mud, Pete reeled drunkenly about moaning, "Oh Lord, Lord, please get me out of here." A farmer with mules was found, the car was dislodged and then taken to an all-night filling station to be washed. The Entity was saved; but Pete's personal salvation was not so easily achieved. He began the second semester at Southwestern, but soon concluded that the attempt was useless. He simply wasn't interested. After getting a job with Van Court Realtors, he withdrew from college on February 8, 1938.[21]

In later years, when Peter Taylor was always buying and selling houses, friends would joke that the most valuable experience of his early years was his job with the real estate firm. But it was really rather grim at the time. He was natty and jaunty, but sales were slow. Various friends with little to do would hang out in his office, or come and sit with him for an afternoon when he was stationed at an open house. Gertrude Smith later realized that for all Pete's joi de vivre, he was really "hurting inside." Late one night he called her, very upset, and asked her to walk to meet him. When they met on Tucker midway between their houses, he burst into tears and sobbed, "I think I'm losing my mind."[22]

Just when everything appeared darkest, Pete received an important piece of news. David McDowell, who had spent some of his early years in a Memphis orphanage, was one of the Vanderbilt students who had followed John Crowe Ransom to Kenyon, having his way paid by a football scholarship. On his return to Memphis the following spring, McDowell got in touch with Pete, who invited him to one of the picnics. Pete learned from David that he had not been forgotten and that Ransom, in fact, was working to get scholarships for a few promising literary students. Pete wrote Ransom immediately. On May 2, he got Ransom's reply, expressing his pleasure that Pete "would compete in the Kenyon literary competition" and adding, "I will say off the record that you are a foregone conclusion, but for the sake of the proprieties we must have a file of manuscripts to represent the competition." In the middle of the month, Pete received the notice that among the three "successful contestants" was "Hillsman Taylor, Southwestern and Vanderbilt University." Ransom had asked the Admissions Committee to forward the proper forms for admission. He concluded: "I hope that you will abide closely by their instructions; from this time on you are in their hands till you get here." Within a few weeks, Pete had been accepted, and his father, perhaps in desperation over his son's future, agreed to let him go. Pete wrote to David McDowell: "I read much at night and go *North* this winter."[23]

Buoyed now by his prospects, Pete was able that summer to complete a draft of his first truly accomplished piece of writing, "A Spinster's Tale." In the 1980s, when Barbara Thompson asked him about the influence of Henry James upon him, Peter Taylor immediately named "A Spinster's Tale" as an example. It is the first of his Jamesian tales and one that is particularly revealing of the way he drew inspiration from James. The work lying behind "A Spinster's Tale" is *The Turn of the Screw.* Influenced by the narration of James' governess, so revealing of her neuroses and fantasies, Peter Taylor took one of his mother's tales of her girlhood and transformed it into the story of a young girl who refuses to accept her passional self and the otherness represented by male sexuality and thus becomes a stifled, repressed spinster. He would later say that the voice was suggested by the prim side of his mother's nature. Perfecting that voice must have been his means into the story.[24]

"A Spinster's Tale" is an exemplary Taylor work in its presentation of both the outer and inner worlds of the character. We see the ugly, heavy late Victorian rooms through which the narrator moves, with their stained-glass windows, antimacassars, and beaded lampshades, and we view her father, her older brother, and the drunken old man, Mr. Speed, the sight of whom disturbs her so much. But beneath the physical realm is the presentation of the girl's hidden life of adolescent confusion, fear, and fantasy. The story is filled with Freudian suggestions, the most obvious being the narrator's linking Mr. Speed with runaway horses. Taylor probably first encountered Freud in Tate's class at Southwestern in which he read *The Turn of the Screw.* Vanderbilt must also have provided discussions of Freudian ideas, for Randall Jarrell was already a deeply interested Freudian, and John Crowe Ransom may well have already begun the reading that would later produce his important essay "Freudianism and Literature." Peter Taylor obviously found in Freud an exploration of some of his own interests: the unconscious and most particularly the dream world. The encounter opened a whole new landscape to him.

So grounded is the work in psychological ideas that in 1988 the *Journal of Evolutionary Psychology* published a psychoanalytic "appreciation" of the story. In the same year, another journal featured a piece giving two readings of "A Spinster's Tale," one Freudian, the other Adlerian, to show the "satisfying" ambiguity of the story. It is doubtful that in 1938 Peter Taylor was familiar with Adler. That he did leave room for the Adlerian reading is due to his habit, apparent as early as "The Party" in 1936, of suggesting both sides of an issue, of throwing crosslights upon his material, of refusing to come to a resolution.[25]

The writing of "A Spinster's Tale" was an exciting experience, and when Pete finished, he asked Virginia Jett to draw illustrations for the story. That summer she had done a watercolor portrait of Felder sitting in a canvas chair with his sleeves rolled up, and she was working on a more formal oil portrait of Pete. Shortly before he left for Kenyon, he went over to the Academy of Art and, in her words, "just took it" unfinished. He was happy and confident when he boarded the train for Ohio: he felt that he was going to a place where the literary life would be appreciated. But he could never have known how profoundly Kenyon would mark him.[26]

5

Kenyon ··

When the young Memphian arrived at Kenyon in the fall of 1938, he was twenty-one years old, a published author who had just completed a story that he knew was far better than anything he had ever done. He felt surer of himself, and the basic persona that he would henceforth present to the world had coalesced. In the first place, he would now be known as Peter Taylor; he had shed both the name he was christened with and the nickname given him shortly after birth. A classmate recalled his first glimpse of Peter Taylor of Memphis, a young man wearing a snap-brim fedora and looking decidedly more sophisticated than the usual undergraduate. The next day, the young man could be seen walking across the campus with a copy of the *Southern Review* tucked conspicuously under his arm. In accompaniment with this literary image was his social one. Peter was like a great comic actor, the same friend commented, playing the role of the aristocratic Southern dandy, like the English artist-dandy, a kind of public act that he could not refrain from then puncturing, such was his sense of humor and irony. He was still, as a Memphis friend had described him, the "world's youngest middle-aged man." But his prudery and his inhibitions were also the subject of self-parody.[1]

Overriding all, Peter Taylor's basic warmth and good spirits were disarming. He drew people to him. To remove the literary students from the usual undergraduate fraternity scene, John Crowe Ransom had arranged that they all live in Douglass House, a ramshackle Carpenter's Gothic residence across from the post office and next door to one of the local cafes. The place housed eleven, including faculty member Randall Jarrell, assigned there as a kind of housemother. The friendships formed in Douglass House would be among the most important of Peter Taylor's life.[2]

Foremost was his bond with the large, scruffy, myopic, yet somehow handsome Bostonian whom he had met once briefly after one of Ransom's classes at Vanderbilt. Robert Traill Spence Lowell had insinuated himself into the inmost Fugitive-Agrarian circles, placing himself in intimate relation to both Tate and Ransom. After Lowell's spending a year and a half at Harvard, the Boston psychiatrist Merrill Moore, himself a Fugitive poet, had suggested that this problem son go south to study under Moore's old mentors and friends. With characteristic doggedness and intensity, Lowell had pitched a pup tent on the front lawn of Benfolly, the Tate's country house, and camped there for three months. At summer's end he had followed a new master, John Crowe Ransom, to Kenyon. Entering Kenyon a year before Peter, Lowell had first roomed with Randall Jarrell in the Ransoms' faculty dwelling until Mrs. Ransom could abide no more students in the house. Lowell and Taylor took to each other immediately and decided to share a large room behind the dormers of Douglass House.[3]

In the view of one of the Douglass House group, a Massachusetts Lowell and a Tennessee Taylor felt an immediate connection. But the bond between the two was based on a great deal more than a sense of class. In the first place, obviously each had heard about the literary promise of the other before that first day at Douglass House—and from those who counted most, their revered mentors. Lowell, whose childhood obsession had been Napoleon, had decided in prep school that he would be a great poet and then imperiously chosen the fields in which his closest friends should make their marks. In Peter Taylor he found not only someone whose dedication to art and to distinction was as strong as his own, but also someone who was just as much his own person.[4]

On the face of things, the two could not have been more unlike. Lowell had been given the name Cal at St. Mark's School, because of his affinity with the creature Caliban, though he had transmuted the origin to a more exalted source in his view, the depraved despot Caligula. Cal was dirty and unkempt, intellectual, intense, and overbearing, a big, loutish figure allowed to play tackle on the football team because of his sheer brute force. The non-athletic Peter, with the streak of the dandy, was engaging rather than assertive, and though having deep literary interests, he lacked Cal's consuming intellectual drive. Still, the friendship sustained the two until Cal's death almost forty years later.

Elizabeth Hardwick has said that Cal loved Peter more than he did any other man. They became not only the best of companions but something like ideal brothers. Peter remarked that he and Cal never had an argument after college and that the ones in college were always over trivial things. One telling example he offered occurred after Peter had petitioned Kenyon's president that he be excused from competitive athletic play because he disapproved of it on principle and the president had granted him the concession of walking around the playing fields for exercise. Cal insisted upon accompanying him, and then tried to dictate the pace. There were also arguments over the time for bed. Often Cal read to Peter much later into the night than his sleepy roommate wanted, and there was recurrent controversy about just when the lights should be turned out. Once when *Peter* refused to observe curfew, "Cal stood over him like a grizzly and with one yank ripped the wires out of the lamp while sparks shot into the darkness." But Peter put up with Cal's so often outrageous behavior because he understood his intense, manic aspirations and also saw another side: his roommate's shyness and difficulty at expressing affection except through teasing. As a result, Peter became a character named "Sub" in the private mythology of bears that Cal compulsively recited, often to the exasperation of friends. Cal of course took the major mythic role, "Arms of the Law," a half-man, half-bear whose endless speeches were delivered in "a funny singsong whine."[5]

"We were regarded by the rest of the community as being just eggheads and longhairs," Peter told Lowell's British biographer Ian Hamilton. "One time, there was a tradition at Kenyon that on Sunday everyone stayed on in the great hall after lunch and sang songs—the college songs of which Kenyon had a great many. But Cal and I got up to leave and as we went out the whole student body booed." But the two had better things to do, and Peter Taylor has left a splendid picture of these occupations: "We walked the country roads for miles in every direction, talking every step of the way about ourselves or about our writing, or if we exhausted those two dearer subjects, we talked about whatever we were reading at the time. We read W. H. Auden and Yvor Winters and Wyndham Lewis and Joyce and Christopher Dawson. We read *The Wings of the Dove* (aloud!) and *The Cosmological Eye* and *The Last Puritan* and *In Dreams Begin Responsibilities.*" No matter what Cal's antics, no matter what the internecine sophomoric arguments, here is encapsulated the bond. As Ian Hamilton has observed, "The two of them were allies in a huge, world-altering adventure."[6]

Much of the essence of the Kenyon experience is captured in Taylor's story "1939" (written in 1955), based on the Thanksgiving trip to New York and Boston made by the roommates actually during their holiday in 1938. The two, so talented but still so green, determined to strike out for the East in an old car abandoned by a Kenyon visitor, ostensibly to confront the larger world—but primarily to see the two young women on whom they had centered their dreams. For Cal, it was Jean Stafford, whom he had met at the Colorado Writers' Conference immediately before he entered Kenyon. For Peter, it was Virginia Jett, who was then taking classes at New York's National Academy of Art. The trip was a disaster. After driving through the night, Cal and Peter appeared at Virginia Jett's door unshaven and disheveled. Virginia had decided in New York that she didn't want to be an artist, that she wanted stability, marriage, and a family. Peter ever afterward linked this decision with her coolness toward him. Jean, who had thrown herself into a bohemian role, was equally unreceptive to Cal. After having left New York for a confused visit to Cal's family in Boston, the two young men were put on a train back to Kenyon by the Lowells. During the long ride, the two roommates, each resentful of the other for seeing his shame and each resisting seeing himself in his deluded and rejected friend, merely glowered at each other. The cathartic culmination of all the resentment was a prolonged shoving match in the club car, finally brought to a close by the conductor's threat to throw both off the train.[7]

Looking back almost twenty years later, Peter Taylor could understand the significance of the trip, what it showed about two young men, gifted but not yet ready to meet successfully the larger world. And he could make the experience into a sort of universal story of those on the threshold of adulthood. But he would have been fascinated to know about the machinations of some of those merely peripherally involved in the action.

In a letter to his mother in the fall of 1938, Robert Lowell had mentioned casually that he "might possibly come to Boston Thanksgiving with a Southern friend of mine named Taylor. His people have been Tennessee governors and he is a prose writer of great talent and accomplishment." Charlotte Lowell, always a controlling and meddling presence, went into action and sought the guidance of Cal's psychiatrist, Merrill Moore. On Friday, November 25, she left a message at Moore's office describing Cal's friend as "very aristocratic, a kind of hot-headed Southerner." Soon mother and doctor had launched an investigation of the Memphis boy. On December 2, Moore wrote Mrs. Lowell: "I will do all I can to find out about Peter Taylor," then adding a Tennessee touch—"It is just remotely possible that he is kin to me." He continued: "You certainly are observant. I have the greatest respect for your observations. Thank you for the notes. They are really helpful. I am awfully glad you got to see them. The best thing to do is to be as nice as possible and feed them well." Letters and phone calls followed between Boston and Tennessee. Then Peter's thank-you note arrived, which apologized for his losing the keys to the old car that the boys had left with the Lowells. Charlotte forwarded it immediately to Merrill Moore. His reply is classic: "Thank you for the note from Peter Taylor. He certainly sounds neurotic. . . . If you will look in the book by Freud 'Introduction to Psychoanalysis' the first chapter is about slips and little things. Little losses are slips. There is some unconscious reason for him losing his keys and gloves. For some reason he either wants to get rid of them or wants to come back."[8]

Peter Taylor ends "1939" as he said the experience did in fact end. The two boys, who had left so fiercely conscious of their independence and their difference even from the Douglass House group, return to find that their housemates have invaded the dormered room to cook, eat, and swap stories. The fictional boys return to discover community. The real young men also found it in Douglass House. The group there was a remarkable one for any college residence at any time. The two other men who remained closest to both Cal and Peter in later life were Robie Macauley and Jack Thompson. Both were from Michigan, and both were holders, along with Peter, of the literary scholarships. Robie would later make a name as both a novelist and editor, and Jack, as a college professor, poet, and critic. David McDowell, a Tennessean first inspired to literary endeavor by Father Flye at St. Andrew's School and Flye's protégé James Agee, had been a student of Ransom's at Vanderbilt. Editor of the literary magazine and quarterback on the football team, McDowell was the only campus leader at Douglass House. He would become an important New York publisher. The most exotic figure was John Nerber, who had already published in *Poetry,* and who could imitate Auden's verse and "invent Metaphysical poems of astonishing ingenuity." Tall, blond, and very handsome, he wore "strange, poetic clothing," and, as Jack Thompson quipped, "You couldn't get a straight story out of him about anything." Nerber never graduated, drifted to New York, published a well-received book of poetry, and died an early death.[9]

Added to this mix of undergraduates was Randall Jarrell, who was serving that year as instructor of English and director of tennis. If any one of them were sui generis, it was Randall. Lowell would sometimes speak of him as "Childe Randall." Kenyon president Gordon Chalmers was shocked on a skiing trip with Jarrell, when flying down the slopes Randall had shouted joyfully, "I feel like an angel!" Accompanying such outbursts of naive ebullience were instances of almost constant intellectual arrogance and the most merciless criticism. Most in Douglass House kept their distance. "Jarrell treated everybody pretty badly," Peter Taylor told Ian Hamilton. "Cal and I were the only ones who stuck by him through thick and thin. We would take his insults because—and I think Cal taught me something here—Cal was *determined to learn what he could from Randall.* From the very beginning, he wouldn't reject him the way other people did." According to Lowell biographer Paul Mariani, "Jarrell was the first person of his own generation Cal genuinely held in awe." Peter, who took Jarrell's American literature course held at eight o'clock on the third floor of Ascension Hall, would join the other students hanging out the windows to see their instructor sprinting down the Middle Path and eating his breakfast as he ran. For Peter, the best sessions were those for which Randall didn't make the bell, and all of the class stampeded out except a devoted half dozen.[10]

Other faculty members who were an influence upon the men of Douglass House and a part of their later Kenyon mythology were Philip Blair Rice and Frederick Santee. Phil Rice, who taught philosophy and was Ransom's second in command at the newly begun *Kenyon Review,* had worked on the Paris *Herald Tribune* and had important New York connections. Because of his knowledge of modern painting, European literature, and avant garde writers, he provided a significant complement to Ransom. Frederick Santee, classics professor, was a strange man with a strange history. A prodigy, he had graduated from Harvard in his teens and received a medical degree from Johns Hopkins, before getting graduate training in classics. Brilliant and weird, he was in the view of many sinister. According to Ransom's daughter, the great Kenyon raconteur Helen Ransom Forman, who believes that Santee was, among other things, a foot fetishist, he had once worked as a door-to-door salesman of silk stockings. Often the classes of these men were made up only of Douglass House intellectuals, a group of four in a Rice philosophy class, or just two in Santee's course in Dante. So intimate did the boys become that they were constantly at the Rice and Santee houses, where they felt free just to wander in and pour themselves a drink.[11]

They would never have taken such liberty with John Crowe Ransom. Kind and generous, he was nonetheless naturally reserved and rather distant. He was the reason they had come to Kenyon, and as Peter Taylor has written, they respected, they adored him: "I suppose it really was a sort of idealized father-sons relationship. He was the father we had not quarrelled with, the father who was not a lawyer or a businessman, and was the man we wished to become. We would no more have addressed him as 'John' than any one of us would have addressed his own father by his Christian name. Yet behind his back, when we were in high spirits, we often referred to him lovingly as 'Pappy.'" The affection, Peter knew, was returned: "I am absolutely certain that he had a parental love for all of us. But I am just as certain that he loved Lowell most of all. When he went for his afternoon walk, he would often stop by Douglass House, stick his head inside the front door and call up the stairway: 'Lowell! Lowell!' Presently, with the hot flames of jealousy blazing up inside us, we would hear Lowell's 'big, ugly feet' on the steps, going down to join 'Pappy' on his walk." What Ransom had to give all of them was not the offering of an inspired or inspiring teacher. "He had a sort of rumpled, unprepared, absent-minded air," Robie Macauley recalled. He would take ten matches to light his pipe; he would then read a text and begin a low-key, apparently random response to it. Four weeks into one term, Robie was upset when a tennis player sitting next to him asked, "Hey, what book are we reading anyway?" Many others in the classes were equally disaffected, but for the best students, Peter insisted, Ransom was wonderful. "Somehow one left him with something inside us moving toward articulation, logic, directness and complexity," Robert Lowell would write later in tribute. And for Peter, as important as anything else was the fact that what he talked about was only the greatest literature, and that was the standard by which you were to judge your own work.[12]

Ransom had little interest in fiction. Once when Peter submitted a story that contained a poem, Ransom gave him an A for the poem, but only a B for the story. The serious students all left a Ransom class with a thorough grasp of New Critical theory: the study of the text in isolation, texture and structure, tenor and vehicle, the seven types of ambiguity. Though Peter would rebel against the constant emphasis upon poetry and against being surrounded by student poets, still he was driven to writing poetry to gain recognition. Years later he would acknowledge that Ransom's teaching him so much about the compression of poetry was what led him to be a short story writer rather than a novelist.[13]

Almost as important as their teachers for the young men was the presence of the *Kenyon Review,* the first issue of which appeared in 1939. Not only was it tangible evidence of the literary discrimination of Ransom and Phil Rice, but it also brought to Kenyon distinguished literary people like Robert Frost, Allen Tate, and Lionel Trilling. Among the highest aspirations of Douglass House was the wish to be published there. In the meantime, the undergraduate literary magazine, *Hika,* was virtually a house organ. Edited for Peter's two years at Kenyon first by David McDowell, and then by Robie, the pages were filled with poetry, fiction, and reviews written at Douglass House, supplemented by the work of known writers who had responded to the entreaties of Douglass House—Ezra Pound, William Carlos Williams, W. H. Auden—or those writers with some personal connection, like George Marion O'Donnell, Merrill Moore, or Cal's teacher at St. Mark's Richard Eberhart.

It is in the pages of *Hika* that one watches Peter Taylor's artistic development at Kenyon.[14] The first issue of the 1938–39 school year included "The Lady Is Civilized," published earlier in *River,* and a review of David Cornel DeJong's *Old Haven,* which Peter published simultaneously in the Memphis *Commercial Appeal.* The next issue contained what one must call merely an abortive Gibson County sketch, significant only for reflecting one of the later recurrent Taylor themes, the leaving behind of the rural past. In February of 1939, he contributed a review of Allen Tate's *The Fathers,* a piece he would point to frequently over the years as the last review he wrote. Like competitive athletic play, reviewing was an activity, he concluded, for which he was not suited. That same number also featured his first published poem, a vaguely Eliotic work beginning

> The surly serving class
> Lift up their trays and eyes
> And take their tips with tighter lips
> Than threaded bolts could screw.

Neither this nor any of the other half-dozen poems that Peter Taylor had in *Hika* is actually as interesting to later readers as an unpublished poem, dated simply 1939, that he wrote in an A. E. Housman vein satirizing the classically saturated verse of his roommate and the shared preoccupations of the two:

A DIDACTIC POEM
    for R.T.S.L.
    With the Proper Accoutrements

Mine is a mean heritage; nay, infamous.
Midas, my grandfather was called. His one wish
Was too strong and his pursuit too strenuous
For getting wise and he died rich and famous.

My great-grandfather, yclept Tithonus—
Even I remember his wrinkled flesh—
Lived a hundred and twenty years with us
Always doctoring to be old and foolish.

Oh, my own father was wiser than they.
Mithridates was his kingly name,
And he died contemning all the foolish tribe
Of zealots, died with all wisdom we say
Except to have known torturous craving for fame,
Madness from love, and disappointment's gibe.[15]

Peter's poetic persistence, however, was finally rewarded by the *Kenyon Review*'s accepting his poem "The Furnishings of a House," the first published piece for which he was paid:

The incommensurate odds and ends arrange
A riotous paisley table by my lounge
And are the most of grace that I can show
To you, critical caller at my infare,
Stiff in my ladder-back, rush-bottom chair.

Those niceties, untabulated bits
One browses out, happens on, or inherits,
Are there in their humorous contiguity—
Sweet alabaster birds, three monkeys in brass,
A repoussé goblet, a gavel cut of glass.

My house though comprehensive is unready;
And should I show what yet may be a study,
A place to breakfast, a bath, we'd have to face
The toothless shelves, the misfit window-shades,
The unappointed pictures, the scattered blades.[16]

In his second semester at Kenyon, Peter Taylor's fiction reflects his experiments in technique. "Memorable Evening," the story appearing in the March 1939 issue of *Hika,* contains his strangest opening:

> When Hubert Lindsey would come upon the division between the personal and the modern, there was an emptiness in his stomach. He would stand up in whatever the white-walled picture shaded drawing room might be and walk shakily between the slippers to a door. He found that the doors became smaller each night as his Negro mammy had done each year until she was now the reasonless little body two feet shorter than he, shut up in the little cabin behind the old house. To destroy the comparison there was only the insulting fact of the truth that he was no longer dwarfing the old marks on the inhumanely unpainted nursery door; and yet the doorways became more hatefully dimensional each night.

The paragraph introduces a short story rendered through a kind of high modernist impressionism. The scene is a dinner party "on the twenty-seventh of the Christmas month," to which are invited both the central figure and the young woman who has rejected him. Through dense prose passages, at times suggestive of late Henry James, at others of Faulkner, we experience the party by means of bits of random conversation, ranging from Tennessee politics, to Parisian experiences, to Harvard suicides—juxtaposed with Hubert's hidden agony and sense of desolation:

> That his own was one of these voices, that he, like the others had another voice, that he like the others had a thousand voices that spoke from no common stomach somehow deprived him of consolation for the loss of a woman with whom he had too hastily filled what might be too simply called his private life. It wasn't that his other voices spoke different languages, but it was that each voice had specialized its vocabulary to the point that it could utter none but its own technical words.

Finally, Hubert leaves the party to seek out Mammy Judie's cabin, where the shrunken old woman, though distracted by her great age and her own pain, recognizes the man's grief and links it with his agony eight years before, after the death of his mother. The story ends with his terror at his failure to sustain feeling.

Peter Taylor's final prose piece of the school year is driven by the same obsession with lost love, centered here upon the recurrent figure of an artist named Caroline. His most self-indulgent effort in fiction, "Mimsy Were the Borogoves" (the title taken from Lewis Carroll's "Jabberwocky"), he would confide, was one of his dreams written down almost precisely as the dream occurred. This venture into surrealism, filled with private symbolism, is incoherent without being particularly interesting. Only years later would Peter Taylor find effective ways to dramatize his interest in the power of the unconscious.[17]

At the end of his first year at Kenyon, Peter returned to Memphis intent on winning Virginia back and occupied with new plans. Robie Macauley's father, a prosperous Grand Rapids businessman, owned a newspaper in Hudsonville, Michigan, and Robie had determined to publish on its press a collection of Peter's stories. Peter had ridden from Kenyon to Memphis with Phil and Kitty Rice, who were then entertained by his parents. The Taylors had moved again, this time to a comfortable Tudor duplex on Stonewall, but some things had not changed. After a long discussion of the *Kenyon Review* with Rice, Hillsman Taylor finally asked him "why in the Devil he had published [his son's] poem."[18]

"I'm hard at work on the stories and am not going to summer school," Peter wrote Robie in late June. "What do you think of giving each story a date instead of a title—1886 and 1900 and 1939?" In July, Peter went to visit the Tates at Monteagle, Tennessee, an old, run-down resort community on the Cumberland plateau. After a teaching stint at Woman's College of North Carolina, at Greensboro, they were going in the fall to Princeton. In the meantime, they had rented a large house called Westwood (renamed by them Wormwood), across the way from the house of Andrew Lytle and his wife. It was Peter's first visit as an adult to a place that would loom large in his life and in his work.[19]

For the first time, he told Robie, Caroline Gordon showed enthusiasm for his work, probably on the basis of "The Life Before," a delicate Jamesian piece about a middle-aged, rather literary couple living at the Maxwell House in Nashville. According to Peter, she "put the word out on the mountain," and as a result he had several interesting encounters, one with "one of the most beautiful girls I've ever seen." Robert Daniel, a young Yale Ph.D. and the grandson of the bishop of Tennessee, also drove the six miles from Sewanee to see him and show him a manuscript. Back in Memphis, the foursome of Peter, Felder, Virginia, and Elizabeth Farnsworth were having dinner together or going to see operettas at the open-air theater in Overton Park. And he was revising the Hubert Lindsey story with a different point of view and "up to my neck in fiction again and I thank God for it."[20]

As the summer drew to a close, Peter realized that he wouldn't have the "new story outlined in my mind" ready before school started. He had been ill and reading the short stories of Balzac and Maupassant and the poetry of Marianne Moore and Matthew Arnold. There were other distractions and milestones. Annie Rose Wallace and Leslie Buchman had been married shortly before he returned from Kenyon, and Bruce Fulton and Gertrude Smith were married on August 26. These first marriages among his circle must have been bittersweet occasions for a young man who was feeling rejected, though a picture taken at the latter wedding shows him with Tommy and Mimi, drink and cigarette in hand, looking happily like a character from a Noël Coward play.[21]

Back amid the spires and turrets of Kenyon College, the Douglass House group were reunited, to compare the summer's experiences and to recite again the stories of the year past. A favorite was Peter's behavior at the Kenyon formal. Haughtily insisting that proper attire for a ball was not black tie, but white tie, he appeared at the dance resplendent in white tie and tails, but with Mexican huaraches on his feet. His date had been Susie Thompson, a girl who would dazzle the other boys and a reminder of the great days in St. Louis. Cal had tried to move in on him, and at one point the boys, each of whom thought he was holding Susie's hand, discovered instead that they were holding hands with each other behind Susie's back. But Cal was far too serious over Jean Stafford now to compete with Peter over another girl. During the Christmas holiday of 1938, Cal had brought her to Boston, and on Christmas night, driving his parents' car, he crashed into a wall at the end of a cul-de-sac in Cambridge, the impact severely damaging Jean's face. Financially, Jean's only recourse was to sue the Lowells. Because of the suit, Cal was not supposed to see her, but in the midst of this complicated situation the two were communicating and becoming increasingly involved. The following November she even visited him at Kenyon.[22]

The increasing seriousness of Cal's romantic involvement no doubt contributed to Peter's brooding over lost love. He began to feel at loose ends and to talk of leaving school and going to New York, even telling Allen Tate of that plan. Tate counseled against such an absurd idea and then commented: "Alas, Pete, I see in this an early marriage; and I should be sad to see you married to a beautiful, charming, and even cultivated girl, who would probably reduce your sensibility and cultivation to the terms of her own. That is the way of American women, and of Southern women today." Ever afterward, Peter would refer to Tate's letter warning him not to marry *a society girl,* while the document actually expressed Tate's own temporary misogyny and probably his present unhappiness in his own marriage.[23]

Peter's mood passed; he would finish the work for his Kenyon degree. Surely he could gauge the effect that the Kenyon experience was having on his writing. He was continuing his experimentation and seeking models among numerous writers, among them Thomas Mann, whom Jean admired so much. The November issue of *Hika* carried his Jamesian story "The Life Before," and the December number a promising piece named "Middle Age," centered on the dinnertime conversation among a faithless husband, his wife struggling to hide from the truth, and their African American cook. Peter was also working on a novel, a chapter of which appeared in March. While really not standing well on its own, the chapter has some remarkable effects, particularly a funeral scene in the Trenton Methodist Church with both white and black mourners joining to sing hymns. Surprisingly, Peter Taylor never attempted anything of this sort again. The graduation issue featured his most accomplished story since "A Spinster's Tale"—"Winged Chariot," a work inspired he later admitted by Mann's "Disorder and Early Sorrow." A totally uncharacteristic Taylor effort in tone, in texture, and in its handling of time, the story is nonetheless a landmark in his career.[24]

It was a fitting literary culmination to the Kenyon years, and Peter had not done badly academically. Cal, the very epitome of competition, finished, as he boasted to his mother, summa cum laude, Phi Beta Kappa, highest honors in classics, first man in his class, and valedictorian. At Kenyon, Peter had been allowed to take pretty much the subjects that interested him—English, Latin, French, history, philosophy, and art—usually under the teachers most sympathetic to him. At the end of his two years, he ranked sixteenth out of the fifty-nine in his class, graduating cum laude. His father should have been pleased. But far more important than his academic record had been his finding at last a group of peers, a group that would stimulate and entertain and sustain each other over the decades. The summer before his final year, he had begun a poem that he first titled "For the Friends in Douglass House." Months later, he submitted it to *Hika.* The final stanza summarizes his feeling for Kenyon:

What we've to learn our hundred little quarrels
Each should reveal some part. And every heart
Opened here would find a bitter failing—
Though I should only look from my dormer
At gingerbread about our eaves and say
I have not loved enough this gingerbread.[25]

6

Limbo

"Let's all go join the French ambulance service," Peter Taylor jotted on a post-card to a friend on June 4, 1940; "this would be something to die for." Every-thing was over at Kenyon except the graduation ceremony, and he wished "this limbo of a life could go on forever; I dread seeing the great real world again." What a mixture of feelings he dashed off on that card: the menace of the world situation, his sense that life had not yet really begun, and his confu-sion over what to do once it did. But he was about to exchange that pleasant "limbo of a life" amidst the Douglass House gingerbread for a more extended and sometimes less pleasant period of suspension.[1]

During the spring holiday before graduation, Robert Lowell had married Jean Stafford in St. Mark's Episcopal Church in the Bowery, with Allen Tate giving the bride away. Cal had then returned to Kenyon and did not see Jean until she came out for his graduation. Through the efforts of John Crowe Ransom, it was arranged that the Lowells would go to Baton Rouge, where Cal had received a fellowship at Louisiana State University to study under Cleanth Brooks and Robert Penn Warren, and Jean had been offered a position as secretary at the *Southern Review*. After the graduation ceremony, Peter and the Lowells boarded a train to Memphis, where Cal and Jean were to stay with the Taylors before continuing on to Louisiana.

"All of this must go," Cal declared as the train pulled into the Southern Railroad freight yard. Peter was outraged at the Bostonian's pronouncement at the first sight of Memphis. He was used to Cal's teasing about Southerners and the South. The first passage that Lowell had ever read aloud to him was the one in *The Education of Henry Adams* about Adams' classmate Rooney Lee: "Strictly, the Southerner had no mind; he had temperament. He was not a scholar; he had no intellectual training; he could not analyze an idea, and he could not conceive of admitting two, but in life one could get along very well without ideas, if one had only the social instinct." There *were* superficial parallels between Rooney Lee and the admittedly unintellectual, gregarious Peter Taylor; and Peter would go along with the teasing much longer than most people would have. But he was not ready to take any anti-Southern comments at the moment from this shaggy-locked friend without even a respectable pair of shoes, whom he was just about to introduce to his parents.[2]

The moment passed. There was too much underlying affection between the two young men, and the Hillsman Taylors, who had sufficient social sense to appreciate having Lowells in their midst, were taken with both Cal and Jean. The nose surgery performed after the automobile accident in Cambridge had altered Jean's appearance in a strange way. "It was her eyes, rather than her nose . . . that struck me," Eileen Simpson recalls in *Poets in Their Youth*. "They seemed to be bathed in an excess of fluid, so that they looked permanently welled-up, giving the impression that she had been crying or might do so at any moment. It may have been this, as well as her expression in repose, that made her look sad." But Simpson, as she continues, captures also the other side of Jean, her animation and charm: "The sadness vanished as she talked, when, depending on what she was saying, she looked sly, shrewd, or mischievous, as she twisted her mouth and blew out her cheeks with suppressed glee at the wickedly funny things she said." Because of Cal's winning teasing of Katherine Taylor and Jean's wonderful wit, the visit was a great success. Peter took a week to show them Memphis, arranging even a gin picnic, at which Cal could meet the fabled Bruce Fulton.[3]

Once the Lowells caught their train south, the question of Peter's future arose again, but more than anything else he was brooding about Virginia Jett's relationship with an up-and-coming young cotton broker. In late June, Peter was escort at the Summer Cotillion for the beautiful, blond Mary Jane Peeples, a family friend with whom he occasionally had platonic dates. One of the important social occasions of the year, the ball was held at the Skyway atop the Peabody Hotel, the place considered the ultimate in Memphis glamour. It was a perfect summer night, and she remembers Peter standing with one foot on the parapet reciting poem after poem, including Yeats' "In Memory of Major Robert Gregory," a favorite of Virginia's. Mary Jane was charmed; Peter was "flamboyant" and "debonair," "never queer or odd or strange, just different in an interesting kind of way."[4]

By that night Peter had taken a temporary job. C. P. Lee, a young English instructor at Southwestern, had had a novel accepted by Macmillan. He had rented a house at Monteagle, where he could revise the manuscript, and he needed a typist. Peter agreed to go to the mountain. As opposed to Memphis, it was cool, but shortly Peter grew to hate the novel and Lee. In seclusion, however, he did have time for his own writing, especially at night when Lee frequently went to the movies in the village. During the weeks at Monteagle, Virginia's engagement was announced, and Peter was back in Memphis before the wedding on August 10, which he and Felder refused to attend, spending the time drinking at a beer garden instead. Afterward, a drunken Peter waked Gertrude Smith Fulton's mother and poured out his sorrows.[5]

As Peter confided later to Robie Macauley, that summer he had begun writing a novel about Virginia:

> I write on it almost like a diary. It is a very wordy attempt to analyse the only very real relationship that I have ever had with another person, to discover for myself, really, what happened to it, who did what, and what was the real nature of our affections at the different times during the four years. I'm trying not to place the responsibility too heavily on either side and not too heavily on society—the responsibility, that is, for the outcome. I still want you to meet her when you come to Memphis. You'll understand why I think what's happened is a calamity.

Despite such disclaimers, Peter Taylor was never able to view the relationship objectively. As a Memphis friend commented, Peter at the time was "no image of stability." If one discounted or failed to account his talent as a writer, he seemed to have no prospects. Certainly Virginia's mother felt that way. Then there was the simple fact that Virginia might care for someone else much more deeply than she did for Peter. But Peter refused to face those facts. He romanticized the situation and made it a central part of his personal myth. The artist had been rejected for the businessman, and his rejection grew out of the very culture that had produced him. He did blame the social order, and this laying of blame distanced him even more from the social world of which he seemed so much a part. Whatever the effect of Virginia Jett's marriage on Peter Taylor personally, it helped make him as a writer.[6]

Mixed with the expressions of heartbreak in his letters was enthusiasm for his writing. "This summer," he told Robie, "I have written my longest and, I think, best short story. It is the tale of the drunk bitch on a week-end party with High Society people." Years later, he would recount just how the story started. He had gotten tired of Robert Lowell's teasing him about how prim and puritanical he was, how little he knew of the world and of the "roughness of life." So he sat down and wrote the sentence, "He wanted no more of her drunken palaver." "I had no idea where I was going from there," Peter Taylor said later, "and then suddenly a whole story based on someone I knew, a father with two boys, just came to me." The father is obviously the high-rolling Mr. Fulton, and the innocent younger son is a quite idealized version of Bruce. Peter Taylor never wrote again about quite the same milieu, but the story showed him new possibilities for using window characters. "From my drunk woman story [which Robie would name "The Fancy Woman"]," Peter reported to his friend, "I have begun to get ideas of how I can write about the folks I know, how I can show what they are and aren't. This drunken hussy, whose best job has been in a second-rate department store in Memphis, can look pretty objectively at things no other person would notice." The story is shaped by the woman's perspective. At end, she has been shamed because she cannot recognize innocence, but that is accounted for in part because of the excess of hypocrisy all about her, to which she is so attuned. "The Fancy Woman" exhibits earmarks of stories by the mature Peter Taylor, especially the exploration of the strengths and limitations of one perspective.[7]

In the same letter, Peter reported that he was hearing once or twice a week from the Lowells, who told him that it was almost certain that the *Southern Review* would publish "A Spinster's Tale," which he had withheld from *Hika* and earlier submitted to the *Atlantic Monthly*. He was leaving that Saturday for a visit to Baton Rouge, "where I may find a fellowship which will answer my needs for the winter." But clouding everything was the threat of war, "that by that time we may all be dead somewhere in Flanders. . . . But this talk of our approaching loss of liberty has made me want to stop this letter. Write me in Baton Rouge."[8]

Peter did get the fellowship. Impressed with "A Spinster's Tale," Cleanth Brooks and Robert Penn Warren had arranged a stipend of thirty dollars a month for grading freshman papers. In addition, the *Southern Review* had taken the story for the princely sum of $145. Peter was set for the next few months as a graduate student at LSU.[9]

Louisiana State University had been a remarkable place in the 1930s. While other institutions of higher learning were languishing during the Depression, Huey Long, the populist governor of Louisiana, determined to make his state university a major center of learning. He erected impressive buildings and provided funds for new faculty and even for the *Southern Review,* founded in 1935. Being at LSU was still another instance of Peter Taylor's recurrent good luck. The June 10, 1940, issue of *Time* had judged the review "superior to any other journal in the English language." In the next few months it would publish three Taylor stories. From that point on, Peter Taylor was known among literary people. The judgment of Katherine Anne Porter was representative. She wrote to an intimate lauding "the short story, really superb, by young Taylor" and commenting that "this Taylor youth should be able to do anything he likes in a few years if he proceeds the way he has begun."[10]

As important to Peter Taylor as the establishing of his literary reputation was his exposure to Brooks and Warren. Almost fifty years later, he called it "a splendid year" for both himself and Cal: "Here we were with two writers not much older than ourselves, yet enough older to know a great deal more about the art of poetry and fiction than we did and to have experienced a great deal more of the world than we had. For ourselves, I will say only this much, that we were sharp enough to see that we must learn from them. I don't know whether we learned more about how to write or how to live." Much of the learning, he recalled, occurred around the dining tables of the Brookses and the Warrens.[11]

Both students of John Crowe Ransom, graduates of Vanderbilt, and Rhodes scholars, Brooks and Warren (or "Brooksandwarren," as Cal called them) had recently published the college textbook *Understanding Poetry,* which applied brilliantly the principles of the New Criticism to the classroom. The two would become one of the most influential academic teams of the twentieth century. They complemented each other in an interesting way. "Face-to-face across their abutting desks they would thrash things out," Warren's biographer writes, "the thirty-one-year-old Brooks, short and compact, chubby-faced yet firm-jawed with a direct gaze from behind wire-rimmed spectacles: Warren, a year older, tall and rawboned." One of their best students has described well their differences in temperament and style: "Warren rather grand and expansive and somewhat roughneck, and Brooks always sort of contained, the prototype of the scholar-gentleman." But he comments, "My goodness did they strike sparks one upon the other."[12]

Peter rented a room in the Warrens' apartment on State Street, registered for courses under both men, and socialized with both couples on the weekends. In early December, he wrote Robie that the past weekend marked "the first one of the Warrens' heavy drinking parties at which neither Cal nor Jean nor I have got sick." He would often tell the tale of the Brookses' driving them home from one party. The drunken trio in the back seat, desperately trying to hide their state, were discussing Donne and Herbert with their distinguished driver, when Jean opened her purse and threw up in it. When the three got out, the movement caused Peter suddenly to get sick on the back of the car. He tore off the jacket of a new gray flannel suit and ran after the car trying to wipe it off. When Peter and Cal entered the apartment, they found Jean rinsing the dollar bills in her purse.[13]

That fall both Warrens were drinking a great deal, but so were Peter and Jean. The two had formed a close bond that remained unshakable over the following decades. Each was a great talker and a great raconteur who appreciated the other's comparable talents. The same intensity and enthusiasm led to the drinking. But there was also their shared devotion to their art. Peter would later say that, after his having endured all the Kenyon poets, Jean was the first talented writer of fiction he had ever known. They respected each other, and Jean, who had studied in Germany, knew a great deal about Thomas Mann, as well as Proust and James, and could talk with Peter on subjects that he relished.[14]

Another of their ties was a shared lack of interest in the academic world. In late June, Jean had written a friend that the "talk in academic gatherings is of . . . (1) language requirements for the degree PhD (2) the deficiencies of the Freshman English curriculum and (3) the necessity of subordinating historical scholarship to criticism or vice versa." "Now mind," she continued, "they were all delightful, charming, amusing people *but* it is a university. It is academic. It is that and nothing more." Six weeks after beginning graduate school, Peter confessed to a friend, "My temperament is as different from an educator's and critic's as it is from an insurance salesman's." By mid-November, he had decided, he told Robie, that "there's certainly no place for me among university people. . . . I think that you have a similar predicament, though your aversion to the university class is not brought about by both boredom *and* incapacity."[15]

At Thanksgiving, Peter quit the graduate program at LSU. Robert Penn Warren recalled the circumstances in which Peter, who possessed "a kindliness and courtesy of manner that in all likelihood would have seemed a bit old-fashioned even when he was a young boy," told him of the decision: "With grave kindness, more like a father explaining the facts of life to a young son than like a student walking across the campus in the dusk with a professor, Peter tactfully explained that graduate work was not for him. He made the blow very soft for me and tried to absolve me of blame. He had to be a writer, he said, and he had to put all his eggs in one basket." Peter chose not to tell his parents until the end of the Christmas holiday, and by then he had decided to remain in Baton Rouge, where he was getting a lot of writing done, until April.[16]

By the time he dropped out, not only had "A Spinster's Tale" already appeared in the *Southern Review,* but the journal had also accepted "The Fancy Woman" and "Winged Chariot" (which Peter had renamed "Sky Line"), and an editor at Houghton Mifflin, who had been in Baton Rouge, had expressed interest in Peter's novel. He was winning a place in the literary world, and he would have enough money to support himself for the next few months.[17]

After Christmas, Robert Penn Warren took a leave without pay in order to teach at the University of Iowa, and the Warrens sublet their apartment to the Lowells. Peter had new landlords, and the male member of the pair was going through a strange period. Cal, who at Kenyon had once scornfully told his roommate that Catholicism was "the religion of Irish servant girls," was taking instruction under Father Schexnayder, the Catholic chaplain at the university. Cal approached his conversion with the kind of zeal that he showed for every new endeavor, and he sought to impose a religious regimen on the other two members of the ménage. As a result, Peter and Jean were placed in the roles of wayward children, with Cal as the stern father. If anything, the situation drew the two even closer. Jean was extremely possessive of Peter, just as she had been of her other male friends in the past. In the fall on the spur of the moment, Peter had invited a rather intellectual young woman whom he had known for many years to come to LSU. She was given a job under Jean at the review. Jean took an immense dislike to the girl, and because of her wicked tongue, made her terribly uncomfortable. Eventually the girl came to feel completely alienated from the three friends. Jean had Peter now to herself. One evening, she told a friend, "Peter & I got incredibly drunk and exchanged words over the extent of Peter's love for me & the peril of it so that Cal, who spent the evening talking with Mr. Brooks about belief, did not speak to Peter for 1 week thereafter." Years later Peter confided to Jack Thompson that "nothing ever happened between him and Jean, but there were many times when something could have."[18]

By March, Jean had fallen ill, the first of a series of illnesses during these years; and Peter boasted that he was cooking two meals a day. To Robie Macauley, he reported on Cal's state: "Cal will be baptized next Sunday in the Catholic Church around the corner. He's really spent the entire winter converting himself (Don't tell this to anyone either.) It's what he's been destined for from the start. He's literally hunted down the most complete sort of orthodoxy; and once he found it, I must say, he gobbled it up as only Cal can gobble—day and night in an earnestness that approaches perversion." On March 29, 1941, Cal was received into the Church, and then, in typical Cal fashion, indulged himself in a lengthy confession, while Jean, Peter, and a few others waited nervously outside the church. Within a week, Peter moved back to Memphis.[19]

Before he left Baton Rouge, Peter had written to Allen Tate that he had been working on two "longish stories" as well as "dabbling as ever with painting. (I've never been able to give up the idea quite completely that I can be a painter and writer too)." But it was time to leave, though Baton Rouge had truly been kind to his genius. "I am starving," he wrote a Memphis friend, "for the taste of sweet gossip, absurd argumentation, intimate Sunday-night suppers, carousing evenings in West Memphis, and an occasional whiff of the rare, rank odor of Memphis High Society."[20]

His return to Memphis, however, was a return to confusion. On the one hand, his career as a writer was taking off. He had the praise of his old mentors, Ransom and Tate. He had been asked to submit part of his novel to the Houghton Mifflin fellowship competition. He now had as agent the firm of Russell and Volkening, and on the basis of "Sky Line," Robert Penn Warren reported that the University of Iowa creative writing program was prepared to offer him a fellowship for the next fall, the only duties being to attend a weekly workshop in fiction and advise students. On the other hand loomed the question of the draft, and each time Peter spoke of the future, he would say that he was going to Iowa, "if not to war." After all he was twenty-four and unmarried.[21]

Many times in later years, Peter would tell the tale of his experience with the draft board. After writing a letter to the board stating that he was a conscientious objector, he arrived at the office to find a college friend working as secretary. She told him that she knew he didn't mean any of that, so she just threw the letter in the wastebasket. It was a good story, but evidently not exactly what happened. At the time he told Robie that he had been sent conscientious objector forms "that were too tricky to fool with (I sent them back unfilled out, for I'd have had to swear that 'by religious *training* etc,' while the Methodist minister and my father are practically calling for war)."[22]

When Peter was called for his physical, the examining doctor had found a problem that needed attention. "More unpleasant than it is serious," Peter described it to Robie, with Jamesian delicacy—the problem was probably hemorrhoids. After surgery, he recuperated at home and felt "like a criminal that is being nursed back to health for the execution." He was bitter that he would be sent to defend "the high minded society which is responsible for the happy conclusion to my late romance." His recovery was rapid, and in early May he received word that he had been drafted and ordered to Fort Oglethorpe, Georgia. Just before he left, Nadine Lenti Parker, the watercolor instructor at the Memphis Academy of Art whom he had met through Virginia and to whom he had grown close, had a farewell picnic for him at La Grange, Tennessee. On June the third, he left for Oglethorpe.[23]

A week later Peter posted a letter to Nadine, begging her to write, refusing to list the "tedious miseries" of army life, and extolling one pleasure—sleeping in a tent, especially during storms: "Last night I went to sleep with a heavy rain falling and the lightning and thunder. . . . On other nights the sky has been beautiful, and I have my cot right by the open flap through which I can see the other tents and the sky. It's a very lush scene, like a scene from a Shakespearean play." Oglethorpe was filled with Memphians. Jimmy Smithwick, with whom Peter had gone to Europe, was there, as well as Felder. The camp, Peter reported to Jean Stafford, was run by "Memphis society boys"; and there were group excursions into Chattanooga, Tennessee, just across the state line, and long drinking sessions there in the bar at the Read House. The editor of the Memphis *Commercial Appeal,* a friend of Millsaps and Sally, had used his influence to have Peter assigned to clerical duty in the transportation section.

On weekends, he and Felder would visit Felder's rich aunt, who lived on Lookout Mountain, a fashionable enclave on the outskirts of the city.[24]

By the middle of July, the two had taken to borrowing the aunt's car and driving up to Monteagle, which Peter described to Robie as "a little, old fashioned mountain resort where the same fine old families have been going for seventy-five years." The two soldiers were dating sisters, daughters of one of those families, the James Knox Polks of Nashville and the Mississippi Delta, and staying at the Polk cottage. Peter had also begun going to Mass "furtively," and he was finding time to read Proust, the first four volumes![25]

In August, Congress passed a law making the term of the draft thirty months. "It was only this morning," he wrote Jean Stafford on the eighteenth, "that I grasped just how long the thirty-months are going to be. . . . Can you understand that the thought that one is confined and occupied by military things for the next two and a half years is more painful than the actual restriction? It's what I'm not going to be able to do that hurts, not so much what I'll have to do." But in point of fact, he was able to lead an active social life, as well as find time for his writing. Jean and Cal came through Tennessee separately en route to New York and a year in the Village. Peter and Jean spent a wonderfully boozy rainy evening in Chattanooga, going from bar to bar in taxis, and he and Cal made a pilgrimage to Monteagle to see Allen Tate, who was staying there briefly. Caroline Gordon received them on the porch of Andrew Lytle's cottage, but would not allow them to wake Tate, who was sleeping after a fishing expedition. "I must say now quite frankly," Peter burst out to Robie, "that Mrs. Tate annoys me. She's friendly to both Cal and myself (more especially to Cal), but is plainly condescending." Another weekend Peter's beautiful longtime friend Elizabeth Farnsworth and her family were in town. "She has money, has been to Vassar, and her family eat dinner at eight by candlelight," Peter wrote in the same letter, and then revealed his old ambivalence. "I am somehow drawn to all the vulgarities and pretensions of society and at the same time despise them."[26]

The Farnsworth visit, however, inspired him to write a very short story, entitled first "Like the Sad Heart of Ruth" and, more aptly later, "A Walled Garden." Peter was still experimenting with form and responding to different influences. With the Farnsworth garden in mind, he wrote a chilling dramatic monologue in prose, much like a Browning piece, in which a mother gradually reveals how she has formed and controlled both her garden and her daughter. He sent it off to Russell and Volkening, who had just placed another story in *American Prefaces*. They were still trying to sell another story, this one about a mute. Peter was thinking deeply about his own fiction, and in a letter to Robie offering constructive criticism of a group of Macauley stories, he offered a rare glimpse of his own evolving theories. "I'm not going to theorize," he began paradoxically, "but I hold that a story ought to have an absolutely natural level and that meaning which can be drawn out of the story should seem mere happy coincidence."[27]

Shortly, the *New Republic* accepted "Like the Sad Heart of Ruth," and Peter was encouraged by his success and the laxity of restrictions at Fort Oglethorpe to take a room in Chattanooga, in an old downtown section amid the "First Churches." He gathered his books, pictures, records, and civilian clothes there and slept there from two to five nights a week, but that was a fact kept from both his sergeant and his family. In early December, he wrote Jean Stafford "on one of those Sunday mornings" after an hilarious drunken evening. He was "very happy to announce that I am once more able to drink without my thoughts turning to the jilting V.J. gave me." Paul Brooks at Houghton Mifflin had returned the chapters of the novel devoted to that painful situation "saying that he was not sure whether I had chosen the right theme and that it had 'static qualities.' " Peter was sorry that he couldn't come to New York at Christmas because he was "confined to this life of a half-soldier/half-clerk." He signed the letter and then was startled by a news flash on the radio. He scrawled at the top: "The announcement of the Japanese attack came as I was writing this letter."[28]

At first it seemed that everything had been changed by the attack on Pearl Harbor. On December 18, Peter wrote Jean: "My last letter, just as camp life before the outbreak of war, now seems like part of a dream. My room in Chattanooga and everything resembling personal freedom is now gone." He reported that his brother was coming into the army after Christmas, and "right now nothing seems so important as keeping Mother's spirits up." The next day he left for a Christmas furlough in Memphis.[29]

When he returned to Oglethorpe, rumors were circulating that his unit would be leaving, and in February he told Jean that "all writing is of course out of the question for me now as it would be for anyone on the twenty-four hour duty we're on. But under the circumstances it doesn't matter, for my writing has been fizzling out anyhow." The transportation section was thrown into a flurry of activity, and in the next couple of months, Peter accompanied convoys of troops to the Far West and to New Orleans, where he mourned with his friend John Palmer over the shutting down of the *Southern Review*. But there was good news too. Martha Foley was including "The Fancy Woman" in

The Best Short Stories of 1942, and the *New Yorker* had written to express interest in seeing some of his fiction.[30]

At the end of March, Peter wrote Robie expressing hopes that his friend had not been called yet: "I count on coming out alive (I mean I have the *feeling* that I'll come out alive) but I don't like to think of coming out myself without the prospect of getting together with you at last and starting our magazine or whatever we choose to do (like attending Iowa graduate school)." Peter might have had that feeling, but he seemed to be covering his bets. He was going to church and reading Catholic literature that Cal had sent, though he was still "by no means a convert." He had also done some writing, turning out "three little stories that are no good . . . [because] I haven't the time to work them out in detail as I should." Nonetheless, he had mailed a story to the *New Yorker*.[31]

By this time, Peter's life had fallen into a pattern not to be broken for some time. In the late spring, he was promoted to corporal and three months later to sergeant. He was head clerk in the transportation section, and there he was satisfied to stay while Felder and others went on to officer candidate school. One of his duties was accompanying companies of troops to their next assignment. In a matter of a few months, he went twice to Washington, D.C., twice to California, and once to Florida. His friends were marrying—Elizabeth Farnsworth, Mary Polk, and Tommy and Mimi—and he wrote Nadine that "now-more-than-ever-I-stand-signally-alone" (quoting a James essay on Balzac). But he was taking out several young women and enjoying his wartime bachelor existence.[32]

On the first trip to Washington, Cal came down from New York to see Peter, and the two stayed with Peter's glamorous Aunt Ret (Loretta), his mother's older sister. Much more worldly than the lively but rather prim Katherine, Ret had married first Campbell Pilcher, a Nashville socialite, and after divorcing him, Jay Hayden, a high-ranking Washington correspondent. Cal found the resemblance between Peter and this aunt striking. On another visit, Peter began a relationship with a Memphis debutante now in Washington, Lila Burr Chapman. Both sojourns in the capital would furnish ideas for later fiction.[33]

In the summer, Peter saw a great deal of Tom and Sarah Booth White, who were living in Chattanooga while Tom was taking an advanced flying course. A brooder and a searcher, Tom revealed depths that his friend had not previously suspected. During these months he would pick up Peter on his motorcycle, and they'd ride into the city for long talks, each unburdening himself to the other. This intimacy continued throughout Peter's life.[34]

The *New Yorker* rejected the two stories that Peter had sent to them, the second being the piece "Middle Age," which had been published in *Hika* and which Peter had renamed "Supper." In that letter of rejection, the editor William Maxwell showed his own cynicism about the typical *New Yorker* story: "The story belongs to a world that is essentially remote from New York City. The editors have in their minds an imaginary map of Manhattan which includes, strangely, all of Connecticut and Long Island, Florida, New Jersey, Hollywood, and wherever New Yorkers go. Since naturally a great many New Yorkers go into the army, the army is a wide open subject, and we have been hoping that you would see your way clear to do some army stories for us." On other fronts, the news was better. In the fall, Russell and Volkening arranged a contract with Doubleday for a novel or a book of stories, with a delivery date of one year after Peter's discharge from the army, and an advance of $250 upon signing.[35]

Peter continued to read a great deal. After finishing Tolstoy's *Resurrection,* he had begun *War and Peace.* He was also reading Turgenev and finding in him a link with James. Increasingly he was thinking about principles of art, and in the National Gallery, he judged Mary Cassatt's painting of a mother, father, and child in a row boat "the most genuine modern picture in the gallery." And such thinking, of course, had brought him back to his own fiction. "It seems to me that I must start over all over and work from the inside out instead of from the outside in," he wrote Robie. "Most of us have made the mistake of selecting themes and pushing them into the lives of such people as we have known (mainly ourselves) instead of writing about the real problems of these people and finding how these problems touch upon the great themes." It was an insight hard won and important for the future of his fiction.[36]

In the spring of 1942, Jean Stafford sold her novel to Harcourt, Brace for an advance of five hundred dollars. Allen Tate and Caroline Gordon were leaving Princeton. They had taken a cottage at Monteagle with five bedrooms that they dubbed "New Wormwood"; and they invited the Lowells to join them for the year. All were working on literary projects. That year (from the summer 1942 to summer 1943) would become another fabled time in this literary group's history, comparable to the summer that Cal had pitched his tent on the lawn of Benfolly. Jean Stafford was expanding and revising the manuscript that became *Boston Adventure,* Caroline Gordon was working on her novel *The Women on the Porch,* Allen Tate was writing a series of sonnets, and Cal had a burst of creative energy and was writing poem after poem. But wherever the Tates were in residence, there was also plenty of entertaining. Peter and a new friend at Fort Oglethorpe, James Waller, an Agrarian economist friend of Allen's, went up frequently on weekends; and Peter revealed to Tom White that "Mrs. Tate has now favored me with real friendship which I used to have the feeling she was withholding."[37]

Among the Tates' many guests that year was a young woman named Eleanor Ross, whom both had taught at the Woman's College of North Carolina, at Greensboro. Their most promising student during their two years at Greensboro, she had grown up on a farm outside Norwood, North Carolina, the third of four talented children—all of whom would eventually become writers. Allen Tate looked upon her as a sort of Emily Brontë, with a strong natural talent; and both the Tates had encouraged her to enter the graduate program at Vanderbilt and work on her writing under Donald Davidson. With their support she won the sole writing fellowship for the 1942–43 school year.[38]

After several invitations, she agreed to come up from Nashville to visit after Christmas. Inexperienced but intelligent and possessed of a writer's eye, she penned the best description ever written of that literary group on the mountain:

> They look the way I suppose aristocrats must look—Jean with her soft blonde hair all frowsy, and no make-up over her freckles, and wearing red knee socks with saddle shoes and a red collarless jacket; Cal with his perpetual sensitive frown and big bony frame and tousled crew haircut and thick-lensed glasses; Mrs. Tate little and not as slender as usual in baggy gray wool slacks and white shirt and an adolescent green jacket of Nancy's that had bright red valentines of leather stitched on the elbows as patches and didn't quite go with her hair that's white at the edges and partly-dyed; Mr. Tate looking spatulate somehow (but he's a sweet lamb) with his slew feet and his hat that's narrow behind & turned up, and flares into a wide brim at the front, and his mustache and an old, old, old striped coat.

Thus she wrote her mother immediately afterward of the scene as the group bade her good-bye at the Monteagle bus station. Even then they were begging her to stay, because "a couple of unattached soldier-writers were coming up for New Year's Day." But she had to get back to duties in Nashville. So they pressed her to come up again at Easter. She agreed, and, as things turned out, in the spring one of the same young men was again also invited. The soldier-writer was Peter Taylor, and neither her life nor his would ever be the same again.[39]

7

Marriage and War ···

Eleanor Ross took the bus from Nashville up to Monteagle on the morning of April 24, Good Friday, and the Tates and their several guests spent that day and the next hiking to mountain coves, gathering mountain laurel, reading, and playing charades. Saturday afternoon they were having cocktails (except for Eleanor, a teetotaler) and awaiting the arrival of Peter Taylor. In the midst of the animated conversation, Eleanor saw a soldier through the glass panes of the front door. She rose and hurried to let him in. Peter Taylor later said that when he saw her walking toward him he knew that he would marry her.[1]

Through the spirited evening, part sophisticated literary talk, part pixilated revelry, Peter was attentive to the girl from the moors of North Carolina. The next day the group drove out of the village and descended by steep mountain ledges the gorge named Fiery Gizzard to a beautiful swift creek, where they picnicked. Later in the afternoon, back at New Wormwood, Cal built a big fire in the living room, and Allen Tate read poetry to everyone. Before the group dispersed, Peter told Eleanor Ross that he was coming to Nashville the next week.

He knew that she was engaged to a young army doctor who had been stationed near the town where she was teaching the year before. But Peter was undeterred, and she wrote her parents to tell them, in an apparently offhand way, that he would be visiting in Nashville. During the intervening week, she read his three stories published in the *Southern Review* and was impressed that each was so accomplished. He surpassed even what the Tates and Lowells had said about him as a writer. Peter and Eleanor spent the next weekend walking and talking for hours in Centennial Park. At one point, he went over to an old man to get a match and stood for a while chatting. When he came back, he apologized and said that he felt he "had to pass the time of day" with the fellow. Peter was winning her; the speech reflected so much the country ways that she knew and valued. Then later, sitting on the bridge, he told her that he had decided to stay in Nashville beyond the weekend. "What are you going to do?" she asked; and when he replied, "Just this," she knew that the situation was getting serious.[2]

Finally he had to leave to spend the rest of his furlough in Memphis as he had promised his mother. But within two weeks he was again in Nashville, and this time he took the manuscript of Eleanor's novel back to Fort Ogle-thorpe. When he reported this news to Jean Stafford, she lashed out: "As for Eleanor—and don't tell Cal I told you—she irritates me a) because she is not so guileless as her blue eyes would have you think, I have decided and b) because she said something extremely catty about me to Nancy [the Tates' six-teen-year-old daughter], I like her even less than I did the second time I saw her in Nashville. However, I can understand how a young man might be fetched by her, so I will say no more." Jean was jealous. She and Peter were close and compatible, they had wonderful times together, and she wanted him to remain unattached.[3]

The next weekend, he was back in Nashville, and Eleanor agreed to marry him. Peter invited Jean to come down to Chattanooga and have dinner with him. Over drinks he broke the news, which Jean conveyed to Monteagle that night. Even before that, letters had gone out to Norwood and Memphis. Elea-nor's parents were shocked and dismayed over the entire affair, not least by the fact that their daughter had known this man only a month. They would not give their blessing. Because Katherine Taylor was visiting in St. Louis, Peter wrote separate letters to his parents, his letter to Hillsman particularly affec-tionate and warm. After assuring his father that Eleanor was "the sort of girl and of the sort of folks that you and Mother will find congenial," he went on to express a son's gratitude: "You have given me everything in the world that I ever could have asked. I have become more and more aware of that during the past two years of associating with various sorts of people in the army. I am especially conscious of the things you and Mother have given me that are not measurable by the dollar, things that neither the boom, nor the depression, nor the war can change. I am glad that I am marrying someone who can appreciate those things." Hillsman's reaction was to take a train to Nashville and confront this young woman. Though a shy country girl, Eleanor Ross knew her own mind. She thought his coming to see her rather crass and was secretly amused at the figure of this big, unwieldy man riding beside her on the streetcar. Peter, he told her, was just not as smart as he thought he was, and he was certainly in no position to get married. The same advice was given her by Caroline Gordon, who felt a maternal responsibility for her protégé. "I just think you'd do better with your doctor than with the Sarge," she said. But none of this moved Eleanor; plans for the wedding went forward.[4]

Cal wrote a jubilant note, Jean had now fallen in line, and the Tates insisted that the wedding be at Monteagle. On May 30, Peter wrote his mother to say that they would be married the next Friday afternoon. Peter was arranging his leave and was apartment hunting in Chattanooga. Eleanor was studying for her exams and grading student papers, while Caroline and Allen were making arrangements for the wedding. Father Flye would perform the ceremony at the Episcopal chapel at St. Andrew's School near Sewanee. That would be followed by a reception at the Tate cottage.[5]

On Thursday, Peter and his army buddy Gid Fryer drove up to the mountain in a new rented coupe, bringing four gallon jugs of sauterne for the reception punch. That night Caroline Gordon sat with the prospective groom on the steps leading down to the kitchen and lectured him about his responsibilities to Eleanor. The following afternoon saw the most literary of weddings. Allen Tate gave the bride away, Caroline took the role of Mother of the Bride, Cal was best man, and Jean, Eleanor's attendant. Eleanor wore a long white dress and veil that she and friends had made, Peter was in uniform, and Allen was dapper in a white suit. Unexpectedly, Peter's parents had driven up bringing Millsaps, Sally, and Louise Fitzhugh, and champagne for the reception. Avery Handly played the organ for the service, and other friends came from Chattanooga and Nashville, including the Donald Davidsons. It was a gay occasion. Peter and Eleanor left soon after the ceremony, but the younger members of the party continued celebrating well into the morning.[6]

By Saturday, the newlyweds were getting settled in their apartment on Missionary Ridge, out from Chattanooga. "I'm sure that ours is the happiest household in the world right now," Peter wrote his mother the next day. During this time of war and upheaval, in the space of six weeks, he had entered into a relationship that would last all his life. Eleanor was small and blond with large blue eyes. People in Memphis would later remark on her resemblance to his sisters. But she was different from them and from all the society girls that Peter had known. She was delicate and refined, a lady—but she was also a country girl who had grown up in a house with books but little more. In opposition to his compulsively social nature, she was retiring. She never touched a drop of anything alcoholic; she never learned to drive a car. She was an unusual and very complicated person, and Peter found her wise. She was his anchor. A poem that she published forty years after they met captures her side of the relationship:

> Love knows but one story.
> It sits in the corner with its book
> and reads it over and over
> lips parted, eyes shining—
> how the face appeared at the window
> > how the door was opened
> > > the eyes met
> > > > and the hands
> Luckily, it is my story.[7]

In the letter to his mother, Peter drew the first of the many floor plans and architectural sketches that he would send out over the years. Their second-floor apartment had three rooms and a view of the Chattanooga valley. It seemed a world away from Fort Oglethorpe. Peter waked at five each morning and rode to the post with Bill Eason, who lived downstairs with his wife and child; then Peter rode the yellow streetcar back in the afternoon, reading *Battles and Leaders of the Civil War* during the trip.[8]

Peter dispatched other letters—to Red Warren, to Robie, to Nadine Lenti Parker, to Tom White—to tell of his marriage, all expressing his joy, some noting that Eleanor felt that she must have a job for the income, but that he wished her to stay at home and have time for her writing. The young couple had now received the blessing of the Rosses, a great relief and satisfaction. They were sending out announcements, and Eleanor had selected patterns of silver and china.[9]

During these first happy weeks of his marriage, Peter Taylor wrote his most

personal story, "Rain in the Heart." It is a remarkable and flawless performance, combining a Hemingway-like precision in the presentation of physical
detail with a Jamesian awareness of the workings of consciousness. The plot
line is simple. A sergeant returns to his barrack from a field maneuver. Amid
his crude and bawdy fellow soldiers, he showers and changes in preparation
to spend a night in town with his young wife. Waiting at a streetcar stop, he
talks with a grotesque, embittered cleaning woman, who thrusts at him a handful of sweet peas that she is carrying. The yellow car takes him to his block,
where he sees his wife in an upper window. A tender reunion follows, then
supper, washing the dishes, reading, and bed, as a shower falls outside the
window. "Rain in the Heart" is the Taylor story most closely drawn from life
and the most careful exploration of the intimacy and empathy of his relationship with Eleanor.

As the sergeant rides the bus to his stop, we encounter Taylor's first passage
on what would become one of his central images—houses, and their relation
to family:

> He bent over now and again and looked out the windows at the neat bungalows
> and larger dwelling houses along the roadside. He would one day have a house
> such as one of those for his own. His own father's house was the like of these,
> with a screened porch on the side and a fine tile roof. He could hear his father
> saying, "A house is only as good as the roof over it." But weren't these the things
> that had once seemed prosaic and too binding for his notions? Before he went
> into the Army had there not been moments when the thought of limiting himself
> to a genteel suburban life seemed intolerable by its restrictions and confine-
> ment? . . . And yet now . . . he dreamed longingly of the warm companionship
> he would find with her and their sober neighbors in a house with a fine roof.[10]

When the soldier reaches his apartment and his soft, gentle, sensitive wife, he
feels that this is his "real life," set apart from all the rest of the day's contin-
gencies. But even here his own inwardness intrudes to mar the perfection of
perfect union. First, his aesthetic sense is stirred as he gazes upon objects his
wife has arranged upon a table, "such a pleasing isolated arrangement of objects" (252). Next, his gaze falls upon the bowl in which the sweet peas have
been placed, bringing to mind all the cleaning woman's grotesque being: "He
was utterly preoccupied with the impression he had just received and he had
a strange desire to sustain the impression long enough to examine it." His
wife senses his distance, and he knows that she too feels "a terrible unrelated

diversity in things." The story ends as he clasps her in his arms. The rain has begun again, isolating them from the rest of the world. "Rain in the Heart" prepares us for the power of effect that Peter Taylor would continue to achieve and for the detachment with which he is capable of viewing the workings of the human psyche, even his own. In a sense, "Rain in the Heart" harks back to his attempt at capturing the moments between husband and wife in "The Party," written for Allen Tate's class. But what a span of experience and technical development separates the two.

Not everything he was producing was equal to "Rain in the Heart." The novelette that he kept revising he was to finish only many years later. But he continued to work, and he had to have complete silence when he did. In August, Peter took his bride for the first time to Memphis. She was apprehensive about meeting his friends and dealing with all the Taylors in a body—she was especially dreading Bob, who had written Peter a letter of complaint that his brother had not chosen him as best man. Much to Peter's delight, Katherine Taylor and Eleanor took to each other immediately, and Eleanor was charmed by Bruce Fulton. Among the other encounters was this scene, which Peter conveyed in a letter to Tom White:

> Right now I feel that it is Monday afternoon again. We have parked the big black car—Eleanor and I—across the street and down a little way from your house. Someone is seated on the grass of your front lawn with Sarah. It is someone in a blue dress and with two little girls hanging about her. Surely it cannot be Virginia. This is all a dream—my approaching the residence of Mr. and Mrs. Tom White and their two and a half year old son for whom I have a special fondness, my approaching their house with my own wife and finding Mrs. Virginia Jett McCallum visiting there with her two daughters. No this was no dream, for I was broad awake. I approach with unsteady foot and with a mouth ready to stammer. . . . But I am already on the lawn making quite smooth and quickly calculated introductions, concealing a thousand regrets and a thousand pleasures from the meeting itself.

Soon Annie Rose Buchman drives up. General conversation and laughter follow, and for Peter, all awkwardness is forgotten in the sociability of the moment. But Eleanor's response is different: "Eleanor, in the black car, reveals that she thinks it would have been better if we had seen Sarah alone. Three are too many to try to get to know at once. She longs for our little apartment in Chattanooga, for the typewriter, for the books, for our record player (her

Bach and Stravinsky), for her own kitchen, for our breakfast room at dawn with the west windows looking out over the green, foggy valley of Chattanooga." This difference in temperament would remain throughout the couple's lives.[11]

For months it had been rumored that Peter's unit would be transferred from Oglethorpe, but he had almost become used to the uncertainty. Through a recommendation from Caroline Gordon, after the return from Memphis Eleanor secured a job at the Chattanooga library at a hundred dollars a month, and the Taylors moved to the center of town. Within a few weeks, they received distressing news about Cal. He and Jean had spent the Fourth of July weekend with the Taylors before they left for the north—Cal to New York to secure an apartment and Jean to the writers colony at Yaddo, where she could finish her novel. Now they learned that Cal was about to be drafted. He had registered for the draft in 1941, and in 1942 he had more than once attempted to enlist so that he could go to officer candidate school, only to be rejected because of his eyes. But by the time he returned to New York in 1943, he had completely changed his position. He was now in total opposition to the war. In July he was ordered to have a physical, and soon afterward he received notice that he would be inducted on September 8. On that day, he sent a letter to President Roosevelt stating his position on the war, refusing the draft, and signing it "your fellow citizen." He sent a copy to Peter.[12]

Then no word came from the Lowells for two weeks. Peter was frantic. On October 13, Cal was arraigned and sentenced to a year and a day at the Federal Correctional Center at Danbury, Connecticut. As Peter was taking in the situation, he received a cryptic note from Tom White, now an officer and a pilot: "Today I walked barefooted in Arabian sand. Regards to Eleanor." It was a shock, the first indication that Tom was no longer in the United States. The war seemed to be moving in on everyone Peter knew. He brooded over the question of just how he would perform if he had to go to the front.[13]

He wrote Jean that he had begun attending services at an Episcopal church; he wanted her to tell Cal, whom he thought about constantly. In the midst of confusion and anxiety, in late October he traveled to Memphis alone to stand as best man in Bob's wedding. During mid-December Peter had a ten-day furlough, which he and Eleanor spent in Memphis. "At times," he reported, his father was "the pure country squire, and (alas) at times he is the disillusioned business man." But during the visit, Hillsman "talked and talked about old times in Tennessee," which both Peter and Eleanor enjoyed. On their return, they put up a Christmas tree in their small living room and entertained four soldiers and a WAC for Christmas dinner. For Peter's birthday on the eighth of January, Eleanor made a chocolate cake decorated with twenty-seven candles. A week later while Caroline Gordon was staying with them, Peter received orders to leave Fort Oglethorpe on January 19 for Camp Butner near Durham, North Carolina, where he would train for overseas duty.[14]

From Butner, Peter wrote a reassuring letter to his mother. Along with Bob Denney, a thirty-seven-year-old married man from a different Memphis social world, with whom he had made friends at Oglethorpe, Peter had been assigned to Headquarters Company, 12th Replacement Depot. "When we do go across, our function will be the handling of other men who come over. We'll remain from fifty to one hundred miles behind the lines and continue to send replacements up. So we'll be comparatively free from danger," Peter told her. Still, he admitted, "This is a rough outfit." Repelled by the incessant profanity of soldiers, Peter also retained his rather formal, old-fashioned manner, so he always stood out among the general soldiery and received his share of insults and heckling. At Butner, the men underwent concentrated training in the field. "Life is only a constant struggle for petty advantages—to be first in some line, to get a newer gun than the next man, to steal an extra pair of pants, to avoid some menial job," he told Jean. "That's life in the U.S. Army." Peter confided to Nadine Parker that the worst part for him was not crawling amid barbed wire, shell holes, and mud under a barrage of live fire, but the enforced participation in sports, especially boxing and wrestling. "I am eager for experiences which I may have, especially if we go to the European theatre," he wrote. "I am frightened at the thought of actual combat, which there is, of course, a chance of my taking part. And I am distraught at the prospect of leaving Eleanor, for these have been the happiest months of my life."[15]

As soon as Peter's train left, Eleanor began packing all of their belongings, most of which she shipped to Memphis, and within ten days she was in Durham, where Peter was able to see her most nights. The first weekend, they spent in Norwood with the Rosses. "I liked them immensely," he told Jean, adding, "They are an anomaly in this age." Then a week later, his mother arrived, staying until he left Butner for an unnamed port near New York, and diverting Eleanor with her dramatic anecdotes while the two women darned Peter's socks and waited to see him for a few hours each evening.[16]

Eleanor had been back in Norwood for almost a week when Peter called and told her that his ship had been delayed indefinitely. Soon she was on the

train to New York, staying first at the Lowell apartment and later in Princeton
with Zandra Ross (the wife of her brother James), to be closer to Fort Dix,
where Peter's company was now being held. So they shared a few more hours
until Peter was confined to camp to prepare for embarkment. He shipped out
on March 12.[17]

In later years Peter Taylor would always say that he had had "an easy war."
But no soldier amid the thousands packed into the Île de France knew what
the future would hold as the ship headed toward the European theater. All
the men were apprehensive. Otherwise, the crossing was marked by just two
unusual incidents. A fellow G.I. recalled that while playing chess with Peter,
a soldier trying to get the attention of the surrounding group read from a story
reprinted in a service publication. To the astonishment of the soldiers, Peter
started to recite the next lines. The story was "The Fancy Woman." The author
just grinned and returned to the chess game. A few nights later, Peter awaked
in shock to find someone groping his body. The advance was easily rebuffed,
but he found sleep difficult for the rest of the night.[18]

The unknown destination of the troop ship turned out to be Northern
Ireland, which Peter judged the most beautiful country he had ever seen. "Just
as Chickamauga and Fort Oglethorpe inspired me with interest in Southern
history," he wrote Jean, "now I am being spurred by the sight of ancient vil-
lages, churches, and what the Irish call castles to draw out volumes of Irish
history." Obviously army life was not getting in the way of his basic aesthetic
and historical appreciation of landscape and place. Nor did it when the group
shipped over to England, where they were billeted in tents in the lovely Somerset countryside. And he was writing. He finished drafts of one story on the
ship and of another in Ireland. In Somerset, he found a room in a church kept
open to give the soldiers a place to write letters. It was his retreat, and there
he began his story "The Scoutmaster."[19]

In the space of a few weeks, he had also managed to make friends among
the local people. First, he came to know the vicar, an Oxford man, likable and
intelligent, and his family; and he was soon spending many evenings at the
vicarage. He had also met an old lady who lived in "an irresistible sixteenth
century country house in a fine state of decay" and whose talk fascinated him.
But the deepest friendship he formed in England was with Charles Abbot, a
gentleman of about sixty with whom he had fallen into conversation as the
two stood looking on at a dance. "His talk revealed that he is a strong reactionary not just to communism, but to capitalism itself," Peter wrote Eleanor.

"Now and then I would feel as though I was talking to Allen or even to Donald Davidson [the most reactionary of the Agrarians]." Evidently it was the talk of this cultivated English gentleman that set off the train of associations and ideas that inspired "The Scoutmaster."[20]

That the charming and impressive Charles Abbot could suggest to the writer the pathos of a character like Uncle Jake in "The Scoutmaster" reveals Peter Taylor's complex transformation of his own experience in his fiction. Beginning the story, the reader finds Uncle Jake no more in the foreground than any one of several members of a Nashville family in the 1930s, for this is Peter Taylor's first venture into the apparently digressive mode that would become one of his hallmarks. Gradually one is led into the world of a ten-year-old boy in the family and his dawning awareness of sex and death, of the roles that people come to play in dealing with these and other issues, and of the difference between the perceived essence of a character and the role that the character adopts in coping with life. At the conclusion, almost all the family have become "strangers" to the boy, above all Uncle Jake in his Scout uniform, delivering his message:

> In that cold, bare bright room he was saying that it was our great misfortune to have been born in these latter days when the morals and manner of the country had been corrupted, born in a time when we could see upon the members of our own families . . . the effects of our failure to cling to the teachings and ways of our forefathers. And he was saying that it was our duty and great privilege, as Boy Scouts, to preserve those honorable things which were left from the golden days when a race of noble gentlemen and gracious ladies inhabited the land of the South. He was saying that we must preserve them until one day we might stand with young men from all over the nation to demand a return to the old ways and the old teachings everywhere.

As Elizabeth Hardwick noted after having reread the story forty years later, among its other qualities, it is one of the saddest Taylor stories of the "unreality of backward longings."[21]

Peter knew that this was a different sort of story for him, containing more of the "elements," as he expressed the matter to Jean Stafford, that he was now interested in. He went on to describe the creative process: "Once I've gotten the idea or maybe just a first sentence for a story in my head I walk around for days or weeks while the tone or level-of-irony-for-the-narration tries to establish itself finally. Then one day I suddenly hear it in somebody's speech, or remember it in something someone has said in the past." In "The Scout-master," he had found how to blend the discursive structure with the proper level of irony, and he was pleased.[22]

Charles Abbot could never have seen himself in Uncle Jake. Locally known as a "cocoa magnate," he spent the weekdays at his business in Bristol, where his residence was a fine eighteenth-century house. At other times, he lived the life of the cultivated country gentleman in Somerset. He was wonderful to Peter. The Saturday after their meeting, he invited the young soldier to his Somerset home, a great thatched-roofed half-timbered house with a splendid library, where Peter spent an evening with Abbot and his spinster sister, an avid sportswoman, Mistress of the Hounds of the local hunt. As he was leaving, his host pointed to a stack of reading matter. "These are for you to take along with you," he said. The stack contained Samuel Butler's *Erewhon* and old issues of the *American Mercury*. In the weeks following, the invitations continued, urging that Peter make use of the "house, books, and bathtub." Soon Peter had both Abbots reading Henry James. One of the many books pressed upon the young soldier was a volume of Trollope, whose works became one of the great pleasures of Peter's life.[23]

Allen Tate had written requesting a story for his first issue as editor of the *Sewanee Review*. Peter felt the honor of such a request, coming from the person "who has taught me most of what I know about writing." Peter had also been invited to apply for a Guggenheim, to begin after his discharge. He submitted a plan for a book of four short novels or long stories. "There would be charac-ters or types of characters linking them, and certainly the general scene would do so," he explained to Eleanor. "All together . . . they'll be my criticisms of life and society in my own region in my time."[24]

But for all the reading, writing, and interesting social contacts that Peter had managed, most of life was still the army routine. He and Denney were still working together and living in the same tent. In a letter to his parents, he asked that they keep in touch with Denney's wife. That would reassure his friend. He added a postscript to a letter to Eleanor: "Just a few minutes ago I learned that our troops have landed in France. Everyone in camp is wild with joy." The dreadful building tension of the past weeks was over; the war had entered a different stage.[25]

By month's end, Headquarters Company moved to a new location, with running water and electricity, near a small city. Peter found the situation ugly, and he missed the lovely country he had left and the friends he had made there, so much he said that he longed for the outhouse and candles of the old camp. While in this lonely, restive mood, beset often with the fears that a person of his imagination would always suffer in time of war, he took the step that he had been contemplating for some time—he was confirmed in the Church of England. Influenced by Cal's example, he had been attending services for the past two years and had felt fortunate to have an Anglo-Catholic chaplain in his company abroad. Under the cleric's direction, he had been reading theology. The chaplain learned that the bishop of Bath and Wells was to conduct Evensong at the little Norman church at Stoke-sub-Hamdon on the last Sunday of August. That afternoon he and Peter drove down into Somerset in a jeep, and Peter was accepted into the Church. After the service, a fat little old lady in black moving slowly out in the line of communicants took his hand and said, "I was confirmed far from home a long time ago in India." "My loneliness is abysmal and my temptations are numberless," Peter confessed to Tom White. But, tellingly, after reporting the event to Jean, he commented: "Perhaps I can get back and try to sketch that Norman arch over the chancel, for I'm really haunted by it." Even during this great spiritual moment, he was ever the artist.[26]

On the first of September, the company moved to a permanent station near London, Camp Tidworth. Tensions were building on the Continent. "I try to think as little as possible about the actual slaughter that is going on across the channel," he told his parents, "for there are necessarily days when you can think of nothing else and you'd go crazy if you didn't purposely turn your thoughts away from it." In November he confided to Eleanor that in his dreams he was usually fighting someone or on his way home. More and more men were being shipped over. At the end of the month, Denney and other close friends received orders for the Continent. On December 17, Peter wrote Eleanor:

> I still have not heard from Denney nor have I heard from any of the others that have gone. All but three or four that are in the group picture have gone now, and they were the best friends I've ever made in the army. I always meant to write you about them individually, but now it would seem pointless to do so. They were the best lot of men I've ever been thrown with. . . . By best friends and best lot I mean that they were all men (though several are under twenty) independent yet generous and considerate, rough and impersonal in their manner but full of kindnesses and real humor. I think I'll always remember the war chiefly as a long series of separations.

The day before the letter, Hitler's panzer brigades had launched the surprise attack that began the Battle of the Bulge.[27]

The bloody battle was still raging the day after Christmas when Peter was told that he was to follow Denney and the others to the Continent. After a day spent gathering personal equipment, he arranged a hurried farewell pass and went to London, where he met Bill Eason, now stationed near Warwick. Spending money lavishly, they ordered a fine meal—martinis, oysters on the half-shell, sauterne, Supreme of Grille with mushrooms in white wine—followed by many hours of talking and drinking scotch in the bar of the Berkeley Hotel. The next morning, while nursing an awful hangover, Peter was recalled to Tidworth. Back at camp he learned that his commanding officer, a colonel priding himself on possessing the best athletic teams in the regiment, had been removed after the discovery that he had been subverting orders by keeping all of his athletes in England while sending men in much worse physical condition, like Denney, to the Continent. Not only had the colonel been removed but all his orders rescinded. "I have much to be thankful for," Peter wrote Eleanor on the last day of 1944.[28]

The whole camp was now filled with activity, and Peter was given much more work to do. But it was clear that he would remain in England. By February, the Allies were pushing the Germans back on all fronts. Victory was in sight. Personal dangers were passed. "Rain in the Heart" appeared in the winter issue of *Sewanee Review,* and Peter's agents, Russell and Volkening, had entered "The Scoutmaster" in the *Partisan Review–Dial* short story competition. He learned that he had been awarded only third place. "I hope you won first (though I'd have liked winning it)," he wrote Jean when he received the news, "so that I'll feel I've been beaten by someone worth being beaten by." He was sincere. Peter Taylor felt little petty jealousy about the successes of his friends. But still, the results of the competition must have exacerbated all sorts of dissatisfactions and tensions. While he was locked into hateful routines with no literary companions, Jean and Cal (now out of prison) were spending evenings with Mary McCarthy and Philip Rahv and making names for themselves in the literary world. Jean's photograph had appeared in *Harper's Bazaar* after her novel *Boston Adventure* made the best-seller list, and critics had responded to Cal's first volume, *Land of Unlikeness,* with respectful attention.[29]

On May 7, peace was proclaimed in Europe. "Somehow I felt no inclination to imbibe or make noise," Peter told his father. "There were a lot of U.S. soldiers who felt about it as I did. Such a halfway peace cannot be the cause of much rejoicing for someone who has already been in uniform for four years and for whom the prospects of getting out of it are entirely remote." But this mood passed, and a month later Peter was writing Nadine a happy letter reporting that he was reading the works of Trollope ("The nineteenth century, I am convinced, was the great age of genius"), traveling to London frequently to haunt the galleries, and writing. After months of starting but being unable to finish his stories, in the weeks after V-E Day he finished two impressive, though quite different efforts.[30]

The first, titled originally "The Spell" and finally "Allegiance," is his most thoroughly Jamesian story, but no matter what his indebtedness, it is a dazzling piece of work. An American serviceman visits his worldly, expatriate aunt in London, whom his rigidly conventional mother has long ago judged guilty of a breach of trust and shunned. Burdened with guilt for even making contact with the aunt, he is still captivated. Caught in the flow of the soldier's consciousness, the reader feels with him the overpowering reality of the present moment, the spell of the aunt. But in the end, the man returns to the constraints of background: "And though my mind is troubled by a doubt of the reality of all things and I am haunted for a while by an unthinkable distrust for the logic and the rarefied judgments of my dead mother, I feel myself still a prisoner in her parlor at Nashville with the great sliding doors closed and the jagged little flames darting from the grate." The germ of the piece apparently lies in the contrast between Peter's sophisticated Aunt Ret in Washington and his mother, but the theme of conflicting allegiance may be traceable to the appeal of a young widow living with relatives at a country house named Chilliwood in Somerset. Because of her, Peter told Tom White, he had to quit visiting the family.[31]

When Allen Tate judged the story "fuss without feathers" and "imitative of James," Peter took umbrage. "I don't often try to write a story of that sort," he told Jean, "but it's certainly enjoyable to try to write something out-of-one's line now and then. I think sometimes, though, that I shouldn't experiment with style at all." Tate, however, accepted the second effort, "A Long Fourth," for the *Sewanee Review*.[32]

A longish story set on an estate off Franklin Pike south of Nashville, "A Long Fourth" returns to what readers would come to know as Peter Taylor's particular milieu, but it examines that world in even more complicated terms than did "The Scoutmaster." The story has elicited some schematic cultural readings. Various of Peter's letters from England do articulate Agrarian views.

"I am only now coming to realize how right Mr. Tate and the Agrarians have been about the South which is the only region where our agricultural traditions have persisted," he wrote his father. And to Robie Macauley, Peter commented that he now found the Southerner a "much more significant type than I ever dreamed that he was." But after advancing the idea that the change from the life on the land (grounded in the family, old social traditions, and traditional religion) to the present industrialized, urbanized, materialistic phase manifested the decline of civilization, Peter followed with this startling statement: "This is neither a negative or pessimistic view." He continued by insisting that his ideas indicated no political position, but reflected instead "the real drama which I want to insinuate in my stories of the happy and unhappy experiences of Southerners." Individual passages from the letters might support an Agrarian or even Spenglerian reading of Taylor's fiction—but one must note in these letters the twists and turns of Peter Taylor's mind.[33]

"Threads snap when I try to develop a theory too far," he admitted to Jean Stafford. He was speaking of literary theories, but the admission relates equally well to cultural matters. Both as an artist and as a man, he operated by instinct, not logic, and certainly not by the dictates of dogma. Though acutely aware of all the degrees of cultural change, he remained primarily concerned with the fate of human beings caught in the ceaseless turnings of time. Thus Harriet Wilson, the central figure in "A Long Fourth," rather than being a representative product of a traditional culture, is more fundamentally a compelling instance of the unexamined life. Decidedly less intelligent than her iconoclastic mother (who is of course more thoroughly the product of the old culture), Harriet unquestioningly accepts her place in a patriarchal structure. In fact, those whose opinions she most reveres she calls not by their names, but by the appellations "Sweetheart" and "Son." When Harriet finally realizes that she has produced three insensitive, uncaring children, the reader lays some of the blame, not to the decline of culture, but to the mother's own shallowness and lack of force. The shallowness is exemplified most dramatically in Harriet's horror when Mattie, her longtime African American maid, finds a parallel between her sorrow over separation from her nephew B.T. (in Harriet's mind, that "sullen, stinking, thieving, fornicating black B.T.") and Harriet's grief over Son's call to military duty. In her rigidity and lack of empathy, Harriet is shown to lack even the humanity of her husband's paternalism.[34]

"A Long Fourth" is a richly textured and complex story, drawing upon Peter Taylor's thorough knowledge of his culture and his sense of human limitation and confusion, as well as his interest in humankind caught in time. It represents his first real treatment of his culture's racial constructs. Like many sensitive American servicemen, the war years marked a change in Peter Taylor's racial attitudes. As strange as it may seem today, the first step for a white Southerner was breaking the taboo against sitting at the same table with African Americans. In January of 1944, he wrote his mother about being seated with two black servicemen in a dining car. His first reaction was rage at the head waiter who had arranged the seating; his second was embarrassment at the situation. Afterward, he was critical of himself. "It was cruel of us not to have talked with them," he realized. Within three months, he reported a dream in which his mother was waiting on the table and Lucille, their beloved St. Louis maid, was seated with the family. She told them that the old order of things was over. That dream, he told his mother, "is indicative, I think." He shared no further racial insights with her, but others no doubt followed in the months before he wrote "A Long Fourth."[35]

Peter would not have expressed even these thoughts directly to his father. They had exchanged affectionate letters when Peter was first in England. "Dad's letter was the best I've ever had from him," he wrote Eleanor in July of 1944, "and he related in it an experience he had recently in Alabama. I'll save the letter for there's really the core of story in it." Peter did save it and wrote the story ("Two Pilgrims") almost twenty years later, but the correspondence took a different turn soon afterward, when Hillsman found that his son had been confirmed in the Anglican Church. Always wanting to remain the patriarch in control, Hillsman was furious, first that Peter had not consulted him before taking this step and second that Peter had rejected his father's religion—never mind that Hillsman had done the very same thing in his own youth. Thereupon ensued a correspondence over Peter's lack of respect for his father's opinions and his father's intelligence (this latter reported to Hillsman by Bob). What tangles of logic Peter got himself into refuting those charges. Then the following spring Peter set his father off again by suggesting that he might well become a serious painter, as well as a writer. "Do not try to be a 'Jack of all trades and good at none,' " Hillsman fired back. "You have made a success of writing and a fine reputation. Do not waste it. Writing will take all of your time and besides I do not believe you would succeed as an artist." This was sound advice, but unfortunately he continued: "You have the temperament, but not the skill. You are not physically skillful."[36]

As the weeks dragged on after the victory in Europe, in addition to the disagreements with his father, Peter was experiencing all sorts of mood swings, as well as being worried about Tom White in India and distressed about Bruce, who had been severely wounded in France. "The best part of my twenties is being spent in the army and absolutely thrown away," he wrote. "Whatever profit was ever to be had from the experience is long since realized." But at the end of the letter, he added: "There are bad days and weeks, but I inherit a happy sort of nature and am likely to go along quietly whatever happens."[37]

He was wrong about the likelihood of new experiences. Early in July he received a membership card for the Churchill Club in London. He began using the club as his outpost in the city, and he was there the evening that the prime minister announced the Japanese surrender. In the next morning's rain, he walked among the crowds in Piccadilly and Trafalgar Square, stopping in St. Martin-in-the-Fields to say a prayer. Finally it was over; life could begin again.[38]

Within two weeks Peter had an opportunity to go for his first visit to Paris. He was enchanted, stimulated, awakened to all sorts of aesthetic experiences. And he had a bit of wonderful luck. Walking down the rue du Rivoli, he spied Gertrude Stein, approached her, introduced himself; and soon they were talking. When she learned that he was a writer of short fiction, she asked what writer he admired. "My first great admiration was for Henry James," he replied. She responded by asking whether he had read Trollope. "How funny that your generation should like those people," she said. "I read Trollope when everyone else was ignoring him. He has the real touch. I think he is the real genius of the nineteenth century." She then invited him home to her apartment on the Left Bank. "She is the reverse of all you would imagine," Peter wrote. "She is sensible and witty and the old word *warmth* is the only one to describe her personality." During the two hours of the visit, Stein returned again and again to the moral reprehensibility of slavery in the South. As he left her apartment and started down the stair, she opened the door and called after him with a smile, "Remember. Face the facts."[39]

Returning to England, Peter found that the depot was being broken up, and the men with low service points assigned to duty on the Continent as part of the army of occupation. By October 6, he was writing his mother that "the old outfit is no more." Peter was temporarily made a librarian before being assigned to teach American literature at an army school, his first stint as a teacher. During the term, he gained another glimpse of a literary giant as one of a group of thirty at a lecture given by T. S. Eliot. Speaking on the writings of Poe, Eliot reminded Peter "of nothing so much as a great lanky raven."[40]

During these weeks, Peter experienced many false hopes about his separation from the army. Again and again, there was delay. The literary news, however, was good. The British critic Herbert Read had asked to reprint "Rain in the Heart" for a collection that he was editing; and Martha Foley had chosen the story for *The Best Short Stories of 1945*, Peter's second appearance in the series. He had not been awarded the Guggenheim, but Paul Engle had written offering a position at the University of Iowa Writing Program, and Eleanor had visited her old professor Marc Friedlaender at Woman's College of North Carolina, who wanted Peter to come there. One thing was certain, Peter wrote his parents: he and Eleanor would spend some time at Monteagle, which he was coming to regard as a second home. He had a final visit with the Abbots and made a last excursion to Salisbury. Finally, on the first of December, he was able to write Eleanor: "We're told that we will sail on the Queen Mary one week from tomorrow. That will be the ninth. We should dock in New York on about the fifteenth." "So," he concluded, "barring any further postponements, you can fairly expect to spend Christmas with a civilian husband."[41]

8

Starting Out in the Forties ···

After the *Queen Mary* landed in New York, Peter's group of soldiers was first sequestered at Camp Kilmer, then shipped by rail to Fort McPherson outside Atlanta. On December 20, he was released from the army, and he took a train to Chattanooga, where he met Eleanor in the lobby of the Read House. A week later he wrote Cal and Jean that he was still "too dazed to try to make any plans." He and Eleanor had gone immediately to Sewanee, where they found only Allen, Caroline having left to secure a divorce. It was "all very sad and disheartening," he told the Lowells, "like coming home to find your house burnt down." After only a few hours with Allen, the Taylors had boarded a night bus with standing room only for Memphis.[1]

The Memphis homecoming was happier than the one on the mountain, but Peter was distressed to see that during the two years he had been overseas his mother's hair had turned white. Peter was the last of his group to return from the war, and throughout the Christmas season one reunion followed another. Bruce Fulton, wounded in France and thus now in his father's favor, had been made vice-president at Fulton Cotton Company. The price of cotton was high, and everyone that Peter knew was prospering.[2]

On the first of the year, Hillsman and Katherine went to California, and

Peter and Eleanor had the Stonewall apartment to themselves for a month. Then in early February, they secured a house, not in Monteagle as planned, but in Sewanee, where they were to take the place Allen had leased and rent him a room. "Our month of luxury and nightlife is up," Peter wrote Jean on the fifth, "and I feel very much like a civilian again." But he was a different civilian. Once when his mother made a remark about Negroes, he had replied, "Why, Mother, I've been a Negro for four years." He reported to Jean that "the nigger-hating continues" in Memphis and like all cities its "solution for the race problem is brutal."[3]

The Tate divorce had gone through on January 8, Peter's birthday, and Allen's name was being linked with a number of women: the young writers Elizabeth Hardwick and Mildred Haun, the mountain girl who was his secretary at the *Sewanee Review,* and Alida Mayo, wife of a history professor at the University of Virginia. Early in the Taylors' stay in Sewanee, Allen received a call from Donald Davidson suggesting that Mildred Haun's mountaineer twin brothers might seek revenge. Turning from the telephone with his consummate sense of the dramatic, Allen said, "We must arm ourselves!" The Tate drama continued for several weeks, ending with Allen's following Caroline to New York, where they were remarried on April 11.[4]

In the meantime, Peter had revised and typed a book of eight stories and sent it to Doubleday. He wanted most now to spend some time in New York, but for the fall he knew that he must take an academic job at either Woman's College in Greensboro or at Iowa, a better choice, he felt, especially if he could persuade Robie Macauley to go there too. At Eleanor's urging, he also made contact with another of the Kenyon group, Randall Jarrell, who came up from Nashville with his wife for a weekend on the mountain. In March, Peter received two bits of disappointing news—first, Doubleday rejected the manuscript, saying that they would wait for a novel from him. "My writing a novel now would be merely a matter of spreading the jam thin," he complained to Jean. "Writing well has always been an up-hill battle for me, and I am far enough advanced now to make no bones about it and I know too well what I am doing to be diverted by agents and publishers." Feeling that his agent Diarmuid Russell had failed to represent him effectively, Peter wrote directly to Doubleday demanding either release from his contract or an immediate thousand-dollar advance, and mentioning three linked stories that he was working on. To his amazement, the publishers agreed to the advance. No sooner had that matter been solved than a letter from Paul Engle reported that the position at Iowa would be little more than a graduate fellowship. Greens-boro seemed now the only option. In early April, Peter and Eleanor left for North Carolina to visit the Rosses and interview at Woman's College.[5]

"The Rosses," as Peter described them to Jean, "are very much like what my own great-grandparents must have been, and life here on the farm can not be very different from what theirs was in Tennessee about a hundred years ago." A rigid old-time Methodist, Mr. Ross allowed no work on the farm on Sundays and talked mainly of his crops and his mules; Mrs. Ross never openly disagreed with him about anything. "A strange and extremely interesting fam-ily," Peter found them, especially Eleanor's three siblings, who were all now writing fiction. They returned his regard, and all must have been delighted when by the middle of the month he had been offered and had accepted the position at Greensboro, just eighty miles from Norwood.[6]

With plans for the future school year settled, Peter drew from the Double-day advance to purchase an old Chevrolet from a fat shade-tree mechanic cousin of Eleanor's. Taking the rest of the money, he and Eleanor headed for New York, to confront the literary world for the first time as a couple. The Tates arranged that they take the apartment of the writer Marguerite Young during her absence from the city, and Allen got Peter a temporary job reading manuscripts at Henry Holt, where he was now an editor. The walk-up flat at 244 West Tenth was dominated by a giant King of Hearts over the living room mantel, with glitter applied, oppressive to both Taylors. But the Tates were just a few blocks away on Perry, and, as always, wherever they settled was the center of social life, even though on Perry the only water source was the bathroom. When the Taylors reached New York, by luck Cal was in town, down from Maine, where he and Jean were living. Soon afterward, the Tates had a wonderful literary party, among the guests poets Howard Nemerov and e. e. cummings, with his beautiful model wife.[7]

The whole Kenyon group was in New York. All except Cal had been in the service, but no one ever talked about life during the war. It was the life now that engaged them. Randall and Mackie Jarrell had been in the city since April, when Randall temporarily assumed the position as literary editor of *The Na-tion*. In New York, for the first time he and Peter became close friends. "I doubt I could have ever got started again after the war," Peter later wrote, "if I had not had Randall to talk to or to listen to." The rest of the group were more wary of and daunted by the holy terror. David McDowell was working for James Laughlin at New Directions, and Robie Macauley at *Gourmet*. The center of activity for the Kenyon men was Jack and Dilly Thompson's apartment on West Sixty-seventh. During the war, Jack had married a rich girl from Grand Rapids, and though Jack was now only a graduate student at Columbia, they lived in a comfortable apartment and drove Dilly's yellow Mercury convertible, one of the last cars made before the war.[8]

A Memphis friend was also working in publishing, Anne Draper, who had been married to and divorced from Jimmy Smithwick, with whom Peter had traveled to Europe after high school. Peter arranged that she meet Robie, and the two of them, along with the Taylors and the Thompsons, crammed themselves into the Mercury and headed south on an excursion that all talked about for years. The plan was to picnic along the Jersey shore, but rain began to fall, and they drove farther and farther, drinking from jugs filled with Tom Collins and consuming sandwiches until they finally reached Delaware and decided to turn around and come home. Drunk, hot, and hilarious, they drove into Manhattan, where Eleanor (the only sober one) declared, "Well, that was better than a really successful picnic."[9]

Despite their differences, Dilly Thompson and Eleanor became close, Eleanor later crediting the worldly and smart Dilly with teaching her all sorts of things that she needed to know. Dilly was also witty, proclaiming at one party that she had had so much to drink that she made a pass at the boorish David McDowell. At another gathering, sick of literary talk, Dilly quipped, "Eleanor, I don't believe in the written word." "Dilly," Eleanor said, "I don't believe in the spoken word." Eleanor's reticence was becoming legendary, especially in contrast to her ebullient husband.[10]

Much of the New York literary talk centered on Red Warren's novel *All the King's Men,* which was creating a sensation. Another literary landmark was being completed that summer at Damariscotta Mills, Maine, where Cal was putting the finishing touches on the manuscript of *Lord Weary's Castle.* At the end of June and of their New York stay, the Taylors went up to Maine to visit Cal and Jean. Then after seeing James and Zandra Ross in Princeton, they left for North Carolina, and Peter's first teaching job.[11]

A year earlier, Peter had written his father: "I am still resolved not to try to make teaching my profession.... To be a good teacher you must be scholarly and you must like to teach. I am not a scholar and I cannot instruct." Further, he noted, "I have seen teaching prevent both Mr. Tate and Mr. Ransom from writing as much as they should have in their lifetime." But like so many of his literary generation, teaching was the means by which he would make his

livelihood. Peter approached the first term at Greensboro with trepidation.
He had been assigned a creative writing seminar, along with a freshman and
a sophomore class. His salary for the year was $2,700, supplemented by what
Eleanor would earn as a librarian.[12]

But even before the fall term began, he and Eleanor were in the midst of
the first of many love affairs with a house, this one the old Lilly place near
Norwood, built by Eleanor's great-great-great-grandfather. It was a two-story
frame dwelling of the late eighteenth century, the interior finished in virgin
pine and oak, which had never known a drop of paint. The paneling and wain-
scoting, he told Robie, "literally beggar description." The Taylors were willing
to live in cramped quarters in Greensboro in order to buy it, Peter said, though
by fall they had rented instead a large and fairly expensive apartment near the
campus. At the start of the school year, "A Long Fourth" appeared in the
Sewanee Review, and Cal wrote praising it as Peter's best effort, or at least
almost his best, next to "The Scoutmaster." Three days later Cal posted another letter from Maine with the news "everything is in chaos with us." He
and Jean were separating.[13]

In the next few months much of Peter's emotional energy was spent in
consoling the Lowells and serving as intermediary between them. He invited
each separately to come to Greensboro for a visit. Neither came, and early in
November a disturbing one-sentence letter arrived from Jean: "Dearest Eleanor and Peter, Please write to me for I am very lost." This was followed by Cal's
letter announcing that they were getting a divorce. Soon afterward, completely
debilitated, Jean entered the Payne Whitney Clinic at New York Hospital for
both psychological problems and alcoholism. Finally two days before Christmas, Peter wrote Cal: "My powers of restraint are just about exhausted. I now
feel compelled to ask you to hold up on the divorce until you and I have met
and talked. . . . Wait a year. Take the matter out of the hands of your lawyers.
Agree not to communicate with each other, except through me." After making
this offer, he revealed the depth of feeling for both of them:

> There has been a bond between the three of us, to which I've never seen anything
> comparable. . . . What is important is the determination each of us has shown
> to forgive the failings, and to learn from, the others. . . . In a sense, our relation-
> ship was the greatest—perhaps our only—mark of humanity during the period
> when we were nearing maturity. It is probably the thing that we each should be
> most proud of, for we had no examples set for us. We had all, one way or another,

isolated ourselves from our families; and the thing that we maintained is just that thing which the generation of writers preceding us—the very people we admired and tried to imitate—were notably lacking.

Though Cal had earlier written that "there is no one else I can talk to in the same way," he responded, "You mustn't idealize what someone else has to live. You mustn't." Peter wrote back, withdrawing his offer, having realized that he would "only complicate matters further and probably add to the misunderstanding." Still he continued to stay in close touch with both Cal and Jean.[14]

Through the fall Peter managed some time for writing, having done "several little Chekovesque things" and "sketched in parts of several longer stories." He had also begun a story covering the thirty hours of Lindbergh's flight to Paris, and he was determined during the Christmas holiday to finish his novelette, begun in Chattanooga and titled at first "Edward, Edward," after the medieval poem. In order to realize that goal, he had to remain in Greensboro. Hillsman was furious that Peter would break the custom of having the family all together, but Peter stayed and completed the work, wishing all the while that Doubleday had revoked his contract.[15]

Between semesters in January, he went to Memphis by train alone. "I wouldn't live in Memphis again for all the cotton on Front Street," he wrote Jean on his return. His friends, many still hard-drinking, were settling into parenthood and prosperous bourgeois routines. Hillsman, once again a rich man, was "more arrogant than ever and more certain of his eighteenth century philosophizing." Peter sketched this portrait of his father:

> The night I left he listed on his ten fingers the ten country squires who set the tone of Trenton society in the 1890's. Each of them, he said, was a classical scholar, a farmer, and a man of business. I felt that all the Agrarians' fiction had come to life for the sole purpose of haunting me. Now I wish you could see my father after a couple of highballs; it's like meeting the ghost of one of the barons who signed at Runnymede. But don't misunderstand me. I love my father and have great sympathy for him. I know so well how his mind works and how impossible it would be for him to strip himself of all the comforts which seeing one's self as part of a tradition offers.

There were compensations for all Peter's listening: he returned with Hillsman's promise to advance the money for the purchase of the Lilly place.[16]

Back in North Carolina, he found that the Lilly farm had been leased for a year to three families, but he continued to negotiate to purchase, and he began writing a one-act play. As he worked on it, he reported to Robie that he had also been reading the plays of Chekhov, Shaw, Synge, O'Casey, and Ibsen. Randall, now teaching at Sarah Lawrence, had expressed interest in coming to Woman's College, and Peter had arranged an interview for him in March. After he left, Peter's time was consumed by frantic last-minute preparations for the college's annual Arts Forum. Peter had secured Robert Penn Warren as the primary literary speaker, and he had stacked the panels with other friends. Jack and Dilly were driving the yellow convertible down and bringing Robie and Cal. At the last moment, Bob Giroux, Cal's editor at Harcourt, Brace, expressed interest in coming, so five people now descended on the Taylors' apartment.[17]

The forum went off well, and socially it was a rousing success. The convivial New Yorkers left after the weekend, but Cal stayed on, and during the Easter break he and the Taylors made a trip down the Carolina coast to Charleston. Peter's story "Allegiance" was appearing in the spring issue of *Kenyon Review,* and Eleanor made her debut in the spring number of *Sewanee Review* with "Mr. Milkman," a story written shortly before Peter returned from England, published under the name Eleanor Ross. Good things continued to happen. Monday, April 14, was an incredible day. The morning's mail contained a letter to Cal announcing that he had won a Guggenheim. Before lunch, Peter informed the English department of a substantial offer Iowa had made him for the next year. That afternoon the advisory committee met and agreed to match the Iowa salary and allow Peter to teach two rather than three courses a term, both writing seminars. At the same time, the committee voted not only to hire Randall but also to give Mackie Jarrell a job. In late afternoon a telegram arrived from Bob Giroux. Harcourt, Brace offered Peter a contract for two books and agreed to repay the Doubleday advance. As Peter wrote Robie, his life seemed completely changed.[18]

Jean's second novel, *The Mountain Lion,* completed before the separation, had appeared to good reviews, and she left the hospital for a few weeks in April. Early in May, the Pulitzer Prizes were announced: Red had won for fiction, and Cal for poetry. All three of these friends were Harcourt, Brace writers. Surely Peter was happy to be among them, but for the rest of his life he was to be unhappy with agents, editors, and publishers. Bob Giroux wrote suggesting that Peter's volume of short stories bear the title *A Long Fourth and*

Other Stories, that it be published with an introduction by Red Warren, and that it appear after the first of the year. Peter was bitterly disappointed that the collection would not appear in the fall, but finally he agreed to the terms.[19]

Peter wrote to Cal to congratulate him on his celebrity, winning the prize and having his picture in *Life.* Katherine Taylor had visited, and Peter and Eleanor had driven her to East Tennessee to see her family. "I adore my mother," he told his friend, "but how a visit with her does exhaust me." Then he sketched another vivid family portrait:

> Her memory is certainly something remarkable; she seems to be living two lives at once. She came here from a long visit with Aunt Ret in Washington, full of all the Capitol gossip which, like all old time Southerners, she takes pretty seriously . . . the ostentatious furnishings of the Joe Davies house, Senator Reynolds' life interest in the McLean house (What a rascal he is!), and exactly at what point behind her ears you can find Wally Simpson's face-lifting scars. She talked about all this as we drove up through Virginia, meanwhile pointing out old houses where she had visited as a girl, once saying, "That's the old Dr. St. John house where George took poor little Emmy as a bride." (Emmy being my late Aunt Em).

Both Taylors were eager for the end of the school year, when Eleanor would quit her job, and Peter told Cal that the Jarrells were arriving in July.[20]

In June, the Taylors went down to visit the Rosses and to investigate the situation with the old Lilly place, which Peter was already giving a name, though he wavered between Lilly Hall and Riverview. The owner was now offering to sell the house and seventy-five acres along the Rocky River. Since Peter was to use his father's money, Hillsman had to be consulted. "Don't agree to any of the things this man is asking for," he advised his son. "Talk with Mr. Ross and your attorney." Then he adopted his pompous classical pose: "I call your attention to the chapter of Bacon's Essays on trading and suggest that you read it. I have not read it in a long time, but I do believe that is one of the best things that I ever read on dealings between buyers and sellers. Bacon's Essays are all, of course, very wonderful commentaries on human relations in business, but I think the one on trading is the best." When the Jarrells reached Greensboro, however, Peter got caught up in another project. By the end of July, Peter and Randall had taken out G.I. loans and bought together a two-story brick duplex. Hillsman judged the purchase a mistake and cautioned against buying the farm now, but his wayward son ignored the practical advice. By the second week in September, the Taylors had moved into one side of the duplex at 1924 Spring Garden; and with a loan of five hundred dollars from Jack Thompson, they had also bought the Rocky River farm. Eleanor was now working in the customer complaint department of Sears and Roebuck to pay for the property.[21]

The Spring Garden duplex is today a central part of Greensboro literary history. The Woman's College literary tradition began in the 1930s when Allen Tate and Caroline Gordon taught there. Now again in 1947, two significant writers were on the faculty—and living in the same house. The Taylors and the Jarrells were young, attractive, and intelligent, though Randall's brilliance always tended to eclipse that of anyone around him. He was mentor during this period to both Peter and Eleanor. He soon had Peter revising his novelette still another time, and he would go over it with Peter sentence by sentence. Eleanor was again writing poetry, and one day Peter led her to the Jarrell's living room. "I've taken this little girl by the hand," he said to Randall, "and made her bring these poems to you." There began a strong literary and psychic bond between Eleanor and Randall that lasted until his death. But of course Randall could also prove difficult. His skill at finding and exposing a person's weaknesses struck terror. His wit was truly rapier sharp. "He found small talk deadly," Eleanor remembered. "Once when Mackie and I were discussing the price of stockings, or brands of coffee, he burst out histrionically, 'Oh, what a petty, ignoble conversation!' " But she also insisted that no one's voice could express "more affection and welcome" than Randall's. Because the Taylors appreciated Randall's talents and his interest in their work, they could minimize difficulties in his personality and the frictions that always result from living in close quarters. They had to say no when Randall wanted the connecting door between the apartments always left open for easy access. One night, however, the Taylors forgot to lock the door. Upon discovering the Jarrells' beloved cat, Kitten, in their bedroom, an enraged Peter attacked the feline with a dust mop. Then there was Randall's record player. Randall played music at full volume, and his Mahler filled both apartments day after day.[22]

Overall, however, the first months on Spring Garden were stimulating, productive, and happy. Peter spent the fall revising the novelette, which he now called "Casa Anna," and working on the proofs for his collection of stories. This complete absorption in his fiction contributed to his first run-in with Allen Tate. A year earlier Tate had asked Peter for a contribution to a special issue of *Sewanee Review* in honor of John Crowe Ransom's sixtieth birthday.

At the last minute in November of 1947, Peter wrote that he simply could not do it. He also felt it necessary to apologize for having changed publishers without consulting Allen. Tate's reply was curt. He made it obvious that Peter had let him down, and he also refused an invitation to the spring Arts Forum. "Again, Peter, you oughtn't to ask us at the last minute," he wrote; "there is a rather distressing inference to be made from it."[23]

Again at Christmas the Taylors did not go to Memphis. They had visited Hillsman and Katherine at Hot Springs, Virginia, in September, and when Peter and Eleanor had driven away in their wretched old car, his father had made a point of hallooing from the central portico, "Good-bye, PROFESSOR! Good-bye, PROFESSOR." Instead, Cal, now poetry consultant at the Library of Congress, came down from Washington, and James Waller came over from Chapel Hill, where he was teaching economics. "We'll all get looping," Peter had told Tom White in anticipation. Early in January, the Taylors took the train to New York to see Jean, who had finally been officially released from Payne Whitney, and to see some plays—*Medea, Volpone* (with Jose Ferrer) and *A Streetcar Named Desire.* Eleanor cautioned Peter that she did not want to waste her time in New York on parties.[24]

By this time, Peter had accepted a position at Indiana University for the next fall to teach graduate and undergraduate courses in creative writing at a significant increase in salary. He was in debt, and the chance to get more money and to have male students carried the day. Another change was also in the offing. "I am still highly skeptical, but Eleanor says it is true and Dr. P. D. Sparrow confirms it," Peter began a letter to Tom White. "It is rather unthinkable, I admit, somehow; yet one must, if he is at all imaginative, *must,* indeed be willing to consider the hypothesis. Especially so when a date, a month of the year—September—has been pointed out as the time when another being shall breathe the impure air of this world." He continued for two pages single spaced with stream-of-consciousness memories, associations, and expressions of exuberance.[25]

Peter had also revealed to Tom, with greater candor than to any of his literary friends, his joy and his hopes over the publication of his first book. "Suddenly I am going to be thrown upon the literary scene in a big way," he said, "and I shall enjoy reading all the silly things—good and bad—that will be written about me in literary journals." *A Long Fourth* was officially released on the first day of the Arts Forum, at which Cal and John Crowe Ransom were the featured literary figures. Upon his arrival, Ransom offered Peter a position at Kenyon, and Peter was now sick that he had accepted the Indiana offer. But his closest friend and his old mentor were both there to share the excitement of the first reviews.[26]

After going over the proofs for the last time, Peter had told Robie that it struck him that the stories were "usually about failure, the failures due to the characters' incredible lack of understanding of themselves and their situations." When Peter read Red Warren's introduction, he found it "just exactly perfect." "I imagine that it is not a common experience for a writer to *know* that he has been read with such intelligence and care by someone so especially qualified to understand the material and the experience in the writing and so able to interpret it," he wrote Red in gratitude. The introduction begins by noting that Peter had broken new ground in treating for the first time "the contemporary, urban, middle-class world of the upper South"—a world "vastly uncertain of itself and the ground of its values." The style, Warren commented, "is a natural style, one based on conversation and the family tale, with the echo of the spoken word, with the texture of some narrator's mind." In the midst of his discussion, he made an assessment of unusual prescience, in regard to both Peter's work and his nature—that Peter had "a disenchanted mind, but a mind that nevertheless understands and values enchantment."[27]

As Cal had predicted, the Warren introduction set the tone of the reviews that followed. The first to appear, on the initial day of the conference, was that in the *New York Times* by Nash K. Burger, who found that the seven stories "reveal an unusual, varied, well-sustained talent." The brief notice in the *New Yorker* called the book "an excellent collection," and the *New Republic* reviewer judged the stories "unusually fine." Coleman Rosenberger, writing in *New York Herald Tribune Books,* found the volume "a little island of excellence in the flood of books from the South," possessing the "qualities of permanence; a fine craftsmanship, integrity, and the imprint of a subtle and original intelligence." Most critics saw Peter as a new sort of Southern writer, not only in subject matter, but also attitude. The reviewer of *Commonweal,* short story writer J. F. Powers, distinguished Peter's subject as not "the people and parts we know already from Faulkner and Caldwell or even from Porter and Welty," and he went on to make sensitive comments on Peter's method, his refusal "to exploit his material to the limit," because, Powers argued, "Taylor knows that life itself has a very weak story line." The *New York Times Book Review* commentator also remarked upon Taylor's originality, especially his removal from the Southern grotesque, and praised the general quality of the stories.

But he voiced a criticism that was to recur among some critics and some read-ers—that a number of the stories were too ordinary, "almost quotidian." This judgment stood in sharp contrast to Marjorie Brace's assessment in the *Satur-day Review*. In what was perhaps the most interesting of all the reviews, she described Peter as writing "with limpid sobriety, of undramatic incidents." She argued that, while on the surface his material appeared to be not very complex, actually he was experimenting "both technically and psychologi-cally, with very difficult approaches to extremely difficult definitions." She found his method odd and daring, "radical in the strangeness of his associative patterns." Closer to home, Hillsman Taylor wrote to tell his son that he had read *A Long Fourth* with "a lot of pride and pleasure."[28]

In the midst of the praise, one negative note was sounded—and, as it turned out, by someone with whom Peter was to be intimately connected for many decades. "Taylor, appearing in book form for the first time, is even now a kind of A student, modest, corrigible, and traditional," Elizabeth Hardwick wrote in the *Partisan Review*. "He is too serene, too precocious. In his stories one longs, now and then, for harshness, indiscretion, that large, early ugliness a young writer can well afford, a battle with the inexpressible." "How could any magazine print the tripe Elizabeth Hardwick writes for criticism?" Peter complained to Cal. "I had never realized how truly dreadful she is till I saw her mind and her prose style at work on my own dear stories."[29]

Hardwick notwithstanding, Peter was reveling in his moment of glory when in the spring, the farmhouse finally cleared of its tenants, he and Eleanor went down to their farm. After having gone through a succession of names (Lilly Hall, Lilly House, Riverbend, Riverview, Pecan Hill), Peter hit upon the final name, Scuppernong, while planting vines of that grape indigenous to the South. In moments of truth, however, Peter had to call the place Scuppernong Camp, so primitive was its condition. But though the house lacked plumbing and a telephone, the Taylors began spending weekends there. They were buy-ing antiques that fit the house—a dough chest, two tables, a dutch oven, two Victorian bowl and pitcher sets. They began a garden with tomato plants and asparagus, put out fig bushes and more pecan trees. Inside, as Peter put it, they were "scrubbing away the filth of generations of white-trash who have occupied it since the decline of the Lillys." Before the end of spring semester, when the strain of living in the "big brick" with the Jarrells had proved too much, they moved down permanently and commuted to Greensboro. In addi-tion to Randall's brutally expressed opinions and biting wit, he neither drank nor smoked, and he was more prudish even than Peter. "For all the 'high level' on which most of the talk was cast this winter," Peter told Cal, "I feel a little as though I've been living in the Y.M.C.A. with St. Ignatius."[30]

Robie had written begging the Taylors to come to New York for his marriage to Anne Draper. The Kenyon crowd was to assemble, but Peter and Eleanor were staying at Scuppernong. The summer began well. Eleanor's sister Jean and her husband, a young poet named Donald Justice, whom she had met and married while both were in graduate school the year before at Chapel Hill, came to live with the Taylors for several weeks and to share household duties and expenses. Almost fifty years later, Justice recalled a warm evening on the porch when Peter spoke of something he was writing or was going to write "in such a way that it seemed to me that suddenly I saw what it was to *think* like a writer." Such idyllic scenes, however, did not last. Eleanor began to develop medical problems connected with her pregnancy, a small tornado blew down trees and tore away part of the roof, and a few weeks later a heat wave set in just as Tom and Sarah White and their son arrived to visit. It was a miserable experience for everyone. The Whites, uncomfortable worrying about the strain of their visit on Eleanor, were also completely unused to such primitive conditions, and of course all were sweltering. The heat continued, Peter complaining in a late-July letter to Red about "this God-awful hot summer" and putting under his return address "Temperature 106 F." Some relief was provided by Eleanor's brothers James and Fred coming down a couple of weekends with supplies of gin and Jack Daniel's, and James, now separated from his wife, rented the place for the winter. By August, Peter was diverting himself by reading the Kinsey report, *Sexual Behavior in the Human Male*. Though he joked about it, the book was disturbing to him in its revelation of the high incidence of promiscuity and the variety of sexual experience.[31]

One promising sign amidst the heat was Peter's ongoing correspondence with the *New Yorker*. In the spring Katharine White, encouraged by Jean Stafford, had written Peter asking that he submit a story. Bob Giroux sent over Peter's short novel, now named *A Woman of Means*, in hopes the magazine might use a part of it. Early in July, Mrs. White responded regretfully that the editors found nothing in it quite suitable. Within two weeks, Peter mailed off a revised version of his *Hika* story "Middle Age." He had sent it to the *New Yorker* in 1942, and it had been rejected. The first week in August, Peter received Mrs. White's response: she was accepting the story.[32]

Late in August, Katharine White mailed the proof of "Middle Age," and in the accompanying letter she offered Peter a "first reading agreement" with the *New Yorker*. The magazine would get first refusal of all his stories, and he would receive a hundred-dollar bonus for signing, a 25 percent increase in payment above their regular rate for his accepted work, and what the magazine termed "a cost of living adjustment," based on the Department of Labor index, which amounted in the case of "Middle Age" to a 30 percent increase over the originally set payment. Addressing Jean as his "blue-eyed press agent," Peter wrote her the news. "I feel that I owe all the luxuries I have to you and to Red Warren," he said. "Believe me, I think that first-reading agreement of the New Yorker's sounds like something pretty wonderful. Was there ever a more beautiful phrase than 'cost of living adjustment?' " With a collection published and enthusiastically received and a contract with *the* prestigious and well-paying magazine, he knew that he was fully launched in his literary career. As Peter and a very pregnant Eleanor drove off to Bloomington, the summer heat was forgotten in their euphoria.[33]

9

Bloomington and Hillsborough ·····································

"I was touched that you should remember that Katie was born in Blooming-ton," Peter wrote to Mary Polk Kirby-Smith in 1967:

> It was a strange year that we spent there, though not strange because of Katie. Cal Lowell had his first crack up while visiting us there, and I found it impossible to like the other people in the English Department. I expressed my dislike by making the University provide us with two houses and me with three offices on campus. And then at the end of the year I turned over all of our furniture to an auction house, where it brought twenty-five dollars, and we left in the early dawn without telling anybody we were going. I usually explain my behavior there by saying it was just after the War and somehow nothing could please me.

A fair enough summing up almost twenty years afterward, but the experience was a bit more complicated.[1]

The Taylors reached Bloomington to find that the university house prom-ised was, instead, an apartment (one of eight) in an old army barrack amid sixty such structures. "All day long," Peter described the situation to Cal, "you could sit in our living room and hear several choruses of children crying and quarrelling, and hear their mothers calling, Kumeer-er, dee-er!" The quiet office promised turned out to be in the music building, next to the piano-tuning room. After Peter blew up and threatened to leave, a university house was secured and another office provided. He was also still having real doubts about himself as a teacher. "What I believe I detest most about it," he told Cal, "is the constant awareness that I am doing a second-rate job of it, and the necessity of always talking down to students and pretending that I am taking the whole thing in my stride. Somewhere along the route (of My Life) I adopted, through necessity or vanity, a fairly self-assured clownish conventionality as my method of dealing with the day-to-day world. But it doesn't work for teaching." Peter was also uneasy around the young intellectual college professors: "I have never felt more out of place. . . . What really bothers me most is their serious reception of all my opinions. How I long to have some of the Kenyon crowd to poke fun at my most serious statements."[2]

Such discontents were temporarily forgotten as the end of September drew closer, the projected time of the baby's arrival. Katherine Taylor came to Bloomington to be on hand. The three of them played endless games of Hearts, Oklahoma, and Casino, and Katherine almost exhausted her stock of tales. Eleanor had a hard time of it. After three days of labor, on September 30 the doctor finally ordered a cesarean section. The baby was a girl, whom they named to no one's surprise after Peter's mother—Katherine Baird Taylor. "I sit and stare and stare at her," Peter admitted to Jean, "and occasionally touch her head with two fingers. She is not pretty, but already I adore her completely."[3]

Early in November Peter went to give a reading at the University of Iowa. While in Iowa City, he enjoyed seeing Robie and Anne, and Paul Engle again tried to get Peter to join the Iowa faculty. Through these years, again and again Iowa would make him offers. He was never to accept them, but they added to his basic restlessness. Once back at Indiana, Peter wrote to Woman's College to see whether he could have his old job back. The head of the English department sent an encouraging response, but noted the misgivings of the patently realistic dean. The dean was opposed to Peter's commuting from Scuppernong, and he wished to know whether once Peter returned he would remain for "any considerable time," given the fact that he would probably continue to receive attractive offers elsewhere.[4]

As Christmas approached, though the administration at Indiana University had no inkling, Peter was still wrestling with the decision of whether to go elsewhere in the fall. He was also uncertain about the summer, and this too would become a recurrent pattern. Just like the year before, he was considering going to Yaddo, or taking an apartment in New York—or various other plans. And what would the Taylors do with their real estate, Scuppernong and the duplex, which were currently rented out? Schemes were proposed, investigated, abandoned, resurrected. Nothing was resolved.

Peter, Jean, and the poet Richard Wilbur constituted the literary panel at the March Arts Forum in Greensboro. Jean flew back with Peter to Bloomington, to visit and to give a reading. The Taylor marriage was settling into a new phase, as marriages do once a baby arrives. "What every marriage needs is some big project, some business the two parties have a mutual interest in—and I don't mean an intellectual interest," he told Jean. "E. and I agree that if we hadn't Scuppernong and Katie we'd have nothing to talk about or think about together [during] long winter evenings." But there was another side to the pleasant, settled picture. At the age of thirty-one, he was beginning to feel too settled—or was it *trapped*? "I have stumbled strangely into a prosperous, comfortable existence that has no meaning for me and which I must in some way escape before it destroys the very essential difference between me and the person I have always been afraid I might become," he confided to Tom White:

> For several years I have watched some sort of worldly success coming toward me and now I see it solidifying into something smaller and uglier than I had expected. I have established some reputation for a particular kind of performance, and now if I will exploit my advantage, I'll have the money and prestige to satisfy a considerable ego. Further, I now have "tenure" in the teaching profession and can be fired only for a "treasonable act" or for "gross immorality." What an awful situation for a man of my temperament to be in at [thirty-one]! The impulse to throw it all overboard grows stronger every day. And if I don't, what's to become of the old search for reality and the pursuance of art for its own sake?

In following decades he would recurrently find himself forced to negotiate between his desire for a secure, ordered life and an impulse to throw it all over and be free.[5]

Repeatedly Peter registered his psychic confusion. "Funny things are happening in my head," Peter told Cal. "My experience, of one sort and another, baffles me and doesn't seem to relate to earlier things." As it was to turn out, Peter's psychic disturbance was mild in comparison with the problems of his friend. Throughout the winter, alarming accounts of Cal's behavior circulated, but Peter doubted them and even wrote to warn Cal about the gossip. By March, Cal had brought charges that Mrs. Elizabeth Ames, director of the writers colony at Yaddo, where he was then in residence, was the center of a Communist plot. Shortly afterward, he experienced a conversion (or reconversion) to Catholicism. "The affair at Yaddo," Jack Thompson wrote Peter on March 29, "induced in him an experience which I'm perfectly willing to accept as a genuine religious conversion . . . [but] it seems to be taking the form of a Crusade. . . . he gets full of zeal and certainty and blind enthusiasm." Jack reported that Cal was on his way to Chicago to visit Allen Tate, who was teaching there. "I hope he can see you," Jack concluded, "because you will know better than anyone how whatever he's going through now relates to how he has been in the past, and so you will be more sensible with him."[6]

On April 4, an agitated Allen Tate telephoned to tell Peter that Cal was deranged, that the Tates had put him on the train to Bloomington, and that Peter must meet the train with a police escort. Knowing Allen's penchant for drama, Peter discounted the account of Cal's behavior. Still, not wanting to have Eleanor and the baby upset, he made a reservation at the Indiana faculty club. As soon as Cal stepped off the train, Peter realized that Allen was right. Using the excuse that the baby was not well, Peter took Cal to the club for dinner. In the midst of the meal, Cal began to sniff: "Do you smell that? . . . I know what it is, it's brimstone. He's over there behind the fern." After getting Cal to his room, Peter raced home to telephone Jack Thompson and Dr. Merrill Moore. As he put down the phone, it rang. The club manager reported that Cal had come down again from his room and run through the kitchen, threatening the cooks, and out of the building. Peter called the police and left the house to search the streets, calling Cal's name at the top of his voice. Finally the police apprehended Lowell after he had grabbed a roll of tickets from a movie theater and fled to a nearby house.[7]

Peter could hardly sleep that night. "I could see he was mad, the things he was saying," Peter told Lowell's biographer, "and I suddenly felt that all of our long conversations about literary things, about what we were going to do with our lives, at Kenyon. I felt they were all nonsense. And I felt that I was about to have a crack-up myself." But the morning was even worse. Peter went to the jail, where he was admitted to Cal's cell. After the guard clanged the door shut and locked the gate to the cell block, Cal began to rave. Terrified, Peter suggested that they pray and that he move to an adjoining cell in the empty block, with the excuse that he could not pray in the same room with anyone else. Subsequently the guard changed, and the new guard thought that Peter too was a prisoner. He was in the cell block for hours, "the most dreadful hours of my life." For days he could not talk about the experience even with Eleanor. "I thought Cal was lost forever," Peter explained to Ian Hamilton. "I really thought that I had lost this friend forever."[8]

The next day Jack, Dr. Merrill Moore, and Cal's mother flew in and took Cal back to Boston. They left behind Cal's belongings confiscated at the jail, including a photograph of Elizabeth Bishop that had been in his coat pocket. Jack wrote soon to reassure Peter about Cal. Chances for his recovery were deemed favorable. The diagnosis was a manic condition with elements described as "shizo-thymic." He had been placed at Baldpate, a small private hospital near Georgetown, Massachusetts. The next day Allen wrote seeking to explain his irresponsibility in putting Cal on the train to Bloomington: he did not want to "engage with" Charlotte Lowell, who already blamed Tate for Cal's marriage and his first conversion to Catholicism. On April 20, Peter wrote to Cal. "Eleanor and I talk of nothing but having you spend the summer with us," the letter begins. It concludes: "You cannot know, Cal, how much I depend upon your affection and understanding. You are the only close friend I have left, and I have a real need for seeing you again and talking as we used to do. I don't have to tell you how much you occupy mine and Eleanor's thoughts or how much we love you." Peter Taylor had a deep capacity for friendship, and he never wavered in his love for his best and most troubled friend.[9]

After the end of the spring semester in June, Peter had agreed to be on the staff of the Missouri Writers' Workshop in Columbia for two weeks—the first of many such engagements. Upon his return, the Taylors left Bloomington for Scuppernong. By mid-summer Peter was telling Jean that this was their best summer in years. Katie slept nearly all morning, while Eleanor worked in her flowers and vegetables and Peter wrote. In the afternoon, they would putter about the place or drive to Norwood for a milkshake and groceries. Katie was in bed by seven, which left the evenings for reading and writing. Peter had finally made up his mind: he was returning to Woman's College in the fall. On August 9, having signed a contract with the college and sold the remaining household goods in Bloomington, Peter informed the English department at Indiana University of his decision.[10]

Shortly afterward, the Taylors moved back into the "big brick" in Greensboro with the Jarrells. Peter was in fine spirits. All the old troubles about living in close proximity, he maintained to Jean, had disappeared: "They no longer try to possess our souls, and yet everything is on the friendliest basis." Then he excoriated some other old friends. "Confound those Tates. What they are telling some people is that they put Cal in the hands of a doctor and sent him back east to a hospital," Peter said, "the thing they were too cowardly to do. *Don't you start seeing them, Jean.*" On July 28, Cal married Elizabeth Hardwick. In his letters to Cal, Peter had made comments about her only in terms of her review of *A Long Fourth* or her relationship with Allen. When Cal wrote of their meeting, Peter had responded: "I wish I knew what Madame Hardwick told you about Allen. After reading Sexual Behavior in the Human Male I can believe anything about anybody." Now he found himself inviting Cal and his new wife to North Carolina. Soon, however, Cal had another episode, and was put in Payne Whitney. "Elizabeth's fidelity and sacrifice is so great that I think it puzzles even her," Jack reported to Peter.[11]

The Taylors had entered a particularly decisive phase. By the middle of September, they had sold Scuppernong, a measure they had debated for a year; and they had purchased a house in Hillsborough, North Carolina. The town was forty miles east of Greensboro over an excellent highway, and a hour away on the Southern Railroad (on which four trains ran a day). Chapel Hill was fourteen miles away, and the Durham airport ten. Peter took nearly a page describing to Jean this "truly enchanting old house in the most charming old town in the South":

> Our house is about the same age as Scuppernong and about the same size, though it seems much larger. It is built in an L shape, and there are steps up and down between various rooms. There is no door between the dining room and kitchen, but there is a sort of dumbwaiter. You have to go out on the porch and down two steps to get to the kitchen. The library is four steps lower than the reception room through which you enter it. Upstairs there are four bedrooms (tiny ones) and a bath. The chimneys are magnificent. The house is built rather close to the street, on a decidedly steep slope. The front porch is six feet or more above the ground, reached by a long flight of steps, and with lattice work underpinnings and a sort of greenhouse underneath. The back of the house—the kitchen door—is level with the ground. Under the main part of the house is a big basement that could be used for living quarters. Above the library is a finished attic with a separate closet stair leading to it. Behind the library in the L is a screened porch. The house is much smaller than it sounds, but it is lovely and exactly what we want. Our trees are indescribably beautiful—all of

them giants: magnolia, maple, elms. We are a few hundred feet from an ancient
Episcopal church and the prettiest old churchyard north of St. Francisville.

In his next letter, Peter included a drawing of the house and detailed floor
plans. With money from the *New Yorker* and the sale of Scuppernong, he was
having repairs made and a furnace installed. The Taylors spent Christmas in
the house, and by the early days of 1950, they had gathered all their possessions
there and moved in permanently. "This is to be our last move," Peter said. It
was not, but the first years in Hillsborough were productive and contented
ones.[12]

Early in February of 1950, the proofs for the novelette, on which Peter had
labored on and off since 1943, arrived in Hillsborough. Begun in Chattanooga,
it had first borne the title "Edward, Edward" and centered on a boy named
Gerald Patton. Allen Tate at the *Sewanee Review* had been the first to reject it;
next, Delmore Schwartz at the *Partisan Review.* Then *Good Housekeeping*
turned it down, commenting that "it is mainly the depressing, grim conclusion
that makes it so very unsuitable for our use." Needing money, Peter had tried
cutting short stories from it, first "Casa Anna," which he published in *Harper's
Bazaar,* and later after signing his *New Yorker* contract, he placed "Dudley for
the Dartmouth Cup" there. By the time that the first story was published, Peter
had settled upon a new name for the protagonist: Quintus Cincinnatus Lovell
Dudley, obviously inspired by Faulkner's Lucius Quintus Carothers McCaslin
of *Go Down, Moses* (in turn inspired by Senator Lucius Quintus Cincinnatus
Lamar of Mississippi), which Peter had read in England. In Bloomington, he
had tried rewriting the whole piece attempting to produce a novel. But in
January of 1949, he wrote to Katharine White: "I have made a rather unexpected decision about my so-called novel and the sections which I have been
trying to make into stories (a decision dictated, I suppose, by temperament).
The decision is that it would be a mistake for me to go on with the project.
The piece was written as a novelette, and though I had not fully realized it,
my design for expanding it was largely a result of the publisher's pressure on
me to produce a novel. I have never felt a real inclination to write anything
of novel-length, and I hope I won't be urged (or lured) into planning a novel
again." Then he asked for any suggestions about making "Dudley for the Dartmouth Cup" a better story, admitting that "I don't feel the same certainty . . .
that I sometimes do when I have written a story from scratch."[13]

After this second story had been accepted and printed, Peter sent the last version of the novelette to Bob Giroux at Harcourt, Brace. The readers' reports expressed reservations. While all praised Peter's achievement, all felt the conclusion too abrupt and suggested that he expand the work. Giroux wrote that Harcourt, Brace would publish the novelette as it was if Peter insisted, but he reminded Peter that his account with the house was still in the red after subtracting his advances from the sales of *A Long Fourth.* The sub-text was that Peter really needed a novel to put his account in the black. By fall, however, Peter had worn Giroux down, and Giroux agreed to publish the novelette (now named *A Woman of Means*) as it stood.[14]

Perhaps because the novelette had been begun so many years before, *A Woman of Means* shares more affinities with Peter's earlier work than with the stories and plays he was presently writing. Quint Dudley's attempt to make sense of his life and to form an identity apart from his beloved stepmother (the woman of means) reflects the interest in the world of childhood and the growth of personality lying behind both "Sky Line" and "The Scoutmaster." In bringing Quint's world to life, Peter drew upon many scenes and experiences of his own childhood—Travellers' Rest out Franklin Road from Nashville, the grand mansion on Portland Place in St. Louis, the sense of repeatedly being the new boy at school, and even, in a sketchy form, Rogers Caldwell's betrayal of Hillsman.

A Woman of Means was finally published on May 4, 1950, in an edition of 2,500 copies, a thousand more than the printing of *A Long Fourth.* It was not, however, as enthusiastically received as the short story volume. The critic of the *Saturday Review* judged it "as slight in effect, in content, and in quality as it is slight in form." She found it lacking "the impact of Peter Taylor's fine stories." The *New Yorker* reviewer called it "a rueful little first novel, faultlessly written," but registered disappointment with the work because Taylor had here "attempted too little rather than too much." Even Coleman Rosenberger of the *Herald Tribune* qualified his praise. He argued that the slightness of the novel was deceptive, that it was a "work of very solid merit." But he added: "It is not, however, the fully realized novel for which a reader of Mr. Taylor's excellent short stories could wish. One suspects that it stands halfway between those short stories and a novel which he will write." A majority of the reviewers found the work's major flaw to be the descent into madness of the title character. They considered it "too feebly foreshadowed," "a glaring weakness," "awkward and superimposed," "ambiguous."[15]

In the midst of such criticism, two reviews stood out as particularly positive and particularly sensitive to Peter Taylor's method. Both came from sources close to Peter Taylor. Writing in the *New York Times Book Review*, Robert Penn Warren praised the novel for its "vividness of characterization" and its "sense of the depth and complication of event." He pointed out the author's skillful involvement of the reader: "He wants, it seems, to make the reader make his own interpretation, or at least to give the reader the illusion of that freedom and that responsibility." Thomas Wilcox, in the *Sewanee Review*, went a step further than Warren, pursuing the issue of the author's irony. "None of these people knows why all this has happened," he wrote, "though none of them is so imperceptive that he cannot find an explanation plausible to him." Then Wilcox offered an insight that illuminates many works both that Peter Taylor had written and that he would write: "What may at first look like simple dramatic irony becomes something different when you begin to explore the tissue of paradoxes Mr. Taylor has contrived. When you try to construe the few events his novel describes you find that no single interpretation will account for everything you have learned and that finally you must credit all the explanations—some of them seemingly contradictory—the characters separately entertain."[16]

Even though the reviews were more mixed than Peter would have wanted, he was happy that the book was out, and *A Woman of Means* was receiving wider notice than his first volume. In the meantime, he was in the midst of work on both plays and short stories. The first play that he had published, the one-act drama "Death of a Kinsman," which appeared in the *Sewanee Review* in winter 1949 while the Taylors were in Bloomington, is one of his weakest pieces. Set in Detroit in the home of expatriate Tennesseans, it centers on the contrast between the rural traditional culture that produced the Wade family (and the values to which they still subscribe) and the urban industrial culture amid which they now live. Representing the two quite schematically are a Wade maiden aunt and the Wade housekeeper, Miss Bluemeyer of Detroit. The context of the play is simply too thin, and the final paradox (that, for all their differences, both characters are isolated women and equally worthy of pity) does not sufficiently complicate and strengthen it. The play is significant, however, as Peter Taylor's first foray into detailed cultural examination. Earlier he had written to Jean Stafford that in his novelette, as well as in the "The Scoutmaster" and "A Long Fourth," he was "trying for nothing but the development of character." That cannot be said of this play, in which cultural patterns and roles dominate.[17]

Peter Taylor began reading anthropology after he had written "Death of a Kinsman," possibly at the suggestion of Randall Jarrell. Naturally he became fascinated, for contemporary anthropologists like Ruth Benedict and Margaret Mead were then occupied with the very matters that he had begun to explore, particularly the roles available to women in the changing American culture. Mead's *Male and Female: A Study of the Sexes in a Changing World* was published while he was living in Bloomington and in the midst of his reading. One finds the influence of contemporary anthropology upon a body of his subsequent work, not in the application of any specific principle, but in the almost clinical detachment of his cultural probings. Like all the other influences upon him, the anthropological was filtered through what Robert Penn Warren has called "the slightly askew angle of vision that is his and his alone."[18]

The most immediate manifestation was his story "A Wife of Nashville," published in the *New Yorker* in December of 1949. Continuing his exploration of race issues by focusing upon a middle-class woman and her black servants, the story looks back to "A Long Fourth." But it brings into question the victimization enacted by an entire social order, one that he knew as well as Benedict or Mead knew any that they had studied. "Mainly I [am] telling the story," Peter revealed to Katharine White, "of a woman in a society where man exploits woman and woman exploits her black servant." He judged the piece "by far the most complicated one I have ever written." It is a powerful and disturbing story.[19]

His next venture into the anthropological was a very different sort of work, a beautifully crafted study of Chekhovian tone, "Their Losses." Published in the *New Yorker* in March of 1950, it concerns three women riding on a train of the Southern Railroad toward Memphis. While the surface of the piece is rendered in splendid naturalistic detail, the symbolic suggestions are clear. During their shared trip through time, these women and the culture that formed them have been left behind, as manifested in the decaying houses and eroding landscapes that flash by the windows. The bulldozers at work near Memphis and the businesspeople who fill the train represent a present and suggest a future in which these three relics of another time have little place.

Interspersed with these stories of women were two stories focused upon men and significant for very different reasons. The first is "Porte Cochere," which appeared in the *New Yorker* in July of 1949. Drawing from the psychological matrix of his own family, Peter created this tale of an encounter between a psychically twisted patriarch and his son. The father, punished by his own father by beatings, has chosen never to punish his own children; but he still wishes to control every part of their lives. The never successfully suppressed rage of the controlling patriarch erupts at the conclusion of this darkly powerful and shocking work. As the French critic Simone Vauthier has argued, Peter's brilliant use of spatial pattern as a gauge of psychic tension, in itself, reflects the high art of "Porte Cochere."[20]

The second piece lacks both the power and the artistry of the first. That story, "Uncles," would haunt Peter for the rest of his life because he wrote it solely for money. On September 13, 1949, Katharine White reminded Peter of a *New Yorker* policy that might benefit him: if the magazine bought six stories of a writer within a twelve-month period, the writer received a 25 percent bonus on all six. She told him that he need produce only two more by November 5. Always short of cash and with the cost of repairs to the Hillsboro house running higher than expected, Peter went to his office and dashed off "Uncles." He mailed it to the *New Yorker,* and the magazine accepted it immediately. It was a bitter irony because the readers had at first turned down, then reversed themselves on "A Wife of Nashville," which Peter considered one of his best works. Peter was so disillusioned and so ashamed of himself that he did not even try to write a sixth story. For the rest of his life he would point to "Uncles" as an example of the economic corruption to which writers were liable. He never included the story in any of his collections. But despite the quality of the piece—and it is the poorest story that Peter Taylor published as an adult—"Uncles" does include one explicit passage that casts light on an aspect of Peter's cultural exploration: "As I put down the receiver, it came over me that I would never again be able to talk to Mother or to Nora or to Grandmother except in the specific role of a man. It suddenly became clear that everything clever, gentle, and light belonged to women and the world they lived in. To men belonged only the more serious things in life, the deadly practical things—constructive ideas, profitable jobs, stories with morals, jokes with points." The passage takes its place easily in the literary tradition examining America's gendered culture, a tradition traceable from Henry James to Louis Auchincloss.[21]

Despite his shame over the episode of greed, Peter still took pleasure in his new financial status. On November 4, 1949, he had incredulously revealed to Tom White that in the last twelve months, his writing had brought in over $6,000. He was earning more from writing than from teaching. Another cause for satisfaction was his relationship with Katharine White. She appreciated his talent, encouraged and sustained him. She was not only a sympathetic *New Yorker* editor, but friend, confidante, and surrogate mother.[22]

The only thing to mar the first spring in the wonderful Hillsborough house was a visit from Hillsman Taylor. When he stepped off the plane at Durham, his first words were "If you'd been home when that last story came out, I'd have knocked you down." He was speaking of "Their Losses" and Peter's drawing upon Hillsman's Aunt Katty's career in Washington and her final madness—a minor part of the overall story. Later Hillsman brought the conversation round to "A Wife of Nashville," in which he saw himself as model for the unsympathetic husband. What he never mentioned, but what he must actually have been seething about for months, was the portrait of the father and grandfather in "Porte Cochere." The visit was filled with unpleasant moments. One particularly Freudian scene occurred when Peter seized Eleanor and prevented her from serving his father breakfast in bed. Finally Hillsman left, but only after having compared everything the Hillsborough Taylors had unfavorably with the possessions, child, and even garden of Peter's brother Bob and Bob's wife Jerry. Though Peter Taylor never acknowledged the fact, Hillsman's behavior caused him to abandon treating in his fiction the central emotional truth of their relationship until after his father's death fifteen years later.[23]

With Hillsman's visit behind him, Peter wrote to Jean, "We are happier here than we have ever been." He told Cal that he felt that he had lived in Hillsborough all his life; Eleanor was even attending church with him, not for religious reasons, she made clear, but to take part in community life. The Taylors now felt affluent enough to hire a cook-nurse for seven days a week, and Peter had encouraged Eleanor to ride with him to Greensboro his three teaching days and take Randall's poetry course. Soon she was writing "all sorts of wild modern poetry," as she put it to Hillsman and Katherine. "It's the ideal way to continue my writing—in a different field from Peter I don't suffer being overshadowed! And it's easier to pick up in little moments of time, and work over and over than longer pieces." Randall was so impressed with her first efforts that he drove the forty miles to tell her.[24]

In the midst of all of life's other satisfactions, Peter learned that "Their Losses" had been chosen for the O. Henry volume of the year's best short stories and that he had been awarded a Guggenheim for the next school year. He immediately put wheels in motion to get Robie appointed to fill his place at Woman's College. Now that Peter was settled, his friends all seemed in flux.

In January, Jean had married Oliver Jensen, a senior editor at *Life;* Tom White, unhappy in the cotton business, had gone to night law school and was preparing to take the bar exam; Cal and Elizabeth were at Iowa for the spring semester, but planning to leave for Europe in the fall; Jack was teaching at Columbia on a year-by-year basis. Peter invited all of them to Hillsborough. Jack and Dilly came in May, Tom and Sarah in mid-summer, and the Lowells in August.[25]

The last was a grand reunion. Peter had not seen Cal since his crack-up in Bloomington a year and a half before. To Peter's relief, he seemed the old Cal, and Elizabeth was "as nice as her voice" on the phone. Cal did persist in bringing up the fact that she had given Peter's book that bad review, and he revealed, with great hilarity, that Randall had recently described Peter as a great white horse doing tatting. Half the night, the two old roommates would sit in the library drinking and talking and laughing.[26]

Shortly after the Lowells left, Robie and Anne arrived. Happy times continued. The Taylors and the Macauleys were congenial, and Peter continued to enjoy the Jarrells, though he had to admit that "under certain circumstances Randall still seems to be a madman." At the times of Randall's greatest arrogance, Peter took comfort in the fact that Jarrell did say "strenth" and "sujections." The Taylors' other intimates were Malcolm and Lucy Hooke, a generation older and friends of the Tates. Malcolm was a genial professor of French, but it was the motherly Lucy, brimming with wit and good stories, who was the great spirit. Two that she told stuck in Peter's mind for years. One concerned the Hookes' finally escaping from her parents' house on Lookout Mountain only to look back and spy the remaining family dancing with joy. In contrast, the other dealt with a Chattanooga cleaning woman who found a human hand in a wastebasket she was emptying. Completing the literary-academic crowd was Frances Gray Patton, also a *New Yorker* writer, who would frequently drive over from Durham.[27]

"Our house is wonderful, we love each other, and we're both getting our writing done," Peter wrote Jean in the fall of 1950. Not only had Eleanor joined a garden club and the altar guild at the little Episcopal church, but *Poetry* had accepted two of her poems. Peter finished three stories. The *New Yorker* rejected one of them, but Katharine White called another, "What You Hear from 'Em," one of her favorites among all his stories, and acceptance of the third, "Two Ladies in Retirement," was equally rapid. Drawing upon Easter Sellers (the Taylor family's beloved "Mammy" in Trenton) in creating the memorable Aunt Munsie in "What You Hear from 'Em," Peter exposed the inherent victimization in the stereotype of the Southern mammy. In "Two

Ladies," he introduced in his fiction the Tolliver family, who had come from Thornton, Tennessee, to live in St. Louis—Taliaferro (pronounced Tolliver) was the name his Aunt Bess had insisted that the Trenton Taylors originally bore. The parallels with his own family are obvious, but he added to the family group two old female cousins. In a reprise and expansion of the theme of his play "Death of a Kinsman," Peter delineated with equal sympathy for his characters the power struggle between the old spinster cousin and the Tolliver's African American cook. He had now begun referring to all the recent stories as constituting his Thornton collection, after the recurring fictional town based on Trenton.[28]

With his *New Yorker* checks, Peter went on a spending spree, buying box-woods and a large Charleston-made plantation desk. By Christmas, floor-to-ceiling bookshelves lined the library walls and "a wonderful red Persian carpet" purchased in Durham covered the floor. Robie and Anne came to Hillsborough for the holidays, which Robie characterized to Cal and Elizabeth as "a rather old-fashioned Christmas" that included afternoon calls upon the local gentry, a party, and "a great gorging Christmas day."[29]

Early in the new year, all three Taylors went for an extended visit to Memphis. Peter was now a celebrity there, and in anticipation of the visit, the afternoon newspaper devoted a full page to the native son. Not surprisingly, most of the piece is an interview with Hillsman, but buried within it is a significant paragraph written by Peter about his work:

> I began by writing about the scenes and the people I know best and much later began to discover what and who they were. I am still in the process of making that discovery and hope to remain so as long as I live. But in the end I don't mean what and who in a political or sociological sense. In my stories, politics and sociology are only incidental, often only accidental. I make the same use of them that I do of customs, manners, household furnishings, or anything else that is part of our culture. But the business of discovery of the real identity of the images that present themselves is the most important thing about writing fiction. Ultimately it is the discovery of what life is all about. As long as one writes, the process must go on. Until a writer learns something from the story he is writing or finds himself making observations he didn't know he was capable of, his story probably won't be any good. This is true, I suspect, for any writer, no matter how practiced, no matter what age.

This is as revealing a statement about his fiction as Peter Taylor ever produced.[30]

The Memphis visit started out well enough with a drinking party at the Fultons' house at Maywood south of Memphis and a drunken return to the city with Peter at the wheel. But soon Katie and then Eleanor fell ill. Housebound, Eleanor now had to suffer all the household stresses in the Hillsman Taylor family, while Peter was gallivanting around town, dancing the Charleston with Gertrude Fulton at the Peabody and talking into the wee hours at Tom White's house. Upon their return to Hillsborough, Eleanor said that she would never "put foot in Memphis again"—a resolve that she stuck to for years.[31]

Back in Hillsborough, the Taylors had a splendid spring. Earlier Peter had been determined that the three would head out for Europe soon and join the Lowells. But that turned out to be what Cal called "one of the trips Peter takes in his head." "We seem pretty permanently dug-in at Hillsboro," Peter told his friend. "I've gotten the feeling I can't write anywhere else, the same feeling I once had about the porch swing at home in Memphis where I wrote my first stories for Allen's class." He reported that he had found the proper rhythm for his workday—writing four hours in the morning and then putting work out of his mind for the rest of the day. He was convinced that was "the only way to write fiction and go on living a normal life."[32]

At the end of March, in a letter brimming with happiness Eleanor told Hillsman and Katherine that Red Warren had come to Greensboro for the Arts Forum and a visit, that Peter had finished a new story and completed doing away with a privet hedge, that Katie at two and a half had taken to assuming imaginary roles, and that Eleanor herself was rereading *War and Peace*. Peter's story was "Bad Dreams," a Kafkaesque piece about the Tollivers' three servants living in rooms above the garage—the very place on Peabody where Peter had done his writing in the months before he left from Kenyon. The *New Yorker* took it immediately, and Peter told Cal that Harcourt would publish "the Thornton collection" in the fall. But he misjudged. It would be three years before he would complete the stories for the volume.[33]

In late spring, Randall surprised both Taylors by bringing to Hillsborough a novel he had been working on called "Pictures from an Institution," a delightful academic satire (though Randall was not pleased with the role-reversal when Peter offered criticism of the manuscript), and to announce that he would be teaching at Princeton during the next academic year. The Macauleys too were leaving Greensboro for a summer in Europe. Suddenly the Taylors were being abandoned. Peter went to Bloomington in July to take part in the writers conference at Indiana University, and immediately afterward the Taylors set out for Cape Cod to visit the Jarrells. The trip was a disaster. They arrived to find Randall and Mackie at each other's throats, and after a day's stay, the Taylors decided to leave. Shocked and upset, they drove straight through the night to North Carolina.[34]

Shortly they learned that Randall and Mackie were filing for a divorce. "What a wonderful writer and teacher and friend he is, but what an impossible husband he must have been," Peter admitted to Cal. Now the Jarrells needed their money out of the duplex, and the Taylors moved back to Greensboro temporarily in order to sell the property. It was a miserable fall. The Taylors too were short on cash, and Peter got two advances from Katharine White, explaining in one request that he found it easier to ask her than Bob Giroux: "To tell the truth, I like to think I'll never again ask Harcourt for an advance— Harcourt or any other book publisher. They always manage to make me feel like a black mailer." Early in December Peter sold the duplex, and the Taylors used their share to pay back the *New Yorker* and to make further repairs to the house in Hillsborough. Peter reported to Cal: "I really don't believe either Eleanor or I could survive another three months in a place like Greensboro."[35]

At the beginning of the Christmas holiday, they moved back to Hillsborough, where they had a twelve-foot tree that took three days to decorate. Posing in front of it (all three with right legs swung forward, in imitation of the famous Christmas picture of the Scott Fitzgeralds and Scottie in Paris), the Taylors had a Christmas photograph made. It was, as Peter reported, "a fine Christmas." But before the end of 1951, Peter was complaining to Jean now about Hillsborough: "In Hillsboro—God bless it—there just isn't no congenial company except on days when we are feeling very Southern and old fashioned. All literary and vaguely youthful society must be imported and must be our houseguests. There's the rub. We have had enough houseguests to last us a long lifetime." All the signs were apparent; the old Peter Taylor restlessness had returned.[36]

For the spring quarter, Peter arranged for Frances Gray Patton to take his writing classes while he taught (lured by a particularly good salary) at the University of Chicago. The Taylors were to leave North Carolina soon after the Arts Forum, at which the principal speaker was Katherine Anne Porter. "There is only one other writer I want as much to meet," he told Cal, "and that is Thomas Mann." When the radiant figure arrived, Peter was smitten. "When she sparkled," Robie later recalled, "she sparkled the way no one else could." He characterized the meeting of Peter and Katherine Anne as "a momentary

affair of great passion that can occur when two great talkers get together." The
situation culminated at a party on the last night of the forum. Every man in
the room had gravitated to Katherine Anne, and Peter was at the center of the
group. When Robie arrived, Anne told him that Eleanor had left and that she
was crying. Writing to Cal from Chicago, Peter admitted that he had made a
fool of himself.[37]

In Chicago, rooms had been arranged in a residential hotel, the Plaisance.
Living in such close quarters with a three-year-old child and having no nurse
for Katie as they had in Hillsboro, tensions were inevitable. The Taylors escaped them occasionally by getting out of town, once to Iowa City to visit
Donald and Jean Ross Justice, who had recently moved there, and another
time to St. Louis for a stay with Mettie Taylor Dobson and her family. And
good news came while they were at the Plaisance: the National Institute of Arts
and Letters had awarded Peter a grant of $1,000. Shortly afterward, President
Chalmers of Kenyon asked the Taylors to drive over to Gambier and talk with
him about Peter's joining the faculty. At the end of the visit Chalmers made
an offer that included an opportunity to teach a class in playwriting.[38]

"I don't know what in the hell I want to do," Peter wrote Cal. It seemed
that his group were all preparing to take up residence in the Midwest. Cal and
Elizabeth were coming to Iowa the next year, Randall would be teaching at
Illinois, the Tates (with whom everyone was now reconciled) were already at
the University of Minnesota. Exciting things were happening at Kenyon's new
theater, and the place itself was appealing. Finally the decision hinged on one
point: would the college provide the Taylors with a house instead of the apartment offered? Peter explained to Chalmers that his practice of writing at home
"puts great restraint on the rest of the family unless we have fairly large quarters." Tellingly, he added in one draft of the letter, "It makes a real tyrant
out of me." Chalmers met the condition, and in mid-May Peter accepted the
Kenyon offer and wrote a letter of resignation to Greensboro.[39]

On May 28, Peter was in New York to accept his grant from the Institute
of Arts and Letters. It was the sort of occasion that he relished, and he especially
enjoyed getting to know Eudora Welty, one of the newly elected members.
Spring quarter ended a week after Peter's return. Happy to be leaving the Plaisance, the Taylors drove back to North Carolina, and then Peter caught a plane,
by way of Memphis, to Salt Lake, for the Utah Writers Conference. The whirl-
wind of activity over and the tensions of Chicago forgotten, he wrote back to
Eleanor after a week's separation, "I hadn't known how dependent on you I

am for all the joy in life." That would be his lifelong response whenever he was away from her.[40]

His letters were filled with news of Caroline Gordon, who was at the Utah conference. Both Tates were now Catholic converts. Peter reported to Cal that "Caroline's Catholic nonsense is too tedious for anything, and it made me realize how tedious her Southern-Agrarianism must have been to people who had no interest in the subject." The twice-lapsed convert Lowell had seen Allen at the Congress for Cultural Freedom in Paris. "It's against nature," he responded. "I mean really, not just Allen's as a wolf, but everything that is honest and intelligent and gay and intuitive in him."[41]

Peter returned from Utah to face the dilemmas he had been experiencing in Hillsborough in the spring. At the first of the year, Katharine White had written Peter that she missed receiving his stories; and the next month she wrote again to reassure him that William Shawn, the new editor of the *New Yorker*, would be as happy to publish his stories as Harold Ross had been. At the end of July, Peter finally finished a story and sent it off, but shortly Mrs. White had to tell him that, regretfully, the four readers were unanimous in turning it down. Two weeks before completing that story, Peter had revealed to Cal that he hadn't finished a story in nearly a year: "The truth is that when there are friends around I can't get much writing done for enjoying their company, and when there is nobody to see I can't do much writing for wanting and plotting to see somebody." Then he veered off to explain that his trouble was that he kept turning stories into plays, before finally lamenting: "My writing is simply a muddle." To this plight, Kenyon seemed more than ever to offer a solution. At summer's end the Taylors, once again filled with hope, left for the Midwest.[42]

10

The Idyll ···

All three Taylors would look back upon the years at Kenyon as an idyll. Though it was not generally a productive period for Peter as a writer, he did have the opportunity to pursue his interest in drama, and he gained the distance to reevaluate what he wanted to do in his fiction. Overriding all was the fact that family life was happy and social life pleasant and stimulating. Peter Tayor later said that the best years of his academic career were those at Kenyon, "when we were all young together." He was speaking of the compatible group whom Gordon Chalmers had drawn to Gambier.[1]

When Chalmers became president of Kenyon in 1937, one of his first moves was to lure John Crowe Ransom away from Vanderbilt, and Chalmers lent his support to the *Kenyon Review* and to other measures strengthening Kenyon's commitment to the arts. The war interrupted his efforts for the college, but in the postwar years Chalmers devoted himself to recruiting an exceptional young faculty. According to Barbara Kreutz, whose husband Irving joined the faculty in the fall of 1952, though they were living in an isolated enclave (a college of 600 in a village of 400), the experience was like being "on a golden mountaintop." Everyone's life was on the rise, all had young children, all were in the same situation economically, and they were among intelligent, attractive people. A gourmet club was formed, but most entertaining was quite simple, just getting together for drinks in late afternoon. The children played outside the host's house or watched television, the conclusion of *Howdy Doody* bringing the cocktail hour to an end.[2]

The college owned most of the property in the village, and the Taylors lived that first year in the house of a faculty member on leave, a two-story clapboard structure with four bedrooms. In addition to the young crowd, the Taylors spent a great deal of time with the John Crowe Ransoms. John Ransom was somewhat distant but kind, a ruminative presence whom former students (including Peter) could never quite bring themselves to call by his first name. Both Ransoms were short and sturdy. She had been a Denver debutante celebrated for her beauty, but she had little vanity and no pretensions. It was often said in Gambier that she simply did not keep house. Plainspoken and quite deaf, generous of spirit, with a wonderful sense of humor and of fun, Robb Reavill Ransom heartily disliked functions like faculty teas. For decades, when faced with some dreaded occasion or duty, Eleanor would protest, "Mrs. Ransom wouldn't do that." Mrs. Ransom was also an avid sportswoman—a champion golfer, a crack shot, a competitor in everything. Since Peter's college days, there had been a croquet court next to Mr. Ransom's garden. So devoted was the family to the game that in warm weather they would play by the light of car headlights until ten at night. Next in importance to croquet came bridge. Mrs. Ransom gave lessons to the younger faculty members, and the Taylors and Ransoms played regularly, the women against the men. A running tally was kept on the back of a closet door, and because of Mrs. Ransom's skill, the women usually won.[3]

Another great social and literary attraction for Peter in Gambier was James Michael, professor of drama. A graduate of the Yale Drama School, he had come to Kenyon just after the war as a result of Chalmers' interest in fostering the arts. Among his early and promising Kenyon students had been Paul Newman and E. L. Doctorow. Jim Michael and Peter occupied the only two offices in the Shaffer Speech Building, which also housed the Hill Theater. For his entire stay at Kenyon, Peter involved himself in the details of Michael's productions, and the two enjoyed long conversations in their offices.[4]

So pleasant was his whole situation that Peter even accepted with relatively good grace the college's misunderstanding in assigning him a freshman English course in the fall semester. But he made sure that it would not happen again in the spring, even though he had to accept a reduction in salary. Still, all his letters expressed his happiness at Kenyon, and he cited the additional class as the reason he'd gotten no writing done. Just before Christmas he received a three-hundred-dollar check from the *New Yorker* for signing a first-reading agreement, and he told Katharine White, "If I haven't produced some new stories by June, I'll have no excuse."[5]

But the next few months were marked by houseguests and reunions. The marriage of Peter's oldest sister, Sally, was going through a rocky stage. A known philanderer, Millsaps Fitzhugh was now making little effort to hide his affairs from his wife. After a suicide attempt and hospitalization, Sally stayed with Peter and Eleanor for the month of January. Blond, petite, and pretty, Sally was living just the kind of life to which she had been bred. After devoting herself in the early years of marriage to rearing Millsaps' daughter Louise, to the Junior League (of which she was president), and the Memphis social whirl, later she began filling her life with travel, taking cruises around the world. Despite this history, Sally was no superficial socialite; rather, she was intelligent, witty, well-read, and winning, like Peter. The weeks in Gambier were just what she needed—an escape from Millsaps and from Memphis society, where everyone knew her situation. The Kenyon crowd was delighted with her, and she and Eleanor became close.[6]

Early in 1953, Jean Stafford divorced her second husband, Oliver Jensen, and Robie's novel, *The Disguises of Love*, made the best-seller list. Peter was keeping in touch with both friends through letters, and that spring brought reunions with Cal and with Randall. Cal stopped by en route to his teaching stint at Iowa, and Peter traveled there in April to give a reading and visit the Lowells. Randall had remarried in the fall to a vivacious dark-haired California divorcee, who brought to the marriage two young daughters and a sleek Ferrari. The Jarrells were at Champaign-Urbana, close enough for an exchange of visits.[7]

Since moving to Gambier, Eleanor had published poems in *Botteghe Oscura* and the *Virginia Quarterly Review*, but Peter was still blocked and distracted. Katharine White sent a letter in March to remind him of his June deadline, and over four weeks later he replied that he was still "wrestling with the story." Mid-summer of 1953 came without his having completed the piece, and Cal and Elizabeth arrived to spend a month in a rented house in Gambier. The Macauleys came for a visit, and the whole group piled into the Lowells' 1936 Packard and went to meet Jack and Dilly Thompson at Gun Lake, Michigan, where Dilly's family kept a summer place comprising several cottages, with sailboats and a motor launch. After much carousing, the Lowells and Taylors returned to Gambier, where Peter determined that despite the fact that the Lowells were still in residence he could no longer live with himself if he didn't finish the promised story before the fall term began. On September 10, he mailed to Katharine White the "last of the stories about Thornton women," entitled "The Dark Walk."[8]

Within two weeks, Peter received a letter from Katharine White. "It is such a pleasure to receive one of your stories after so long a silence that it is terribly disappointing . . . ," she began. They had rejected it. Peter was so happy to be through with the story that completed the Thornton collection that he was not particularly upset. He mailed the story to Bob Giroux at Harcourt, Brace, so that the book would be delayed no further, and asked Giroux to see about placing this final piece. *Harper's Bazaar* took it, but insisted upon cuts, which Peter grudgingly made for the magazine printing. He had grown tired of both the story and the binding theme of the volume long before either appeared. The story concerns Sylvia Harrison's dilemma after the death of her husband, Nate, a Chicago businessman, over moving back to her birthplace, Thornton, Tennessee, which has always been the source of her values and her great nostalgia. The piece is overly long for its substance. It draws upon all Peter's parents' moves and locates the impulse behind bringing along the possessions of many generations as a failure to live in the present. The use he makes of a Hillsborough landmark, the Dark Walk, where lovers court, is too portentous, as evidenced by the final authorial commentary on its significance. Sylvia returns to the cherished image of her courtship:

> She found it had changed. She and the other young girls no longer seemed to be beginning life anew in the Dark Walk. They were all dressed in black, and it seemed that the experience they had shared there was really the beginning of widowhood. From the moment they pledged their love they were all, somehow, widows; and she herself had become a widow not the day Nate was found dead in his office but the day he asked her to marry him, in the Dark Walk. . . . The men of Nate's time had crossed over a border, had pushed into a new country, or fled into a new country. And their brides lived as widows clinging to things the men would never come back to and from which they could not free themselves.

Such were Peter's reservations about the story that, after its appearance in the collection for which it was written, he would never agree to its being reprinted.[9]

With the *Harper's Bazaar* version of the story and the new collection both in press, Peter could devote himself fully to his consuming interest—the theater. Jim Michael was doing Chekhov's *Uncle Vanya,* and Peter went to all rehearsals and conferred with Michael daily on "many wonderful problems." "It's my whole life right now," he told Jack Thompson in December. In the fall Peter had achieved another housing coup. For his second year at Kenyon, he had arranged for the college to lease for him a big brick house built in the 1830s on Brooklyn Street. A substantial place of eleven rooms with walls three bricks thick, the house he described to Katharine White as "just to our taste." After bringing the furniture from Hillsborough to the Brooklyn Street house, he went to two auctions, where he bought "three enormous beds, an eight foot divan of the 1840 period, [and] an elaborate marble-top walnut dresser with a huge mirror and much carving." Such a house seemed all that he had needed to make his happiness complete, and the Taylors immediately planted flower and vegetable gardens.[10]

The shortened version of "The Dark Walk" appeared in the March 1954 issue of *Harper's Bazaar,* the first Taylor story to see print since May of 1951. He had written Katharine White after the first of the year to ask for a year's extension on repaying his $500 loan and to tell her that he was planning a new book of stories about growing up during the Depression. But most of his creative effort was actually going into a long play, set in St. Louis on Jackson Day, January 8, 1939. Cal and Elizabeth had come through from the East for their next teaching jaunt in the Midwest, this time at the University of Cincinnati from January to June. Soon after the visit Cal's mother died suddenly. The death precipitated another manic episode, and Cal was hospitalized, first in Cincinnati, before transfer to Payne Whitney. About the same time, Peter learned that Robie, after various dissatisfactions including problems with Randall, had left Woman's College and joined the United States intelligence agency.[11]

The Widows of Thornton was published on April 29 with a dedication to Allen and Caroline. The exact spirit behind the dedication is difficult to gauge, given Peter's very mixed feelings about the volume. But *Widows* is his most Southern collection and therefore appropriate, and he did feel old obligations to the Tates. The collection was reviewed less widely than Peter's first two volumes, and Peter was disappointed by that and by the quality of the reviews. Some were good: the *Herald Tribune* critic called him "a first-rate writer," "possibly the most interesting and accomplished writer to come out of the South in the last ten years," and the *Chicago Tribune* writer praised the collection as another volume "by which Mr. Taylor enriches American fiction." But the *New York Times Book Review* concluded its discussion oddly by interpreting the author's message in these terms: "If the sanctity of the home is preserved, all will be well with mankind." And Peter was enraged by the *Saturday Review* piece, which spent four paragraphs lingering over the contents of Southern pantries and then paralleled their piquant odors to the effect of Peter's stories.[12]

"Before I finished *The Widows* I was pretty well fed up with the subject," Peter protested, "and now that the book is out I have to endure phrases like 'the flavor of nutmeg and cinnamon' in the reviews." He wrote Jean that he would never use another place name in a piece of fiction, and he made the sweeping statement, "To me the South is an old lady, and along with Aunt Annie Tyree and Cousin Latta Jetton I have buried her. Writing that book nearly ruined me." He meant what he said in regard to his fiction, but strangely enough he was at the same time writing a play with many of the same elements as *The Widows of Thornton*.[13]

The spring brought more houseguests and traveling. Sally arrived for a long April visit, Peter's mother joining her toward the end. Eleanor began feeling ill, and Sally proved a great help, fixing breakfast and taking charge of Katie. When Katherine Taylor arrived, Mrs. Ransom kept her busy playing bridge day after day. After Eleanor recovered, Jean Stafford came for a May weekend, and the week before commencement, the Taylors left Katie with friends and took a week's trip to New York. They saw a play, went to museums, spent a great deal of time with the Thompsons and Jean, and visited Cal at Payne Whitney. "He seems quite normal in most ways," Eleanor told her parents, "but on some fixed subjects, he gets tense, his face clouds, and he is really incapable of logic."[14]

At the end of June, Peter learned that he had won a $3,000 Rockefeller Foundation fellowship awarded through the University of Iowa Writing Program. Another of the winners was Eleanor's brother-in-law Donald Justice. Peter had also been promoted to associate professor and given a raise. As soon as he learned of the grant, he arranged with President Chalmers to teach half-time at half his salary for the 1954–55 school year. Katie went to day camp that summer, and both adult Taylors were productive. Peter worked on his play with an enthusiasm that he hadn't felt in years, and Eleanor completed several poems and a story. By mid-summer the doctor confirmed what Eleanor had suspected: she was pregnant.[15]

In late August, they made a brief trip to North Carolina to see Eleanor's parents and to check on the Hillsborough house and their tenants, arriving back home just days before Katie started the first grade. Eleanor was continuing to write so that, she told her parents, "editors will begin to know who I am"; then, she said, she'd " 'retire' again for a couple of years." Within a month, Peter had finished his play, *The Southern Colony*. Katharine White had written in July asking for a story. She was probably dismayed to receive, instead, a long, four-act drama. She replied quickly that unfortunately the *New Yorker* could use neither the whole play nor any single scene or act. Then very tactfully she approached the matter of Peter's foray into drama. "Naturally I have done some pondering about which form—the dramatic or the fictional—seems to me to do more for the themes and characters you have made so much your own," she ended her letter. "I find that for me the fictional treatment seems to be richer and subtler."[16]

After he had mailed off the play, Peter had an experience that he had never had before and was never to have again. At a Gambier cocktail party, the wife of a Spanish professor asked him why he had never written about his college days at Kenyon. He went home and immediately began a story. In contrast to his usual long process of composition, so inspired was he that he finished it within a few days. To Jean he characterized the story as "a long rambling thing . . . all about Douglass House days and a fateful trip to New York which two undergraduates took one Thanksgiving." Katharine White accepted it immediately, and, even after his $500 debt was subtracted, the remaining part of the payment was munificent. "There has never been anything like *The New Yorker* for American writers, or for any writers," Peter wrote back in gratitude.[17]

To celebrate the sale, the Taylors gave two large cocktail parties the week before Christmas, inviting forty people to each. Just "a big bowl of punch and a ham and a turkey—simple, but big," Eleanor described the occasions to her mother. These were the first of the parties for which the Taylors became so celebrated everywhere they lived. All were delightful, convivial affairs, but none of the guests would ever forget that second party on Brooklyn Street. David McDowell was to be in Gambier, and Peter naturally invited him. Only at the last minute did the Taylors learn the identity of McDowell's traveling companion, who was the father of a Kenyon undergraduate. It was Whittaker Chambers, at the moment infamous as the informant in the Alger Hiss trial. Hurriedly Peter called the guests to tell them that he would understand if they chose not to come. All came, and many, like the Taylors' close friends Bill and Monique Transue, went hating Chambers and left pitying the pathetic figure they found him to be.[18]

By the date set for Eleanor's cesarean, Gambier had suffered four big snows and the temperature had dropped to near zero. On February 7, the Taylors' second child was born, a son. As soon as she had learned she was pregnant, Eleanor told her parents that the child "would have Ross in its name somewhere," and later she determined that it would be named either Jenny Ross or Williamson Ross. When the child arrived, he was named Peter Ross Taylor. Eleanor had an even more difficult delivery than her first, requiring this time four blood transfusions. After coming home she was laid up for another two weeks, while a cook–cleaning woman and Peter ran the household and cared for Katie. Cal sent the child silver-backed military hairbrushes that had been his father's and then his. Peter wrote his thanks, saying, "I hadn't dreamed how crazy I would be about this baby, and I don't dare get started on the subject."[19]

The March 12, 1955, issue of the *New Yorker* contained Peter's Kenyon story, entitled "A Sentimental Journey." Four years earlier Cal had asked Peter why he could not write something about a character closer to himself. But now that Peter had used not only himself but his closest friends, he worried about how both Jean and Cal would respond to this story. It was, as Peter mused, "neither fiction nor fact," but it contained unflattering truths about all of them at that period. "At first I was, how shall I put it, *surprised and hurt*," Cal retorted with some irony. "Were we really quite such monsters?" But then he admitted that he was himself "trying to do some of the same sort of thing" and that he was impressed with Peter's effort. Lowell was referring to the poems later collected in *Life Studies*, the volume that would announce an age of "confessional poetry."[20]

For "A Sentimental Journey," Peter had taken material close to a memoir and shaped it so that it resonated beyond its subject. In his hands it became a story of youth and promise and illusion. It is a consummate fictional achievement, as well as a story that holds a place in literary history. From the outset, Peter had set the piece in 1939, rather than 1938, when the events had actually occurred—just one of many facts that he altered. When he collected the story in a volume four years later, he gave it the name "1939," suggesting a world just about to be swept away by the forces of history.

Within a month Peter learned that he had been awarded a Fulbright grant

for the 1955–56 school year. He had proposed to write a novel about the Southern expatriate colony in Paris immediately after the Civil War and asked for
funds to support a year's stay in France. The committee agreed to fund the
project, but imposed one condition: he must participate in the American Studies Conference at Oxford University before going to Paris. For Peter, given his
longtime fears of academic inadequacy, this was an unexpected and horrifying
requirement. But Eleanor very much wanted to go, and after receiving a sympathetic, encouraging ten-page letter from Eudora Welty, who had participated in the conference the year before, Peter finally accepted.[21]

On June 29, the Taylor family of four sailed for England on the *Queen
Elizabeth*. The experience of being in Oxford was fascinating. Though Peter
continued to dread the lectures he was to give, even that was assuaged by his
responses to English life. Fortunately another lecturer was Barry Bingham,
editor and publisher of the Louisville *Courier Journal,* an engaging figure and
a friend of Sally Fitzhugh. Bingham and his wife contributed greatly to the
Taylors' enjoyment of the time, as did Mrs. Graham Greene. Later Peter would
say that, after delivering his final lecture, he tore it to bits, such was his embarrassment. After the conference, the Taylors moved to London for two weeks.
Peter found the city transformed since the war, and he joyed in the English
theater. His benefactor and friend Charles Abbot had died shortly after the
war, but the Taylors managed an excursion to revisit old sites in Somerset.[22]

They crossed the Channel in September. In Paris they had secured temporary housing at 17 avenue Theophile Gautier, the palatial apartment of Monique Transue's aunt the viscountess D'Orgeix, leased while she was away from
Paris. They left after a month for a flat close to Katie's school—six rooms, up
four floors at 20 boulevard St. Michel. The cleaning woman, Marie, followed
them. The essence of the whole Parisian experience Peter Taylor would capture
in his story "A Pair of Bright Blue Eyes," later renamed "*Je Suis Perdu.*" Like
"Rain in the Heart," it provides an intimate glimpse of family life, the couple's
joy in the new baby, and the happiness of the months in Paris.[23]

"We are still starry eyed and wonderfully happy here," Peter wrote Tom
White at year's end, and he described his first impressions, "formed . . . while
I was reading The Ambassadors (retracing poor, dear old Strether's steps
through the rue de Bellechasse) and The Sun Also Rises (hopping on a bus
somewhere along Montparnasse and standing out on the open back end,
smoking, wearing my English raincoat and my new moustache, riding across
town to the Place de l'Opera) and Tender Is the Night (lingering in the lobby

of the Ritz after a cocktail and then crossing Place Vendome to cash a check at Morgan & Company)." Blair Clark, Cal's friend since prep school now with CBS in Paris, and his wife, Holly, entertained the Taylors, and once had them to lunch with Mary McCarthy. Through a cultural attaché, the Taylors were invited to glamorous state dinners, and they went to hear Faulkner talk about his writing and attended a performance of *The Sea Gull* in French. They were reading (in English) French history, Balzac, and Victor Hugo. Before sailing for England, they had arranged to sell the Hillsborough house to the doctor and his wife who had been renting it, and now the Taylors fantasized about buying a house on the Île St. Louis.[24]

In January, Peter admitted to Cal and Elizabeth that he had abandoned all plans for the novel on the expatriate Confederates in Paris. Instead he had written a new story and was revising still another time his four-act play *The Southern Colony*, now retitled *Tennessee Day in St. Louis*. John Crowe Ransom had accepted the first act for the winter 1956 issue of *Kenyon Review*. The play had drawn most of Peter's creative energy for the past two years, and now it proved the stimulus for his decision to change publishers. Harcourt, Brace had been his publisher since 1948, bringing out his novella and two volumes of short stories. The firm had been patient and flexible about his changing plans as a writer. Like every publisher he would deal with, Harcourt was willing to publish the volumes of short fiction in hopes that he would eventually write a novel, and whether consciously or unconsciously, he had strung the company along with promises. Harcourt had also been generous in giving him advances. By the end of 1955, however, Peter decided to go to David McDowell at Random House with his play. "I think that Dave will do better by me," he told Cal. Random House agreed to pay Harcourt over $4,000 in advances, and on February 26, 1956, Peter signed a contract to publish with Random House his play, a promised novel, and a volume of short stories.[25]

He wrote Jean the news, and he commented: "I feel that my last five years have been a great mistake, and as much as anything else it is that book The Widows of Thornton that I don't want to come home to." He was right: the collection was damaging to his career because it seemed to mark him as a regionalist, a label that he was never afterward quite able to shake. But he continued by telling Jean that for the next five years he intended to write plays. He seemed unaware that the play that he had worked on for so long bore out the label.[26]

The editors at Random House were attempting to interest New York producers in *Tennessee Day,* though during the spring they tried to conceal their horror at Peter's idea of devoting himself exclusively to drama. In April, Albert Erskine (Katherine Anne Porter's ex-husband and a senior editor at Random House) even suggested that Peter consider redoing the play as a short novel. Remarkably, Peter did not take umbrage, probably because he was diverted by other things. Shortly before, the Taylors had learned that Phil Rice, an early faculty friend at Kenyon and now a colleague, had died. Both Taylors felt the loss. On April 11, Katharine White turned down a story that Peter had written in Paris, but at the same time she offered him an editorial position at the *New Yorker.* "I believe that the New Yorker intends (like the New Republic with Henry Wallace) to ruthlessly cash in on your unrivaled literature connections," Cal teased. By the time Cal's letter arrived, Peter had already written Gordon Chalmers to say that he wanted to accept the offer, and Chalmers responded with hopes that Peter could do the work from Gambier and eventually succeed John Crowe Ransom as editor of the *Kenyon Review.* In May, as Peter pondered what to do, the four Taylors set out for Rapallo, where they had rented a house, the Villa Gemma, complete with a cook-housekeeper-nurse.[27]

They had just settled when they received the shocking message that Gordon Chalmers was dead of a cerebral hemorrhage. Now Peter felt that he must return to Gambier in the fall, and he wrote to Katharine White. Even with the sad news, the immediate future was settled, and summer at the Villa Gemma was a delightful and productive time. Though Peter would comment that they were "prisoners of the children" that summer, he sent one of his new stories (which he had characterized to Tom White as "about Depression days in a city called Mero, quite realistic, hard, and dramatic") to Katharine White, who took it immediately. Social life was provided by Cal's friend Robert Fitzgerald, who with his wife, Sally, and a burgeoning family was living nearby. On August 23, the Taylors sailed home from Genoa on the *Cristoforo Columbo.* They were met in New York by Cal and a very pregnant Elizabeth.[28]

Initially the changes that Peter had feared were coming after Gordon Chalmers' death were nowhere apparent at Kenyon. The promised teaching schedule was still in place, and Peter was pleased when Jim Michael asked that Peter's course in playwriting be transferred to the Drama department. As opposed to the New York producers, Michael was enthusiastic about *Tennessee Day* and wanted to produce it at Kenyon in the spring. The ideas for stories that had come in Europe continued to germinate, and Peter worked diligently through the fall on one story that grew longer and longer. In February 1957, the *New Yorker* published the first of his Depression stories, "The Other Times." It was, as Peter had described it, a different kind of story for him. Gone was the Southern setting, and in its place was the city of Mero vaguely fixed in America's heartland, described as "being not thoroughly Midwestern and yet not thoroughly Southern either." The theme was not change, loss, or role, but the stifling effect of class prejudices upon human development. The story was indeed dramatic, and it introduced a new kind of Peter Taylor narrator—a man looking back on his own past and still unable to understand his failures, seeking to blame too much on the forces of history, those Other Times, the Great Depression. It is one of the most underrated pieces of Taylor's fiction, and over twenty years later the sort of exploration begun here would lead him to produce the great story "The Old Forest."[29]

Both Randall and Cal praised "The Other Times" and saw it as a new direction for Peter. But they could hardly have been prepared for what came next. Five days after the publication of "The Other Times," Peter mailed to Katharine White "In a Bower of Paper Flowers," the story that he had labored on so long. Also set in Mero, at first it too appears to have a hard, dramatic surface; but as the tale unfolds it becomes increasingly complex, suggestive, symbolic, and allegorical. Katharine White was on vacation, and the other editors hardly knew what to make of the story, though they were unanimous in turning it down.[30]

The spring was full of event. The future of the *Kenyon Review* was now uncertain, and Peter had agreed that, if money could be raised to keep it going, he would accept the editorship. *Tennessee Day in St. Louis,* published in February by Random House, with a dedication to Hillsman and Katherine, was in rehearsal at Kenyon's Hill Theater. An elaborate party followed the opening on April 24, but some of Peter's intimates, such as the Transues, had to admit that the play was not a complete success. A year before the play was published, Randall had given it a thorough reading and written a ten-page critique full of sound advice. "*Can* you afford to have so many people so articulate about how a member of a Southern family plays a role?" he asked. "It's your own especial discovery—should so many of them know it so clearly and articulately?" The most devastating point he made with great tact. "I would look with a very cold eye," he wrote, "at so many long speeches in which characters understand a lot." He ended: "I think it needs more work, but I think it's a good play (with flaws) as it is and can surely be made into a marvellous one."

Astoundingly for Randall Jarrell, he had pulled his punches. *Tennessee Day* remains a talky, entangled play, far too long with far too many characters and plot lines. The only significant review of the volume was Andrew Lytle's essay in the *Sewanee Review*. While Ransom, Tate, and Warren had all moderated the conservative Agrarian positions of their youth, Donald Davidson and Lytle were becoming more reactionary. Lytle was, in fact, on his way to perfecting the image of Professional Southerner that he enjoyed so in old age. His essay casts no light on the real play, but introduces a neo-Agrarian line of Taylor criticism—establishing a cultural context for the work by drawing comparisons between North and South, tracing the causes of social change back to the "military defeat of the South," contrasting the situation of "the family on the land" with that in the city, and speaking of the function of the family in a Christian society as opposed to a modern material one. These were of course Lytle's preoccupations, not Peter Taylor's. It is strange that, at the very moment when Taylor was leaving the South in his fiction in order to make clearer that his themes transcended place, this confused play, only in part concerned with Southern identity, should elicit such a retrograde reading.[31]

The spring also brought visitors. Sally had come up for the premiere. Cal, now the proud father of a daughter and in the midst of a revolution in his poetic practice, came through on his way back from a West Coast reading tour. In Monique Transue's view, Cal and Peter were like children when they got together. "I had a grand time talking Peter down and being talked down by him," Cal wrote after the visit, later commenting, "There is no one in the world I can pour out to as I do to Peter." Finally, David McDowell arrived for a couple of days. He had left Random House and, with Ivan Obolensky, formed McDowell, Obolensky. Dave pressed Peter to break his contract and sign with the new publishers.[32]

But at the moment, Peter was occupied with other matters. In the months after his return from Europe, many of the faculty were distressed to learn that Dean of Men Frank Bailey, then acting president, was being seriously considered for a permanent appointment. A group had visited Peter to get him to ask John Crowe Ransom to help block such a move by the trustees. Peter agreed to do it, the campaign was successful, and the trustees chose another candidate. Bailey, however, still had several months in office. Although initially he had honored Chalmers' plan to appoint Peter editor of the *Kenyon Review* after Ransom's retirement in two years, now he seemed less certain about the fate of the *Review*. Finally, apparently also in retaliation, Bailey intervened in the area particularly important to Peter Taylor—housing. He placed the Brooklyn Street house on the general faculty housing list to be assigned solely on the basis of rank. Peter reacted by calling upon the faculty group who had visited him earlier. They agreed to sign a petition against such a measure, which they would present at the next faculty meeting. The day arrived, and Peter watched as these friends and colleagues entered the meeting singly, and he sat in stunned silence as he realized that they had reneged on their promise: they were not going to present the petition. The house would be assigned to a full professor. Peter felt an overwhelming sense of betrayal.[33]

During the years at Kenyon, a number of academic institutions had approached Peter about joining their faculty, the most recent being Ohio State University. In January, Peter had even driven the fifty miles over to Columbus and talked with Robert Estrich, head of the English department, about his plans to add someone in creative writing. Now he wrote Estrich to say that he was ready to accept the position. In July the Taylors purchased a house in Columbus, and in August they moved from Gambier. The idyll had come to a startling and bitter conclusion.[34]

11

The Middle Years

Just as Peter, Eleanor, and Katie would regard the years at Gambier as among the brightest of their lives, so all would remember the period in Columbus as generally the unhappiest. Though all three made good friends, though both Peter and Eleanor achieved triumphs in their careers, though the family spent glorious long periods in Europe, still there was something deeply unsatisfying about Peter's tenure at Ohio State.[1]

At forty, Peter had suffered a devastating blow. He had returned to his alma mater in glory and left feeling betrayed and shamed. The parallels between his situation and that of his father in 1932, when he had been forced to leave St. Louis, weighed upon him. Peter had successfully negotiated just the terms he wanted with Ohio State. He would teach only half a year, from January to June, receive a salary of $6,876 (over $2,000 more than he had made at Kenyon), and never be asked to serve on a committee. Hired to introduce creative writing at Ohio State, he was viewed as a star in the English department. But he arranged to live as far away from the university as possible, an indication of the cold eye that he now cast on the academic world.[2]

The Taylors had moved from a village to a sizable American city, from a small college of 600 to one of the largest state universities, with a student body of almost 23,000. The sustaining communal life of Gambier was left behind; for the first time the Taylors had to find their place in an urban environment. The house that Peter purchased, at 25 Bullitt Park Place, was near the private school where Katie had been enrolled, Columbus School for Girls. The house lay in Bexley, the most fashionable Columbus suburb, located to the southeast, a considerable distance from Ohio State to the northwest.

The Columbus years began well enough. As Peter had written his father during the war, he inherited "a happy sort of nature" and he was so intensely social that he was likely to find pleasure wherever he was. Though he was a Democrat and had voted enthusiastically for Adlai Stevenson twice, the English faculty were markedly more liberal, and Peter reacted against that. Among the group, he immediately gravitated to Andy Wright, a Columbus Ivy Leaguer, his father a corporation lawyer, his mother on the board at Wellesley. Andy's wife, Gina, was English, a daughter of the actor Leslie Banks. Wright had already published a book on Jane Austen and was a student of Trollope. It seemed inevitable that he and Peter would become close, and quickly an intimacy developed between the two couples.[3]

Almost immediately after the move, Peter asked Random House to release him from his contract so that he could sign with McDowell, Obolensky. Albert Erskine was stunned. Random House had agreed to publish Peter's play only in hopes that the firm would recover its losses later with his promised novel and short story collection. In addition the firm had given a $4,000 advance. Correspondence about the issue continued well into the next year. At the very time that he wrote Random House, Peter was having financial troubles. The move had been expensive, and, by his own choice, his salary would not begin until January. He needed a thousand dollars to get him through. He wrote to Katharine White, and once again she provided the funds. Financial crises would continue to mark the years in Columbus. Eleanor was the very soul of frugality, but Peter had a tendency to do what he wanted—whether it be buying houses or traveling abroad—and only later worry about finances. For this reason he was recurrently strapped for money. Though Eleanor was often unaware of the full extent of his financial concerns, she would feel the resulting disquietude.[4]

Within ten days after Katharine White arranged the advance, she wrote that she was leaving the fiction department. She had been Peter's stalwart supporter, an ideal editor, a good friend. Just how fortunate he had been he would fully realize only in later years. But her immediate replacement at the *New*

Yorker, the novelist William Maxwell, also proved sympathetic, as evidenced by the first of his letters to Columbus, showing a knowledge of Tolstoy and Turgenev, and an appreciation of Peter Taylor.[5]

At the moment Peter was revising three stories—"The Public School Boy" (later titled "The Unforgiveable" and finally "Promise of Rain"), "A Pair of Bright Blue Eyes" (later "*Je Suis Perdu*"), and the long story "In a Bower of Paper Flowers" (later to become "Venus, Cupid, Folly and Time"). All were markedly different from the stories in *The Widows of Thornton,* but also different from each other. The correspondence regarding them is revealing in a number of ways.

"Promise of Rain" is another of the Depression stories set in the mid-American city of Mero. While not the achievement that "The Other Times" represents, it too is an attempt at a new kind of story. Replying to Katharine White's reading that the story, which is concerned with a conventional father's reaction to an unconventional, artistic son, had three disparate explanations, Peter wrote: "The essential thing about the story—the thing that makes it a story in my eyes—is the very existence of the three main facets, the fact of their coincidence in the story. That is where the meaning and the poetry—if I may use the word—of the story ought to be found." Though in this instance, the instinct Peter articulated did not produce a significant piece of fiction, in later years it led him to abandon completely the sort of story that attempts to be a seamless whole.[6]

"*Je Suis Perdu*" William Maxwell characterized as a "mood piece" and offered excellent suggestions (which Peter took) on developing it into a more substantial story. Drawing closely upon family life in Paris the year before, it renders the contradictory impulses, the dramatic mood swings of a protagonist who is, in this case, very clearly the author. The story ends happily and, as Peter was aware, perhaps too sentimentally, too piously. But the solipsism and perversity explored were just the beginning of a new direction in his fiction.[7]

Some judge the third story, "Venus, Cupid, Folly and Time" (as it had been renamed by late September), to be Peter Taylor's masterpiece. During the fall, he continued working on it. Though the *New Yorker* had rejected this long, strange tale—Peter felt because of the incest theme—it was now in the hands of a splendid critic: John Crowe Ransom. "I've never seen a short story covering a greater range of characters who report for it, or figure in it," Ransom wrote on September 25, concluding with some suggestions and questions. After receiving still another revision in November, he responded: "Now I read into this story a meaning which I must have been aware of but not too consciously: the symbolic relationship between incest and the aggressive exclusiveness of Great Families, or even of the institution of Aristocracy." It must have been wonderful to see a great literary mind only slowly and carefully come to comprehend one's most ambitious and complex effort. Ransom ended his assessment: "I think you've done a new kind of story and it is very formidable indeed."[8]

"Venus, Cupid, Folly and Time" is a profound statement about class illusions and the material basis for class in the United States, and Peter Taylor underscored the point by setting this story too in Mero—in the middle of America. The core event, the parties for select teenagers given by two eccentrics, Peter took from such entertainments actually given by a Hillsborough couple. But to complete the rich texturing of the story, he drew upon his whole range of experience—using a house remembered in St. Louis, the behavior of two spinster sisters in Memphis, a Chattanooga landlady's practice of vacuuming in the nude. He worked and reworked the piece, adding layers and frames, enhancing symbols, deepening and complicating suggestion.[9]

Interestingly enough (though it is quite characteristic of Peter Taylor's nature), at the same time that he writing this devastating commentary on class in America, he was boasting to Cal and Elizabeth about his social success in Columbus. "We are in Society here," he effused. "About three weeks ago a formal dinner party for fifty was given in our honor—a seated-dinner, no less, with two hours of good solid drinking before dinner and a choice of eight kinds of brandy offered afterward (all having been in their private cellar for forty years)—given in our honor by family friends (the wife, incidentally, was president of Mrs. Ransom's class at Wellesley) and with only one other academic couple present!" The other couple was of course Gina and Andy Wright, whose parents had given the party. Katharine Timberman Wright, Columbus social and civic leader, had taken the Taylors up. At that very party among the guests were attorney James Seymour and his wife, Jane Farrar Seymour, who soon took a place among Peter and Eleanor's closest friends. During all the years in Columbus, Mrs. Wright was the Taylors' sponsor, and she always included them in the small group invited to her house on Christmas Eve.[10]

The Taylors were driving the fifty miles to Gambier several times a month to visit the Ransoms, the Transues, and Kreutzes; but Peter told the Lowells that "Columbus is an OK place. . . . it is exactly as though I'd gone back to

Memphis to live—but without my past to haunt me." Later in the same letter, he presented a variation on that theme: "I have come home to live again—or at least the half of me that is a mid-western city boy has." And he revealed to Randall that he was "writing furiously on a novel" and "smoking a package of cigarettes a day."[11]

Donald and Jean Ross Justice came from Iowa for Christmas, and early in 1958 Peter flew to Memphis for his parents' golden wedding anniversary on January 8. "Two hundred relatives assembled from all parts of Tennessee," Peter told William Maxwell, "And I felt that all the characters from my own stories had joined forces." The South made itself felt again shortly, when Peter learned that an old Agrarian friend of Allen Tate's, Brainard Cheney, had arranged for a Nashville production of *Tennessee Day* at the end of March. Before the time came, Peter was involved in correspondence about Ransom's successor as editor of the *Kenyon Review*. Randall, Jack, and Robie were all being considered. Randall received the offer, which he subsequently refused, and eventually Robie was chosen. The whole situation was a sensitive one and finally hurtful to both Jack and Robie. The news from Cal was also disturbing. In December, for the first time in four years, he had entered a manic phase and been hospitalized. Shortly after his release came a relapse. He wrote Peter on March 15: "It's not much fun writing about these breakdowns after they themselves have broken and one stands stickily splattered with patches of momentary bubble."[12]

At the end of winter quarter, the Taylors left for a trip south to visit the Rosses at Norwood and the Taylors in Memphis, and to attend the opening of Peter's play. Andy and Gina came down to Nashville, and Hillsman, Katherine, and Sally drove over from Memphis. A clipping from a Nashville newspaper shows the two generations of Taylors before the performance—Eleanor in a smart black dress and pearls, Katherine in a dress with lace bodice, the two men towering above their wives. Afterward a grand reception was held in a Belle Meade mansion. But Peter considered the production a disaster. "Finally I was so embarrassed," he later told a Memphian, "that I just sneaked away into the night."[13]

On May 12, Peter wrote William Maxwell, again asking the *New Yorker* for an advance, another thousand dollars. "Last year it was to help pay for my house," he said. "This year it is for the trip to Europe." Again, he received the money. The Taylors had determined to spend the summer and fall in Italy. They had contacted Robert Fitzgerald, who was living at Levanto and working on his famous translation of *The Odyssey* and who had offered to find accommodations for the Taylors and for the Jarrells, whom the Taylors had persuaded to join them. He secured a villa for the Taylors at nearby Bonassola, and one for the Jarrells at Levanto. This summer filled with literary people was to have its perils.[14]

The Jarrells sailed from America first and settled themselves in Italy. By the time the Taylors arrived, a struggle for ascendancy was under way. Awaiting them were invitations to Fourth of July picnics from both the Fitzgeralds and the Jarrells. After much social discomfort, Peter (with a logic that was his alone) told the Jarrells that, since he had known them longer, he felt bound to accept the Fitzgeralds' invitation. That hurdle was cleared, but others lay ahead.[15]

Shortly before Randall married his second wife, Mary, he wrote her this description of Peter Taylor: "Peter is as original, odd, and attractive as anybody you ever saw—you never saw anybody at *all* like him. Though, now that I think of it, Red Warren's speech and bone-formation are like his, rather." Randall felt great affection for his old friend, despite what Mary saw as their vast differences. "They weren't much alike," she would write twenty years later. "Peter was romantic and Randall was an intellectual. Peter loved England and drank whiskey; Randall loved Germany and drank Riesling. Peter had children and Randall had cats. Peter quoted people and played bridge. Randall quoted books and played tennis." What she did not write was that many people feared Randall's wounding wit, but that Peter could somehow handle it.[16]

Peter had looked forward to this reunion and was determined to enjoy it. Eleanor and Katie also felt special bonds with Randall. A component of their long friendship, Eleanor felt, was his respect for her individuality (apart from her marriage) and his wonderful interest in her poetry, which she was gathering this summer for her first volume. Mary recalled the Italian afternoons spent on the beach—she, Peter, and the children at one end, Randall and Eleanor far off: "Randall read [Eleanor's poems], head down and then exclaimed, head up, and then bent toward [her] admiringly, and talked to her in a fiercely determined way: Eleanor, knees under, and speechless, gazed out to sea smiling her half-believing, half-embarrassed smile." Katie too found in Randall a rare empathy. He alone seemed to know how unhappy she was after a year in Columbus, and he made all sorts of efforts to give her pleasure, arranging that Mary's younger daughter, Beatrice, include her in everything.[17]

Soon, however, the summer was just not working out as all had hoped.

"Venus, Cupid, Folly and Time" had appeared in the *Kenyon Review*. The next time that Peter saw Randall at a distance in the village, Jarrell turned away and would not speak. Peter later learned that Randall disliked the story so much that he could not bear to see the author. Within a few days, however, cordial relations resumed, and Randall was enthusiastic about the story that Peter wrote later that summer. By August, Peter was telling William Maxwell that they were disappointed with Bonassola, though perhaps the main trouble was "having a three year old along and no nurse." Petie would have nothing to do with anyone who did not speak English, and he didn't like the beach, where the Taylors would join the Fitzgeralds and Jarrells every day after lunch. After listing his complaints, Peter ended by saying that still "it is certainly a more stimulating atmosphere than that of Columbus, Ohio."[18]

The atmosphere, however, would shortly begin to thicken. In mid-August, the Jack Thompsons, their three children, and a nurse arrived for a stay in a Levanto hotel. The added strain of another entourage was too much. Randall had never particularly appreciated Jack, and now Randall succeeded in making him as uncomfortable as he had made Robie two years before. Sally Fitzgerald also irritated Jarrell. He objected to the fact that, though from Texas, she had an English accent, and he was offended when *she* tried to tell *him* about Flannery O'Connor's literary value. The social situation became simply miserable. In Jack's judgment, "Randall was a real prick."[19]

At summer's end, when the Taylors and Jarrells parted, the Taylors were all close to tears. The others, however, parted with Randall gladly. The Taylors spent a splendid fall in Rome that included a reunion with Red Warren, his wife Eleanor Clark, and their young children. Warren characterized Peter to Cal as "a superlative companion" and the occasion as filled "with lots of grub, booze, and conversation." On the way to Le Havre for a December 15 sailing, the Taylors stopped in Paris to see Robie and Anne, who were spending their last weeks abroad before coming to Gambier and the *Kenyon Review*.[20]

For months Peter had been on a writing spree. On August 3, he had mailed to the *New Yorker* a powerful story written in Italy about the subconscious gratification found by a genteel couple in their black retainer's criminal actions, a story that questions the basis of Southern paternalism. It was quickly rejected. Peter responded with changes and additions more than once, but the answer was still no. He knew that it was a good story, and he remembered the rejection of "Venus, Cupid, Folly and Time," which he learned had been chosen for the *O. Henry Prize Stories of 1959*. But at the moment he needed money, as he wrote William Maxwell in September—"the difference between our present debts and $2,000." "We can already see that next summer and fall we'll have to stick pretty close to Columbus, Ohio, and live off our vegetable garden," he explained. "But in the meantime, nobody ever got a bigger thrill out of Italy than we're getting." He received the money, and November 14 he mailed another story, "Guests," and ten days later a mediocre piece set at the Veiled Prophet's Ball in St. Louis. But by the end of November, he was writing Maxwell that he found himself in a "terrible predicament"—his account in Columbus was overdrawn, and he needed another thousand. Three days later an airmail check arrived for the sum, an initial payment on "Guests," and before the sailing, the Veiled Prophet story was accepted. "The answer is Yes," Maxwell cabled. "Welcome home, if you can bear it." So the Taylors sailed back to reality—Columbus and Ohio State and their debts.[21]

They were back in Ohio for Christmas and the beginning of the winter quarter. Just after the first of the year, the Longview Foundation wrote that Peter had been given an award of $300 for "Venus, Cupid"; and during 1959, he would receive requests to reprint the story in anthologies, both in America and abroad. In March the news appeared in the Memphis newspaper that the story had garnered the top O. Henry award for the year. Letters came from old friends. "In the seventeen years since I've seen you, I've been reading you. I am so very proud of you," Elizabeth Farnsworth wrote. There had been little correspondence from Tom White since Tom had entered medical school five years earlier, but now he wrote congratulating Peter on the award and on his placement between F. Scott Fitzgerald and Thomas Mann in Tommy White's freshman English textbook at Southwestern.[22]

Though Peter was immersed in his teaching, he realized that he now had enough new stories for another collection, and he and David McDowell were corresponding about that. In March, Cal came to Columbus to give a reading from his revolutionary new volume *Life Studies*. "I enjoyed our wrangling more than anything else and have gone on wrangling with you in your absence," Peter wrote afterward. "You don't know it but you really hit on something that has been disturbing me for some time: my inhibitions. I could never do what you do [in your poetry], but I've been trying to find a way [in my fiction] around the business." It would be two more years before his efforts were successful, but it is interesting to reflect here on the complicated dynamics of influence at work between the two friends—a line to be traced from "1939" to *Life Studies* and then back into Peter Taylor's later fiction.[23]

In the meantime, Peter had returned to the South in two stories that the *New Yorker* would publish in the fall of 1959—"Guests" and "Heads of Houses," set in Nashville and Monteagle, respectively. The germ of the first goes back to the old family joke that someday one of the many visiting Taylor relatives would die at their house. Taking such a situation, Peter wove a story of cultural change and two lost men of different generations. The second piece originated with the anecdote told by Lucy Hooke of Greensboro about an awful visit to her family on Lookout Mountain—a visit that concluded with the Hookes' looking back as they drove off and seeing her family dancing in a ring with joy that they were finally leaving. Peter first merely expanded and developed Lucy's tale, then tore it up when he realized that the character who really interested him was a bachelor brother. Despite the power struggles and tensions between the two married couples, all have roles, certainties—while the bachelor is denied both by his family and the world at large.[24]

The Taylors stayed in Columbus that summer, as Peter had said they would have to. They had undertaken various repairs and renovations on their house, which was a smaller version of Hillsman Taylor's place on Peabody when Peter was in high school—and almost as ugly. Peter was writing a new story and working on the galleys of the collection for McDowell, Obolensky, which had been titled (from Tolstoy's *Anna Karenina*) *Happy Families Are All Alike.* Eleanor's collection was complete, and Randall was to write an introduction. She reported to him that Peter was "reading at your Freud assignments with the result that he blushes every time he forgets something, which is practically every other paragraph." She had just read *The Wisdom of Insecurity,* which "explains myself to me better, too." In a letter from the same period, Peter detailed to Jack Thompson his progress in Freud. Beginning with *The Psychopathology of Everyday Life,* he then went to the *Introductory Lectures* and continued with readings in the *Collected Papers.* "I am completely converted," he told Jack.[25]

The fall was a mixture of the good and the bad. It began badly with an audit of Peter's income tax returns for the last few years by the Internal Revenue Service in the person of "a really loathsome man," who allowed Peter no deductions as a writer and decided that he owed fifteen hundred dollars in additional taxes. The Hillsman Taylors came for a week at Thanksgiving ("Seven Days That Shook Columbus," Peter dubbed it), and all the Taylors went over to Gambier for a big party, where Hillsman was much taken with Barbara Kreutz's mother, the Broadway star Irene Castle. But Peter returned to Columbus disturbed. He was not getting along with Robie, who seemed consistently condescending. "It seems that I had to be forty before I could see how much pettiness and spitefulness there is in most people," Peter burst out to Randall. "I feel that most of my old friends have hated me for years and years, feeling a mixture of jealousy and contempt, but wouldn't leave off seeing me for fear I might be a name someday." Certainly there must always have been stresses and conflicts among the Kenyon group, and in the last few years fissures were becoming apparent, but Peter's outburst reflects too his own general psychic uneasiness. Before November ended, he wrote Robie, resigning from the board of the *Kenyon Review*.[26]

But now came a turn in fortune. On November 25, Peter's collection was published, and the same day the *New Yorker* wrote accepting Peter's new long story, "Miss Leonora When Last Seen." "The new story is wonderful," William Maxwell began. "A kind of modern Morality play is what it is. I see it acted on the steps of the cathedral of Salzburg." The fourth story that the magazine had taken that year, "Miss Leonora" brought, in addition to a large payment because of its length, a hefty year's end bonus—the sum earned from the magazine in 1959 coming to a total of $13,464.44. Immediate debts could be paid and more Christmas presents bought.[27]

The old year ended and 1960 began for the Taylors with reviews of *Happy Families Are All Alike*. The collection was more widely noticed than *The Widows of Thornton*, and the reviews were of a different quality. Gene Baro, writing in the *New York Herald Tribune*, described the author as "one of our best short story writers," one "curiously enough . . . unlike most of his prominent contemporaries." Then endeavoring to suggest the essence of the fiction, he commented: "One understands Mr. Taylor's characters and their individual situations through understanding the social context of their lives; one sees them through a typical circumstance that is itself the expression of social tension or change." William Du Bois of the *New York Times* made a similar attempt, after pronouncing the volume "a literary event of first importance" and Taylor "a master of the short story form," though known to only "a small but devoted public." "Each of these stories," he remarked, "surveys an experience that is not only accurately reconstructed but also deeply understood. Each centers on a turning point, a moment of controlled crisis that is the hallmark of any effective work of fiction." Commenting in the *Christian Science Monitor*, Ruth Blackman offered a particularly astute analysis of Peter Taylor's method and of the experience of reading his fiction. He loads "his narrative with detail," she suggested, "like detective stories in which clues and unimportant trivia are given equal mention, and it is up to the reader to pick up the clues." She found rereading rewarding because "so complex are the layers of meaning in Mr. Taylor's stories that what seemed like trivia on the first reading are apt to turn up as clues on the second."[28]

Adding to the satisfaction of the reviews came the judgments of respected friends. Red Warren called the collection Peter's best book, and Cal wrote, "You know so much more about people than I do. I always marvel at how you keep your feet on the ground without loss of fierceness, grotesqueness and magic." Two months later, he returned to the subject: "No one writes better about families, the pull of our diffent [sic] temporal selves, all leaping like fish out of water for extinction and dominance." To cap things off, David McDowell reported that the book was having a good sale, better than any of Peter's other volumes, and that it had been nominated for the National Book Award.[29]

In February, the Taylors received more good news. Peter's application for a Ford Foundation program offering an opportunity for poets, novelists, and short story writers to "spend some time in a close working relationship with a theatre or opera house" in either America or Europe was accepted. He would be attached to the Royal Court Theatre, and the family would spend the next school year in London. He got the news shortly before Allen Tate arrived for a reading at Ohio State. In the years since the Taylors had seen Allen and Caroline, they had again separated. Cal had kept in closer touch with Tate and would provide from time to time "another installment of Allen's endlessly picaresque and phallic life." Finally the previous summer the Tates were again divorced, and on August 27, Allen married the poet Isabella Gardner of Boston. He brought Isabella to Columbus, and Peter and Eleanor enjoyed her immensely. The reading was a resounding success, and Allen charmed everyone at the parties. To Peter, Tate looked ten years younger, and he was the old Allen, particularly in his penchant for gossip—he wanted to know everything about everyone in Bullitt Park Place, down to the postman.[30]

When the National Book Awards were announced, Cal had won for *Life Studies,* but Peter had not. The situation was all too familiar. Peter stood by graciously as close friends won honors that he was denied. He must have felt a pang, though he never expressed it. He made four trips to the South that spring. In late March, he and eleven-year-old Katie flew to Memphis, Katie particularly to visit the other Katherine Taylor, and Peter to give readings and classes at Southwestern. The next month he had reading engagements at Vanderbilt and at Duke. Early in June, Peter traveled again to Memphis to receive his first honorary degree, a doctor of letters from Southwestern. This was followed by the twentieth reunion of his class at Kenyon—one of those milestones where one looks back and takes stock. Feeling depressed, Peter telephoned Cal. "You shouldn't feel dead," Lowell responded. "Of all people you seem to have escaped the kind of hollowness and airy disorder that so vexes me." But during all the years in Columbus while he was in his forties, there were signs that Peter was having a difficult middle passage. Despite successes, there were regrets, misgivings, and self-doubts.[31]

At the end of the school term, the whole family set out for Tennessee. They had rented for the summer the Monteagle cottage where Peter and Eleanor met and from which they were married seventeen years before. Being on the mountain cheered all the Taylors, and before a month was out, they were considering buying a cottage with five bedrooms and two baths, formerly owned by the Lincoln sisters, one of whom had taken Mettie and Sally to Europe in 1930. Peter was trying to be more careful about his finances. At the moment, he was out of debt. Of course he was about to leave for nine months abroad, but the Lincoln cottage was too good to miss. He made the down payment, and on August 3, the four Taylors sailed once more for Europe.[32]

12

London and Ohio State ···

With his customary relish for new experiences, Peter began his months in London. The English Stage Company at the Royal Court Theatre had become a major influence in the theatrical world beginning in 1956 with its production of *Look Back in Anger,* the work of an unknown writer, the "angry young man" John Osborne. The Royal Court was now known as a writers' theater, and Peter was delighted with the prospect of observing and perhaps working in such a place. The Taylors were also anticipating living in London for the first time. The Wrights and Kreutzes were to be in residence, and the Transues in Paris—"our crowd," as Peter dubbed the group to Cal.[1]

London living the Taylors found much to their taste. They leased a house at 25 Kensington Gate, just two blocks from Miss Ironside's School, where both Katie and Petie had been enrolled. The house was on a small square with a garden behind a locked gate to which all residents had a key. The tall, narrow structure had a living room on the second floor with huge French windows and a balcony, and two floors above on the top level was a study, "blissfully quiet," Peter told William Maxwell, "with wonderful light." Peter was writing afternoons and evenings and attending rehearsals at the theater mornings, feeling particularly fortunate that the first production of the season was Chekhov's early play *Platonov*.[2]

At the beginning of fall, Eleanor's collection *Wilderness of Ladies* was published and received an excellent review in the *New York Herald Tribune*. At Thanksgiving, Peter's story "Miss Leonora When Last Seen" appeared in the *New Yorker* and was met with widespread admiration. A carefully wrought allegory like "Venus, Cupid, Folly and Time," "Miss Leonora" Peter considered one of his most ambitious works, marking the culmination of his exploration of women's roles in the Southern culture of his youth. The three stories engaging his attention that fall centered upon men. "Nerves," which he continued to revise for months, became finally a monologue about the violence and impersonality of modern life delivered by one man to another as they watch their children at play in a park. The other two stories deal with the sexual tension of the wedding night. "Reservations," though evidencing a totally convincing realistic surface, is one of Peter Taylor's most playfully worked out pieces—abounding with Freudian passageways, rooms, doors, keys, egg-shaped locks, and doppelgangers. These two stories the *New Yorker* accepted. The third was rejected. "An Overwhelming Question" left the editors "disturbed and puzzled." Well it might have. Reversing the usual situation, it has a bride-to-be, bent upon sexual gratification before marriage, chasing her prospective husband through the debris of a building site until he leaps from a pile of lumber and breaks his neck, safe from her at last. The editorial comment that it was a "harlequinade" was apt; it is as macabre as anything Peter Taylor ever wrote. He was finally to place it with the prestigious English journal *Encounter*.[3]

Eric Solomon, a young assistant professor at Ohio State, also in London for the year, would occasionally meet Peter and Andy Wright for tea. Peter's fiction was going well, and Solomon found him very much in his element in London. When the Transues came over from Paris for Christmas, they learned that Peter had resigned from Ohio State. He was giving up teaching to devote himself completely to his writing. This was the peak of the curve of the London year. But there were already signs of bad weather ahead. Peter had come to London with hopes that the Royal Court would produce one of his plays. Though George Devine, the artistic director, had rarely been less than cool and peremptory with Peter, after the first of the year he at last agreed to read the plays. The verdict was brutal and staggering. Devine found "no place for them in the modern theatre."[4]

"I am enjoying my bitterness a good deal," Peter wrote Jean Stafford, and he also told her of his disgust with London literary life. This he also detailed to Cal, after experiences with the C. Day Lewises and the Marcus Cunliffes. "I simply can't take the fierceness of literary society," he said. "If you do meet someone who has a bigger reputation than you have (as most do in my case) they seem to be afraid you are going to ask a favor, and if rarely you meet someone with less, then sure as fire you get a note in the next morning's mail asking you to send a manuscript to an American magazine or publisher." But toward the end of the letter, he returned to the real source of his pain, Devine's judgment on his plays.[5]

Early in February, returning home in a taxi and fuming over the stupidity of the popular J. P. Donleavy play he and Eleanor had just seen, Peter announced that he was going back to teaching. "I'm not sure whether I felt more that I needed my students or that my students needed me," he explained to Randall and Mary. Immediately he wrote to Ohio State and was reinstated, and the Taylors moved their return passage up from July to May. In the meantime they traveled in the British Isles and the Low Countries as much as possible, though in April Peter again was forced to ask the *New Yorker* for an advance of a thousand dollars. By mid-June, the Taylors had dropped their luggage in Columbus and settled for the summer at Monteagle.[6]

Peter would complain at first about "everything revolving around children's activities." But as he explained to the Jarrells, "Katie and Petie are happier here than anywhere else we have dragged them, and so we are determined to stick it out." In addition, all the Taylors loved the cottage. They kept finding treasures in the cellar—old picture frames, iron bedsteads, and (by Petie's count) fifteen rocking chairs. Soon Peter and Eleanor were planting laurel and rhododendrons and ferns. Less than a week later, Peter wrote friends: "Suddenly all of Memphis and Nashville and Birmingham has arrived on the Mountain—old ladies with black chauffeurs and big black cars, young mothers with black nurses and station wagons, and teen agers [sic] with each other and with fancy little wagon cars with fringed tops. We had lunch at the Inn today—our one meal out a week—and did lots of handshaking with all ages." The social scene was a needed stimulus, and, in addition, Peter persuaded the Jarrells to take a cottage for two weeks in August.[7]

Before they arrived, Peter finished a story he had worked on all summer,

"There," and mailed it off. It was rejected, and Peter had to write back, rather shamefaced, that he understood the rejection, but that his real trouble at the moment was money. The *New Yorker* continued to act as his bank and advanced a thousand dollars. While the Taylors were in London, it had been determined that William Maxwell's editorial load was too heavy, and William Shawn, editor of the magazine, had assigned a number of Maxwell's writers to other people. Peter had fallen to Roger Angell, Katharine White's son. At first it appeared that this new arrangement might work well, and Roger Angell continued to meet Peter's requests for money with the necessary advances, but as time passed, it would become evident that author and editor were not compatible and that Angell did not care much for Peter's work. "There," the rejected story, Peter put in the back of his drawer. When he eventually took it out and revised it a couple of years later, it was published in the *Kenyon Review,* and later selected for both *The O. Henry Prize Stories 1965* and *Best American Short Stories of 1965*—joining "Venus, Cupid, Folly and Time" and "A Friend and Protector" as pieces turned down by the *New Yorker* and eventually included in prize-winning collections. "There," a very Jamesian tale (putting one in mind of both "Daisy Miller" and "The Jolly Corner"), represents a significant step in Peter Taylor's experimentation with the unreliable narrator, one who as he tells his tale of the past is "like a man delving into a trunk he had packed away years ago and who did not know, himself, what he would come upon next."[8]

The pleasant summer over, the family returned to Columbus. "We enjoy being back in our house," Peter told the Jarrells, "but we hate Columbus. I really think another year is all we'll be able to take of it. Everything and everybody is so damned dull—so damned unpretentious. Ohio State seems more enormous and more anonymous even than before."[9]

Shortly after "Reservations" had appeared in the *New Yorker,* the Theatre Guild purchased the television rights. In early September, the *United States Steel Hour* presented an adaptation, "Delayed Honeymoon." Peter took no pleasure in seeing his work performed. Gone were all subtle Freudian probings; the tone was that of a situation comedy. "Never again," Peter commented to Roger Angell. In the same letter he requested another thousand-dollar advance; he was "fairly strapped." "No matter how large the fellowship is," he confessed, "we always manage to spend about twice the amount."[10]

Petie had started the first grade, and Peter now had three and a half months in which to immerse himself in his writing before his teaching duties began in January. He needed to reduce his debt to the *New Yorker,* and he had promised Andrew Lytle (recently named editor of the *Sewanee Review*) a story for a Peter Taylor issue. At any given time now, Peter would have a number of projects at various stages of development. He had decided to turn *Tennessee Day* into a scenario, and he was toying with a section of a novel, but most compelling was his desire to finish some long stories begun in London. By November he had completed one, which he called "Demons," and mailed it off to Roger Angell. Surprisingly, Angell accepted it immediately. "I suppose," Peter told the Jarrells, "my new stories are not as 'different and complicated' as I thought."[11]

But this effort indeed was, and, given some earlier rejections, it is puzzling that the *New Yorker* took the story. "Demons" has the disjointed quality of the memories that Peter poured into a 1948 letter to the Tom Whites, after Eleanor's first pregnancy threw him into a meditation on time and identity. Some of the same experiences are even touched upon, like the moment when, hiding in the sideboard in St. Louis, Peter realized with absolute certainty that there was no God. Ostensibly held together by a contrast between the world of childhood and the adult world, the story contains outlines of several later Peter Taylor works and disparate passages dealing with the mystery of instinctual art, with betrayal, with sibling tensions, with changing relationships as a marriage progresses. Actually a sort of riff on various psychic and developmental mysteries and conflicts, the story is brought into focus by its title as much as by any other linking device.[12]

The next story that Peter submitted, however, is one of his most powerful. "A Successful Life," later titled "At the Drugstore," is the culmination of his explorations of the psychic unease of middle-aged male figures. The theme was first engaged in the Parisian story *"Je Suis Perdu."* There a man's tendencies toward self-indulgence and solipsistic encasement are held in check—a love of others and the ties of family bringing the character out of narcissistic reverie, and sustaining a balanced social self. "Nerves" and "Demons" (the very titles are revealing) continued the psychic chartings. But "A Successful Life"/"At the Drugstore" is much more complex and much more deeply probing. Also a culmination of his Freudian stories of the period ("Reservations" and "An Overwhelming Question"), the work draws upon the theories of the id, ego, and superego and touches upon Oedipal issues, but not in an overly schematic way. It is a haunting tale of a man on a visit to his parents' home leaving his wife, children, and parents asleep in their beds to set out on a journey of self-discovery, represented by a dream-like trip to the old drugstore frequented in his boyhood. Gradually he gains unsettling knowledge of the multiple selves all existing within him and of the irrational and self-destructive claims of the unconscious. Home again among his family, he sees in a momentary reflection in a glass the terrible thing he has uncovered, so at war with the claims of the others upon him and with his effort to live a "successful" life. "How dearly he loved them all!" he thinks. "And how bitterly the Thing showing its face in the glass hated them!" But rather than engaging his monstrous self, he merely represses it again and retreats into the lulling comforts of the quotidian.[13]

The editors at the *New Yorker* reached a quick decision on this submission. Telling the author that they were "quite baffled by your intentions in the story," they turned it down. At least now Peter had something to give the *Sewanee Review,* but in January, he was forced to ask Angell for another thousand-dollar advance, this time to pay the final installment on the Monteagle cottage, a matter that he "had conveniently forgotten about."[14]

He was now constantly in demand for college readings, as he would be for the remainder of his career. He would sandwich the engagements in between other obligations, and after the beginning of the winter quarter of 1962 he flew to Memphis for a reading and to see his parents. Hillsman had been in bad health for the last two years, suffering the effects of adult-onset diabetes and debilitating neuropathy in his legs. In the last few months, he had been confined to a wheelchair without hope of walking again. Peter found him "feeble, but indomitable still"—or as he joked to Cal, "still hell on wheels."[15]

Cal and Elizabeth stopped off in Columbus in late winter, and then Jack Thompson, who was in the process of getting a divorce and was planning to marry again when it was final. Next came a visit engineered by Peter. Jean Stafford had not been out to see the Taylors since her marriage to A. J. Liebling in 1959. Peter arranged for her to give a reading at Ohio State. By this period, both Lieblings were drinking heavily, and at a sizable dinner party given by the Taylors, both got very drunk. Years later Andy Wright still marveled as he recalled Eleanor's imperturbability throughout the evening, even when Liebling's head hit the dining table and Jean reached over and picked it up.[16]

Such an outrageous occasion was actually a bright spot in the year back in Columbus. Peter and Eleanor were both trying to feel content, and they had projects under way to improve the house. But Eleanor had her hands full with the children's activities, many of them at Katie's school, where she did not

find the other mothers especially congenial. Coupled with that was her awareness that the years were passing and she could find no time for her writing.
Peter seemed always either up in his third-floor study writing or far away in
his campus office. She would remember this as a miserable time. Before Jack's
visit, Peter had expressed similar feelings to him. "Our existence here seems
much more isolated and rather queerer than it has other places. . . . And as
always we tend to shut ourselves off in different rooms of the house. Even
Katie does it now." Peter was also increasingly unhappy at Ohio State. Any
graduate of a state high school was admitted to the university, and Peter found
the students the worst that he had ever taught. Making matters worse, in the
spring of 1962 came a dramatic confrontation between the president and the
faculty over the issue of freedom of speech. Forsaking his usual apolitical position, Peter joined a majority of the English department in protesting the re-
pressive policies of the administration and the board of trustees. Some of the
liberal faculty were surprised at Peter's support, but throughout his career
he would be consistently on the side of the individual faculty member. The
controversy, however, politicized the department and destroyed morale and
feelings of collegiality. The English department at Ohio State became a particularly dispiriting place to work.[17]

At the end of the school year, the Taylors gladly escaped Columbus for the
cottage at Monteagle. Spending the summer months on the mountain was
now a greatly anticipated part of their yearly schedule. The children loved
the place and spoke of their friends there as "the cousins." Patterned after the
Chautauqua Sunday School Assembly at Lake Chautauqua, New York, the
Monteagle Assembly had been founded in 1882. By the 1960s, it was one of
the few "Chautauquas" remaining in the country, "still combining," as its
historian notes, "religion, education, art, theatre, discussions on literary and
public affairs, and wholesome summer relaxation." Over the years much of
the Protestant highmindedness had dissipated, along with strictures against
card-playing, dancing, and drinking. Entered through a stone gatehouse, the
hundred acres of assembly grounds held 160 cottages along roads that wound
to a central mall, where the chapel, auditorium, and bandstand stood. The
assembly was a relaxed place with constant activities for children and an easy,
casual social life, much of it enjoyed on the wide verandas of the cottages. Peter
loved its shabbiness and was fascinated by the kind of people that returned year
after year, preferring it to the more fashionable resorts of a newer America.[18]

Handlys, Bagleys, and other Nashville families from Peter's past gathered at Monteagle, and his relatives were constantly coming and going. A couple of years before, Hillsman Taylor had encountered Rogers Caldwell there, and after a rupture of nearly thirty years, the two had renewed their friendship. When Andrew Lytle came back to the mountain to edit the *Sewanee Review,* he decided to live permanently in the large log house in the assembly that his family had occupied as summer quarters since the turn of the century. Thus the literary associations of the place were renewed. Allen Tate would come for visits, and, at Peter's urging, the Jarrells would usually take a cottage for a week or two. For Peter, among the most interesting of all those associated with Monteagle was Mrs. James K. Polk. When her husband lost his business in Nashville during the Great Depression, the Polks moved to her family's plantation in the Mississippi Delta. There she supervised the construction of a charming house built of trees cut from the bayou and managed to sustain her family gracefully on very little money. Citing the example of her mother and others of that generation, a Polk daughter in later years would declare, "Women ran the South." Mrs. Polk, endowed with artistic sensibilities and wonderful taste, was quick to recognize merit and generous in her gestures and responses to people. She held delightful entertainments on her porch, where she received visitors every day as she sat mending oriental rugs. Peter frequently quoted Mrs. Polk, and some readers would later see glimpses of her in his work.[19]

To Eleanor, Mrs. Polk was "one of the distinguished people of this world," but as a general rule Eleanor was content to stay at home while Peter made the cocktail circuit in the assembly grounds, satisfying his social cravings and hearing talk that fed his creative life. By mid-summer he wrote Roger Angell that he was working on a story set at the old resort. "Coming here," he noted, "has given me all kinds of new detail that I want to use in it, which will make it considerably more complicated." He continued to work on the story as the summer stretched on.[20]

Shortly before Labor Day, the family was back in Columbus. Peter's promotion to full professor was effective in September, bringing an increase in salary. But he was disturbed to learn on his return that the congenial head of the English department was resigning, and he worried about his situation under a new man. In October, he sent the *New Yorker* a new story, "Two Pilgrims," which he significantly revised twice before it was finally accepted almost three months later. In the meantime, he had begun his first story set in Columbus, called "At the Art Theatre." For various reasons, the first story did not appear in the *New Yorker* for a year; the second piece Peter put away and did not publish until it was rediscovered in the 1990s.[21]

During the fall, the Taylors made several trips to visit the Macauleys (Peter and Robie had long before reconciled completely) and other Gambier friends, and sometimes on weekends they would go out to Jim and Jane Seymour's farm north of Columbus, where Petie loved running through the woods and playing in a stream flowing in a rocky ravine. Shortly after Christmas, Peter went to New York for Jack Thompson's wedding to Susan Otis. He stayed for a very social and stimulating three days with the Lowells, who took him to a round of parties (one at Lillian Hellman's apartment), where he mingled with Alfred Kazin, William Alfred, William Meredith, Richard Poirier, and Jacob and Barbara Epstein (with whom Elizabeth would shortly found the *New York Review of Books*). On New Year's Day 1963, writing to thank Cal and Elizabeth, he headed his letter "Nowhere, No Place." "Eleanor and I agree," he wrote, "that this *must* be our last year in Columbus."[22]

The Taylors had been in Ohio for more than ten years, and often unhappy in Columbus for over five of them. At the urging of the Lowells, Peter began corresponding about a position at Vassar. But there were already unmistakable signs that they were also feeling the pull of old familiar places. The previous spring, when Peter had gone for a reading at Duke, Eleanor had encouraged him to look at houses in Hillsborough; that summer en route to Eleanor's parents in Norwood, they had fallen in love with an old house in Pittsboro, North Carolina, and even contacted a realtor; and at Christmas, when the *Greensboro Daily News* asked Eleanor for a holiday recipe, her response was tinged with nostalgia. During a February visit in Columbus, Randall Jarrell learned of the Taylors' discontent and of the Vassar negotiations and decided that this was the time to lure them back to Greensboro. Fifteen years before, when Randall was unhappy at Sarah Lawrence, Peter had set in motion the process that brought him to Woman's College. Now Randall determined to return the favor. The college had already integrated, and in a year it was sched-uled to admit men under a new name, the University of North Carolina at Greensboro. Both changes made the school more attractive to Peter, and by mid-March the administration had agreed to Peter's terms, and he had ac-cepted the offer.[23]

Since Peter was to teach a creative writing seminar just one day a week, the Taylors first considered living again in Hillsborough. But when they went down to North Carolina in April for the Arts Forum and a house-hunting expedition, they settled upon Greensboro. A month later the Columbus residence sold, and they purchased a large clapboard Greensboro house built in 1905. After two weeks in June for Peter at the Utah Writers Conference and the remainder of the summer at the Monteagle cottage, by September the Taylors were in residence at 114 Fisher Park Circle, Greensboro. That fall Peter wrote Cal an exuberant letter. After describing "this fine Edwardian ruin we have bought [as] . . . our biggest and ugliest house yet," he launched into the other delights of Greensboro. Both the town and the school were much livelier places than they had been ten years earlier; people in the neighborhood were already claiming kin; the husband of Eleanor's old classmate was running for governor, and both Taylors were campaigning for him. After the anonymity of Columbus and Ohio State, the Taylors felt that they had truly come home.[24]

13

Greensboro ···

This third stint on the faculty at Greensboro was the Taylors' most prolonged
period of actually living in the city. Earlier, much of the time they had lived
in other places, at Scuppernong or in Hillsborough; but this time they were
settled at 114 Fisher Park Circle, located in an old, once-fashionable section
near the heart of town, for the duration. "We are delighted with Greensboro,"
Peter wrote Robie in October of 1963. "How wonderful it is," he told Cal, "to
be uncloistered again, especially after a mid-western cloistering of ten years.
My class at the College one day a week is just what I need." But his situation
would not prove the perfect environment for writing that he hoped. During
this final period in North Carolina, which was enlivened by new experiences
and new personalities but marked also by strains and tragedies, he produced
very little successful fiction.[1]

All through the fall Peter was involved in irritating negotiations with Ivan
Obolensky (David McDowell having left the firm) over his next volume of
short stories. Peter had very much wanted a gathering of his fiction, a volume
of selected stories to be named simply "Twenty-Three Stories." Obolensky
balked at the idea, finally agreeing to take stories from the two earliest volumes
(now out of print) and include them with six uncollected pieces. Still, publica-

tion of the volume was repeatedly delayed. Finally only after Peter asked to be released from his contract was *Miss Leonora When Last Seen and Fifteen Other Stories* published at the end of February 1964.[2]

Miss Leonora received good reviews. *Time* featured Peter's photograph with a glowing notice. Reviewers recognized the author as "a unique literary personality" and "an important American artist," and several remarked upon the high quality of his art from the very beginning of his career—calling attention to the "solidity of the work from the earlier volumes" and commending his consistent mastery of form over twenty-five years. In the *New York Times Book Review,* Gene Baro noted that the fiction had the "quality of transcending the literal, the limited or the everyday circumstance, even in the act of establishing it." More critics than ever before discovered deeply pessimistic strains in the fiction, one citing Peter's recurrent theme as "the failures of intimacy." The darkest reading ever presented was Jack Thompson's in the *New York Review of Books,* charting the emotional geography of the fiction centering on the family: "This warm circle is a desperate one," Jack wrote, "surrounded by a cold vacuum and surrounding a cold vacuum." While not venturing that far, the critic in the *Sewanee Review* found the frequent ground of the stories to be "a quotidian reality whose chief quality is a kind of emotional deception." Peter Taylor could not have hoped for more respectful and serious attention.[3]

The appearance of two stories in the *New Yorker* during the first two months in Greensboro, coupled with the critical success of *Miss Leonora,* made Peter Taylor a local celebrity. Ironically, these would be the only *New Yorker* stories during the Greensboro years, and the publication of *Miss Leonora* would signal the beginning of a period of drought and frustration in Peter's life as a writer.

Miss Leonora contained several stories (reprinted from earlier collections) that thoughtfully treated racial issues. But from this point, race would never again be an important theme in Peter Taylor's fiction. In later years Greensboro was called "the birthplace of the sit-in movement." The Taylors discovered that they had moved to a city that in 1963 was second only to Birmingham in the number of demonstrators. Out of the continuing Greensboro racial strife, a young local minister, Jesse Jackson, emerged as a national leader. Peter Taylor had long believed in racial justice, but he deplored mass movements. His feelings about the civil rights movement are reflected in the letter of recommendation he sent to Iowa for Diane Oliver, his one African American writing student that first semester in Greensboro. He wrote John Gerber that he very much wished her to go to Iowa so that "she not become preoccupied with the topical quarrels that completely dominate circles she might move in else-where."[4]

His position ran counter to that of his closest friend, for especially after the assassination of John F. Kennedy in November of 1963, Robert Lowell became increasingly an activist. The shock of the assassination also worsened the psy-chological instabilities that both Randall and Cal were experiencing. Jarrell had just returned home from Europe, feeling enervated. Throughout the weekend after Kennedy's murder, he sat in front of the television set weeping. He soon sought the help of a psychiatrist, who prescribed a high dosage of a newly marketed mood-elevating drug. In the early weeks of November, Cal again began behaving strangely. Just a few days after the assassination, a friend talk-ing with the poet at the opera was startled when Cal smiled and said, "Lyndon Johnson has asked me to be in the cabinet." Within another week Lowell had been committed to the hospital, where he remained for two months.[5]

It was with some anxiety that the Taylors looked forward to the Greensboro Arts Forum in early March of 1964, which was to feature both Randall and Cal. A month earlier, Eleanor went into the hospital for surgery. Her convales-cence was barely over when Cal and Elizabeth arrived for the forum. Also taking part was a Duke graduate student named Fred Chappell, who had just published a first novel. Chappell remembers well the literary panel on which he appeared with Lowell, who "seemed completely bewildered by the words on the page [before him] and would fix upon words in his mind more familiar and more comforting." Neither of the Taylors, however, betrayed by the slight-est sign that anything was amiss with their friend.[6]

Despite Cal's problems, it was an affectionate reunion. Peter had just been invited to teach the fall term at Harvard, where Lowell too would be in resi-dence. Both were delighted. The invitation also offered Peter an escape from Randall, whose strange behavior was becoming a burden. Later that spring Peter and Cal were both booked for a program at the University of Delaware, after which Peter rode with Lowell back to New York, to see Jean Stafford in the hospital. Her emotional devastation at the death of her husband, A. J. Liebling, in December had led to months of little food and little sleep, heavy drinking and chain-smoking. On April 5, she had suffered a heart attack. "Jean is *very* thin and very sad to *see*," Peter reported to Eleanor. Most of Liebling's estate went to his first wife, as provided in his divorce, and Jean was brooding about how she would make a living. These were troubled times for Peter's old friends.[7]

In June when the Taylors left for Monteagle, though both children had been accepted at the Buckingham School in Cambridge, Peter was still waiting for the Harvard English department to find the family adequate housing. The summer started well. In the past two years, Monteagle had been transformed, many of the cottages painted and rehabilitated and the site where the old hotel had burned given to the assembly for a park. The Taylors could miss the old run-down atmosphere a bit while still enjoying the brightening-up of the place. Both Peter and Eleanor were absorbed in gardening and landscaping projects. He was building beds in the ravine behind the cottage, and she laying out a garden on the slope above. The middle of the month, Peter sent a warm letter to Randall and Mary, inquiring after Randall's health and inviting them to visit later in the summer.[8]

Katie's Monteagle friends remember the Taylor cottage as a place where they had to be quiet so as not to disturb her father, who was writing. Peter may have been unusually severe about noise that summer because of his failure to produce salable fiction in the past few months. The previous fall he had made good a promise to Robie and sent a story for the twenty-fifth-anniversary issue of the *Kenyon Review*—"There," a piece the *New Yorker* had earlier refused. In January, Roger Angell turned down "The Throughway," a dark story about an aging couple's despairing recognition of their isolation from both the outside world and each other. Peter sent it to the *Sewanee Review,* and Andrew Lytle hurried to accept it. Peter was pleased to appear in either the *Kenyon* or the *Sewanee,* but there was a great difference between what these journals paid and a fat check from the *New Yorker.* In the spring Roger Angell also said no to "At the Art Theatre," a charming and provocative sketch of one tense and apparently inconsequential moment experienced by a young engaged pair—traceable to her rearing in an academic family and his country club background. The summer's political conventions inspired Peter to write "The End of Play"—set in the Washington Terrace house in St. Louis during the conventions of 1932, when his father was wrestling with the problems of a business failure and his own future. This was the first time that Peter had treated more than obliquely the effects of the Caldwell and Company debacle upon his family, and probably he would not have done so if Hillsman were not so debilitated that he could no longer read his son's fiction. This story too Roger Angell turned down.[9]

This rejection had its effects. Though earlier Peter had demanded perfect working conditions at Monteagle, he began to feel socially deprived and insisted that the Taylors give a party. After that, Eleanor told her parents, they were deluged with invitations, which she predicted Peter would eventually start finding excuses to get out of. Peter grew increasingly restive and irritable, and when Eleanor suggested that it would not be wise to uproot the children again and move them to Cambridge, Peter threatened a divorce. The threat only worsened the situation and increased Eleanor's resolve. The rest of the family would remain in Greensboro while Peter went to Harvard alone.[10]

The year before, when Peter was in Utah, he had written his wife—"You *are* my life." The early letters of the penitent husband away in Cambridge struck the same note. But between the lines it was also obvious that he was stimulated in the Harvard setting. His apartment on the eleventh floor of Leverett House (one reserved for visiting faculty) was lined with windows offering spectacular views of the Charles River. He raved about the beauty of the town, the wonderful ancient trees along Brattle Street; and he had never been so favorably impressed by students after just the first meeting. Time would prove that these were an exceptional group.[11]

The most unusual of them was James Thackara, son of a grandson of General William Tecumseh Sherman born in Argentina and the female diving champion of China, divorced before their child's birth. Walking through Harvard Yard, Thackara had encountered a close friend, Jim Toback, who told him, "There's a writer that I think you should know who's teaching a course here." Toback, a great networker, who arrived at Harvard already knowing Aaron Copland, Leonard Bernstein, and Norman Mailer and who subsequently became a filmmaker, was a man to heed; and both students enrolled in Peter's undergraduate writing course. From the first day, Thackara was awed by Peter's power to "produce an atmosphere of tolerance and decency among an incredibly rivalrous group of people." It was not, however, until the conference on his first story that teacher and student came to know each other, a meeting for which Peter was not atypically late. "The person Peter found sitting in his hall," as Thackara paints himself, "was somebody incredibly angry. I had trekked across the world like some sort of twentieth-century refugee. I was someone who had been in ten schools, several different cultures, several different languages, who had no sense whatsoever of any place in the sense of geo-political place or *patria*." Literature had filled the void created by rootlessness and family instability. "For me," he says, "it was a great gift, having a private audience with a genuine writer. And he was forty-five minutes late!" Finally Peter appeared mumbling gracious words of apology. "But," as

Thackara tells it, "I was pissed off and said to him, 'It is really unforgivable. I hope you never do that again.' " A look of great interest transformed Peter's face. "Well, please come in, young man," he smiled widely, "and let me find out about *you*." Here was a rare bird for a man who appreciated rare birds.[12]

Soon Peter was being taken to ice hockey games by Toback, Thackara, and Thackara's current girlfriend (later a *Vogue* model who married a British movie actor). It was from this Harvard group that Peter first began to number students among his close friends. Another, from this same class, was a young married man named Tom Molyneux. In the graduate writing class, there was John Casey, a law student, who appeared at Peter's door the first day of class with a 350-page manuscript. But much as he enjoyed his students, Peter was also having a lively social life among his contemporaries. Cal was up from New York during the week and staying at Quincy House just across the street. William Alfred, the legendary Harvard English professor and playwright, lived in a little nineteenth-century house on Athens Street nearby. The three men were soon meeting regularly for drinks and meals. Alfred noted the contrast between the two old friends, Peter "such an elegant man with such dash," and Cal "just a touch untidy"; but he found that the two were like brothers. By the middle of October Peter could report that he had invitations for every night the following week. Robert and Sally Fitzgerald entertained him, as well as Peter and Esther Brooks and Lee and Bob Gardner (the latter Allen Tate's brother-in-law and a friend of Cal's). Cal had also arranged that Peter go to dinner at Mrs. Sally Sedgewick's on Beacon Hill, promising that she was the Boston equivalent of Mrs. James K. Polk. Of all those he was thrown with, Peter was becoming particularly fond of Alfred Conrad, the Harvard philosophy professor, and his wife, the poet Adrienne Rich, whom the Taylors had first met in Greensboro through Randall.[13]

In late October, Peter flew down to Monteagle to pack up and place in storage the furnishings of their cottage, which at the end of the previous summer they had decided to sell. Eleanor and Petie came to Cambridge for the Thanksgiving holiday, and the three had Thanksgiving dinner with the Conrads and were entertained by the Gardners and Brookses as well. By that time, Peter had all sorts of experiences to relate. At first Cal had seemed fine, though naturally excited about the publication of his new volume of poetry, *For the Union Dead,* and the off-Broadway opening of his play, *Old Glory,* based on two Hawthorne short stories and Melville's "Benito Cereno." The Jarrells were in the Northeast for a series of lectures, and it was agreed that Peter would join them for Cal's opening. When the day came, Randall failed to return any of Peter's calls to his New York hotel, so Peter decided not to go down. Two hours before curtain time, Elizabeth Hardwick called in a fury. As Peter was trying to explain his absence, she upbraided him, "Oh, but it's too late now. You're missing something that's great and important—not just another off-Broadway production!" Later Peter unburdened himself to Eleanor: "Randall is a great writer-critic-teacher, but he is no good as a friend, except when it is perfectly convenient for him. Cal is competitive and 'tricky,' but he is not forever making these choices that hurt or destroy somebody or something." Peter, however, was putting up with a lot from Cal too. It had seemed at first that Cal was almost moving in with Peter, so often was he in the apartment. That proved to be a problem, since Lowell helped himself to everything, even Peter's razor. Peter also had to endure often merciless teasing and put-downs. Sally Fitzgerald remembers a dinner at their house when Cal said to Peter, "You have a lot of charm, but you haven't any brains." After an evening at the Conrads, Adrienne called Peter's apartment to express her displeasure at Cal's needling of him. "Had it been anyone else," she said, "I would have asked him to leave my house." After a series of non-committal replies from Peter, she finally said, "Oh! He's with you right now—isn't he?" "Yes," Peter answered, looking at his friend across the breakfast table.[14]

One of the minor subjects of Cal's teasing was that Peter was being pursued by women in Cambridge. He was much sought after, he had charmed everyone, and some felt that one Cambridge wife was quite smitten. But as Helen Ransom Forman later commented, Peter Taylor in his maturity was like a great peacock who had a beautiful tail to spread, but was very circumspect with it. He would do nothing to endanger his marriage.[15]

Early in December Peter woke to find the Charles River frozen over and snow fallen on the ice. Everything was beautiful from his windows. He had agreed to recommend one of John Casey's stories to the New Yorker. Casey, who had been writing in secret for years, was embarking on a legal career because of parental pressure. On election day, Casey had come for a conference. Peter saw in Casey the same conflict between individual talent and family aspirations that he himself had experienced. At the end of the conference, Peter said to him, "You shouldn't be a lawyer; you should be a writer." In a strange twist of events, Peter went that evening with the Gardners to an election-night party at the Ritz Carlton, where he was discussing with an attractive Washington couple this talented student and Peter's advice to him. The three looked up to see the couple's son approaching—it was John Casey. Peter, as Casey remembers the moment, "became brilliantly active. He was charming, witty, quickly moving to the higher ground of loftiness, then back in a flash to the lower ground of practical matters." The parents were stunned, and Casey felt that his life had been changed.[16]

Peter deeply affected other students also. "I needed what I needed from Peter so desperately, and he was such a profound person that he seemed to sense that," James Thackara remembers. "Within the first few minutes of my first conference, the roles of professor and student were dropped. He must have known that I was a homicidal writer, that for me being a writer was a matter of life and death," Thackara says. "He was going to share with me the writer's life, and he must have known that he could, perhaps by very small gestures, lead me toward it." Over the years that was a service that Peter Taylor performed for many talented young people. Another that term at Harvard was Tom Molyneux, who decided to bring his wife and young family to Greensboro the following fall and enroll in the new writing program.[17]

Harvard had been a wonderful experience in every way, but Peter wrote Eleanor that he had never looked forward to anything as he had to spending Christmas with her. Randall Jarrell arranged to be in New York in order to avoid Peter and Eleanor's Christmas party. Now it was clear why he had not returned Peter's calls: Randall was still angry about Peter's lack of support earlier in the fall for Jarrell's mad plan to oust the head of the English department and several faculty members. It was actually a relief not to have to see Randall.[18]

Back in Cambridge after the New Year, Peter discovered that Cal was not returning for the final two weeks of the semester, even to pick up his students' papers. After talking with Lowell on the phone, Peter reported to Eleanor that his friend sounded "in bad shape and heavily tranquilized." A week later, despondently he wrote her, "Cal and Randall are both hopelessly mad." But another old friend appeared in Boston in fine fettle. Allen Tate and Isabella arrived to visit the Gardners, and a large group had a wonderful night on the town, ending with dinner at the Somerset Club. "Allen outshone all others," Peter told Cal. "Surely [the walls of the Somerset Club] had never heard such loud Southern voices at such late hours—and saying things no Yankee walls were meant to hear. The Gardners were a model of tolerance." It was a fine end to the Harvard experience, marked also by a wonderful letter from Adrienne. "You did turn out to be one of the best things to come through Cambridge in years—and we are going to miss you very much," she wrote. She had been rereading his fiction and she found him "closer than I ever realized to the ones we can call great . . . who set down tones of moral twilight and the flashes of lightning we occasionally see by." She continued: "I don't know who else nowadays has written about family life, for instance, with such refusals of ready-to-hand assumptions yet such awareness of what a strange mixture it all is. And your women are marvellous."[19]

Upon Peter's return to Greensboro, Peter found Randall waiting for him at the Fisher Park house, seeming completely himself again—"like the old, old Randall, merely changing the subject when I say something stupid and not suffering so much from it." This Peter reported to Cal in a characteristically generous and supportive letter, telling his old roommate how much he missed him. Soon, however, Cal was again admitted to the hospital, as was Randall. Peter had arranged that Jean Stafford be featured at the Arts Forum. "Such gloom as we have been living in could only be dispelled by a visit from you," he wrote her a few days before the event. "I promise we'll all be gay and keep off the heart-breaking subject." In April, Randall was again back home, and Peter was relieved to report that "he doesn't seem manic and he doesn't seem sedated," and that the marital troubles that Randall and Mary had been having were apparently over. Within two weeks, however, deeply depressed, Randall cut his wrists in a suicide attempt. Peter was finding it increasingly difficult to cope with Randall's dizzyingly up-and-down states. Jarrell returned from the hospital again in July, and shortly afterward, the Taylors went to Monteagle, where they rented a cottage for a couple of weeks.[20]

The spring term had been hard. In addition to dealing with Randall's instability, Peter was working with poet Bob Watson putting finishing touches on the MFA Writing Program that would begin in the fall, and there was ongoing trouble with the Obolensky organization. Just as Peter was leaving for Harvard the previous September, he received a curt note from Ivan Obolensky stating that the firm had contracted with Peter and brought out two collections of short stories, but "the whole objective on my part was to do your novel." He then asked that Peter send him immediately the part he had completed. The old issue of a promised novel had resurfaced again, but the firm was truly acting strangely. Despite the excellent reviews, the publishers had not advertised *Miss Leonora* well. Bookstores had complained about not being able to obtain copies, and Peter had still not received one penny from royalties. In June, Peter wrote Ivan that he must sever his ties with the publishing house.

For four years, Cal had been urging Peter to go again with Bob Giroux, now at Farrar, Straus and Giroux. On the first of July, Peter signed a contract with Giroux's firm for a work of fiction named "The Pilgrim Sons," to be completed by September 1, 1966, and bringing an advance of $6,000 over twelve monthly installments. It was the largest sum Peter had ever received for a projected work.[21]

For some time Peter had been working on several long stories that he was hoping to turn into this novel. He was also under obligation to the *New Yorker*. Though he had renewed his first-reading contract with them for 1965, he had submitted no stories, and he owed the magazine $700. But that summer he devoted to the play set in Monteagle that he had begun two years before. That was one reason he wanted to go to the mountain for a short visit. By fall, he had finished "The Girl from Forked Deer," and Farrar, Straus and Giroux was sending it the rounds of theatrical producers.[22]

Peter had just learned that he had been awarded a grant from the Rockefeller Foundation to take the 1966–67 school year off from teaching, when he was summoned to Memphis on October 7. After a long struggle with cancer, Millsaps Fitzhugh was dead at the age of sixty-two. Peter grieved, remembering his brother-in-law's friendship dating from his own teenage years, but he was most concerned about his sister Sally. The marriage had not been untroubled, but Sally had loved Millsaps deeply. She was herself suffering from emphysema, and she looked ravaged. Upon returning to Greensboro, Peter learned that Randall, who had returned to teaching that fall, had checked into the North Carolina Memorial Hospital at Chapel Hill because of an injured wrist. Three days later on October 14, when Peter and Eleanor returned from a party, a badly shaken Katie was standing at the front door. There had been a phone call. Randall was dead.[23]

The facts were puzzling. Between treatments for the wrist, Randall was allowed strolls outside the hospital. On Thursday evening, a driver on the bypass saw a man walking on the edge of the highway suddenly "lunge out into the path of the car." Cal came down for the funeral. Randall was "our own special thorn and pearl," he told Eleanor, "vexing and noble beyond all of our acquaintance." The Taylors and Lowell talked for hours, trying to understand, to make sense of the last year in Randall's life. After Cal left, Peter poured his grief and his confusion into letters to close friends he had shared with Randall—Adrienne Rich and Robert Fitzgerald and Allen Tate. "Eleanor and I never knew precisely how he was suffering," he told Adrienne. "And we are not certain whether his death was by accident or by suicide." The worst part of grieving was the guilt Peter was feeling especially after mutual friends told him that in the spring Randall had asked why Eleanor and Peter no longer liked him. Gradually as Peter wrote the letters, he moved toward his own sort of clarity about everything. "I don't know whether or not his death was suicide," he wrote Robert Fitzgerald. "Probably no one will ever know. I think it was." To Allen Tate, Peter disclosed that he was writing about Randall's last year in a notebook, on the left hand of the page listing "facts," and on the right, "speculations." "I am afraid," he confessed to Tate, "that in the future I might confuse the two." But earlier in the letter Peter had referred quite simply to "Randall's suicide." This was the view he adopted, and he would hold to it for the rest of his life.[24]

While still grieving and brooding over Randall's death, Peter had to face another sorrow. When he had gone down to Memphis for Millsaps' funeral, he had been saddened to see his father. An invalid for several years, now Hillsman was unable to speak, and whenever Peter came into his room, he could only gaze at his son as great tears rolled down his cheeks. A month after Randall's death, Sally called to say that Hillsman was dying. As Peter boarded the plane in Greensboro, he wished only that his father could live until he reached Memphis. At the Memphis airport, Peter learned that his father was dead. He felt surrounded by the dead. His grief was awful. "All my father figures gone in one blow almost," he told Mary Jarrell. "I was suddenly reminded that it was Millsaps who introduced me to Tolstoy and Chekhov, Randall who taught me how to read them, and my father who made it possible for me to understand a good deal of the subject matter. I loved all three of them."[25]

Immediately after Randall's death, Robert Penn Warren began gathering essays for a memorial issue in one of the quarterlies, and two months later he began to plan a memorial service for Randall at Yale on February 28. He wanted Peter to participate. About the same time, Peter received an invitation to give the annual Hopwood Lecture at the University of Michigan, the sort of request that he customarily refused. This time he accepted because, as he explained, "I shall have something important to say." He planned to talk about "the place of creative writing in the university curriculum, about the role of the writer as teacher in the university, and about the place of the student in the life of the writer-teacher," all to be developed through comments on Randall's career.[26]

Randall's death, Peter wrote to Robert Fitzgerald, "is the greatest personal loss I have known, and I feel that it must and will change my whole life." He expressed to both Adrienne and Cal his thankfulness that at Harvard he had learned to make friends among his students, "instead of keeping them at arm's length." He mused about why he had done that, given the examples of Allen and Red Warren. He had been too unbending—had it been the influence of Mr. Ransom? But the reasons did not matter. In this time of loss, he had found a new source of friendship. After his neglect of the past weeks, he would turn his mind to his students now.[27]

Just before Peter's father's death, his mother had sold the suburban house that Hillsman purchased after he fully recovered his financial losses, and she had rented an apartment, to which she now had to move. During Christmas Peter flew down to help get her settled before Sally and Katherine went to spend the winter at the Fitzhugh house in Arizona. The English department had decided to fill Randall's position for the fall term with a distinguished poet or critic, and Peter now wrote Allen Tate to ask whether he was interested. Cal had taken to telephoning and talking excitedly for an hour at a time, reading letters he had received from Jackie Kennedy or announcing that for $3,500 he had purchased a bust of Tecumseh, which he had put in his dining room replacing a bust of Napoleon. Soon Jean called to say that Cal had again been committed after standing up in a box at the opera and attempting to lead the orchestra. "One has to laugh at his antics, but it is heartbreaking," Peter confessed to Allen. "I keep wondering if there is nothing more that can be done for him than is being done. And I wonder how long his health and his luck can hold out. Some sort of violent end seems almost inevitable."[28]

Peter's response to the losses of the fall and his worries about the troubles of those remaining who were so close to him was to throw himself wholeheartedly into every aspect of living. Peter's interest in what he spoke of as "ril estate" was never sated. He could see a "one-time *mar*-velous End-chimney house or Center-hall house in every forlorn old farm dwelling stuffed with hay," Mary Jarrell recalls. It was part of his maintaining "a kind of *sparkling* interest in all the little life around us." Peter was continually embarking on excursions out from Greensboro, with friends, family, or alone, just to see what he might find. A year earlier, seventy miles and three thousand feet above the city, he had found a cabin, built of chestnut logs, near the Blue Ridge Parkway just across the state line in Virginia. He had to have it. The new year, 1966, began with a trek by all four Taylors up to the cabin. Work continued there for months.[29]

As he had for the last few years, a month later he went to Memphis to hold classes at Southwestern's Adult Education Center. Usually that gave him a chance to see his family. This time, though his mother and sister were out of town, he did enjoy the customary long lunch at the Four Flames Restaurant with old friends Jim Roper and Ann Watkins Boatner. Memphis law still prohibited mixed drinks, but patrons were allowed to "brown bag" (bring their own liquor). Ann always arrived with a large fruit jar of martinis, and once that and oyster omelettes were consumed, all three went home for naps. On February 28, many of Randall's friends in the literary world gathered at Yale for the memorial service. Red Warren had been so successful in soliciting essays and reminiscences that Farrar, Straus and Giroux was eager to publish a memorial volume to be edited by Red, Peter, and Cal. A month later, Peter delivered another tribute to Randall as the Hopwood Lecture at Michigan.[30]

Back in Greensboro, Katie received news that she had won an Angier Biddle Duke Scholarship to Duke University for the fall. "To our conservative eyes," Peter told Allen Tate, "she seems a wild liberal. She says her generation is in search of freedom." Both she and eleven-year-old Petie had always been excellent students, and this substantial scholarship relieved the Taylors of any financial anxiety during her college years. Celebrating, Peter decided to have a bulls-eye window cut in the second story of the front facade of the Fisher Park house. The brow of the house, as he explained it, was too blank.[31]

Peter also reported to Tate that he had begun "hanging out" at a local bar called the Pickwick with literary colleagues and the "wonderful bunch" of students who had been attracted to the MFA program. Among the colleagues were Bob Watson; Fred Chappell, the mountain-bred young writer now on the faculty; and poet Gibbons Ruark. The students included Tom Molyneux, Angela Davis, William Pitt Root, and Lawrence Judson Reynolds, whom Peter would enlist for various building projects and who would remain a devoted friend. Like many of the others, Fred Chappell was awed by Peter, though the older man neither realized it nor would accept such reverence. "Peter Taylor as an artist and as a man was, to me, one of the shining examples of what a life in literature should be," Chappell has written; and he has set down a splendid description of Peter during these Greensboro days:

> He was one of those whose physical appearance seemed to have originated directly from character. His face was unique. Not handsome in any ordinary sense because it looked slightly twisted, it became more askew when he grinned one of his encouraging wide grins. All his words were underscored with a continuous

wide chuckle, and he had one of the brightest gazes I have ever observed. I couldn't decide whether his eyes were gray or light blue or green, tinted with brown. But they were wise and willing, set into a face humor-lines had made as crinkled as a favorite leather-covered armchair. He liked academic tweed and wore it comfortably, suede elbow patches and all. His personality was complex and the way he looked was complex. If I had to choose an artist to make a portrait of Peter Taylor, I think I might light upon the illustrator Arthur Rackham. Peter could sit as a model for a lore-steeped scholar or kindhearted cobbler.

Peter was interested in everything and everyone. In those days, Greensboro was amazed when Peter Taylor, the aggressively self-proclaimed non-sports-man was seen at games of the local hockey team with Tom Molyneux. Fred Chappell posits that this can be explained not only by Peter's marked fondness for the student, but because Molyneux's enthusiasm reflected "a mode of life and an outlook very different from his own." Peter, in Chappell's view, "pos-sessed a mercurial envy for all other ways of life he couldn't pursue, for all the other personalities he couldn't be." Just the physical aura of dramatic person-alities could draw Peter's keen interest. One day at the entrance of the striking brunette beauty Kelly Cherry (a poetry student) into the Pickwick, Peter leaned forward and said, "I know there's a story there."[32]

The guest lists for the Fisher Park parties were filled with people who might have stories. Because of the Taylors' wide connections in the town, they could draw upon a varied array of personalities. By this time, Eleanor's family had been dubbed "The Writing Rosses of North Carolina." Her oldest brother, Fred, a radio announcer and newspaperman, had also written a successful novel. His daughter Heather Ross (now Miller), a former student of Randall's, was attracting attention as a poet. Eleanor's younger sister, Jean Justice, an-other product of Woman's College, was producing fiction. James Ross, Elea-nor's beloved older brother, who had been Caroline Gordon's protégé and written an early novel of great promise, was a reporter for the Greensboro paper. Recently married to Marnie Polk, of the distinguished Warren County Polks, he lived across the park from the Taylors. Like Eleanor, he had never learned to drive, and he charged the paper for shoe leather. Described as a "classic newspaper type wonderfully sardonic and full of good tales," James and now Marnie were always among the guests. They provided a link to other journalists, like Bill Snyder, publisher of the paper; Edwin Yoder, later a re-spected columnist for the Washington Post Writers Group; the young book reviewer Jonathan Yardley, subsequently to become one of the country's preeminent literary journalists and one of Peter's greatest advocates. There were always a sprinkling of political figures (though political affiliation was an irrelevance): Richardson Preyer, the Democratic congressman; Blackwell Robinson, a conservative Republican who ran for the Senate; as well as Norman Smith, chairman of the local chapter of the American Civil Liberties Union. There were the socially prominent, among them Eleanor's friend Cornelia Cannon, of the North Carolina textile family. Added to the mix were Peter's colleagues. Here Peter displayed none of the petty snobbery or rank-consciousness of some academics. He was just as warm to young members of the department, like Randolph "Mack" Bulgin and his wife, Kathleen Mather Bulgin, as to the chairman. From the department, the Taylors always invited Bob Watson and his wife, Betty, a talented painter who had done two splendid portraits of Randall Jarrell, numerous studies of Kelly Cherry, and a portrait hanging in the Fisher Park house of all four members of the Taylor family. Added to the mix were Peter's writing students. Randall Jarrell had hated such affairs and had grumbled that "Peter likes too many people."[33]

Eleanor, though maintaining privately lifelong that she too hated parties, insisted on preparing everything herself. Laboring for two days in the kitchen, she would produce a sumptuous table of delicacies amid a setting, as one guest described it, "sparkling like a diamond necklace." And she was a perfect hostess, warm, solicitous, making sure that people who would enjoy each other met. Peter—who might possibly have spent a hot afternoon laying a brick walk up to the front steps—would appear, in Mary Jarrell's words, "showered, flanneled and radiant; in love with the party, and hoping it would last all night." "He loved to listen to stories and he loved to tell them," Jonathan Yardley remembers. "In his pronunciation the word emerged as stOHry; speaking the word he often lingered over it, stretching it out, savoring the pleasures and possibilities that lay ahead in the telling." Mack Bulgin's favorite anecdote from a Taylor party was hearing Peter, reveling in the moment, say to a guest, "Wait a minute. I was just making up something for you to say."[34]

To be invited to a party at 114 Fisher Park was an honor much sought in Greensboro. Among the greatest of these events was that honoring the panel for the Arts Forum—Jean, Eudora Welty, and James Dickey. Though Dickey was then writing some of the best poetry of his career, Peter found his "crude jocularity . . . no less than outrageous." Still, for Greensboro, here too was a celebrity, and Eudora Welty was a great hit, as she sipped her bourbon and told her wonderful tales. She and Peter realized anew their profound affinities, and the guests were dazzled by the affair.[35]

Toward the end of the semester, Peter again flew to Memphis. Sally was very ill. The emphysema had now affected her heart. "There is little chance of improvement," he told Allen Tate. Tate had recently divorced Isabella Gardner and was planning a summer wedding to Helen Heinz, a former nun and one of his students at the University of Minnesota. He had agreed to teach at Greensboro in the fall. The Taylors were staying in town that summer—Petie going to day camp, Katie working, and Peter writing in his office through the week and taking the family up to the cabin in Virginia on the weekends. "Saturday morning found me seventy-five miles north of Greensboro whacking away at alder bushes along our creek and pulling fox-grapevines off the rhododendrons," he wrote Sally on June 19, "and Eleanor seventy-five miles south of Greensboro working in her mother's vegetables and flowers." Both of Eleanor's parents were now infirm, and she was making frequent trips down to Norwood.[36]

Amid all the events of the past year, Peter had still found time to write. Early in January, after the trips to Memphis for funerals, Peter sent Roger Angell "A Cheerful Disposition," a wry tale of a man so superficial that he can feel nothing at the funerals in his family. Angell returned the story with the comment that it was not one of Peter's better efforts. Few would disagree, though Peter later placed it in the *Sewanee Review*. Subsequently Peter did receive one bit of good news. "There," rejected by Angell two years earlier and then published in the *Kenyon Review*, had been chosen for Martha Foley's *Best American Short Stories of 1965*. At summer's end, after what he called a vacation from his novel, Peter sent the *New Yorker* two stories—"Tom, Tell Him" and "Mrs. Billingsby's Wine." The first, centering on the fate of a baptismal font from a deconsecrated Episcopal church in a small West Tennessee town, Roger Angell judged the more complex, but less clear of the two. "Mrs. Billingsby's Wine" Angell accepted on the condition that it be cut. Peter's response was unprecedented: he told Angell to cut the story as he wished and just return it for his approval. Both stories are rather slight treatments of social distinctions amid changes in time; both lack the more profound probing of the great Peter Taylor fiction. Peter's entire letter to Angell, in which he also muses whether all stories should not be written quickly (as opposed to his usual practice), reflects a general lassitude.[37]

This may be traceable to his preoccupation with both the writing of his novel "The Pilgrim Sons" and the fate of his play "The Girl from Forked Deer." He had finished a draft of the play a year before, after a trip to New York to see the Moscow Art Theatre's productions of *The Cherry Orchard* and *Three Sisters* and a final stay at Monteagle. Peter would remain proud of the way the characters in his play (like Chekhov's) talked *over* each other, voluble but never communicating. As opposed to the novel and the stories he was now writing, he had poured his profundity into the play; and he never lost faith in the work through all his disappointment with its reception. Roger Straus had refused to publish it until it was performed. Despite attempts by Farrar, Straus and Giroux and Peter's own efforts, no theatrical producer expressed interest. When he sent it to Andrew Lytle, even the *Sewanee Review*, a place Peter could usually depend upon, turned it down.[38]

On September 3, Peter wrote Bob Giroux telling him that not only had he missed the promised deadline for delivery of "The Pilgrim Sons," but that he would be lucky to deliver it in another year and a half. He was having a terrible time with the novel. By that date Allen and Helen had arrived for the fall semester. Peter did not teach for the 1966–67 school year because of his Rockefeller Foundation grant, but his writing during the fall term was hindered a bit by his delight in Allen's company. In the middle of the term, it was announced that Peter had been made the first Alumni Distinguished Professor at the university—a reward for his distinguished career of thirty years. At the moment, however, he was not writing at the peak of his powers. The end of November Peter mailed to Roger Angell "The Elect," which he hoped would be "the first of a new series" of political stories. A week at the Georgetown University Writers Conference in July had stirred his long-dormant idea of drawing upon his family's political history for his fiction. The story, which again is not one of his best, does suggest the changes in political life and political image over the century and the sacrifices required in the personal life of a politician's wife. Despite the rejection of the story, Peter wrote Cal that he wanted to find an apartment in Georgetown for the spring and that he was reading *Reveille in Washington* and *Advise and Consent*, preparing to write "my long-awaited (awaited by me) Washington stories."[39]

The spring of 1967 was filled with trips back and forth to Washington, and to Memphis and Norwood to spend time with the ill. Still, wherever he was, Peter worked on the novel three hours every morning, and he was musing over the offer of a chaired professorship in creative writing at the University of Virginia. All the members of the family had been often miserable in Columbus, where Peter had nonetheless written some of his best stories. Despite the recent sadness over deaths, family life had been wonderfully happy in Greensboro, where Peter had written little of first quality. Eleanor did not want to leave Greensboro. They were really settled there for the first time in years, the children were happy, she had close friends, she was near her elderly parents, and she was again writing poetry. But she could see that in a sense the city, because of her long connection, might be more her place than his. During their visit to Charlottesville, the dean of the faculty had made Peter feel fully the honor and advantage of the offer. A highlight of the visit was an evening spent in the company of Mrs. Dabney, the ninety-year-old doyenne of Charlottesville. Virginia had done everything right, and Peter was impressed with the university and attracted by the idea of Charlottesville social life. He had reached a pinnacle in Greensboro. Would he not be simply repeating himself? As for academic ties, his cherished writing students were graduating and leaving Greensboro, including the beautiful, golden Molyneuxs—Tom and his wife and their two children. Finally, what Southerner of Peter's sort could resist the University of Virginia? Peter decided to take the offer.[40]

In the midst of the confusion and elation of the decision, Peter had to rush to Memphis. Sally was dying. Sally had been a buffer against his father when Peter was struggling to find his vocation, and dating from the Kenyon faculty years, she had become an important part of the life of his own family. As he told Mary Polk Kirby-Smith, the close friendship that had developed between Sally and Eleanor was one of his "greatest satisfactions." Both Peter and Eleanor were distraught. Seeing Sally suffer was agony for Peter, but during the last days he was able to tell her just what she had meant to him. On March 19, she died. "Life doesn't seem the same without Sally," he confessed to Cal two months later. "The loss of Randall and Dad was hard, but with Sally it won't go away."[41]

So Peter buried himself in his work, distracted himself with trips to Charlottesville to find housing, and in July went again to the Utah Writers Conference, where James Dickey shocked the participants both by his on-stage performances and by living with a woman in the dormitory where the male writers were housed. Unsuccessful at finding a place to purchase in Charlottesville, Peter decided to rent out the Fisher Park house and to take a year's leave of absence, rather than resign at Greensboro. The Taylors rented a large house in Charlottesville (the largest that they had ever occupied) at 1101 Rugby Road near the campus. They would have the year to decide whether they would remain. But Virginia offered great possibilities for Peter as he entered his sixth decade, and the place appealed to all sides of his nature. Charlottesville would be his permanent residence for the rest of his life. Here he would make more close friends, and here he would write some of his greatest works.[42]

This large portrait of the Reverend Nathaniel Greene Taylor, along with a similar one of his wife, hung proudly in Hillsman Taylor's residences and later in Peter Taylor's own houses in Charlottesville.
Courtesy Eleanor Ross Taylor

Newspaper lithograph inspired by Tennessee's "War of the Roses,"
when Peter Taylor's maternal grandfather, Robert Love Taylor, ran
against his brother for the governorship
Courtesy Eleanor Ross Taylor

The four children of Hillsman and Katherine Taylor Taylor. *Left to right:* Mettie, Pete, Sallie, and Bob.
Courtesy Eleanor Ross Taylor

Hillsman and Katherine Taylor on their fiftieth anniversary in 1958
Courtesy Tennessee State Library and Archives

Portrait of Peter Taylor painted in 1938 by Virginia Jett
Courtesy Eleanor Ross Taylor

Peter Taylor and Eleanor Ross on their wedding day, June 4, 1943, with Allen Tate
Courtesy Eleanor Ross Taylor

Peter and Eleanor Ross Taylor at the door of St. Andrew's Chapel, Monteagle,
Tennessee, with Allen Tate, who gave the bride away, and best man Robert
Lowell
Courtesy Eleanor Ross Taylor

Allen Tate and Caroline Gordon
Courtesy Eleanor Ross Taylor

Jean Stafford
Courtesy Eleanor Ross Taylor

Randall Jarrell and Peter Taylor in front of the duplex owned by the
two families on Spring Garden in Greensboro, North Carolina
Courtesy Eleanor Ross Taylor

This collage of views taken at Scuppernong, the country house the Taylors owned from 1949 to 1951 near Norwood, North Carolina, hung in Peter Taylor's study.

Courtesy Eleanor Ross Taylor

Peter Taylor, Ross Taylor, Randall Jarrell, Mary Jarrell, and Katie Taylor on a picnic at Monteagle in the early 1960s
Courtesy Eleanor Ross Taylor

Peter Taylor and Robert Lowell at John Crowe Ransom's eightieth birthday celebration at Kenyon in 1968
Kenyon College Alumni Bulletin *11 (September 1987).*

John Crowe Ransom on the same occasion
Kenyon College Alumni Bulletin *11 (September 1987)*

Peter Taylor photographed in Key West by Wright Langley in the 1970s
Copyright © Wright Langley

Peter Taylor toasting Henderson Hayward at his seventy-fifth birthday party in 1990.
Eleanor Taylor is third from the left and Hayward at the extreme right.
Courtesy Eleanor Ross Taylor

14

Charlottesville ···

"Just don't think for a moment you are going to get me on a horse," a resigned Eleanor had told Peter when he announced the decision to move to Charlottesville. Through the ensuing decades, both Taylors were able to avoid riding, though the foxhunting set was one of several in which they moved. The spring before the Taylors' arrival, the *Washington Post* Sunday magazine featured a piece on Albemarle County, calling it "the last great bastion of the aristocracy" and noting that it was the fourth-richest county in the country. Mr. Jefferson's university was a magnet for the wealthy, the worldly, and the cultivated, as was the beautiful rolling Albemarle countryside dotted with charming country estates. A number of Virginia faculty had independent incomes, many diplomats had retired to Albemarle, and there were sizable colonies both of English and of Germans who had fled the Nazi regime. Charlottesville was the center of a cosmopolitan mix of town, gown, and county—the categories often overlapping. For social variety and complexity, it far exceeded any place Peter had lived. Naturally he delighted in that.[1]

The interest of Virginians in horse-breeding and sport can be traced as far back as the historic race run at Bermuda Hundred in 1677 between steeds belonging to Abraham Womack and Richard Ligon. For decades Albemarle

County had been home to two hunt clubs, Keswick and Farmington. The University's most famous writer-in-residence, William Faulkner, had ridden with both and proudly posed for pictures in his hunting pinks. Soon after the Taylors' coming, bachelor bon vivant John Coleman, who taught writing courses in the English department, threw a party to introduce them to some of the old Faulkner circle (including Mrs. Faulkner, her daughter, and son-in-law), as well as other county people. Among the Faulkner intimates were the amazing Katinka Hume of Hunting Ridge Farm (who had been Lady Willoughby and who rode to the hounds up into her eighties) and her husband Charlie, and David Yalden-Thompson of Clunie Farm (a Highlander, native of Argyle, graduate of Cambridge, now on the philosophy faculty) and his wife, Barbara. Mary Scott Blake (an Albemarle divorcee and socialite descended from Alexander Spotswood, early eighteenth century governor of Virginia), whom John Coleman often squired, was there, and two couples with whom the Taylors would become especially close. Henderson Heyward, a Charlottesville architect born in Memphis, was full of stories of family and of intricate old Virginia connections. He, his wife Jane (née Gamble, of Boston), and their five children lived at Foxhaven Farm. Peter's old Memphis friend Mary Jane Peeples had already made the Taylors known to the other couple, the Bedford Moores. A graduate of Princeton, he taught English in the engineering school. His wife, Jane, had come to Virginia for college from Mobile. They lived at Shack Mountain in a beautiful red-brick Jeffersonian house designed by the former director of Monticello, which they had filled with fine antiques. "Now, Bedford, you're from Charleston," Peter said upon meeting Moore, and he laughed at the witty reply: "No, Columbia, but we are *received* in Charleston."[2]

The primary form of entertaining among the group was the seated dinner for eight or ten people. The Taylors responded in kind, but they continued to give their customary cocktail parties, at which they would mix their county and town friends with Peter's students and his colleagues. Foremost among the latter was the legendary head of the English department Fredson Bowers, known for his often ruthless policies in building a distinguished department. Proud of proclaiming that he was born on the wrong side of the tracks in New Haven, he had an emphatic voice and a commanding presence, evidencing total self-control. Strangely enough, considering the declaiming of humble origin, he was given to wearing ascots and taking snuff. His wife, the writer Nancy Hale, was an Englishwoman. The Taylors also almost always included two other couples whom both found congenial, the E. D. Hirsches and the

Tony Winners. As Tony Winner recalls, one component of every Taylor party was the ninety-year-old matriarch Mrs. Dabney, to whom everyone was introduced on his way to the bar. She had taken the Taylors up, including them often in her weekly Sunday luncheons for eight. Upon her death, the town finally got into the kitchen, where they found only a primitive sink, a woodstove, and one table. But Mrs. Dabney and her almost equally aged butler, Leonard, had brought off the elegant affairs, the only hitch being that Leonard frequently had to come into the dining room and remove Mrs. Dabney's foot from the buzzer that was continually sounding in the kitchen.[3]

Peter Taylor himself soon owned a collection of ascots, and he had concocted a wonderful story connecting him with the University. For decades he had dreamed of purchasing the two-story red-brick house outside Trenton once owned by his great-uncle Will Taylor, whom he had watched at the dinner table in childhood maneuver the hooks substituted for his hands blown off in a Civil War battle. In 1951, Hillsman had written his son suggesting Will Taylor as the subject for a story. According to Hillsman, Will originally wanted to be an artist, purchased the brick house after the Civil War, and refused to wear a tie to his own wedding. Once in Charlottesville, Peter turned the rough-hewn Will Taylor into a graduate of the University who had studied to be an architect and built a house near Trenton based upon those in the Pavilions running south from the central Rotunda, before losing his hands in the war. So dedicated to reaching an underlying psychological truth in his fiction, Peter was also capable of transforming a tale in conversation for his own benefit and pleasure.[4]

Just as had happened when he moved to Greensboro, a Peter Taylor story appeared in the *New Yorker* shortly after his arrival in Charlottesville—"Mrs. Billingsby's Wine" on October 14—adding luster to his name and establishing him in the eyes of his colleagues as a *New Yorker* writer. But it was the last story to appear there for nine years. Plainly Roger Angell was not a fan, and Peter was particularly bitter about Angell's rejections of his political stories, "The Elect" and "Sweat" (later renamed "First Heat"). The previous January, Peter had argued for his knowledge of political families in defending "The Elect," and in September he concluded a letter, "We are never going to agree about certain types of men who enter politics and who (with their families) suffer for being what they are."[5]

Before leaving Greensboro, Peter had mailed to Bob Giroux roughly a hundred pages of his novel, mainly, he wrote, so that Giroux could see that "my novel is not just a myth." Months earlier Peter had confided to Giroux: "People have often told me that I am not very smart (principally Cal) but I never fully realized it till I began trying to organize this thing." He went on to divulge that Anne Macauley once said to Cal, "Robie and Jack are both smarter than Peter," to which Cal replied, "What difference does that make!" "That's what's *really* wonderful about [Cal]," Peter commented. But Peter was facing an impossible task in turning what he had written into a novel. He was so basically a short story writer, and he had simply written stories set in Memphis very loosely tied together by one character, a middle-aged college professor who has returned home for visits over twenty-five years—and hoped that the project would finally coalesce and satisfy his publishers. In Charlottesville he continued his labors on the novel, though he clung to his long-held desire to assemble and publish a collected-stories volume.[6]

The *Kenyon Review* had agreed to publish his Monteagle play, still named *The Girl from Forked Deer,* and upon the editor's request, Peter was writing a preface for it. Jim Michael was also enthusiastic about doing the play at Kenyon's Hill Theater. As 1967 turned into 1968, Peter worked on the preface. During the two years' of frustration with the supposed novel and the pain of the *New Yorker*'s rejections, he had written an important play. Now laboring on the preface, he produced a piece of historiography memorable in texture and sweep. Take this passage, in which the author contrasts the fate of the settlers of Owl Mountain (Monteagle) with those of the lowland South:

> Life, instead of getting better for them after the first years, got worse. The early cabins they built might look very much like the early cabins built by the families who pushed on to the low country, but as the years went by the mountain man did not add to his cabin room after room, wing after wing until the cabin had become something that could be called a Southern big house. Instead, the original log cabin on the Mountain generally deteriorated until it had to be abandoned—abandoned for a shanty-like structure with cheap siding from the saw mill, a tin roof that would soon rust out and have to be patched with flattened tin cans, and a jointed stovepipe in place of the old rock chimney. Though here and there one of the old cabins remains to this day, preserved by chance or by the assiduous attentions of some particularly industrious family, for the most part the only signs left of these cabins are the crumbling stone chimneys or chimney bases that one stumbles upon when hunting or fishing or picnicking. (10–11)

Such a passage draws upon a knowledge of region achieved over a lifetime, and what rich suggestions of historical process, of economics and sociology, he conveys through architecture. Another paragraph delineating the lowland cottage owners at the old resort offers Peter Taylor's best gloss on the social subjects of his entire canon:

> They are not, to be sure, ne'er-do-well, down-at-the heel, old-line Southern gentry. Yet they are figuratively, and in many cases literally, the first cousins or even the brothers and sisters of that well-known breed. They have the same names as those you will find lingering in the old homeplaces in the lowlands. But they are the sons and daughters of the old regime who have had too much energy, too much vitality to be willing to accept shabby gentility as the way of life for the women or—for the men—either the frustrations of idleness or the dwindling rewards for farming or for practicing law in a country town. They are for the most part those whose forebears left the land a generation or so ago, and with their good names and their connections and their natural endowments went to the new Southern cities and towns to make a place for themselves. (17)

But the play has to do with a group within this larger body—a "class unto themselves," who still retain a fondness for the "old patterns of existence." That is their attraction to Owl Mountain. Just as the shabby old resort came into being as a refuge from the yellow fever epidemics that scourged the lowlands in the nineteenth century, so now it offers the nostalgic city-bred summer people "a retreat from the fever of modern life" (18). As Peter was writing the preface, he changed the name of the play to *A Stand in the Mountains*, suggested by Donald Davidson's poem "Lee in the Mountains," which in turn draws upon the advice (rejected by Robert E. Lee) that, instead of surrendering, he gather his troops and make one final stand in the Blue Ridge.[7]

As Peter finished the preface, the fever was increasing. Early in 1968, Peter began a letter to Cal, "The news is so bad these days that it is hard to write a cheerful letter." The world seemed to be breaking apart, and 1968 would come down as one of the key years of the twentieth century in American history. Demonstrators blanketed the country, galvanized by the Tet Offensive in the Vietnam War, the assassinations of Martin Luther King and Robert Kennedy, and the violent experience of the Democratic convention in Chicago. In September, Adrienne Rich wrote Peter from New York, "Life is tenser, more grilling than ever and yet one feels that here, if anywhere, there might be a chance of salvation, a vision of something freer, more open, more daring than any-

thing our society has known. Also of course it's a razor-edge. Come walk it
with us, when you can." *That* Peter did not choose to do; instead, in Charlottesville he pondered the political and social upheaval as he continued to
revise his play. It is his most violent work. Though the violence is all off-stage,
the play begins as what seems a Chekhovian study of ineptitude and helpless-
ness, then changes to a work with Ibsen-like fissures and terrors. Drawing
upon central themes of his fiction, here Peter Taylor dramatizes conflicts rising
from the displacements effected by time, the choice of role offered by a changing social order, the struggle between men and women for power, and the
tensions within the family unit. Nowhere are the obsessions of the Taylor
canon—history, gender, and the family—brought together in a more disturbing way.[8]

As an escape from both current events and the tortured world of his play,
Peter was reading Trollope. When the bulk of Sally Taylor Fitzhugh's estate was
to be disbursed after her mother's death, Peter was to receive almost seventy
thousand dollars. In the meantime, Sally's personal possessions had already
been divided. Louise Fitzhugh (Sally's foster daughter, born to Millsaps and
his first wife, the dancer from Mississippi) was now a successful New York
writer. She wanted nothing from the Fitzhugh home, so embittered was she
about the years she had spent there; thus Sally's things fell to her three siblings.
Peter's lot contained Sally's portrait and her books, including her set of Trollope. Since receiving this particularly meaningful part of his legacy, Peter had
read *The Small House at Allington* and *Phineas Finn*. "I don't know how I'd
live without Trollope," Peter told Cal.[9]

The early spring was enlivened by visits from Jean, Cal, and Allen, all at
Virginia to give readings. Katherine Taylor's health was deteriorating, and
Peter flew to Memphis periodically to visit her. Whereas formerly he would
appear and spirit her away to Trenton to visit her dear friend Miss Helen Freed,
now he most often simply sat and talked with her in her apartment. One day,
remembering Peter's affection for the huge portraits of her grandparents,
which were now in storage, she went to her desk and wrote a statement that
they were to go to him at her death, an action with interesting later consequences.[10]

At the end of April, Peter and Eleanor joined the rest of the old Kenyon
crowd in Gambier to celebrate John Crowe Ransom's eightieth birthday. The
occasion, which was covered by *Life*, was a memorable event. Upon the return
to Charlottesville, Peter wrote the editor of the *Kenyon Review*: "It had been

years since I was in the room with so many people I like. My main memories are of Jack Thompson's booming voice and Cal's dancing all about like an enlarged leprechaun." Mr. Ransom's young editor at Knopf, however, remembered above all Peter's graciousness to her—in contrast to her treatment by Allen, Cal, and some of the others.[11]

Peter knew almost immediately that he would remain at Virginia, and he tried unsuccessfully to buy the large house he was renting at 1101 Rugby Road. At the urging of "Miss Estelle" Faulkner, the Taylors finally purchased from the Faulkner biographer Joseph Blotner the property at 917 Rugby Road that Faulkner had occupied in Charlottesville, a two-story brick Georgian house built in the 1930s. But that venture did not completely satisfy Peter's yen for real estate, and shortly he had also purchased a ramshackle thirteen-room house on thirty acres overlooking the James River at Palmyra, in the next county. Fortunately, soon afterward the Taylors were able to sell their Greensboro house to Mack and Kathleen Mather Bulgin. Peter named the Palmyra place first "Blue Ruin," then changed the name to "Stoneleigh." He had more trouble with the designation of his house in town. Throughout their tenure at 917, everyone continued to call the property the Faulkner house, which infuriated Peter. Cal's teasing Peter about living in the old master's own house of course made matters worse.[12]

Mother's Day found the Taylors scattered. Eleanor was in Norwood visiting her parents, Katie was at Duke—Peter wrote a friend—"protesting," and Petie was on a camping trip. Peter was at home working on a second draft of a story drawing upon his resignation from Kenyon, entitled "Dean of Men." He had placed the two political stories that the *New Yorker* had rejected: "First Heat" was appearing in *Shenandoah* (and would later be selected for the annual O. Henry Prize volume); and "The Elect" was sold to *McCall's*. On July 26, Roger Angell refused "Dean of Men," one of Peter's major stories, dealing with definitions of manhood, the breakup of patriarchy, and the cultural changes forming a gulf between a contemporary father and son. Angell judged the story "in some curious way, . . . both too long and too short" and found that "the connection between the young man to whom the tale is addressed and the events within the story . . . hard to understand." The *New Yorker* was now publishing the experimental stories of Donald Barthelme, and Angell, never a Taylor fan, clearly was finding Peter Taylor dry and dated. What a disappointment this rejection must have been.[13]

But the fall began well. On September 9, Peter signed a new contract with

Farrar, Straus and Giroux for a volume of collected stories to be published within a year. The social scene was enhanced by James Waller, Peter's friend from Fort Oglethorpe days, who had joined the economics faculty. Another highlight came at the end of October—the production of *A Stand in the Mountains* at Kenyon. Jim Michaels did well by the play, and Peter was deeply satisfied to see it at last performed. At Thanksgiving, the *Washington Post* Sunday magazine featured an article on Peter and an excerpt from the novel-in-progress, along with several pictures. "An enthusiastic tale-swapper in his staccato conversation as well as his writing, Taylor is at 51 a deceptively mild man in both appearance and speech," the reporter described Peter. "He is tall, solidly built, given to British tweeds. . . . His quizzical eyes jump from object to object; his phrases often tumble over each other, his mind darting past ideas faster than he can express them. He gives a surface impression of disorganized otherworldliness until he zeroes in on a subject." Peter Taylor was now a celebrity in the region.[14]

He continued to keep in close contact with his favorite students. James Thackara had settled in London, the Molyneuxs were at the University of Delaware, and Lawrence and Margie Reynolds had moved to Annapolis. Both the couples had open invitations (which they frequently used) to vacation at the Taylors' cabin, Hornet's Nest, in southwestern Virginia. Lawrence, in fact, had been responsible for the rehabilitation of the place. A country boy from southside Virginia who had worked in the tobacco fields, the strong, handsome young man had followed his future wife, Margie Halstead, to Greensboro and enrolled in the MFA program. Finding that Reynolds was short of money, Peter asked whether he knew anything about carpentry. When, on the first day of class, Peter had read Chekhov's "Gusev," Lawrence was deeply moved. "It was not the story I remember—though it is a story I have come to love—it was the way he read it," Reynolds has written. "His voice created the story for me in a way my own reading had never done, he made it real, he made it matter." But their intimacy developed at Hornet's Nest, as Peter (not particularly competent, but enthusiastic) worked alongside his student. Reynolds, who with age has come to resemble Peter Taylor, regards those weekends of work as the turning point in his life: "Peter became my father, my brother, my second self." The older man opened a whole new world for him, helping to form his sensibility and his tastes. Just as Peter himself had found surrogate fathers in Allen Tate, Robert Penn Warren, and John Crowe Ransom to replace a stern and unsympathetic parent, so Peter filled that role for a number of younger men. James Thackara admits seeking a figure at Harvard to replace the absent parent of his childhood; Lawrence Reynolds found in Peter a father-friend who appreciated the undeveloped side of a shy and modest young man who never put himself forward. And in the fall of 1968, another young seeker had arrived in Charlottesville with whom Peter would form close ties.[15]

Stephen Goodwin (who had grown up in Alabama, attended a Catholic prep school in Rhode Island, and been at Harvard with Tom Molyneux) was a married man serving in the army in Germany when he began applying to M.A. programs. Delighted with the Molyneux connection, Peter was also impressed with Goodwin's writing. Goodwin was attracted to the University of Virginia not only because of Peter's personal interest in him, but also because his own Harvard tutor, Walter Cowen, had moved to Charlottesville as editor of the University of Virginia Press. Sent away to school when just a boy, Goodwin was marked by his parents' divorce when he was in high school. Here was another young man who gravitated to mentors. In September of 1968, Steve and his pretty wife, Lucia (called Cinder), arrived in Charlottesville. Blond and athletic, with rather a James Dean appeal, and deadly attractive to women, Goodwin was immediately among the favored included in the Taylor parties. Peter sponsored Steve for a Rockefeller grant and recommended his fiction to both *Shenandoah* and the *Sewanee Review,* while never once calling attention to his good offices.[16]

"Having Peter as your writing teacher must be like having Ted Williams as your batting coach," Goodwin has commented. "They make it sound so easy—and of course it is if you have their talent." The other member of the class with whom Peter formed a warm friendship was Susan Richards Shreve, who was fascinated with Peter's wearing tweeds, ascots, and English shoes and still not coming across as a dandy or a snob. Finally it came to her that he looked like an "elegant mountaineer." Goodwin found the image apt: "Peter has broad hands and large, expressive features; he has a comfortable walk as if he is always moving down a slight incline. His face is lined but calm and open, and his eyes are a light blue; my classmate found it easy to imagine him on a ridge, wearing buckskins and resting on his musket gazing into Appalachian distances."[17]

In November, Peter sent the *New Yorker* a chapter from the novel, which was turned down within a week; but two weeks later Peter submitted another, entitled "Daphne's Lover." His accompanying cover letter is revealing. "Since it seems almost certain that you won't want to use pieces from this book, I wonder whether it wouldn't be better for me not to sign a contract for the coming year," he ventured. "I suggest this because even when I feel fairly certain that the *New Yorker* won't accept a story, the rejection is still a rather depressing business. (After a certain age one avoids unnecessary moments of depression. It is too easy for those moments to mount up to something worse.)" Nine days later Peter received Angell's letter rejecting "Daphne's Lover." While judging it "my favorite chapter from the book so far" and the writing of "exceptional quality," Angell found "the construction and pace ... entirely novelistic." Despite still another rejection, Peter did sign the first-reading agreement; but the experience increased his problems with the novel and his worries over his writing in general.[18]

At such times, social life was even more important to Peter than usual. On the morning of Christmas Eve, the Taylors gave a big Irish coffee party, with turkey, a country ham (a favorite of Peter's) ordered from Kentucky, and goose pâté. Two days after Christmas, Eleanor's father died. The family spent the next two weeks either in Norwood or on the road back and forth. On January 6, 1969, however, Peter flew to Washington for Katherine Anne Porter's annual glittering Twelfth Night party. Katherine Anne, Peter told Lawrence Reynolds, was in "fine fettle," wearing black satin pajamas and the fabulous emeralds purchased with the profits from *Ship of Fools*. Peter sat at a table with Red and Eleanor Warren and was transported by the whole affair. A month later he learned that he had been elected to membership in the National Institute of Arts and Letters. Here was acknowledgment of the judgment of his peers upon his work—something that he sorely needed at the moment.[19]

Cal came for a reading in April, and the Taylors naturally gave a party. On this occasion, Peter's legendary tolerance of Cal and good grace at his friend's fame was sorely tested. Known now as the greatest poet of his generation, his picture having appeared on the cover of *Time*, Robert Lowell was always lionized in Charlottesville. As Cal sat and talked in a monotone surrounded by people hanging on his every word, Peter stood in a corner telling Steve Goodwin about Lowell's first crack-up in Bloomington twenty years earlier. Finally, unable to bear Lowell's dominating the party one minute longer, Peter walked to the buffet table, cut an enormous hunk of cheese, placed it on a cracker and shoved it in Cal's mouth.[20]

When May arrived, Peter realized that he could not go to New York for his induction into the Institute; Katherine Taylor was failing, and he flew to Memphis to be with her. Loving his mother as deeply as he did, he found the protracted process of her dying almost unbearable, and tensions with his brother added to his distress. On her last day, Bob (who was preparing an ill-advised campaign for governor of Tennessee) brought a former governor, Gordon Browning, to the hospital. Furious, Peter stormed out of the room. His sister Mettie followed him and finally was able to quiet him. The family situation only worsened after Katherine's death. Grief-stricken as Peter and Mettie were, they were constantly outraged at Bob's behavior. The culmination came over Katherine Taylor's will. Lula, Katherine's devoted servant and nurse, had told Peter and Mettie that Bob was always harassing his mother about various bequests. When time came for the reading of the will, Bob made a great show of looking for the document and being unable to find it. Only when Mettie threatened to contest the will was the document produced. With her life interest in Sally's estate and Hillsman's, Katherine left close to a million dollars to be divided more or less equally among the three children. But to the amazement and fury of the other two, Katherine's personal possessions— including all memorabilia from her father, all family pictures and scrapbooks, and even the monogrammed set of flat silver long promised to her namesake, Katie—was left to Bob. Peter then drew from his pocket the statement written by his mother bequeathing the portraits of her grandparents and all furniture and other items in storage to him. Now Bob sat in shock. At the conclusion of the reading, Peter and Mettie rose and left the apartment. Neither ever spoke to Bob again.[21]

After Peter's return to Charlottesville, he was still haunted by his grief for his mother and his fury at Bob. Most of June was spent at Norwood with Eleanor's mother, relieved by a week's stint for Peter at the University of South Carolina writers conference and a weekend spent by Peter and Petie at Edisto Beach, South Carolina. On June 27, Peter wrote Jean that he had now come back to his "personal gloom," but that the three Taylors were to spend the month of August at Monteagle, where they had rented a cottage. Monteagle restored him. Peter went fishing nearly every day with Allen Tate, and the Taylors had been in residence hardly a week when they bought the century-old, double-galleried Brooks House on the main street in Sewanee. At the beginning of the year, they had sold the Palmyra house, though they had also rented a farm in northern Albemarle County with a view of the Blue Ridge, on which stood a two-story log house. So Taylor holdings in real estate were growing apace, always something that made Peter happy.[22]

In mid-October, Farrar, Straus and Giroux gave a launching party for *The*

Collected Stories of Peter Taylor, which included sixteen stories from Peter's earlier volumes, along with five previously uncollected works. It bore a dedication to "Katherine Taylor Taylor, who was the best teller of tales I know and from whose lips I first heard many of the stories in this book." Peter's long-held dream of a collection reflecting his entire career was finally realized, and friends gathered about him to celebrate the occasion. Now he had only to wait for the reviews.[23]

From the outset, they were mixed. Writing in the *Chicago Tribune Book World,* R. V. Cassill, the foremost student of this country's short fiction, cited Peter's collection as evidence that a "Golden Age for the American short story began soon after World War II." He judged Peter Taylor's concerns "very large," and he argued that in "the fascinating configuration of the whole collection, we see how the world spins out from Tennessee and closes its vast circles there"—how the regional forms the universal. The poet and critic Richard Howard acclaimed Peter Taylor in the *New York Times Book Review* as "one of the very best writers America has ever produced"; and Geoffrey Wolff of *Newsweek* called him "an artist of the first rank" and suggested that he had no living peer among short story writers. Then came the negative reviews. The *New Republic* reviewer Barbara Raskin judged the stories "respectable, careful, craftsmanlike, but ultimately mind-deadening." She then offered the bizarre notion that Taylor's characters were reminiscent of those of Tennessee Williams and Truman Capote. In the rest of the piece she attacked the patronizing portrayal of African Americans in the stories. A later issue of the magazine featured a letter from Jonathan Yardley refuting Raskin's judgments. Attacking first her "fundamentally untenable premise that all Southern fiction is alike" and her "racing Dixiephobia," Yardley went on to point out just how she had failed to understand the meaning or value of Taylor's work. But the year 1969, with its social unrest and extremism, was not the time for an appreciation of Peter Taylor's kind of quiet, subtle (though often actually radical) examinations of the social order. Too often his subtlety was neither recognized nor appreciated. "The world has passed Taylor by," noted Roger Sale in the *Hudson Review,* and in the *New York Review of Books,* Christopher Ricks described the stories as "slices of life" and noted that "sliced life often has the vapidity of sliced bread."[24]

Among Peter's old friends, Jack Thompson had always been the one most attuned to Peter's intent in his fiction. In Jack's review in *Harper's,* he described the background of the fiction as "the long serenity of our middle class" and argued that the stories revealed that "all culture, all social contrivance, country club or Army, family or corporation, knife and fork and automobile, all those are only the fragile and necessary contrivances that stand between us and the essential horror of our animal condition." The much later reviews in the quarterlies were also often filled with praise. Stephen Goodwin's review in *Shenandoah* is one of the most insightful short pieces ever written on Peter Taylor's fiction. "Taylor never distorts, never diminishes life to secure a resolution for art," he wrote. "The convenient and indulgent fiction of most storytelling—that emotions may be permanent, that revelations may be lasting—is never invoked." Goodwin was the first critic to make the point that the best of Peter Taylor's stories possess the amplitude of novels. But it was left to Joyce Carol Oates in a review two years later in the *Southern Review* (which had published Peter's first important stories) to offer the highest praise. Oates called the collection "one of the major books of our literature."[25]

But Oates' encomium, though sweet, would come only after Peter had faced disappointments and frustrations, and in the meantime he would remember that, even in some of the generally positive notices, his latest stories were judged his weakest. Thanking Robert Penn Warren for his letter praising the collection, he said that he'd like to frame it and hang it on the wall of his study: "It would be especially good to see it there on those mornings when I feel that I have done nothing and won't ever finish the book I am working on." As the reviews were appearing, in reaction to the response to his recent stories and to the intractability of the novel, he found himself writing plays.[26]

These were plays different from the ones he had formerly written. After Randall's death, Peter told Robert Fitzgerald, "I know that it is a strange thing for me to say, but I have never been so near to believing in ghosts. There have been moments when I have felt the presence of both Randall and [Millsaps]." That is his only statement on the subject, but in the intervening years, he had lost Sally and his mother, people even closer to him. These losses likely contributed to the turn his writing now took. During the fall, he wrote three one-act ghost plays (two of them thoroughly Freudian) presenting sexually conflicted families. On December 9, he mailed the plays to the *New Yorker*. Surely it was no surprise ten days later to receive Roger Angell's response that the works were "not quite right for us." Finally Peter acted as he had been inclined to do for the last few years; he refused to sign the annual first-reading agreement with the magazine. His long, close relationship with the *New Yorker* was over.[27]

One of the plays concerned the rivalry between a son and a red-headed father deemed unworthy of the mother's love. Early in 1970, Peter the son played out a similar Oedipally charged scene. Katherine Anne Porter again invited the Taylors to her Twelfth Night party on January 6. Twenty years ago in Greensboro, Peter had gotten himself in trouble because of Katherine Anne. She was now eighty, about the age of Katherine Taylor, and there were other parallels besides their names and ages. In elocution class both women had learned the nineteenth-century chestnut "Lasca," for decades an important piece in Peter's mother's repertoire. To Peter's delight, Katherine Anne had once declaimed the poem, and he had joined in. Still beautiful and still a sexual creature, Katherine Anne sparkled the night of the party. Peter again went too far in responding to her charm. Years later, he told Porter's friend Barbara Thompson that he had "danced too long and too close" with the old beauty and that Eleanor had left the party. What a macabre dance it must have been. At the time, he must have realized some of the implications of such dancing with his mother's double, for the courtship of a much older woman was one theme of the novel he was writing, a strand that he would soon rework in his play "The Early Guest." And twenty years later he would draw directly upon the doubling of the Katherines in his last novel.[28]

In the spring the Pulitzer Prize winners were announced. Peter had hardly dared to hope. Still he must have felt a pang when he learned that the prize for fiction had been given to *The Collected Stories of Jean Stafford*. Late in March, Peter made another sad trip to Memphis, this time to gather the possessions inherited from his mother and have most of them moved to the Brooks House in Sewanee. The large portraits, however, he sent back to Rugby Road to hang in the Faulkner house. A month later, he helped initiate the North Dakota Writers Conference. For the last few years, he had been serving on panels at such meetings and conferences, often three or four a year, in addition to giving readings at various colleges and universities. Immediately before leaving for a summer in Sewanee, he participated in a conference on literature and film that George Garrett had organized at Hollins College.[29]

"Welcome to the Magic Mountain. May your convalescence be prolonged" began the note from Allen Tate affixed to the front door of the Sewanee house. "We're having a small cocktail party for you all on Saturday, followed by a small dinner. Drop by today if you can." In his seventieth year with two sons under the age of three by his third wife, the intensely social Allen had established himself as the reigning presence in Sewanee. On the same mountain, six miles to the east, Andrew Lytle reigned at Monteagle, where he had bought

back his family's large log house with its huge central hall. The Taylors celebrated the Fourth at Andrew's, the guests drinking bourbon from silver goblets
from noon until five. Between social activities, Peter and Petie worked at clear-
ing the underbrush in the two acres behind the Sewanee house, and Peter told
Lawrence Reynolds that he was still "plugging away" on the novel.[30]

In Peter's writing workshop at the Garrett conference at Hollins had been
Anne Hobson Freeman of Richmond, now in her middle thirties. A graduate
of Bryn Mawr, Anne had—like Sylvia Plath—won the *Mademoiselle* fiction
award and a Fulbright, in Anne's case to the University of London. In 1958,
she had given up graduate study when she married a prominent Richmond
attorney, and in the intervening years, she had been occupied rearing three
children. Peter Taylor was the first person in years to recognize her talent and
offer encouragement. At his urging, she entered the graduate program in Charlottesville that fall, commuting from Richmond. Intelligent and warm, belonging to an old Virginia family (she was a descendant of George Marshall), but
totally without pretension, Anne was soon numbered among the student intimates.[31]

She describes Peter's class during the period as always following the same
format. The course assignment was three short stories. During the first sessions, while the students were writing their own fiction, Peter read to them
stories that he considered masterpieces—Chekhov, D. H. Lawrence's "The
Horse Dealer's Daughter," and Malamud tales from *The Magic Barrel*. He was
filling their minds with the writing of masters. The remainder of the course
was occupied by Peter's reading student efforts aloud (the author never being
identified). Discussion followed, with Peter offering his opinions only at the
end. He never read his own stories, but he did talk about what he was writing.
One of his teaching strategies was particularly effective: when he came to a
four-letter word in a student story, he would simply sound a "bleep." Soon
no student story contained profanity, because the bleeps simply wrecked the
effect. Anne also learned quickly that the worst response Peter could give a
student was "You are very smart." This answer to a student defense of a story
meant simply: "Though you are intelligent enough at argumentation, I find
you simply unteachable."[32]

The student counterculture, components of which were the questioning of
all authority and a rejection of tradition and traditional behavior, was now in
full swing. Anne Freeman remembers dropping her pencil one day and noting
that she and Peter were the only ones at the table wearing shoes. On another

occasion, Peter burst out, "Will the gentlemen, if there *are* any gentlemen, please get up and give Anne a seat." Nor was his scorn directed only at student behavior. "I am tempted to write a little essay on college professors," he told Allen Tate. "My opinion of them—all except my very own friends among them—gets lower every year. It is they who are responsible for all the upheaval in the universities now. They love the excitement, because they are timid men and it is the only excitement they have; and they love all the attention to academic life, because it makes them seem important. They love the image of themselves as bold revolutionaries, yet they have chosen a very protected life, and how they cherish their tenure!" Yet Peter was popular among his colleagues, and, as one friend reports, often at a student wedding, held in a meadow in the Blue Ridge, the principals festooned with garlands, the only person over thirty would be Peter.[33]

The first book-length study of Peter's work was published in 1970, a volume in the Twayne series by Albert Griffith, and occasional critical articles on Peter's fiction continued to appear in academic journals. But he was now devoting himself to writing one-act plays, and he hoped that Bob Giroux would publish a "Collected Plays of Peter Taylor." Jim Boatwright, a faculty member at Washington and Lee and editor of the university's literary quarterly, *Shenandoah,* was now a fixture at every Taylor party. Not only had Boatwright published the first three ghost plays, but he was also deeply interested in Eleanor as a poet. In addition, he was responsible for Steve Goodwin's being recently hired by Washington and Lee. In October, Boatwright brought over to Charlottesville the recent Pulitzer Prize winner for poetry Richard Howard, who had written the fine review of the *Collected Stories* in the *New York Times Book Review,* to confer with Eleanor about publishing a second volume of her poetry in a series that he was editing for the publisher George Braziller. Peter described Richard to Cal as "wonderfully brilliant . . . a combination of R. Jarrell and M. Proust." Allen had earlier returned from England to report that Cal was getting a divorce from Elizabeth Hardwick to marry Lady Caroline Blackwood. In November, Lowell wrote Peter: "I fell in love part manic, was sick in a hospital a good part of summer, got well, stayed in love. There has been great joy in it all, great harm to everyone." The day after Christmas, Jack Thompson sent a letter from New York saying, "Poor Cal is here dismantling his life."[34]

Katherine Taylor's estate had now been settled. Peter paid off the mortgage on 917 Rugby Road, and for the first time the Taylors actually owned their own home. He was putting all the rest of the funds in the hands of the bank to invest, but first he had to indulge himself in one more real estate transaction. On December 2, his purchase of the farm he had been renting became final. Previously he had dubbed it Sugar Hollow, but soon he began calling it Cohee, in reaction, he said, to Virginia elegance. A "Cohee," he explained to Cal, was the opposite of a "Tuckahoe," or aristocrat. A Cohee was an upcountry man—the term thought to be a corruption of "Quoth he," an expression used "only by old-fashioned upcountry people." Peter loved the little farm and planned to fix up the log farmhouse and do all his writing there.[35]

The year 1971 Peter Taylor devoted to the theater. With the aid of Bob Giroux, Peter was accepted for membership in The Players club in New York. Founded in 1888, when the actor Edwin Booth gave his 1844 townhouse (with its extensive library and many paintings) to the group, The Players still occupied 16 Gramercy Park, though the structure had been later remodeled under the supervision of Stanford White. The square in which the townhouse stands is lined with Greek Revival, Italianate, Gothic Revival, and Victorian Gothic structures, including the city's oldest apartment house. In the center is New York's only surviving private park, its gates locked to all except residents of the surrounding buildings. Boxwood lines the paths that run among a variety of specimen trees and flowering plants, and great cast-iron urns are scattered throughout. A statue of Booth stands in the center facing north toward the Chrysler Building. Club, square, and park—all provide an ambiance that Peter Taylor could fully appreciate. It was agreed between the Taylors that Peter would now spend a weekend a month in New York, to attend meetings of the Institute of Arts and Letters, to see his friends, and especially to keep abreast of the New York theater.[36]

Eleanor was worn out from a year of traveling between Charlottesville and Norwood to care for her eighty-eight-year-old mother. She wanted to bring Mrs. Ross to the Rugby Road house, but Peter would hear nothing of it. Finally it was decided that Mrs. Ross would be moved to a Charlottesville nursing home. In late February, having transformed their station wagon into a kind of ambulance, Peter drove to Norwood and brought Eleanor and her mother back to Virginia.[37]

"I may never write anything but plays from here out," Peter confided to Jean. "They are a great release for me, because in fiction I have got so I become completely carried away by context, whereas what I aspire to is characters, characters, characters and the interplay thereof." He was now working on three more one-act dramas, often incorporating parts of his novel in them. He was also revising *A Stand in the Mountains* for its production the last week of May at the Barter Theatre in Abingdon, Virginia. The oldest repertory theater in America, the Barter (now the state theater of Virginia) had been founded during the Great Depression. In the beginning, the price of a ticket was often paid in produce, an exchange gratefully accepted by the theatrical folk. The theater's founder and guiding spirit, Robert Porterfield, admired Peter's play. Also a member of The Players, he met Peter at the club, and over dinner it was decided that *A Stand in the Mountains* would introduce the 1971 season, under the direction of Michael Norell of New York. Peter enjoyed working with Norell and responding to many of his suggested revisions, but on one matter he was adamant: "It must end the way it does," he insisted, "with everyone at loose ends, nobody achieving satisfaction." This statement offers a key to understanding not only the play, but many of the great late Peter Taylor works.[38]

The production was a wonderful experience for Peter. Abingdon is just over the Virginia line from the Watauga region of East Tennessee, where his mother's family had settled in the eighteenth century. Peter was delighted to receive an invitation to tea from an Abingdon cousin, daughter of one of Senator Taylor's twin sisters, whom the senator had to pay off when they too threatened to go on the lecture circuit and to whom he never spoke again. The cousin, daughter of Rhoda Taylor Reeves (who in old age wore a red wig, which she frequently took off in public), bore an amazing resemblance to Katherine Taylor, both physically and in her mannerisms.[39]

To the grand, rowdy party that he gave on opening night in the parlors of the Martha Washington Inn, Peter had invited scores of his friends. Many came—Felder Heflin (whom Peter called his "oldest friend," now retired from the military and living in Washington) and his wife, Nancy; Tony and Violet Winner from the English department; Bedford and Jane Moore; and among Peter's students, the Reynoldses and the Goodwins, who spent that night at Hornet's Nest in the Blue Ridge. Abingdon was situated in a "dry" county, with no liquor sales, so Peter had brought a case of Jack Daniel's. Discovering that a member of the cast had stolen a half-gallon, Peter was first outraged, then delighted as he turned the theft into a tale. Steve Goodwin remembers an inebriated conversation among himself, Peter, and Bedford lasting into the early morning. For Peter, it was a triumphant, happy night.[40]

A few days afterward, Peter flew to Ohio to receive a doctor of letters conferred by Kenyon—in the words of the citation—upon "a gentle, humane, literate, truly civilized man." It was an honor, but of equal significance for Peter was Jim Michael's staging that week at the Hill Theater of his first three ghost plays. He was well pleased with the production, and it stimulated him as he worked on more plays.[41]

In June, Peter told Robert Giroux that he was "attacking the novel again" and readying the manuscript of a book of plays to show him. But two weeks later he wrote Tom White: "I have no more ideas for stories or novels. When I sit at my desk, I can think only of lines and scenes and themes for plays. And so, in a sense, I am setting out all over again, on a new career. I'm at the bottom of the ladder, content at the moment with little provincial successes. . . . God in Heaven, give me ten more years." Nearly six months later, on December 2, 1971, Peter mailed to Farrar, Straus and Giroux the manuscript of "The Collected Plays of Peter Taylor." Somewhat guiltily he ended the accompanying letter: "I'm on the novel again now. And if I don't have it finished by September . . . , you will never hear me mention it again."[42]

15

An Extension of Time ···

By mid-January of 1972, Peter was pushing Bob Giroux for an answer on the volume of collected plays and admitting, "I don't ever want to write that long novel." On February 1, Bob responded, explaining that since there was little market for plays except Broadway successes, he regretfully had to say no, though he found the one-act plays "a new and provocative departure" in Peter's work. Rancor marks none of the subsequent correspondence leading to the breaking of the Farrar, Straus and Giroux contract. These were two people who had known each other long and rather well and who felt loyalties and obligations. Having his plays published simply meant more to Peter at the moment than any other consideration. By the end of March, he had signed a contract with Houghton Mifflin for a book of fiction and a volume of one-act plays.[1]

Eleanor's mother had died the first week of February. After the strain of months of devoted attention, Eleanor now felt at loose ends, unable to return to her writing or any of the other things she had neglected. Immediately Peter began making plans for the two of them and Petie (who was now insisting that he be called Ross Taylor) to spend six weeks in England. On April 3, they flew to London to meet Lady Caroline Blackwood and see the six-month-old son, Sheridan, she had borne Cal. Lowell they found very happy, and the Taylors were taken with the baby and with Caroline, who had arranged that they occupy a flat in her townhouse at 80 Redcliff Square. London, Peter wrote Jean, "is the only city in the world. I have never loved it more." The Taylors spent most of their time there, though they did make trips to Milgate Park, Caroline's home in Kent; to Oxford (where the Tony Winners were living that year); to Salisbury; and, for a week, to Scotland. Toward the end of the stay, Ross took his College Boards at the American School, and Peter browsed the shops along Porto Bello Road collecting antique doorknobs for the Brooks House at Sewanee.[2]

In May, Peter went to New York for the meeting of the Institute of Arts and Letters and long, very liquid sessions with Jack and Jean. He returned home in time for the party he and Eleanor were giving for James Dickey. It would be another memorable occasion. Peter had now known Dickey for years, admired his poetry and his novel *Deliverance,* and put up with his antics. Shortly after the Taylors moved to Charlottesville, Dickey's oldest child, Christopher, entered the university. He had taken two classes from Peter, who thought highly of him. It was a matter of course that the Taylors would entertain the Dickeys when they came up for Christopher's graduation. Everyone gathered at the Rugby Road house before the morning ceremony. Jim Dickey, who had been drinking beer for a couple of hours, was wearing a large cowboy hat. Peter was impressed with Christopher's handling of his father. Not embarrassed by the big, bluff, boozy parent, on the way to the university Christopher quietly took the beer from his father's hand and then the hat from his head. Dickey was not so easily muted that evening.[3]

Eudora Welty had received an honorary degree at Washington and Lee the same day, and Steve Goodwin was called into service to bring her and her close friend Reynolds Price over to Charlottesville for the party. Peter was looking forward to seeing Eudora ("Knowing her is one of the joys of life," he told Red Warren), but Dickey dominated the evening. First he embarrassed Peter by bellowing, "You remember that time in Salt Lake City when we were out with those two broads," referring to Peter's accompanying him, one of his paramours, and her unattractive friend to dinner. Eleanor no doubt understood. She and Dickey valued each other's work, she found him entertaining, and she was amused when he sidled over to her and loudly whispered, "Let's you and me run away together." He was just warming up, and he began pouring tumblers of bourbon and imitating Marlon Brando, Jonathan Winters, and finally the radio in a policeman's car in Columbia, South Carolina. Then he proceeded, for no apparent reason—as Reynolds Price recalls—to lift the 175-pound Price into the air, deposit him in an armchair and say, "I've never done so but if I were ever to sleep with a man, I'd want it to be either you or Ned Rorem."[4]

Within a few days, Peter and Eleanor left for Sewanee with the seventeen-year-old Ross for the first time at the wheel. Eleanor's second volume of poetry, *Welcome Eumenides,* had now appeared with a splendid introduction by Richard Howard. Cal wrote, praising "the beautiful Southern voice of old fashioned religious atheism, a good thing to have, to be," and Eleanor learned that Adrienne Rich was reviewing it for the *New York Times Book Review.* Two years before, Adrienne told Peter that she and Alfred Conrad had decided to live separately, though they were not considering a divorce. A year later, when Cal reported Alfred's suicide, he commented, "I thought everything was too frenetic with them, but never guessed," and then he revealed his own attitude toward her increasing feminism: "I guess she has weathered it, but she writes me odd unasked for woman-libish advice and seems to feel that Alf somehow unfairly injured her by killing himself." Rich's review of *Welcome Eumenides* begins, "Maybe the spirit of the times is catching up to Eleanor Ross Taylor," and, in her sensitive appraisal of the title poem, she comments that Eleanor "has brought together the waste of women in society and the waste of men in wars and twisted them inseparably." Adrienne was soon to write her important feminist poem "Diving into the Wreck," and she concluded one letter to Eleanor on this personal note: "I'm not convinced it helps one writer to be married to another. . . . Men seem to need all kinds of help but women have written while making calf's foot jelly, keeping house, nursing children and the aged, etc. etc. etc."[5]

Peter clearly relied on Eleanor's support. It was one reason that Peter could continue to write, even during that social summer in Sewanee. In August, he told Jean that for three weeks there had been a party every day, but he had written a "good first act" of a new long play drawn from his abandoned novel. "Hope springs eternal in my stage-struck breast," he admitted to Bob Giroux. As was now customary, Peter was also engaged in building projects—having "acres of lattice repaired" and a gas furnace installed so that they could rent the house out the following winter. Allen Tate, suffering now with emphysema, had been hospitalized for ten days; but he had returned to the mountain, still enraged about what he called "a conspiracy" on the part of Andrew Lytle to influence the selection of the next editor of the *Sewanee Review*—a power struggle into which Peter would eventually be drawn.[6]

On October 10, Peter returned to the mountain to give the Founders Day address at the University of the South, entitled "Literature, Sewanee, and the World." The title offered simply an umbrella under which Peter could talk about the old three divisions of the state of Tennessee, invoke the ghosts of old friends (James Waller and Avery Handly), and confess his sentiment about the place. "My feelings are both that this region of the upper South is very much a part of me and that I am very much a part of it," he said. "Why a writer should be so egotistical as to have such feelings about a whole region and so crass as to express these feelings is a mystery. But nearly everything about art is a mystery and must ever be so, and yet this is *my* mystery."[7]

Close friends since youth, Allen Tate and Andrew Lytle were no longer speaking. Always irascible, always a gossip, always a manipulator, Allen in old age had fallen out with a number of old friends, including Cal a year earlier. During Peter's visit, both Allen and Andrew approached him about becoming editor of the *Sewanee Review*. Knowing Peter as they did, it was a surprising action on the part of both men, and equally surprising that Peter gave the position serious consideration. Absentminded, forgetful, often somewhat disorganized, and generally unable to meet deadlines, Peter lacked the temperament of an editor. But again, as he had years before when offered the editorship at Kenyon, he first came to the decision that he would accept. At 8:15 A.M. on November 13, Peter called a delighted Andrew Lytle, the present editor, with his answer. Lytle had an appointment with the vice-chancellor that afternoon, and the matter was to be settled then. After hanging up the phone, Peter decided that he must now call Allen. But when he did, Allen scolded him for taking so long to decide and revealed that, though he had no authority, a few days before he had made an offer to someone else, who had accepted. These conversations were the first two of ten telephone calls over two days, as much of Sewanee became enmeshed in the controversy. Eventually Peter withdrew his name, and the vice-chancellor allowed Allen's offer to stand. But Allen was furious with Peter and made calls to a number of common friends, including Jean Stafford, accusing Peter of treachery and duplicity.[8]

Of course the friends reported Allen's calls to Peter, who telephoned Tate and asked him to explain himself, whereupon he could give only stammering, tenuous explanations. On November 30, Tate sent a letter. "I think I may owe you an apology," he admitted. Then immediately his old antagonisms took over: "You not only offered your services to the *Review* too late; you would have rejoiced Andrew's conspiratorial heart had you taken the job." Peter's reply a week later began, "You owe me no apology. You would never owe me an apology for anything you might say or do. My affection for you is such that you would be hard-put to offend me and my debt to you is so great for your enlightening words thirty-five years ago." This is what Peter no doubt believed that he should feel, but the truth is that he simply could not forgive Allen's perfidy, and he still brooded about it.[9]

Another distinguished former Southwestern professor had retired to Charlottesville—Sam Monk, now alcoholic, lonely, bitter, and difficult. The Taylors included him on the guest list for Thanksgiving dinner, to which they had also invited Jean and Jean's glamorous friends the Jean Ribouds (who arrived in a private jet), along with John and Mary Polk Kirby-Smith, now settled in Georgetown. Peter reported to Cal (whom he had seen briefly in New York when Lowell was over from England divorcing Elizabeth Hardwick in order to marry Caroline) that Jean Stafford and Sam Monk, both drunk and vying for attention, simulated heart attacks. Initially Eleanor had them in separate rooms ministering to them. Finally Peter drove Monk home and put him to bed there. Jean he took to the emergency room of University Hospital, where she was observed and tested from 2 to 5 A.M. "I think," Peter told Cal, "finally they just gave her a cold shower and sent her home."[10]

By the first of December, it was settled that Peter would teach at Harvard the following fall. Lowell would again be in residence, and the two wrote back and forth discussing the anticipated reunion with schoolboyish enthusiasm. Peter was eyeing a house in Hot Springs, Virginia, where he had been going for his rheumatism. "Is the Hot Springs your final house, like my final marriage?" Cal responded. "A book will be written (Houses in P. H. Taylor's life) a unique history about a unique person, in which all is told without ever getting off the subject of the houses you bought or thought of buying, and failed to buy." This house turned out to be one of those Peter failed to buy, but as compensation he contracted to have three ponds built at Cohee Farm. He ended the year 1972 planning the playwriting course he was to teach in the spring semester (the texts including Lowell's *Old Glory,* along with Synge, Strindberg, Ibsen, and Chekhov) and looking forward to the publication of his book of plays.[11]

Presences: Seven Dramatic Pieces was released by Houghton Mifflin on Valentine's Day, 1973. As Peter might have expected, no notice was taken by the

New York Times or by any of the important New York magazines. The *Washing-*
ton Post Book World carried a positive, though unexciting, review written by
Paul Theroux, a new colleague at Virginia. The *Library Journal* commented
that "followers of Taylor's well-regarded stories will be dissatisfied, drama
buffs unable to see actability." Nearer to home, the *Virginia Quarterly Review*
notice found the pieces "as drama . . . thin as ghosts." The most intelligent
review, not surprisingly, came from Richard Howard writing in *Shenandoah.*
Aware of the "range of experiment" in the volume, Howard unerringly goes
to the core of the works: "[Taylor] knows that just when we are 'safest' is when
danger comes, just when we are most nearly comfortable and acknowledged
that we are subject to fits, to misfits, to the radical and uprooting discovery
that we have merely invented our lives, imagined the other people we think
we live for and by. The *presences* in Peter Taylor's theatre . . . are *absences* in
the life conceived as replete, the life delusionally figured as real. . . . [H]e sees
all life as haunted: no relation, no alliance is exempt." While appreciating the
plays (and Howard to this day believes them underrated), he still accurately
judged them "by no means the masterpiece of Taylor's long and still-looming
career." Peter Taylor could not be buoyed by one such notice in the midst of
the general silence and the few other pedestrian or hostile evaluations. "I don't
really expect people to like what I write nowadays—or even to read it," he
told Robert Penn Warren later that spring.[12]

    In an interview with Steve Goodwin the previous fall (the first real Taylor
interview and still one of the best), Peter had said, "I doubt that I'll write many
more short stories. I feel that I've done what I want to do as a short story
writer. . . . I have a horror of repeating myself, of imitating myself." His sense
that his fiction was going stale was an impetus behind his playwriting, about
which the mass of critics were either silent or displeased. The plays also reflect
new thematic directions in his writing, dealing with such contemporary issues
as drugs, incest, and homosexuality. An attempt to blur genres was shown in
his next published work, "The Early Guest," which he would later speak of as
a kind of synopsis of the aborted novel. It appeared in the spring issue of
Shenandoah with the subtitle "a sort of story, a sort of play, a sort of dream."
But he would need to experiment further before he found a bridge to bring
him back to the short story.[13]

    In the meantime, he tried to distance himself from bitterness by finding
diversion in the world around him. Luckily, there were new people that year
to offer stimulation. Shortly after *Presences* was released, Elizabeth Bishop

came to Charlottesville for a reading and, as Peter told Cal, left "Eleanor and me in the best spirts we have been in for an age." Cal responded that he knew the three would like each other because "she has forever been my dearest friend along with you." Bishop was now living in Boston, another reason to look forward to the fall term.[14]

There were new faces on the Virginia faculty as well. Foremost was Peter's old Harvard student John Casey, whom he had helped bring to Virginia the previous fall. Since Peter's term at Harvard, Casey had completed Harvard Law School, been admitted to the Washington, D.C., bar, married Jane Barnes, and entered the MFA program at Iowa. Upon graduation in 1968, the Caseys moved to an island of four and a half acres in Narragansett Bay off Rhode Island, where John worked with old fishermen and devoted himself to his writing. During the next three years, he published five excellent short stories, while the couple slowly depleted all available funds. In December of 1971, Peter's letter inviting Casey to be interviewed for a position at Virginia arrived while he was in Vermont cross-country skiing with John Irving. Casey knew that the Fox Island life had to come to an end, and he was desperate about what to do next. The letter was a godsend. Once again Peter had intervened in John Casey's life at just the right time.[15]

John Casey would be Peter Taylor's colleague for the rest of his teaching career and one of his closest friends. Voluble and kinetic, Casey is an athlete. Like another Taylor protégé, James Thackara, he is a non-drinker, needing nothing to increase his energy level or raise his mood. Jane Barnes, also a writer, equally brilliant, warm, and charming, Peter and Eleanor liked immediately. The Caseys added considerably to the Taylors' Charlottesville life. They came to dinner four times that fall, sometimes with another faculty couple, poet Alan Williamson and his wife, Anne Winters, also a gifted poet. The Williamsons were a few years younger than the Caseys and more decidedly products of the sixties in their basic radicalism. All four were fascinated with Peter because of his energy, verve, and wit, and because they found him a kindred soul. In conversation with Alan, Peter once said that, in order to be interesting, people didn't need to act out their anarchic impulses, but just to realize their existence. Alan, the probing psychological critic, felt that with great urbanity Peter displayed aspects of his inner life that one would not expect. He cites a large English department party at which Peter, drink in hand, regaled a group with a discussion of his middle-age insomnia and how lately he waked often to thoughts of suicide; then he moved on to other conversations and more drinks.[16]

Williamson had come to Virginia in the fall of 1969, and Peter may actually have avoided him initially because Alan so idealized Cal, who had taught him at Harvard. Lowell's initial influence upon him was immense, and Alan admits that he came to Virginia feeling that, like Lowell, he would be soon acclaimed the most important poet of his generation. But Williamson soon became intrigued by Cal's old roommate as well. He recalls that the first time (and one of the few times) that he saw Peter "anywhere near out of control" was during the period when Eleanor's mother was dying and Peter came alone to a dinner for the Cambridge poet Frank Bidart. While waiting interminably for Alan to finish cooking a leg of lamb, Peter after quantities of bourbon got on the subject of Alan's adulation, proclaiming that Alan thought "Cal hung God." He went on to detail Cal's first breakdown in Bloomington and then, before the evening was over, to make a long telephone call to Katherine Anne Porter. Though he had twice gotten in trouble about her, he was still enthralled. When Richard Howard once launched into criticism of her often difficult behavior, Peter replied, "But we all love her. She's our Cleopatra." Peter displayed still another side of himself to Alan when the Beat poet Gary Snyder came to visit. Over many glasses of Jack Daniel's, Taylor and Snyder, clearly enjoying each other, were just getting into interesting areas of speculation when Eleanor found it time to bring the evening to an end.[17]

For the last few years, Peter had looked forward to the twice-yearly meetings of the Institute. For several days he would be in residence at The Players, and frequently Lawrence Reynolds and Tom Molyneux would come up to New York, staying with various acquaintances. Peter would then bring together some of his oldest literary friends with two of his newest. Reynolds remembers one such gathering in the spring of 1973. A group met at the Cosmopolitan Club, where Jean was staying, and drank and drank waiting for Jean Riboud, who was flying in from Paris on the Concorde. Jack Thompson finally slid off the sofa onto the floor, where he remained for the next few hours, bellowing from time to time, "When is that frog getting here?" Late at night Riboud arrived. The group had a midnight dinner at the Four Ways, then one of the most fashionable restaurants in the city, and in compensation Riboud picked up the tab—$400.[18]

The spring semester and Peter's playwriting course were capped off by a production in Charlottesville of "The Early Guest" and the settling of the matter of college for Ross. For the last ten years, Peter had planned that his son go to Harvard, but Peter should have remembered his own independence about choice of colleges. Ross simply put off applying to Harvard until it was too late, so the Taylors had to accept his going to the University of Virginia, the place he had wished to go all along.[19]

Now there was just one more enterprise to be settled before Peter's leaving for Harvard in the fall. A knowledgeable observer could have predicted that Peter was primed to make a move in real estate. It was his most grandiose. He found for sale, out ten miles from Charlottesville, a country estate of nine acres named Clover Hill. On it stood a late-eighteenth-century clapboard house ("the oldest and biggest we have ever had," he told Cal, "and the last we shall ever have") and a number of dependencies, including a brick summer kitchen. With bewildering speed, Peter divested himself of all his other holdings—the Faulkner house on Rugby Road, Cohee Farm at ADvance Mills (the local pronunciation that Peter insisted upon), the Brooks House at Sewanee, and the cabin in the Blue Ridge. "A grand sweep," Peter described it, involving "many tedious hours with lawyers and trust officers." The Taylors moved to Clover Hill shortly after the Fourth of July. In August, they took a cottage at Monteagle in order to remove the Brooks House furniture. Peter commented that he knew Allen would never forgive him for living again in the domain of Andrew Lytle. "Isn't it just how one might have predicted Allen would spend his senile years," Peter wrote Cal. Peter still remembered the past and felt grateful for Allen's "generosity when I was young. In a way, he saved me from Memphis. We were lucky to have him for a teacher." But then came a turn: "He also was lucky to have us." So it was with some detachment that Peter negotiated his two weeks on the mountain. Before the return to Charlottesville, the Taylors had purchased another house, Wren's Nest, a large two-story structure out from the village of Monteagle. They were to spend only one night there, but it was a convenient place to store the Brooks House furniture.[20]

By the middle of September, they were installed in a furnished apartment, one of three in a house at 19 Ware Street in Cambridge. That fall was a delightful and stimulating time for both of the Taylors. The students were good, though Peter did not find them as talented as the group in 1964; on the other hand, social life was splendid. Much time was spent with Caroline and Cal, who was on a kind of emotional plateau. For the past three years, lithium had prevented any deeply manic phase, though he was always edgy and subject to periods of nervous excitement. Still, during the term he wrote nine poems, including an early draft of the mordant "Afterlife," dedicated to Peter. The Taylors also saw a great deal of other literary people, all poets—Robert Fitzgerald, John Malcolm Brinnin, Octavio Paz, Frank Bidart, and Elizabeth Bishop. As early as the publication of Peter's Kenyon story "1939," Elizabeth had been an admirer of Peter's fiction. "Peter Taylor sounds like a very sympathetic man—I wish I'd see more things by him," she had written Randall Jarrell. The first meeting in Charlottesville earlier in 1973 had deepened her regard, and during the fall she and Eleanor also became good friends. Heavy drinking characterized all the entertaining. Peter did more than his share, but others far surpassed him. When Ross came up for Thanksgiving, Elizabeth invited the Taylors for the holiday meal. Shortly before they left Ware Street, Frank Bidart (who tended to be the caretaker of all of his friends) called from the Bishop apartment to say that he had arrived to find Elizabeth passed out. The Taylors had their Thanksgiving meal at Grendel's Kitchen in Cambridge. Also a confirmed alcoholic now, Jean Stafford came for a visit shortly afterward. Compulsively demanding to be the center of attention, toward the end of one evening she got on the floor, flailing her arms and legs in an imitation of Muhammad Ali. Looking down upon the display, Octavio Paz muttered, "Such jokes are for sophomores, aren't they."[21]

For Christmas the Taylors returned to Clover Hill, where most of their belongings were still in crates. Ross, now in the middle of his freshman year, had gotten a haircut under the influence of a new girlfriend, much to the relief of both his parents. Katie, who had dropped out of Duke after her junior year and gone to live on a commune-like farm in southwestern Virginia, had become interested in raising cows. Both children and a male friend of Katie's spent the holiday with Peter and Eleanor. Peter returned alone to Cambridge in January to finish the term. Just before term's end, he was offered a permanent appointment at Harvard. It would take much of 1974 before he could decide what to do about the matter.[22]

Peter got back in time for birthday dinners—for John Casey's thirty-fifth birthday and Alan Williamson's thirtieth. Casey's sisters were in town for his celebration. Later Peter would tell John how interested he was to meet the two women. "I collect families, you know," he smiled. Alan's party was a less happy occasion. He had just had a manuscript rejected, and during the fall, despite the support of Peter and other friends, he had been denied tenure. Alan would later acknowledge that it was Peter (not his idol, Robert Lowell) who made it possible for him to live with bitter disappointments and to keep on his chosen path in the knowledge that he "was writing the kind of thing that only he could write." He had watched Peter bear just such disappointments stoically and with dignity and (Alan felt) without losing confidence in himself.[23]

Something remarkable happened after Peter's return from Harvard. He began writing stories again, but he was writing them in verse, or at least writing stories "so arranged on the page that they *look* like poems." "I don't kid myself that they *are* poems," he told Cal. Had he been influenced by being surrounded by poets for the last few months, or was he in a sense returning to his roots? Almost a year earlier, he had explained to Steve Goodwin how his training with John Crowe Ransom in the concentration of poetry had probably led to his becoming primarily a short story writer. Whatever the cause, Peter Taylor was writing again. By March he had finished drafts of three story-poems, which he sometimes called "stoems."[24]

Cal flew over in April to give a reading in Charlottesville, and then he and Peter went to Nashville to participate in the Vanderbilt Writing Program and then to Sewanee (Peter selling Wren's Nest while he was briefly on the mountain). In May, Peter was in New York, where he was joined by Lawrence Reynolds and Tom Molyneux, for the Institute meeting. He was busy, drinking no more than usual, happy with his writing. At the end of May, working at Clover Hill, Peter began having trouble breathing. He told Eleanor that he thought he had better go to the hospital. By the time he reached Charlottesville, he was having a heart attack.[25]

It was Peter's good luck that the physician on call was Dick Crampton, an excellent heart specialist who became also a good friend. Crampton's prognosis was that Peter would have his full strength back within six months and be able to live normally, if he changed some of his habits. Crampton particularly advised that Peter quit smoking and cut down his drinking. For a time, he was forbidden to climb stairs or to drive. A month before the attack, Peter and Eleanor had decided that they should not try to keep a place in the country, especially if they were to be away at Harvard for half of each year. At the moment, 1101 Rugby Road was up for sale, the house they had rented when they came to Charlottesville. They bought it and put Clover Hill on the market. Lawrence Reynolds, now again living in Virginia, was on hand to help with the sale and the move during Peter's hospitalization. Fortunately the back stairs of the Rugby Road house had an electric elevator chair.[26]

The move between the houses taken care of, there was another matter to face. As soon as Peter left the intensive care unit, he went into a deep depression that lasted for a month. He had experienced depression before, and three years earlier he had even had Tom White prescribe something for it. But this was different. "I never before had such dark thoughts or such terrible nightmares," he confided to Cal. "I was so weak that I would wake in the night, blubbering—or the first thing in the morning. And that would send me into deeper despair." He told Lowell that when he had gone out to Sewanee the second time that spring (to see a dreadful production of *A Stand in the Mountains*), Allen Tate called and begged Peter to visit him before he went into the Vanderbilt hospital the next day. Seeing the diminished, pathetic figure, Peter was moved to make a complete reconciliation. "Lying in the hospital, I went over my life in my own mind—again and again, trying harder than ever before to understand it and myself," Peter told Cal, "trying to understand the pattern of my behavior with other people. . . . Allen was in my thoughts a lot then, as you were too of course—you more than anyone else, except Eleanor." The depression and the intensity of questioning Peter eventually left behind, but the experience affected his writing. In the best of his subsequent works, primal conflicts are explored in markedly more violent and disturbing images.[27]

Soon after Peter came home to Rugby Road, he received the news that John Crowe Ransom had died in his sleep. "To me it seems almost inevitable that he should have died in a way to cause those near him the least possible pain. It seems that even in the way he died there was a certain courtesy," Peter wrote in tribute. Peter's negotiations with Harvard continued apace throughout the summer. In the early spring he had accepted a five-year appointment (renewable) to teach at Harvard one semester a year. Then later he wrote changing his mind. Now in early August he reversed himself again, agreeing to begin in January of 1975. At the same time, he mailed copies of the three story-poems to Robert Penn Warren and to Robert Lowell for their judgment. He had not done anything of the sort for decades. It was as though he were just beginning to write.[28]

The earliest, "Instruction of a Mistress," had already been accepted by a new journal recommended by Cal, the *New Review*. The second, "The Hand of Emmagene," he had sent to *Esquire*, from whose editor he received this reply: "Yes, yes, yes: you feel the form is organic to the materials, and I simply don't. Moreover, such a format raises the question of space, the which, in these parts, is at a premium. Further, I might point to a number of the short stories I run and claim their close proximity to poetry—hence, why set this particular piece in such form—and then risk the charge of pretension?" But Peter was undeterred, and shortly he received a response from Red Warren, who had suggestions for some revisions on "The Hand of Emmagene," but felt that in it "you outdo yourself." The third piece (on Katherine Taylor's last days), Warren found "working from practically every cliche possible," but somehow succeeding "in redeeming them all." Peter wrote expressing his profound gratitude for Warren's readings and admitting a heavy element of the melodramatic in these recent efforts. "But what I am determined to get away from—in form and subject—is my usual, old kind of subtlety and the kind of irony that has long since put restriction on the kind of subject I can handle."[29]

Peter had reentered life with confidence and enthusiasm. He was back at building fences and chopping wood, though he confined this to the back yard, since Dick Crampton lived nearby and might see him. The University of Virginia had met Peter's attempt to resign his position with an offer to let him teach just one term a year, the term he would not be employed at Harvard. He was mulling that over, and he was in the midst of a story about his paternal grandfather Taylor's abduction by the Night Riders, the subject of his prizewinning essay at Miss Rossman's School over fifty years before. In addition, he had written two poems (as opposed to the story-poems). The conclusion of one, "Peach Trees Gone Wild in the Lane," casts an interesting light on his present state:

> The lane is walled
> With dogwood of course and judas and sassafras
> With wild cherry and sometimes even
> A peach tree gone wild and trying
> To imagine itself like the really wild things
> It has gone back to. Only my worldly old eyes
> Can detect the deception.
> It will not bear fruit.
>
> It is a lost lane I have found again
> Just by chance. I walk on and on
> In this innocent, wild garden
> Alone and unseen
> In my utter delight
> Imagining or merely pretending that I
> Am young, innocent, excited and gone wild again.

He told Cal that he had given up liquor and was drinking watered wine, but that he and Eleanor had been out looking at another Albemarle County farm and had decided that they had to have another house at either Sewanee or Monteagle, since all that family furniture was still down there. He was not ready to leave all his wildness behind.[30]

Peter decided that he could not go that fall to John Crowe Ransom's memorial service or to Allen Tate's seventy-fifth-birthday celebration, though he wrote a warm letter to Allen thanking him for opening "up the world to me in Memphis." But when Millsaps Fitzhugh's daughter Louise died in late November, he determined that he must go to New York and participate in her memorial service. The child of Millsaps' brief first marriage to the dancer from the Mississippi Delta, Louise had seemed like a younger sister during Peter's adolescence, and it was Peter who suggested that Louise, who wanted to be a writer, and her like-minded friend Joan Williams leave Southwestern and go to Bard College, where they were taught by James Merrill. Now widely known as the author of *Harriet the Spy* and other children's books, Louise had always felt grateful to Peter for his early support and encouragement and for his complete acceptance of her lesbianism. Peter met Jimmy Merrill at the service, the beginning of another long friendship.[31]

It had been a year of deaths—Anne Macauley, Mr. Ransom, Mrs. Dabney, Louise—and Cal kept sending Peter revised versions of the poem dedicated to him, "Afterlife." Lowell seemed preoccupied with death. "For several years," he told Peter, "I haven't felt my 'true self.' Most embarrassing, when I get out of one of the large taxis, the driver sometimes asks if I need help." (How the last statement must have resonated in Peter's mind in later years!) In contrast to his friend, Peter was full of news of the present and plans for the future. Waiting for the turkey to get done, Peter wrote Cal on Thanksgiving Day that Katie and Ross, both now poets, were home "with their friends or sweethearts or whatever one should call them." Peter was looking forward to seeing Cal and Caroline again in January. Between Christmas and the beginning of the term, Peter and Eleanor were going to Key West to visit their Greensboro friends the Watsons: "We are led to believe that its climate will cure all rheumatic and heart ailments." A month later in his next letter, Peter said that the poem-story about his grandfather was now a prose piece and seemed to be developing into a novella. "All these new things of mine make me feel that I have taken up writing again after an abstinence of many years," he confided. "And everything I write seems closer to A Spinster's Tale and The Fancy Woman than anything I have done during the intervening years. I really feel that at some point I got off on the wrong track. I feel that for a quarter of a century I actually was a great white horse doing tatting."[32]

"I feel fifteen years younger. I write all the time," Peter reported after three weeks in Key West. The Taylors had even made an unsuccessful offer on a house. Then he was off for Cambridge, Eleanor to remain behind for a few weeks as her writing too was going well and she didn't want to be uprooted at the moment. As opposed to the previous two terms at Harvard, this one turned out to be simply miserable. The temperature in the Taylor apartment in Eliot House was freezing all through the brutal winter. Suffering with his rheumatism, Peter would wrap up in blankets, but he could never get warm. The students also failed to interest him. "My students are brilliant. But now and then I stop and say to myself, so what?" he told Lawrence Reynolds. "They are such infants, so articulate and so devoid of experience." Still, there was the wonderful Cambridge social life. Once Eleanor arrived, the Taylors were dining with Cal and Caroline every other day, and the old roommates talked on the phone every morning. Elizabeth Bishop had the Taylors to an Easter lunch, which this time did come off, and Peter came to know John Updike. But at the first of April, Eleanor had to fly down to southwestern Virginia, where Katie had been hospitalized and was recovering from an attack of peritonitis. In the midst of the Taylors' concern about Katie, Cal had what Peter described to Jack as a "mild crack-up." After Katie was released from the hospital, Peter flew down and drove Eleanor back to Cambridge. Four days later Katie suffered a relapse. She was taken to Charlottesville, and Eleanor again flew down to care for her. Shortly afterward, Peter resigned the appointment at Harvard. It was with no regret that he returned to Charlottesville.[33]

The months in Cambridge had seen several publications. "The Hand of Emmagene" appeared in the winter 1975 issue of *Shenandoah*. It would be collected in the *Best American Short Stories of 1976,* the first appearance of a Peter Taylor story in that annual collection since 1963. "Three Heroines," the story-poem centered upon Peter's mother, his great-grandmother, and his mother's servant Lula, was published in the spring *Virginia Quarterly Review,* with a dedication to Mrs. Dabney. The Boston-based little magazine *Ploughshares* brought out three Peter Taylor poems, as well as two of Eleanor's (one of these being "New Dust," devoted to Randall's death).

Back in Charlottesville, he continued to write, having produced by the end of the summer a fifty-page story-poem, tentatively titled "A Fable of Nashville and Memphis," which he had soon converted to prose. A fully recovered daughter was now back at her commune, and Peter found it "wonderful having Katie in her old Sally-like spirits again." Peter had now dubbed 1101 Rugby Road Sweetgum Villa, an indication that he had embraced the house finally. On September 6, he mailed to William Maxwell at the *New Yorker* "A Fable of Memphis and Nashville," the first story submitted there in seven years. Maxwell was in the hospital for a hernia, and Roger Angell replied instead. The answer was yes![34]

An ebullient Peter Taylor threw himself into his fall classes at Virginia. He planned to reward himself afterward with a month in Key West, but by Thanksgiving Eleanor declared that she wished to stay at home, and he decided upon taking a two-week jaunt to England, a package deal with a Sewanee group. He woke on January 1, 1975, at the Vanderbilt Hotel in London. The Sewanee group he found congenial, especially Willie Cocke and John Reishman, members of the English department who saw to his luggage and generally made the trip go smoothly for him. He visited every gallery on his list, saw nine plays, and spent time with friends now living in England, like Paul Theroux and James Thackara, now married to Davina Millard ("I so enjoy the beautiful wives of my students," Peter whispered to Thackara). The only difficulty in the whole trip was provided by Cal, who was in the midst of another breakdown. "I have never seen him quite the way he is this time," Peter reported to Allen Tate. "He'll be perfectly fine one day and quite mad the next." Cal was in and out of the hospital several times during the two weeks, and a badly distraught Caroline was constantly changing her mind about how she wanted Peter to deal with Lowell. Despite all that, the two friends did have some good talks on Cal's calm days.[35]

While Peter was in England, "A Fable of Nashville and Memphis," now titled "The Captain's Son," appeared in the *New Yorker*. It had been years since one of his works had elicited such response. The letters poured in—from his old friends and from former students. A drunken pair of expatriate Mississippians, Willie Morris (the editor of *Harper's*) and Craig Claiborne (food editor of the *New York Times*), telephoned. Even the brilliant Irvin Ehrenpreis, the terror of the Virginia English department, wrote a note of appreciation. The story is one of Peter Taylor's subtlest in its digressive quality and use of an unreliable narrator. Beginning with one focus and ending with another, the real story lies hidden in between. The narrative voice, an apparent innocent not realizing the implication of the tale he tells, emerges finally as callous and complicit in his parents' willed blindness to the dilemma of their daughter

and her psychically arrested husband as they descend into alcoholism. Like
the earlier "Hand of Emmagene," the story centers on an upper-middle-class
impulse toward exclusion of the embarrassing or the troubled that leads the
excluded toward madness and destruction. The violence in Peter Taylor's fiction had now reached the surface.[36]

The next story he was writing dealt with the "eternal chaos we live in" on
a broad cultural level. Drawing upon his paternal grandfather's hallucinations
in Reelfoot Lake after escaping from the Night Riders and his own nightmares
and visions after the heart attack, he presents a figure from the Civil War era
who constructs a code to keep at bay the horrors that lurk for all humankind.
The next generation, secure in their wealth and respectability, implicitly reject
the values of old Major Manley (a perfect name found in the genealogy of the
Trenton Taylors), living comfortable, shallow, unexamined lives. Thus they
offer nothing to guide their twentieth-century son as he moves through the
confusion of adolescence. In the course of the story, he will reject the value
system of his grandfather only to discover as an adult that he has found nothing
to put in its stead. But this is only one of many levels that Peter Taylor was
creating in what he first called "Major Manley," and later, "In the Miro District." Another dimension was literary—a coming to terms with the epic
Faulkner tradition in Southern letters. Peter was self-consciously laying that
to rest, just as he had to lay the man's ghost to rest while he lived in the Faulkner
house on Rugby Road.

He continued to work on the story during a peripatetic spring. The Taylors
had rented an apartment in Washington, where they spent occasional weekends. Peter went down to the mountain in March, where there was trouble
with the tenants of a Monteagle cottage purchased the year before. As it turned
out, he made a bid on a house at Sewanee (the Torain place, a two-story stone
house on South Carolina Avenue), and arranged to sell the Monteagle cottage.
In early May, Peter and Eleanor traveled to Greensboro, where both received
honorary doctorates; and in late May, Peter went to New York for the Institute
meeting. While there, he had a meeting at Alfred A. Knopf—he was considering a change of publishers once again. Jonathan Coleman, a recent Virginia
graduate and now a junior editor at Knopf, had called Peter just after the
publication of "The Captain's Son" about the possibility of Knopf's publishing the next Taylor collection. Obviously pleased with the attention, Peter
found it easy to forget that Houghton Mifflin had generously published *Presences* (which as expected sold very poorly) in hopes of then doing a volume

of fiction. True, the editor who had seen *Presences* through the press had left the company, but a new editor was eager to bring out the second volume that Peter had promised. After some negotiation, Peter paid back the Houghton Mifflin advance, and the contract was canceled. On June 7, 1976, Peter signed with Knopf—for an advance of $10,000—a contract for two works of fiction, one to be delivered within one month.[37]

Now Peter went into seclusion at 1101 Rugby Road, keeping the big gates at the driveway entrance shut and locked, determined to finish "In the Miro District" and include it in the new collection. On July 27, Peter mailed the story to the *New Yorker,* surely knowing that it was a masterpiece. It was accepted six days later, and he sent a copy off to Knopf.[38]

Peter was teaching the fall semester at Virginia. Before the term began, he and Eleanor made short trips to Tennessee and to North Carolina, where Eleanor had purchased an antebellum house in Norwood with her modest inheritance. They were going to move some of the Tennessee furniture there. "I can see that I am going to regret the day that I indoctrinated her with old-house fever," Peter wrote Cal. "I have a feeling that some day all these houses will have to be sold for taxes." But Peter's remarks were disingenuous; the Taylors were ready to make their most adventurous move in real estate. They had subscribed to the Key West newspaper simply for the real estate ads, and in December, when an interesting house of the right size at the right price came on the market, they made an offer sight unseen. The bid was accepted, and they prepared to move down, to stay from January through April. Before leaving, Peter finished the proofs of his new volume, his first collection of totally original stories since *Happy Families Are All Alike* had appeared in 1959—and the volume that he would always regard as his best. Before putting the proofs in the mail, he added the dedication—"to Dick Crampton, in appreciation for an extension of time."[39]

16

Fruition

Peter's sixtieth birthday, January 8, 1977, found the Taylors renovating still another house: 1207 Pine Street, Key West. Later in the month, their friend Jim Boatwright came for a weekend visit, to confer with Eleanor on taking the position as poetry editor of *Shenandoah* and with Peter on the *Shenandoah* issue planned as a sixtieth-birthday tribute. The Taylors' enthusiasm for the place was infectious, and before he left, Boatwright too had made an offer on a house.[1]

Since they planned to spend extended periods each year in Key West and at Sewanee, the Taylors decided to dispose of the large Rugby Road house in Charlottesville. By April the place had attracted a buyer. There was other good news. Much to their satisfaction, Katie had returned to Greensboro to finish a degree in French, and Peter was most pleased with a development in the larger family. Mettie Taylor Dobson's son-in-law, John Danforth, was now a United States senator from Missouri—the family was represented on Capitol Hill once again.[2]

Knopf released *In the Miro District and Other Stories* in April, and as the Taylors were packing up to leave Key West for Charlottesville, the first review appeared in the *New York Times Book Review*. It was a shock. The reviewer,

Anatole Broyard, judged the author "at his best . . . a conventional regional writer" and found that the title story moved like a heavily loaded wagon full of cotton. By the time the Taylors had reached Charlottesville, however, other opinions were in. Writing in the *Washington Post Book World,* Jonathan Yardley began by stating that Peter Taylor was a "principal contender for the peculiar distinction of being the most thoroughly undiscovered major writer in American literature." Reviews in the *Los Angeles Times, Boston Globe,* and *Philadelphia Inquirer* all expressed similar opinions. Waiting in Charlottesville was also a letter from Allen Tate, who never offered fulsome praise. "This is your finest and most profound book," he wrote.[3]

Within a week, Peter flew off to Memphis and Nashville on a promotional tour. He had a fine time, even managing a visit with Allen Tate, who had moved to Nashville the year before to be near his doctors. Only one thing marred the trip. At dinner at the Nashville home of Tom and Grace Benedict Paine, Peter had a strange fainting spell. The next day he was back to normal, and as soon as he returned home, he and Eleanor set out for her Norwood house, where they did a week of outdoor work. They returned for a visit from Cal, whom Peter found in "relatively good spirits," considering the upheaval of his life in the last months. Separated from Lady Caroline Blackwood, Lowell was now planning to return to Elizabeth Hardwick. After putting Lowell on a plane, the Taylors again went down to Norwood. On May 19, Peter received a call there—Tom Molyneux had killed himself.[4]

Two weeks before, Peter had received a letter from Tom. His new novel had been rejected, his second wife had left him, and he was feeling trapped in academic life. But the letter contained no clue to the depth of his despair. Still shaken, Peter called Lawrence Reynolds' house in Richmond and spoke to Margie; then after hurriedly packing, he and Eleanor got in the car for Charlottesville, Peter weeping as he drove. As soon as they arrived home, Peter again called Lawrence asking whether they could go up to Delaware together for the services the next day; he just didn't think he could make another long drive. Lawrence could hear the indecision in his voice. Though Peter said, "We really *have* to go," he was dreading it. "It will be awful. I know how these things are," he added, and Lawrence knew that Peter was thinking of Randall Jarrell. The next morning, Peter called the Reynoldses to say that he had been ill all night and could not go. They went on alone. Within an hour, Peter changed his mind. He drove as far as the Delaware line before realizing that he could never make the service in time and turning around.[5]

Three days later, he expressed his grief over Molyneux's death in a letter to Allen Tate. He also gave Allen news of Cal and of Katherine Anne Porter, whom he had spoken with on the telephone recently. Calmly she had told him that she would be put on trial within a few days for some mysterious offense and would probably be sent to prison. The only good news he had to convey was in regard to Jean—and that was qualified. The previous November she had suffered a left frontal ischemic stroke. Continuing to smoke and to drink, she had been hospitalized several times since her initial release. At the moment, she had gathered strength and was living alone again and cooking for herself. "She can barely speak," Peter told Allen, "but somehow her acid wit comes through."[6]

The Taylors had now purchased a smaller house in Charlottesville at 1841 Wayside Place, surprisingly their final Charlottesville house. They took possession on June 15, but Peter and a student left soon afterward in an Avis rental truck to move some of the excess furniture to the Torian house in Sewanee. This transferring of furniture among a variety of houses would now become a recurring routine. Within a few days, Peter called Eleanor in Charlottesville. He was experiencing alarmingly high blood pressure and temporary numbness. He sent the student back alone with the truck, and Eleanor hurried to get to the mountain. "The whole house looks like an attic," she told Cal, "but will have to until September I suppose."[7]

By the time Eleanor arrived, Peter was feeling better, and he was watching his diet and trying to quit drinking. Allen had taken to calling every few days. Sometimes he raved against Cal and Elizabeth, and he was also beside himself that Andrew Lytle, who had been teaching elsewhere since his retirement, was moving back to the mountain. Allen was convinced that Andrew would get control of the *Sewanee Review* again. "They are like the King and the Duke," Peter quipped to Jack Thompson, "and I'm Huck."[8]

The *Shenandoah* number devoted to Peter and his career arrived in Sewanee. It was filled with warm, affectionate tributes from mentors, peers, and students, including one by Tom Molyneux. Peter was touched. Cal's volume *Day by Day* also appeared that summer, the poems filled with the people in Lowell's life, including Peter. It ended with the poem "Epilogue," voicing an issue that Peter remembered from one of Lowell's letters the year before. "I've been thinking lately that what happened is all we have to draw on, yet that isn't art, isn't enough for art," Lowell had written. "What happened is always there with its riches of inharmonious material, its fragmented sharpness—the stuff of life with weirdly its artificial imposed limits like a hard rhyme scheme, or a novel plot."[9]

After an absence of nine months from the classroom, in September, Peter returned to Charlottesville and to teaching. Eleanor was also teaching a poetry-writing course at the university that fall, her only such venture. A recent Kenyon graduate, David Lynn, who was in Peter's fiction workshop, remembers well the morning of September 13. As the class took their accustomed places, all were wondering whether their teacher would appear. The evening before, Robert Lowell had been found dead in the taxi that had carried him from Kennedy Airport to the West Sixty-seventh Street apartment he was to share again with Elizabeth Hardwick. He had suffered a fatal heart attack. Images of taxis (now a haunting pattern) filled a number of Cal's last letters to Peter and his poem dedicated to Peter in *Shenandoah*. The class heard familiar footsteps. Peter came in the door, looking "drawn, shaken, and somewhat distracted." His plane for Boston did not leave until afternoon; he was keeping himself occupied. He drew a handful of papers from a battered old briefcase. "These are thirty-some years' worth of letters from Cal," he explained. "I've been looking through them, for bits and pieces to read in Boston. I thought you might be interested, as writers, in what he has to say about writing." Gradually Lynn realized that, as Peter went through the letters, he had begun shaping a story, "making sense of Lowell's death by telling us a tale."[10]

Six hundred people filled the Church of the Advent on Beacon Hill in the neighborhood where Cal had spent his early years. Both Caroline and Elizabeth were there with their children by Lowell, and among those gathered to say farewell were Elizabeth Bishop, Richard Wilbur, Saul Bellow, William Alfred, John Malcolm Brinnin, and Derek Walcott. Peter read from the pulpit, not selections from letters, but the last poem from Lowell's volume *Lord Weary's Castle*. At the end of the service, ten pallbearers followed the coffin out: Blair Clark, Frank Parker, Frank Bidart, Peter Brooks, Robert Fitzgerald, Robert Gardner, Grey Gowrie, Bob Giroux, Jack Thompson, and Peter. Stopped by a reporter outside the church, Peter could say only, "We were friends for forty years," and then, "He was absolutely the best friend." Later Jack would write Peter, "You and Cal loved each other as neither of you could have loved anyone else and it was a marvel and something to be proud of even seeing."[11]

The day that Peter received the news of Cal's death, he had called to postpone a session with a *Washington Star* interviewer and photographer. Asked whether he wanted more time before the session was reset, he had said, "No,

I've been through the worst. Life must go on. I must keep busy." A week after
the funeral, reporter Ruth Dean arrived for the interview and recorded her
impressions of the Taylors. Peter answered the bell. "The doorway frames all
six feet of him," she wrote, noting "a smile that crinkles the laugh lines around
his clear eyes; an easy, mobile mouth." He introduced Dean to Eleanor, who
quickly left the room, pleading errands to finish. "She is a pretty woman,"
Dean commented, "small and slight (she comes just up to his shoulder) with
soft graying hair and a cool reserve that contrasts with his warm rush of
words."[12]

Robert Wilson, a former student of Steve Goodwin and Jim Boatwright at
Washington and Lee, had entered the writing program at Virginia in 1975.
His sketch in *Shenandoah* characterized the overall impression Peter Taylor
conveyed as one of youthfulness. "He seems to *feel* young," Wilson judged,
but then noted that Peter was "not really young physically" and sometimes
appeared "somewhat gray and tired." Most people credited those moments
to Peter's heart condition, but there was an additional cause. Soon after the
Star interview, in the midst of a cocktail party at a nearby residence, Peter
began to feel weak and suggested to Eleanor that they leave. Walking home
down Wayside Place, he became quite pale and distracted and began perspiring
heavily. Once at home, Eleanor called their general practitioner, who said that
Peter was showing all the classic symptoms of adult onset diabetes, the same
disease that had ravaged his father. The next day a specialist confirmed the
diagnosis and prescribed a strict regimen that included medication, though
not yet injections of insulin.[13]

Troubled to discover this legacy, Peter turned his mind to his teaching and
to the tribute to Cal that he was to deliver at the Institute in November. He
went through several drafts before arriving at the final version, touching on
the paradoxes in Lowell's nature, his humor, and his loyalty. He ended with
lines from William Cory's translation of Callimachus' "Heraclitus" that
Lowell had read to him on that last visit in London:

> They told me, Heraclitus, they told me you were dead,
> They brought me bitter news to hear and bitter tears to shed.
> I wept as I remembered how often you and I
> Had tired the sun with talking and sent him down the sky.
>
> And now that thou art lying, my dear old Carian Guest,
> A handful of grey ashes, long, long ago at rest,

Still are thy pleasant voices, thy nightingales, awake;
For Death, he taketh all away, but them he cannot take.

Peter had first planned to fly up and back the same day. But he wanted to spend some time with Elizabeth and her daughter Harriet, and when he discovered that both Jean and Caroline would also be in the city, he felt that he should extend the stay. That is what he did, dividing his time among Lowell's three wives. How characteristic that was of Peter Taylor—and exactly what Cal would have wanted and expected of him.[14]

After Christmas, Peter and Eleanor set out for Key West, where Peter received the news that he was to be awarded the Gold Medal for the Short Story at the May meeting of the American Academy and Institute of Arts and Letters. A year earlier, he had complained to Allen Tate that he had been writing short stories for forty years and never received a prize. Now one of the most respected awards had come to him. In his acceptance speech, he addressed the issue of his lack of a wide reputation and his own particular compensation. "I have always had a wide circle of highly intelligent, greatly gifted literary friends whom I have respected and whose respect I have enjoyed, and that had been the kind of glory that I have had," Peter said. "You want some kind of glory, you know." He viewed the medal as an extension of that regard: "It is not a prize won in the market place which would give me more sales, but it represents the esteem of my peers, and I think that is the ultimate glory that any artist wants." It was a great moment for him.[15]

Lawrence Reynolds had come up for the ceremony, staying with a friend on Eleventh Street in the Village. Returning to the apartment the night before, the two had been mugged at the door; then catching their assailants off guard, they began to fight back and finally chased the muggers through the streets of the Village. Peter was at his most social and voluble, and Lawrence arrived for the final cocktail party at the Institute to find himself the toast of the occasion—Peter had told the tale to everyone.[16]

In addition to Lawrence, the Taylors' other Virginia guests for the ceremony and reception were John and Elizabeth Meade Howard (the latter once Peter's student), John and Jane Barnes Casey, and James Alan and Sarah McPherson. John Casey, who had known McPherson at Iowa, had recruited him for the writing program at Virginia two years earlier. A number of faculty members voiced apprehension about how Peter and Jim McPherson would get along—two Southerners, one high-born white, the other working-class African

American. Casey remembers well the first meeting. Peter was subtly sympathetic and winning. After a time, Peter asked, "Do you remember from your
youth 'Womanless Weddings' [a kind of drag event in which men assumed
all roles]?" As McPherson laughed and said yes, a bond was cemented. Peter
had made it clear that the two shared the same culture, in all its manifestations
and aberrations. Peter took great satisfaction in the fact that the two became
friends, and McPherson's letters to Peter testify to his deep feelings for the
older man. John Casey would recall fondly how the three of them, most often
staring off into space, could always reach unanimous decisions on which fiction candidates to admit to the Virginia writing program. Theirs was a rare
academic collegiality sustained during the years McPherson spent at the university.[17]

Back from two years in France, Alan Williamson and wife Anne Winters
were also on hand for the ceremony. Later that year Alan and Jane Barnes
Casey would publish two of the most provocative essays on Peter Taylor's
fiction. Both these young friends were remarkably intelligent observers as well
as readers. Jane disagreed with Alan's view of Peter as living so much of his
inner life on the surface. She felt that the paradox of Peter's charm was that
he was "so incredibly appealing with the power to draw you to him, but at
the same time so distant." Despite the charge of his personality, she intuited
a "gap between his social relationships and his emotional life."[18]

Jane Barnes Casey's essay appeared first—in the spring 1978 issue of the
Virginia Quarterly Review. Commissioned as a review of *In the Miro District,*
the essay actually ranges over the entire career. It locates the primary impulse
behind the fiction as "the great modern problem of how to incorporate the
most vital, but also the most anarchic urges into civilized life." The first critic
to note the shift in Taylor's fictional interest from women to men, she argues
for the central importance of "At the Drugstore," in which he confronts and
explores chaotic, bestial male impulses. "Bourgeois morality is insufficient—it
cannot embrace the whole complexity," she writes. "Nonetheless, it is all there
is to see us through the chaos between birth and death." In the fall *Shenandoah,*
Alan Williamson's piece took a somewhat different tack. Seeing Peter's "subject *par excellence*" as the "tenuously erotic bonds and imaginative identifica-
tions between people," Williamson explores the treatment of the theme over
the career and finds Peter Taylor's most memorable stories to be those "in
which some person, or, more commonly, some feeling or human potentiality,

is excluded or killed in the dangers ensuing from the wider extensions of love."[19]

The exclusion of feeling and human potentiality was, in fact, one theme that Peter was treating in the long story "The Old Forest" that he told Robert Penn Warren he planned to finish that summer at Sewanee. Significantly, in the same letter Peter gave Red Warren a sketch of his friend Tom White, for Tom (as many people would realize) was one of the models for the male protagonist. Another was Peter himself. Years later, he would discuss the origin of the story. In the mid-1970s, Memphians had mobilized to change the course of an interstate highway slated to go through Overton Park. The campaign stirred Peter's musings about the ancient trees there in the heart of the city, the contrast of urban and primitive. The forest also brought back memories of an automobile accident Peter had in the park while taking courses at Southwestern. From these vague beginnings emerged his carefully plotted masterpiece about the search to find a lost girl and the effect on three lives—a young man, his fiancée, and the girl in his car at the time of the accident. Employing a character like Tom White, who had changed careers in mid-life, Peter presented as setting the Memphis of his youth and the position of different sorts of young women within the Southern patriarchy. When asked to explain her Southern background, a woman of a later generation, a graduate of Harvard Law School, once said in my hearing, "Read that story. It's all there in one place." But the social delineation, however astute, is but one accomplishment of "The Old Forest"; more broadly the story represents Peter Taylor's ultimate statement on the question of freedom and limitation. On August 1 (the deadline he had set for himself), he mailed the completed story from Sewanee to Frances Kiernan, his new editor at the *New Yorker*. The letter of acceptance arrived within ten days.[20]

Two weeks later the Taylors drove back to Charlottesville for the fall semester. Having graduated from the University of North Carolina at Greensboro, Katie was now running a dairy farm near Chapel Hill with a male companion and writing a novel. After a year in library science school at the University of Maryland, Ross had entered the MFA program at Iowa in poetry. Peter was enjoying his students, and Eleanor's student from the previous fall, Evie Wright, had begun inviting the Taylors out to her family's home, Bremo. Peter found the house, designed by Thomas Jefferson for John Hartwell Cocke and still in the hands of Cocke's descendants, his favorite in all of Virginia. Eleanor had also begun spending time by herself in Norwood, sometimes taking the bus down. Peter described her in one letter as "relishing her isolation" down at what he called her "Mad House."[21]

Peter and Eleanor spent Christmas in Sewanee with the children before driving south for their third winter in Key West. They had now transformed the Pine Street house. They had painted much of it themselves, had portions rebuilt to make a study for each of them, and enclosed the large side yard with a fence entered through large gates of Peter's design. Within the fence, brick walks wound through a kind of botanical garden of tropical flora, most of the specimens brought in by the Taylors. The climate of the southernmost point in the continental United States was wonderful, and the social life pleasant. The place was just becoming fashionable (though it had yet to reach its zenith), and it was already quite literary. Richard and Charlee Wilbur had been wintering there for twelve years, sharing a compound on Windsor Lane with the John Ciardis, the John Herseys, and the Ralph Ellisons. Key West was also a magnet for gays, one of its appeals for the Taylors' friend Jim Boatwright. In early January, Bob and Martha Wilson, Steve Goodwin (now divorced) and the woman he was living with came down to visit. The Taylors had the group to dinner with the Wilburs, the Ciardis and Boatwright, who later took the younger crowd to the Monster, a gay bar. Jim Boatwright, who was devoted to both Taylors, spent a great deal of time at the Pine Street house. Someone spoke of the generous and kind Boatwright as a big alley cat in the Taylor household—mild and sweet during the day, but living a wild life after sundown. Bob Wilson found Peter intrigued by Jim's two sides, just as he had always been fascinated by dual lives.[22]

It was after the Wilsons and Goodwin left that the literary crowd began to swell. The novelist Alison Lurie and David Jackson, the companion of poet James Merrill, both purchased houses on the island that year. Alison Lurie, who had met Peter a few years earlier when both were on the Harvard Board of Visitors, was delighted to find him in Key West. "It was wonderful to see him come into a room," she recalls, "because you knew that you were going to have a good time." Interested in everything, including all gossip, he was always up for anything proposed. Frequently a crowd of literary folk would go out on the town to dance and drink away the evening. Peter often joined them, but Eleanor preferred to stay at home. It seemed a classic case, Richard Wilbur said, of the Episcopal husband and the Presbyterian wife, though (according to both Wilbur and Lurie) Peter was never really wild and Eleanor was strong and independent, rather than controlling. In the dynamic of the marriage, Peter actually depended upon Eleanor to keep him in line. As Elizabeth Hardwick saw it, "She restrained him a bit, but no more than he wanted."[23]

Added to the mixture was Peter's primness. He would speak of himself as "old ladyish" in his refusal to use four-letter words. Richard Wilbur remembers a time when John Ciardi (who knew no such restraints) told a raw story in front of the wives and Peter responded, "John, you're no gentleman." "I never said I was," Ciardi countered—and Peter broke into laughter. Again and again, Peter would show diametrically opposed sides of himself, expressing one view and then immediately undercutting it. Later the same evening, Peter leaned back from the table and effused, "Isn't it wonderful not to be in a respectable Southern town!"[24]

All the Key West crowd were struck by Peter's remarkable curiosity about every aspect of the place. On coming to the island, he immediately set out to purchase a bicycle. Unknowingly, he bought a racing bike. When friends advised that he replace the handlebars, he delightedly substituted some resembling the horns of a mountain goat and began to explore the island from end to end. His frequent companion and guide was photographer Wright Langley, a Key West native.[25]

In the midst of all the fun in the tropical climate came news of two deaths— Allen Tate's on February 9 and Jean Stafford's on March 26. Both had become pathetic toward the end, Allen bedridden and nearly blind and hardly able to breathe, and Jean shrunken, ravaged, and hardly able to speak. Fully reconciled with Allen, Peter had visited him frequently in his last months. He did not go to the funeral; he had already said good-bye. He had visited Jean the previous summer too, and he had kept in touch by telephone. Jack Thompson would say that toward the end Peter could get along with Jean when no one else could. In that instance, despite Peter's plea, Jean's lawyer would not delay the service until Peter could get there; in November, however, Peter delivered his tribute to her at the Institute. With her death, most of Peter's closest ties with the past were gone.[26]

The Taylors returned to Charlottesville within a few days of the funeral. Ten days later a tragedy occurred. Breece Pancake, a young West Virginian, had made a sensation in the writing program with his bleak Appalachian short stories. Though he had taken a course from Peter and become a friend, he was particularly close to James Alan McPherson and even closer to John Casey. This year Pancake was renting a cottage on the farm of Everard Meade, father of Elizabeth Howard. On the evening of Palm Sunday, the Taylors had invited John and Elizabeth Howard and the Meades to dinner. Mrs. Meade, a semi-invalid, had not been able to come. Early in the evening, John Casey had a telephone call from Elizabeth. "Mother has just called us at Peter's," she said. "Your Breece is out shooting his gun. You better go out. She's called the police." Within minutes Casey's phone rang again. It was Peter. "John, the police have called. You mustn't go out there. Breece has killed himself." It was the beginning of the worst year of Casey's life. His father was dying; his marriage was already troubled, and before the end of the year it would be dissolved. Peter was a stalwart support throughout the painful months.[27]

"The Old Forest" appeared in the *New Yorker* on May 14, 1979, one of the longest stories the magazine had ever published. Three weeks later Frances Kiernan wrote to say that the fan letters were surpassing even the response to "In the Miro District." Peter's output had declined markedly from that in the 1960s, but he knew that he was at the top of his form. The Taylors went down to Sewanee for June and July, and Peter went to Yaddo for the month of August, to escape the heat and try to finish a new story before the beginning of the fall semester.[28]

Peter delighted in finding in that fall's writing workshop a young man named Dan O'Neill. A native of Albemarle County and a graduate of Groton and Harvard, he had studied at Cambridge University for a year and then taken an M.A. at Yale. He was a talented writer, and of equal importance, Peter had seen his name in the newspaper as a licensed realtor. Within a few weeks Peter asked whether Dan would be interested in driving him around and looking at property, and soon O'Neill joined Peter Taylor's coterie of young friends.[29]

The Key West season of 1980 was marred by health problems. In February, Peter's Florida doctor advised that he must begin taking insulin. He was depressed that his condition had worsened, worried about the techniques of injecting himself, and finally very upset when he began experiencing allergic reactions. In March he came back to Charlottesville to see his regular specialist, though he hated to leave Florida because even in the warm sun he was suffering with his rheumatism. In Virginia, that pain worsened. To complicate matters, doctors determined that he had a hernia, and surgery was scheduled, which further weakened him.[30]

An interviewer in July found him pale, but just as charming and gracious and entertaining as ever. He had also begun smoking again—after thirteen years of abstinence, he said. Fortunately there was something to take great pleasure in: due to the success of *In the Miro District,* Farrar, Straus and Giroux had reissued the *Collected Stories* in both cloth and paper. The Taylors had also found a buyer for the Torian house in Sewanee, which they had been trying to dispose of. That was all taken care of before Peter left for another August at Yaddo. A photograph taken of the August residents shows a shockingly frail-looking Peter Taylor, his hands crossed on a cane. He did, however, manage a visit to Red Warren and Eleanor Clark at their place in West Wardsboro, Vermont, for which Red expressed his profound gratitude. "Your gifts are princely, but your presence more so," he wrote. Despite his health problems, this August Peter did finish a story.[31]

On September 7, from Charlottesville, Peter mailed to Frances Kiernan "The Gift of the Prodigal." For the last few years, he had begun everything he wrote in broken-line prose. That was the way he had found his voice again, and he clung to this means of reentry into his art. This new story he felt should be kept as a story-poem, but he told Frances Kiernan that he would be willing to put this piece (as opposed to some of the earlier ones) in "more conventional prose." She requested that he do that, and over the fall he made further revisions. Finally, the *New Yorker* called for an additional change. This situation was the greatest of ironies. For the first time Peter Taylor had used four-letter words in a story. Toward the conclusion, the profligate son, Ricky, turns to his enfeebled father and says, "Man, you've got problems enough of your own. Even the world's greatest asshole can see that. One thing sure, you don't need to hear *my* shit." Peter Taylor's ear is perfect; the speech is right for the character. But he had used words not allowed in a *New Yorker* story. "If we let him say that," William Shawn said to Frances Kiernan, "Pauline Kael cannot be stopped." Changes were made.[32]

Peter now knew that "The Old Forest" had been selected for both *The Best American Short Stories, 1980* and the O. Henry Prize collection for 1980—the first time that a Peter Taylor story had made both. When *Time* reviewed the two volumes together, the magazine included pictures of Peter, Jean Stafford, Elizabeth Hardwick, Saul Bellow, John Updike, and William Gass. Under the Taylor photograph ran the caption "A Southerner who summons the ghost of Henry James." Another review in that issue was devoted to *The Collected Stories of Eudora Welty.* It noted that Welty "and Peter Taylor are surviving members of an extraordinary group of Southern storytellers, of whom William Faulkner and Katherine Anne Porter were the elders and Flannery O'Connor the youngster." It was good company and a well-deserved ranking. Eudora and Peter had gathered earlier that fall to pay tribute to another of the group. Katherine Anne Porter had died at ninety on September 18. Feeling unable to make the trip to Maryland by himself, Peter enlisted Bob Wilson, now at the *Washington Post,* to drive him up. Peter found Eudora Welty seated in a pew ahead of him. After the service, as Peter, Bob, Eudora, Robert Penn Warren's wife, Eleanor Clark, and daughter, Rosanna, stood in a group making the proper funeral remarks, Miss Welty said in a soft voice, "I brought along a little extra money. Why don't we go somewhere and eat some crabs. I think that is what Katherine Anne would want us to do." "Well, Katherine Anne would not have gone for that guitar business," Eleanor Clark said of the folk mass they had sat through—and then they were off, laughing and telling stories on their way to Obrysky's in Baltimore.[33]

By the end of 1980, Eleanor Taylor was absorbed in writing poetry and reluctant to leave for Key West, where, she had told Bob and Betty Watson, "there are just too many dinner parties to give and go to." Peter went down alone, but he always needed company, so he invited Tom White to come for the first week. Tom arrived for the New Year's Eve party that Jimmy Merrill and David Jackson always gave. Peter got a bit tipsy and fell into a flowerbed. As he got up with mock dignity, Tom registered the charm Peter so often demonstrated in making himself the butt of a joke or in puncturing his own potential pomposity. Peter also took Tom to the Monster. Peter had told Alan Williamson and Anne Winters earlier that year that, after closely observing the Key West gay scene, he had concluded that homosexuality was love of an ideal self or of one's self projected onto another person. Anne was struck by how close Peter came to Freud's position. Still Peter was fascinated by gay life in Key West, this other mode of being. All their adult lives, Peter and Eleanor had had gay and lesbian friends, but never had Peter been exposed to a network like that in Key West. Eventually he wrote a story about Key West homosexuals (with two working titles, "Accommodations" and "A Season in Key West") and submitted it to Jim Boatwright, who Peter thought was angered by it. Boatwright did subsequently misplace the story, and it was never found.[34]

After Tom left, Peter arranged to have a second bathroom built in the Pine Street house. Work on that project continued even after Peter went back north for a five-day writing workshop at American University. Among those enrolled was Barbara Thompson, who had also been at Katherine Anne's memorial service, though she and Peter had not met. A California-born graduate of

Wellesley, she was a vibrant, intelligent woman with an interesting history that included a first marriage to a senior civil servant in Pakistan, where she had spent a number of years. The previous fall she had married Ned Davis, a Wall Street lawyer. Charmed by her and impressed with her fiction (which he recommended to Jim Boatwright at *Shenandoah*), Peter was pleased to find that she had been a close friend of Katherine Anne, the friendship dating back to 1960, when Barbara did an important Porter interview for the *Paris Review*. The next step was only natural: Barbara proposed that she do a similar interview with Peter. The first session took place at the Cosmos Club in Washington on April 9, 1981. These would continue into the next year.[35]

Waiting for him back in Charlottesville was a letter from Jean Stafford's lawyer. The estate had finally been probated, and the lawyer asked that the Taylors remove the Belter settee and chair bequeathed to them. Dan O'Neill arranged for a truck and agreed to drive Peter, and the two set out for Long Island. This was a vintage Peter Taylor excursion, filled with stories and punctuated by stops for hamburgers, french fries, and other "people food," as Jack Thompson called such fare. Jean had left Peter and Eleanor what she considered her most valuable pieces. Once placed in 1841 Wayside Place, the furniture seemed awfully mid-nineteenth-century rococo. But the bequest possessed such sentimental value that the settee and chair found a permanent place in the library.[36]

A dramatic change had occurred in Peter's health and spirits since the spring of 1980, when at the age of sixty-three he had experienced an awful foretaste of the sufferings of old age. The June 1, 1981, issue of the *New Yorker* carried "The Gift of the Prodigal," the story written out of that time of pain and fear. Over ten years before, when Peter explored the issue of vicarious living in "Daphne's Lover," his narrator had concluded with this justification: "I tell myself that a healthy imagination is like a healthy appetite and must be fed. If you do not feed it the lives of your friends, I maintain, then you are apt to feed it your own life, and live in your imagination rather than upon it." In this recent companion piece, "The Gift of the Prodigal," the whole basis for vicarious experience has shifted. A pain-wracked father at first responds with outrage to the latest scrape of his wastrel son, before acknowledging the gift that the young rake brings him: "I hear him beginning," the father thinks, "I am listening. I am listening gratefully to all he will tell me about himself, about any life that is not my own."

But now it seemed that old age could be put off a bit longer. Peter had gone

to New York for the Institute meeting and for another session with Barbara
Thompson, this time at the new apartment that she and Ned had just taken
at The Osborne on Fifty-seventh Street, a grand turn-of-the century New York
landmark, just the sort of setting that Peter Taylor appreciated. Barbara's en-
lightened view of his work and of the problems of art made the interviews a
pleasure. Peter was relaxed and enjoying himself, especially after a lunch of
vodka and blinis down the street at the Russian Tea Room. Back in Charlottesville, he learned that James Alan McPherson had decided to leave the university
and go to Iowa. During the past several months of a bitter divorce, Jim had
cut himself off from everyone except three friends—John Casey, Bill Abbot
(a Georgian in the history department), and Peter. Right before Jim left, Peter
lent him a thousand dollars, a loan that in Peter's view Jim requested as a test
of his friendship.[37]

It was a good fall. A few years earlier, Peter had made this protest about
his dealings in real estate. "The world blames these moves and changes on
me," he wrote a friend, "but I think it's mostly Eleanor's doing. When she
sees an old house or an attractive house for sale she clips the advertisement
and puts it beside my plate at the table. It's like setting a glass of liquor before
an alcoholic." But that fall, he could offer no such excuse. Dan O'Neill had
called. There was a property that he thought Peter should see several miles
out from Charlottesville. There was no road into the place, and as Dan was
backing the car up and pulling off the highway, Peter leapt from the car and
began climbing a chain-link fence. When Dan reached him, Peter turned and
said only, "Eleanor will never forgive me." In the distance stood the shell of
a little eighteenth-century brick house, just two rooms above an English basement. Peter immediately named it "The Ruin," and stood for some time just
savoring the enchanting views. He first decided to make an offer on just the
land where the house stood, but that night he called Dan. "I have to have the
quarry too," he said. Peter paid $55,000, and never regretted it—for a house
that was never made habitable and a flooded quarry nearby.[38]

Other new experiences came Peter's way that autumn. Stuart Wright of
Winston-Salem contacted him about putting out a limited autographed edition of one of his works. Peter failed to reply to the letter. Even when Wright
telephoned, he showed little interest until Wright mentioned Peter's plays.
Then Peter responded with great enthusiasm. Over the course of a few weeks,
the two agreed upon the "The Early Guest," and production of the little book
was soon under way. Peter also received an inquiry about movie rights to "The

Old Forest" from a young man in the department of theater and communication arts at Memphis State University. A native New Yorker of Italian background, Steve Ross had been vacationing on Cape Cod the summer before taking the position in Memphis, when he read "The Old Forest" in the O. Henry collection and decided it would be his next film. Telephone conversations with Peter were promising, and it was arranged that he come to Charlottesville during the Thanksgiving holiday for further discussions. Peter was taken with Ross' grasp of the complexity of the story and his knowledge of his medium, his ability to visualize "The Old Forest." On the second day, Peter signed over the movie rights. Steve Ross would later characterize their relationship as "a collaborative dream."[39]

As the good year drew to an end, Peter learned that "The Gift of the Prodigal" had been chosen for the O. Henry Prize collection for 1982. His last three stories had all been selected for at least one of the prestigious short story annuals. But now he found himself going in a new direction. On December 10, Barbara Thompson arrived for two days of follow-up interviews. "My stories get longer and longer," he told her the first morning. He had tried to compress them, one means being to write them first in broken-line prose. "But I'm not trying to write *short* stories now," he admitted. He was working on three long stories "that may be novels, all of them." The first began with his grandfather's fabled funeral cortege, the second one grew from *A Stand in the Mountains,* and the third (which he was calling "The Duelist") concerned a man who doesn't fight a duel and as a result takes his bitterness over a betrayal out on his family. This last work would occupy him for the next few years. It would prove his greatest commercial success, the novel that would finally bring him fame.[40]

17

Turning Points ··

On January 27, 1982, Peter wrote Stuart Wright from Key West, enclosing the proofs of "The Early Guest." He was deep into his novel. "This morning," he told Wright, "I have sat on the porch swing for two hours, smoking cigarettes and in my mind rearranging passages." Barbara Thompson and her husband, Ned Davis, were visiting the island, and the Taylors had thrown a big literary party for them. It was one of their last at 1207 Pine Street. Since rentals were so easily available in Key West, they had decided to sell the house. They disposed of the property on March 13. Purchased for $45,000, the Pine Street house brought $149,000—the only real estate transaction on which the Taylors realized a sizable profit.[1]

After the return to Charlottesville, Peter was on the road almost constantly, giving readings. Then in May he went to New York for the Institute meeting, staying at the apartment of Jimmy Merrill's mother on the Upper East Side. There Barbara Thompson conducted a final interview. When questioned about his and Eleanor's long, stable marriage, such an anomaly among literary people, Peter gave the credit to Eleanor, who had refused to slight her roles as wife and mother for her writing. "After the children were gone, after we had played the traditional roles completely," he commented, "we were in complete agreement that now we each were going to pursue our own selves, express our own tastes, live as we want to, exactly, for some part of the year, and to write independently." He concluded, "The marriage was so cemented that it works for us."[2]

During the summer in Charlottesville, Peter began having excruciating pains in his feet and legs, diagnosed as diabetic neuropathy. This was what Hillsman had suffered toward the end. For a time, Peter was able to sleep no more than a couple of hours each night. Eventually a neurologist prescribed a pain killer that made sleep possible but left Peter with a hangover and with leg pains until early afternoon. "I am told that this ailment will pass," he wrote Judith Jones at Knopf, "or that at least there will be long remissions." He would suffer with this condition sporadically for the rest of his life. This initial episode lasted for weeks. Even by August 1, he was uncertain whether he would be able to teach the fall semester.[3]

But he was determined to send Knopf a gathering of stories. His contract, signed in August of 1980, called for, first, a short novel (to be delivered January 1, 1981) and, second, a collection of stories (to be delivered January 1, 1982). He had missed both deadlines. Now eight months after the second, Peter submitted a collection of fourteen stories, twelve of which had been published earlier in either *A Long Fourth, The Widows of Thornton,* or *Happy Families Are All Alike.* Only two were recent efforts that had never appeared in a collection—"The Old Forest" and "The Gift of the Prodigal." The response in the upper echelons at Alfred A. Knopf was fury at Peter Taylor's cheek. While Peter was teaching that fall, he received word that the collection had been rejected.[4]

On other fronts, things were brighter. Steve Ross called to tell Peter about settings for the movie version of "The Old Forest." Peter was electrified when Steve described a house in Morningside Park he had chosen—it was the very house that the Taylors had occupied when they first came to Memphis. In December, Peter received word that he was to be inducted into the American Academy of Arts and Letters. Restricted to 50 members of the 250-member parent body (the National Institute of Arts and Letters), election to the Academy was the highest recognition of artistic merit in the United States. Peter's primary sponsor was Isaac Singer.[5]

By the end of 1982, Peter had decided to retire from the University of Virginia effective the following June. He and Eleanor were debating whether they should continue to live in Charlottesville or settle somewhere else. But the immediate future was clear enough: they would spend the winter of 1983 in an apartment they had rented on Simonton Lane in Key West. Once on the island, Peter began to feeling so well that he accepted a teaching stint in the fall at Memphis State University. Stories of the filming of "The Old Forest" filled the Memphis newspapers, and the Taylors were receiving clippings daily. These had increased Peter's interest in a return to Memphis after all these years, and he also wanted to gather impressions for the novel he was writing, which was set primarily in contemporary Memphis.[6]

Eleanor's new collection of poetry, entitled *New and Selected Poems,* was published in the spring of 1983 by Stuart Wright. The product of a new imprint with no marketing program, the volume was largely ignored—a dreadful lack of recognition for what some distinguished later critics would see as a second poetic flowering. Despite her experience with a little press, Peter was delighted to be approached by another new publisher, Frederic C. Beil, a Sewanee graduate who wished to bring out *A Woman of Means,* which had been out of print for almost thirty years. He immediately signed an agreement with Beil for the reissuing of the novel. Sewanee was making itself felt in other ways that spring. The Taylors learned that a small Sewanee house originally built as a private chapel by a retired clergyman was for sale, and they bought it. Again they had a residence on the mountain.[7]

Peter was also discovering young literary relatives. An Oklahoman teaching at Bucknell named Robert Taylor had been publishing stories about the East Tennessee Taylors. Peter began a correspondence and discovered that this Robert Taylor was the great-grandson of James Patton Taylor, the brother of Senator Bob and Alf. At a cocktail party given when Peter made his yearly visit to Jim Boatwright's writing class at Washington and Lee, a young poet and visiting instructor introduced himself. His name was Wyatt Prunty and his grandmother had been Hillsman's first cousin. The two men settled on a sofa to talk about Trenton and the Taylors, Peter evidencing particular interest in Prunty's "afflicted" great-aunt, Fanchon Taylor, a beautiful young girl who had gone mad. Before the evening was over, Peter urged Prunty to come to Charlottesville and visit. A few weeks later while Eleanor was away planting boxwood in Norwood, Prunty drove over for lunch. The visit turned out to be a vintage Peter Taylor marathon event. After an hour or so, Peter suggested that they have a drink. Others followed. At six-thirty, Peter thought that they'd probably better have that lunch. He drank some grape juice, excused himself and injected his insulin, and they were off to the B. & O. Restaurant. When they returned to Wayside Place, Peter was clearly ready to stay up all night talking and drinking. The evening came to an end only because Wyatt Prunty had an early appointment the next morning. Both days are still etched in Prunty's memory. He recalls that in Boatwright's class Peter read a passage from the novel-in-progress devoted to the narrator's father's wardrobe and his collection of shoes. "I know that it's too long," he had told the class. "I can cut it down later, but I allowed myself to do this to see just what it would provoke." Prunty felt it an important lesson for an established writer to give students. During the Charlottesville visit, Peter remarked more than once on Wyatt's resemblance to Hillsman Taylor in his coloring, his mannerisms, even his movements. Prunty also remembers Peter Taylor's revealing that he was as happy in Charlottesville as he had ever been anywhere, but that he inevitably became at war with the structure of any place—one manifestation of his basic inability to be satisfied.[8]

The fall semester at Memphis State proved to be a great success. Eleanor came with Peter to help him get settled into the apartment that had been arranged for him. It was perfect. The Edinborough Apartments were filled with, Peter told Steve Ross, "either friends of my mother's or mothers of my friends." Both the Taylors enjoyed Ross. They were impressed by his incisive artistic sense, and he reminded them of Randall Jarrell. There were moments when seeing him was like looking at Randall again. Here was another ghost. The filming now completed, Ross and his associates were doing the editing. There were ongoing talks with Peter about the process. After Eleanor went back, Peter's friends determined to fill any lonely hours. Peter had not been in touch with Tommy and Mimi Bennett Mitchell for many years, but now the friendship was renewed as if there had been no interruption. The other members of The Entity, Bruce and Gertrude Fulton, were living out of the city and no longer went out at night. But Tom and Sarah White, Ward Archer (who had been at Southwestern with the group) and his wife, and Annie Rose Buchman (now widowed) all entertained for Peter. He would later say that he had been out to dinner that fall twenty-one nights in a row.[9]

His teaching, however, did not suffer. Among the fifteen or so in his fiction writing workshop was Brian Griffin, a native of Soddy-Daisy, Tennessee, a small place between Chattanooga and Knoxville. A few years out of college, Griffin was working unhappily as a freelance photographer in Memphis when he enrolled in the course. The first day Peter was typically late. He arrived red-faced and perspiring heavily, apologized, and, without much further ado, began reading from Chekhov's "The Lament." Griffin has written that from that moment his life was changed. "From the simple experience of hearing him read I learned more about writing than from all my literature classes put together," he says; "while listening to Peter I began to realize that what matters most in fiction is the word, the sentence, the movement, the telling—the *voice.*" Not everyone was so captivated. Some would complain as the course progressed that Peter gave no reading assignments and that they heard nothing on which to take notes. Further, Peter never offered criticism—or at least some thought that he didn't. One session after reading aloud a student story that was really just an anecdote about hunting, Peter then read to the class Caroline Gordon's fine hunting story "A Day in the Field." Griffin considers what Peter did "the most brilliant teaching I have ever seen." During the conferences on Griffin's stories, he came to know Peter better, but he was still unprepared for what Peter did on the last day. He read a story that Griffin had written about a fistfight between his father and his uncle and then, as the class was leaving, Peter took Griffin aside and said simply, "If you should ever consider going to graduate school, you should think about the University of Iowa and the University of Virginia." Remembering Peter's words, five years later that is exactly what the young man would do.[10]

After dispensing with the services of an agent for thirty years, Peter had signed in 1976 with Tim Seldes at Russell and Volkening. During 1983, at Peter's instruction, Seldes attempted to place Peter's collection with Farrar, Straus and Giroux, but, like Knopf, the firm turned it down. Dan O'Neill remembers well Peter's saying, "Well, since Bob Giroux didn't take it, I'll just send it to your friend Allen Peacock at Doubleday." While he was at Memphis State, he signed a contract with Doubleday to publish his collection, to be entitled *New and Selected Stories.* Before the end of the year, because of his interest in Steve Ross' film, Peter requested that the title be changed to *The Old Forest and Other Stories.*[11]

On February 15, 1984, Allen Peacock wrote to suggest that if the film would not appear on television until the spring of 1985, perhaps the publication of the collection should be delayed. He also conveyed news with which Peter was not pleased—Peacock had left Doubleday. Peter did, however, agree to the delay. When Peter received the letter, he and Eleanor were spending their first winter at a house they had purchased in Gainesville, Florida. Donald and Jean Ross Justice had left the University of Iowa for the University of Florida in the fall of 1982. The following winter on their way to Key West, the Taylors had stopped over in Gainesville and had a realtor show them houses. When they saw a small house (more like an apartment, Eleanor remarked) in an old section with a view of a local landmark, the Duck Pond, they bought the place. The Ross sisters were happy to be reunited, and the Taylors also found compatible companions among the writers and academics at the university.[12]

Now in good health and spirits, Peter was actually away from Gainesville much of the time giving readings at various Southern colleges and universities. The week of April 23 he spent at the University of Georgia in Athens, and the groundwork for this biography was laid. As a member of the English department, I was assigned to be Peter's host his first evening. Driving him to my house for dinner, I registered the full force of his charm as he turned the conversation toward me, making a great deal of our connection, the fact that I was from Holly Springs, Mississippi, near Memphis. My upstate New York wife was equally captivated, and by the end of the evening I felt that a friendship had been formed. The next morning, I told him that I wished to be his biographer. "Oh, no," he said, "I haven't had a very interesting life"—and then he proceeded to start telling me stories. These continued during our frequent meetings that week, and before Peter left, it was settled that I would visit the Taylors in Sewanee that summer.

Back in Charlottesville, Peter wrote James Thackara to congratulate him on his novel *America's Children,* recently published in England. "Keep them coming, young man. I haven't got all eternity," he said. But at the moment he seemed his old self and looked fit and jaunty. A few months earlier the Taylors had sold Father Luke's Chapel in Sewanee, but they still went down for the month of August and stayed at a friend's house while she was in Europe. Steve Ross brought a crew up to record Peter's voice-over for the beginning of the film version of "The Old Forest." This proved a master touch, giving the film some of the sense of a Peter Taylor story. Subsequently I arrived for a couple of days, just in time to witness the purchase of still another Sewanee house (one that they sold within a few months without occupying). While on the mountain, Peter learned that the National Endowment for the Arts had awarded him a grant of $25,000, and it was settled that he would teach the following spring quarter in Athens. He talked a lot that visit about two of his works—his novel *A Summons to Memphis* (opening paragraphs were currently appearing in an *Esquire* feature on works-in-progress by established writers) and his play *A Stand in the Mountains*—telling me the story of Rogers Caldwell's betrayal of his father and driving me to Monteagle to take in the setting of the play.[13]

The advance copies of *The Old Forest and Other Stories* went out before Thanksgiving. One of the first recipients to respond was Red Warren, who wrote that Peter was "a real master, one of the few." Red also felt that he could now tell Peter something that had happened long ago. In Memphis for a few days in 1940, Warren had been called one morning by Hillsman Taylor. Admitting that he had no literary judgment himself, Hillsman expressed concern about his son's future and asked Warren's opinion. When Warren replied that Peter was a natural-born writer, a splendid talent, Hillsman said something like "I'll trust you" or "I'll believe you." Then he thanked Warren and hung up. Peter appreciated Warren's tact in not telling him about the incident at the time, and he was moved to learn about it now. "I hate to think what I would have said to him then," Peter wrote. "But nowadays, with a son of my own trying to write poetry and a daughter trying to write fiction, I am very sympathetic to his behavior. In the middle of the night I lie awake wondering if these children of mine are wasting their energies and their lives." Increasingly Peter was coming to identify with his father and almost to forgive him—one of the feelings that lay behind the novel he was writing.[14]

In February, he flew up from Gainesville for the launching party for *The Old Forest*. Doubleday was doing well by the volume. The early notice of the book in *Publishers Weekly* suggested its importance, and the firm had also arranged for an interview with Peter in the same publication. The launching day included a screening of Steve Ross' film, followed by a dinner atop the Doubleday bookstore building. After a shot of the wind-blown, unconventional Lee Ann Dehart, a visibly moved Peter leaned over to Steve and said, "Lee Ann died yesterday." He was speaking of Mimi Bennett Mitchell, who had been diagnosed with cancer soon after Peter's term at Memphis State. During her illness, Peter had called her almost every day. Mimi was not the only model for the character. Peter would admit to Steve that he had drawn upon several women to create Lee Ann—taking her intellectual qualities from Eleanor, her wild unconventionality from a girl he had known at Southwestern, her spirit from Mimi. He had also, in fact, collapsed several sub-classes into one group (that he called the demimonde) in order to create his social allegory. But it was Mimi that the wind-blown actress brought so vividly back to life.[15]

The year 1985 marked the rediscovery of Peter Taylor. One of the earliest reviews of *The Old Forest* appeared in the January 26 edition of *USA Today*, where Anne Tyler acclaimed the author as "the undisputed master of the short story form." She placed herself among a generation of writers "who have practically memorized all he has produced." Writing in *Newsweek*, Walter Clemons offered an appreciation of the whole career. "Like Poe's purloined letter," he quipped, "Peter Taylor is hidden in plain sight." Concluding a long review in the *Washington Post Book World* detailing Taylor's central themes and arguing that the long late stories represented his finest achievement, Jonathan Yardley wrote: "In the literature of his own country, Taylor can be compared to no one except himself: he is, as every word in this book testifies, an American master." Notices in the *New York Times Book Review* and *Time* were almost equally glowing.[16]

February was filled with interviews—the Voice of America, National Public Radio, various newspapers. The most extensive was a five-hour session with Bill Broadway of the *Atlanta Constitution*. Broadway was a Taylor fan with a master's degree in English. Peter liked the young man and entered upon a marathon conversation ranging over his whole history and career and revealing to Broadway even his severing of ties with his brother Bob. In the middle of the February 15 session in Gainesville, Peter had to excuse himself to take a telephone call. It was an offer on The Ruin in Albemarle County, and Peter returned to the room, still musing about it. Since he could no longer do the sort of hard outdoor work that he had long enjoyed, like digging ditches and putting up fences, he knew that he could no longer keep the place up himself. Still, he hated to sell it. Then he jumped back to literary matters—his own fiction and his reminiscences of Cal and Randall. During the five hours of taping, Broadway had a fascinating exposure to varied aspects of the writer and the man Peter Taylor.[17]

A week later, Peter was in Chattanooga for a third biennial Conference on Southern Literature, along with James Dickey, Rosellen Brown, Lee Smith, and Louis Rubin. As Dickey saw Peter across the room at the opening session, he was heard to say, "Peter Taylor—he's an original." Peter's reading on the first night was given before a crowd of six hundred in the ballroom of the Read House. The gathering could never know just how many memories Peter Taylor was experiencing as he rose and began his remarks with a long sigh, "Ah, the Read House!" He read from the opening to *A Summons to Memphis*, and then from passages dealing with the father's secret visit to the narrator's fiancée in Chattanooga. A few days later, he was in Johnson City (near the original Taylor

settlement) to give a reading at a branch of the university, but more impor-
tantly to speak to his favorite aunt's book club. Aunt Louise, whom Peter
described as a "feminist Goucher girl of 1905," was now in her nineties, as
were several of the other women. She introduced Peter standing in her walker,
and later Louise's cook shared memories with Peter, remembering her brothers playing with Uncle Alf's boys down on "Chucky." It was a day to remember. In late March he learned that the Lyndhurst Foundation of Chattanooga
had awarded him one of its $25,000 grants for recognition of achievement and
that Doubleday was releasing a fifth printing of *The Old Forest*. Twenty-one
thousand copies were now in print—not a huge run for commercially successful writers, but unprecedented for Peter Taylor. Apparently he was benefiting
from a change in literary climate surrounding "the once neglected and now
again fashionable short story," as J. D. McClatchy described the form in the
Saturday Review of Literature. But as McClatchy pointed out, Taylor was virtually a counterfigure to the "new hard-bitten breed of storyteller," represented by Raymond Carver and Ann Beattie.[18]

Late in the afternoon of March 26, the Taylors' station wagon pulled into
Athens, Georgia. It was packed, filled with luggage of every description, condition, and vintage—some pieces strapped to the roof. Visibly weary from the
trip from Gainesville, Peter and Eleanor still refused offers of help in unload-
ing, asking just to be taken to the furnished townhouse rented for them. That
night Peter slept fitfully because of pains in his legs. Early the next morning,
I received a call. He was not feeling well, the townhouse was too far removed
from town, there were other complications—he didn't see how he could stay
and teach the term. I asked time to think. Quickly I arranged for handicapped
parking, alerted a physician, tried to find other quarters. In thirty minutes I
called back, conveying all that information and begging that he meet the classes
just once and give me his decision then. It worked! Within a few hours he was
feeling better and he was hooked—taken with the students and stimulated by
the new environment. That afternoon the Taylors rented an apartment in a
downtown highrise to use during the day. They now had two Athens residences.

The year before, on his visit to the University of Georgia, Peter had been
in splendid health and in appearance quite dashing. (According to the testi-
mony of a noted Athens beauty, for whom Reynolds Price named a novel,
Peter also was still quite appealing to women.) This time, for all his charm,
he seemed more his age, and on many days he walked with a cane. One of his

reasons for returning to the University of Georgia was the prospect of seeing more Georgia architecture, so trips to the quaint towns of Washington and Madison were scheduled. A luncheon was given at the estate of Bob and Carroll Leavell outside Washington, followed by a tour of the group of houses they had saved and moved to their Wilkes County farm. In Madison, the Taylors were feted at a meal lasting for three hours, beginning with Bloody Marys in stirrup cups of English silver and ending with candied violets, the hostess of the High Victorian house in properly Pre-Raphaelite dress. Somehow Peter Taylor inspired such events. Among the Athens entertainments in his honor was a cocktail party at the home of Milton and Kammy Leathers. Afterwards, Peter spoke of his regard for young Leathers, who had chosen to purchase his great-grandfather's house and to take an Hawaiian wife, thereby both honoring the past and choosing his own path.

Over the ten weeks, Peter was wonderful company, playful with children, and with adults, easy in manner, enthusiastic, engaging. While Eleanor was away in Norwood, a festival of Georgia writers brought James Dickey to the campus. Dickey got Peter aside to scold him for being insensitive to Eleanor's disappointment over the reception of her last volume. The next day Peter told of a resulting dream in which Dickey appeared as a bluff, red-faced country squire vying with him for the attentions of Eleanor, a demure figure out of a Jane Austen novel—while her parents attempted to show Peter their house recently put on the market.

During his stay in Athens, Peter wrote little except an essay, "Tennessee Caravan," about his family's moves within the state for the volume *Tennessee: A Homecoming*. These same memories he was drawing upon for *A Summons to Memphis*, and once back in Charlottesville he plunged into the novel again. As he prepared to type the manuscript through one last time revising as he went, he took great pleasure in the Peter Taylor revival in progress. Chatto and Windus was bringing out *The Old Forest* in England. The American publisher Carroll and Graf, which specialized in reprints, had purchased the paperback rights to *In the Miro District* and released it on its summer list. Frederic C. Beil, after selling the paperback rights to *A Woman of Means* to Avon, had contracted with Peter to publish *A Stand in the Mountains* in a deluxe limited edition. Most significantly, Penguin was bringing *Collected Stories* out in paperback. Soon a great majority of Peter Taylor work would be back in print.[19]

At the end of November, Peter wrote Tom White a letter reflecting his zest for life at the moment and his many plans for the future—new houses to buy, new places to go, new people to meet. He had finished the novel and was already thinking about writing another one. After some correspondence with Alfred A. Knopf, in which he chided the firm for not taking *The Old Forest*, he agreed to submit the novel to them. The first week in February of 1986, his agent Tim Seldes sent Knopf the manuscript. Within a few days, his editor Judith Jones wrote Peter. "There really is no one writing today as you do, and what a pleasure it is to read you. We will certainly publish the book with great pride and give it all that it deserves." It was not too late to get the book on the fall list, and Judith proposed that Peter be given a larger advance than the one called for in the original contract. She would prove to be the perfect editor for Peter Taylor's late works.[20]

Peter received Judith Jones' letter in Key West. After Christmas the Taylors had gone to Gainesville, where Eleanor was content to remain. But John Hersey had arranged for Peter to take the actor Roy Scheider's Key West house for three weeks in February. Steve Goodwin, at present unattached and on a Guggenheim for the year, was pleased when Peter called and suggested that they go down together. Peter spent many of the days wrapped in a blanket in a deck chair on the beach reading in his recently acquired eight-volume set of Chekhov. On a strict diet, he was drinking only moderately and could no longer stay up the late hours that he had enjoyed. But he was still active socially and quite interested in Steve's involvement with Karen Walter, a young woman Steve met the first week.[21]

By the time the Taylors returned to Charlottesville in the spring, Peter was engrossed in a new novel, to be entitled "To the Lost State." The initial focus was the progress of the 1916 funeral train of a Tennessee senator (who had just lost a bid for reelection) bringing his body home from Washington. The novel was to range back and forth over two hundred years in the history of a family and the state of Tennessee. On May 10, Peter himself was in Washington to receive the PEN/Faulkner Award for fiction for *The Old Forest* at the Folger Library. Steve Goodwin and Karen Walter, now engaged, were on hand, and afterward they joined Peter's group at a bar on Capitol Hill. On leaving the bar, they were robbed by an armed man who shot Karen in the leg. Three weeks later, however, the wedding took place as planned, at St. Patrick's Cathedral in New York, with Peter as best man.[22]

On Sunday, July 20, I called Peter for a long chat. He was pleased by a recent letter from Eudora Welty responding to her advance copy of *A Summons to Memphis*. "So sustained in its tone & mood & pace & march," she had written, "so *con*tained, so thin the ice and so dark and deep below." He was working well on the new novel, and Eleanor had poems coming out in the *Paris Review* and the *Partisan Review*. Obviously very happy, they were going out to dinner later, and Peter said that overhead he could hear Eleanor's bathwater running and her typewriter going. A week later Eleanor called. On Thursday, Peter had suffered a stroke. His speech was impaired, and his right side was paralyzed.[23]

By mid-August, when he was released from the hospital, Peter could speak slowly and haltingly and he was regaining the use of his right hand. A speech therapist was coming to the house for daily sessions. Two weeks later, answering the telephone, he was trying to speak very slowly so that he could be understood. "That's hard for me," he joked. "I like to talk." Characteristically, he was already making plans. The August lease the Taylors had taken on a house in Georgetown had been canceled, but they had been able to lease another place for the month of October. They would be only a few blocks away from Ross, who was now working at the Library of Congress. Expressions of concern were pouring in. Ann Beattie, whom the Taylors had known well since she had first lived in Charlottesville ten years before, during her first marriage, had come for a brief visit, as had John Casey and George Garrett. Eudora had written, as had Elizabeth Hardwick, and Jack Thompson was calling constantly.[24]

A feature in the August issue of *Esquire*, a "Guide to the Literary Universe," listed Peter Taylor, along with Richard Ford and Louise Erdrich, as "Rising Stars." Eighteen months earlier, in his *Time* review of *The Old Forest*, Paul Gray had suggested that a successful novel was needed to bring more attention to Peter's overall achievement. That novel was now about to appear. *A Summons to Memphis* was officially released on October 6. It is a tour de force much like Ford Madox Ford's impressionist masterwork *The Good Soldier*, a novel that requires a great deal of the reader, who is led through a series of the narrator's delusions, false epiphanies, rationalizations—finally to wonder, as Peter Taylor expressed the matter to me, "how successful are we ever in understanding what has happened to us?" The novel represents the furthest development of the late reflective Peter Taylor narrator. Drawing upon the primal struggle between his own father and himself, the work presents a son who has not openly rebelled, who has chosen not to confront life, but to retreat from it, who has avoided the quickness of life (with all its pain as well as pleasure) for a serene and deadening withdrawal.[25]

"Master raconteur Taylor casts implications—far wider than his novel's setting—about the invidious undercurrents in family relationships," concluded the first review in the August 1 issue of *Publishers Weekly*. "This is a wise book, and despite its deliberate understatement, a profoundly affecting one." That was followed by Jonathan Yardley's review in *Washington Post Book World* calling the work "not merely a novel of immense intelligence, psychological acuity and emotional power, but a work that manages to summarize and embody its author's entire career." The enthusiasm of this response was matched by that of most of the other reviewers, including those in *Time, Newsweek, USA Today*, and the *New York Times*. Among the early notices, only Robert Towers in the *New York Review of Books* expressed reservations. He had less tolerance for Peter Taylor's method in the novel, finding that his "way of circling a subject repeatedly before revealing its fictional core—a technique that contributes much to the distinctiveness of the stories—leads in the novel to prolixity and repetition." Despite this criticism, Towers concluded that the novel possessed "passages of considerable power, humor, and pathos."[26]

But the reservations voiced in the Towers piece were little preparation for what was to come in the pages of the *New Yorker*. "After a lifetime of tracing teacup tempests among genteel Tennesseans, Mr. Taylor retains an unslaked appetite for the local nuance," John Updike wrote near the beginning of his excoriation of *A Summons to Memphis*. A fellow *New Yorker* writer and Knopf author and an often distinguished critic of American literature (particularly of the nineteenth century), Updike in the course of the review reveals a cluster of puritan prejudices. Focusing, first, on regional and class distinctions that both puzzle him and make him resentful, he then misunderstands Peter Taylor's narrative strategies, often misjudges authorial tone, and is misled by some of the meretricious epiphanies in the novel. Finally one suspects that at the core of his objection to the novel is Peter Taylor's limning and acceptance of a world, in Updike's phrase, "drained of the blood of the sacred." It was a devastating review, and one that could not fail to upset Peter Taylor.[27]

He could, however, take pleasure in two other pieces of criticism appearing immediately before and after the Updike piece. "Peter Taylor's fiction is full of rewards," judged novelist Marilynne Robinson in a front-page review in the *New York Times Book Review*. "It is hard for a reviewer to do justice to the powers of understatement. Mr. Taylor's tact in preserving narrative surface, allowing fictional 'meaning' to remain immersed in its element and preventing the degeneration of question into statement, leaves him open to being seen as another interpreter of an important tradition, when in fact he is as sui generis as middle Tennessee." Concluding her Darwinian reading of the novel, she wrote: " 'A Summons to Memphis' is not so much a tale of human weakness, as of the power of larger patterns, human also, that engulf individual character, a current subsumed in a tide." Writing in the *New Republic,* Ann Hulbert, after commenting on Peter Taylor's interest in "distortions of perspective," offered the most detailed and sensitive understanding of the author's narrative method in the novel. She concluded: "The trauma of maturity, Taylor's fiction has always proposed, involves more than seeing through the oppressive pieties and pretensions of the past. But he has rarely so starkly dramatized the real, and more daunting, challenge: to find some human way of living with precisely the terrifying truth that those family and social customs are meant to camouflage—the chasms between selves."[28]

By the time of the Hulbert review, Peter had the satisfaction of knowing that *A Summons to Memphis* was going into its fourth printing and that the paperback rights had been sold for $150,000. He was also embroiled in a controversy. In mid-October, the American Book Award committee announced their three nominees for the fiction award: E. L. Doctorow, Peter Taylor, and Norman Rush. After learning a few days before the ceremony that he had not won, Peter sent a telegram asking that his name be in no way associated with the awards. "I consider the naming of three candidates in advance for publicity's sake an invidious practice." It is true that he had read a similar statement when he accepted the PEN/Faulkner Award the year before. But now, his timing seemed strange—withdrawing only after learning that he had not won the top award. The withdrawal brought media attention, and Peter's gesture dominated conversation the evening of November 17, when Doctorow was presented the award at the Waldorf-Astoria.[29]

By the end of 1986, Peter had made some progress in recovering from the effects of the stroke. He was driving again and hoping that during the winter in Florida he would be almost completely rehabilitated. But the Florida sun did not prove quite the cure he had wished, and by the middle of March 1987, the Taylors had returned to Charlottesville for conferences with Peter's doctors. Within a few days, however, news came that proved more effective than any of the medical treatments. Peter learned that he had been given the $50,000 Ritz-Hemingway Prize for *A Summons to Memphis,* to be awarded in Paris on April 8. He was determined to go. Ross, who had driven his parents to and from Gainesville, was now teaching a course at George Washington University and could not accompany his father. So Peter called his former student Bob

Wilson, saying that he really needed someone to go along to button the cuff of his left sleeve. On April 3, Peter and Wilson boarded the Concorde for Paris.[30]

They were put up at the Ritz Hotel, which had been purchased by the Egyptian billionaire Mohamed Al-Fayed, who had also endowed the prize, now being awarded for the third year. Arriving at their sumptuous quarters at three in the morning, the travelers were served a four-course meal. Peter was very much in his element during the five days, enchanted to be in Paris again and reveling in the red-carpet treatment. He enjoyed every moment, every cocktail party, every dinner. But during most of the day, he stayed in his room, storing up his energy for the events. One thing, however, he was determined to do. Raymond Carver was reading at a Left Bank bookstore, and Peter showed up on the front row to offer his support. Carver was amazed. All was climaxed by the final ceremony when Peter, before a bank of television cameras and an audience of several hundred, received the award from Hemingway's beautiful granddaughter Mariel.[31]

One afternoon a week later in Charlottesville, while John and Mary Polk Kirby-Smith were visiting the Taylors, Peter received a telephone call. *A Summons to Memphis* had won the Pulitzer Prize. Peter opened a bottle of champagne brought from Paris, and Mary Kirby-Smith noted that Eleanor put her glass to her lips. There were, not unexpectedly, murmurs that Peter Taylor had shown no scruples about accepting his latest honors. Even Jonathan Yardley made note of the fact in the *Washington Post,* though he was still very pleased that Peter Taylor was finally receiving the attention that he deserved. When Ross called to say that he wished his father had had this recognition years before, Peter replied philosophically, "No, better for it to come now. When you're younger, you have a wider range of pleasures and experiences. As you get older the range diminishes. . . . it is much better for me to be getting the attention now." Now of course reporters were calling, letters and telegrams were arriving. One of the best came from Eudora Welty. "I'll toast you tonight with my dinner," she wrote, "and the only thing I can think of to say now is Hot Damn!"[32]

18

Art and Life ··

The excitement of the awards and all the media attention carried Peter Taylor through the next months. In May, he spent three weeks in New York and was on hand for the Pulitzer ceremony and the meeting of the Institute. Roy Scheider had again offered his quarters, this time appropriately his apartment in the old Pulitzer mansion on East Seventy-third Street. Steve and Karen Goodwin were living on the Upper West Side, and Peter and Steve met nearly every day, often going to galleries or walking back and forth across the park. One night Steve had tickets for *Les Miserables*. Toward the end of the play after the slaughter on the barricades, as "Empty Chairs at Empty Tables" was sung memorializing the young artists and intellectuals who had been killed, Peter became overcome with emotion, and Steve turned to see tears streaming down his face. "It struck me suddenly," Peter said, "about our group." A few days later he summoned his strength and took a train from Grand Central to see Robert Penn Warren in Connecticut. It was heartbreaking to see Red a housebound, feeble old man, but Peter was glad that he had gone.[1]

Back in New York, though he was occasionally having terrible headaches, he was pleased with his independence and his ability to get around. Barbara Thompson gave a dinner party at The Osborne for Peter and playwright Horton Foote, an inspired match. Peter also conferred with Kent Paul, who was interested in staging *A Stand in the Mountains,* and went to the play Paul was then doing in Manhattan. Peter even had a cocktail party for a small group that included Dick Crampton's daughter, an aspiring actress.[2]

During the summer he tried to return to his writing. A typist came two days a week to do Peter's correspondence and to take down what Peter read him from longhand notes on the fifty pages of the novel written before the stroke. It was a laborious effort. Though there was still some stammering and slurring when he spoke, he agreed to do a reading in Memphis. Sponsored by his old friend Ward Archer, a Memphis financier and publisher of *Memphis Magazine,* the September event was a great success. In the grand ballroom of the Peabody Hotel, four hundred people gathered for a banquet in Peter's honor followed by his reading of the first ten pages of "Miss Leonora When Last Seen," selected because his spinster teachers at Central High School, all now dead, had contributed to his creation of Miss Leonora. Reporters swarmed in the crowd and television cameras whirred. Despite occasional pauses on some words, Peter read well. He was at his convivial best, obviously enjoying his moment. At an intimate dinner the next evening at the Memphis Country Club, he was drinking moderately, cadging cigarettes, and noting how aged the dancers in the next room seemed, almost the ghosts of the MCC.[3]

The success of this first reading since the stroke made him more confident about the one at the Library of Congress scheduled for late October. Again the Taylors had rented a townhouse in Washington for the fall months. Because of the long family connection with the capital city, Peter had a particular affection for Washington and enjoyed being in residence there, revisiting old scenes, going to the galleries, being entertained by recently made friends like the Roger Mudds. The ambiance stimulated him, suggesting ideas not only for "To the Lost State," but also for stories. Intending to put his Aunt Katty on the senator's funeral train, he was delighted to receive clippings revealing that she had actually been on it; and in November he got a letter from Bess Gore, aunt of the senator from Tennessee, containing her mother's reminiscences of the train.[4]

He was also having final sittings for a portrait by Marcella Combs, who had painted a series of literary people, beginning with her mother-in-law, Anne Godwin Winslow of Memphis, and the Allen Tate group. One day she told Peter that Robert Lowell had at first been reluctant to sit for her, explaining that he had already promised Henrietta Stackpole that she could do his portrait.

Hearing this joke from the grave, Peter could barely contain himself: Jean and Cal had often invoked the Henry James character to get themselves out of things. His friends were also haunting his life in other ways. Increasingly their biographers were asking for interviews, three biographies of Jean being under way at the moment. This was a strange dimension of the present phase of life.[5]

Toward the end of the Washington stay, on November 7, Ross Taylor was married to Elizabeth Kelleher, the daughter of a large Catholic family, at St. Augustine Catholic Church. Fond of Elizabeth, both Peter and Eleanor were pleased at the marriage, which sent Peter back to one of his favorite set pieces, the flirtation of the paternal Baptist Taylors with Catholicism. Peter himself had long ago broken all ties with religion. In protest over the Passing of the Peace in the Episcopal Church, in the late 1960s, he had quit attending church services. Subsequently he realized that it had meant little to him for years. John Updike had been right in charging that Peter Taylor's world was one "drained of the blood of the sacred."[6]

Three days after Christmas, Ross again drove his parents to Gainesville, where Peter celebrated his seventy-first birthday, on January 8, 1988. The change of scene stimulated him. Eleanor was working in the yard every day, and Peter was happily supervising carpenters who were turning the garage into a study (he was always delighted to have workmen about). And Peter was working again on "his opus," as he put it, writing laboriously on a legal pad and then dictating what he had written to a typist. He had read the first section of the novel (fundamentally completed before the stroke and later designated "Cousin Aubrey") at the Library of Congress, and now he had begun a second section, which he was calling "Lasca." It concerned the narrator's attraction to an actress of his mother's generation, a woman much like his mother, but one who had not chosen his mother's path of dependence on men, but had established her own independence through her art. The piece followed in close outline his own platonic attraction to Katherine Anne Porter (whom Peter always described as resembling an actress), down to the very poem that linked the two Katherines. One eerie note is struck by a scene in which the young man must view the corpse of the actress—eerie because Peter Taylor could never be brought to view his mother's corpse and strange too because he would revisit this viewing of corpses in a later story.[7]

He had almost completed the story before he went down to Key West for the month of March to stay again at the rented place on Simonton Lane. "I am partly going," he wrote Robert Penn Warren, "just to give [Eleanor] a vacation from looking after me." But he had to have company, so he invited James Thackara, Tommy Mitchell, and Cal's good friend Blair Clark, each to come for a week. Peter apparently seemed much the old Peter to the Key West crowd. Alison Lurie would comment that he never spoke of being ill and obviously had no intention of living that way. But his former student James Thackara, who had been paying yearly visits, was shocked at the older man's condition. Quartered for the first time in the same house as Peter, Thackara was privy to all the routines and procedures now so necessary to Peter's well-being—the dietary practices, the checking of blood sugar, and the injections of insulin to be followed in a prescribed number of minutes by the ingestion of food. As though in reaction to his careful regimen, one night at a party given by John and Barbara Hersey, Peter got so drunk that Thackara had to support him back to Simonton Lane. When they reached the house, Peter became vituperative. Thackara came to view the evening as his one glimpse of the anger—in this instance at Peter's own physical state, at the moral condition of the world, and at Thackara's liberalism—contained beneath his friend's wonderful urbanity and control. The following morning Peter apologized, and the rest of the visit went pleasantly.[8]

The next week Tommy Mitchell arrived at the peak of the season, one literary party following another. In the space of a few days he met the Herseys, the Wilburs, Alison Lurie, and Jimmy Merrill, the last at a dinner attended by both his old lover and his new one. To Tommy, the Key West scene was quite glittering, but people who had known the place before the AIDS epidemic felt differently. The Taylors' friend Jim Boatwright had now been added to the growing list of the ill, and Peter grieved over Jim's condition.[9]

Immediately before returning to Gainesville, Peter and Dick Wilbur gave a joint reading, and Peter had now booked others and promised "Lasca," now called "Something in Her Instep High," to the newly founded Key West Review. He was throwing himself back into life, determined to live as he always had. In late April, he traveled to Birmingham for a writers conference and, in May, back to New York for the Institute meeting. By the end of the summer, he had completed over a hundred pages of the novel, but he was experiencing terrible headaches and periods of depression and crying. In the midst of a conversation, he would suddenly begin sobbing for no apparent reason. He saw a series of doctors and was given various tests. Then, in late September, following news of the death of two friends, Nancy Hale Bowers and Jim Boatwright, Peter collapsed. Rushed to the hospital, he was diagnosed with a bleeding ulcer.

Once back at home, he was still terribly weak because of the loss of blood, and thus unable to spend the autumn months in Georgetown as hoped and forced to cancel readings for the fall. Since the stroke, Peter had been accepting engagements pretty freely and then canceling if he had to. He refused to let any realistic assessment of his condition influence decisions about the future. He was operating by hope and will. The travel and the public appearances seemed to him necessary stimuli if he was to go on.[10]

Before the stroke, he had submitted "Cousin Aubrey," which he admitted privately was a section of the novel, not really a story, to the *New Yorker*. Frances Kiernan, who had been his editor there for his renaissance in the magazine, had left at the end of the previous year. The new editor, Pat Strachan, had been solicitous, but she, as tactfully as possible, rejected "Cousin Aubrey." The second honeymoon with the *New Yorker* was now over.[11]

Mercedes Kelleher Taylor was born to Ross and Elizabeth on October 13. Before the Taylors left by train for Gainesville on December 11, the child had been brought to visit three times. Since leaving the hospital, Peter had been untroubled by headaches. He was feeling stronger and looked forward to the full schedule of the next few months—just ten days in January this time in Key West, readings in California in both February and March, a visit to Kenyon in early April, and in late April an appearance at the third Flannery O'Connor Writers Forum, held at Georgia College in Milledgeville. Peter arranged that I be put on the program for the latter event, and we were housed in adjoining rooms in the old Georgia governor's mansion there, until recently home to the president of the college.[12]

Though frailer than the last time I had seen him, Peter was still wonderful company, telling me that he suspected Flannery had been in love with Cal, showing such a sophisticated appreciation of our quarters, enjoying so fully every entertainment. Though I felt that I was there in part to protect him from excessive calls on his time and energy, I was surprised at what he was still capable of doing. He held up better than I at a protracted reception followed by an endless seated dinner at an antebellum mansion far out in the Georgia countryside. The next morning, he was delighted when invited to tea by the formidable Miss Regina, Flannery O'Connor's ninety-year-old mother. That evening he read "Cousin Aubrey." He delivered the old magic. I was spellbound, carried away not only by the piece itself but what it suggested about the larger work. At the reception following the reading, an older woman introduced herself as former secretary to the president of a Nashville insurance company. She had recognized one of the vanishing men cited in the story as a man insured by the company. Peter was beside himself, never dreaming that someone in Milledgeville, Georgia, would recognize Horace Buntyn, who had disappeared from Nashville in the 1930s. The joy he took in other things was characteristic. In earlier years, I had seen his interest in an elaborately coiffed and painted woman of heroic size glimpsed in a coffee shop ("Isn't she magnificent!") or a waiter in a club seen talking to himself. This time, he appreciated the good humor of a man walking to the reading who had just discovered that the back seam of his coat had come apart. Always such a close observer, he was entertained by matters that most people scarcely notice. The last morning at breakfast, he was particularly pleased when a student came up to say how much he had enjoyed the reading. That was the sort of person he wanted to reach, Peter commented, and so often youthful shyness prevented any such encounter.

In May, he went to Italy as one of the three finalists for the International Literary Prize Chianti Ruffino Antico Fattore. Not bothered this time by being one of three named finalists, Peter had never been to Venice, and the ceremony presented a perfect opportunity. Eleanor could not be talked into accompanying him, but Tommy Mitchell, now usually ready for a trip, was game. The two flew to Venice and stayed two weeks at the Gritti Palace Hotel. Tommy proved the perfect traveling companion. After an hour at the opera one night, he leaned over and said, "Don't you think this is enough?" and they left, laughing as they reached the street. Each morning they would breakfast on the roof garden. After the first few days, they began talking with people there, and soon every morning a group would be assembled just waiting for Peter to appear. The afternoons they spent on the terrace of the Gritti Palace, watching the boats, sipping drinks, and, as Tommy put it, "filling in the blank areas of each of our lives." When Gaetano Prampolini, Peter's Italian translator, arrived to take them to Florence, he suggested that first they go north for a tour of villas designed by Palladio. They reached Florence three days before the awards ceremony for an elaborate dinner party in the penthouse of Ambrogio Polinari across from the Pitti Palace. The ceremony itself in the Palazzo Vecchio began with a fanfare of trumpets as the three writers honored—Tahar Ben Jelloun for *La Nuit Sacrée,* Juan Eslava Valan for *En Busca del Unicorno,* and Peter for *A Summons to Memphis*—strode into the hall. After learning that he had won the prize, Peter whispered to Tommy that he just didn't think he would be able to go to the party afterward. But when he saw the liveried footmen and five huge white tents each seating a hundred people, he changed his mind. The sybaritic Peter, the young boy who had so marveled at the Veiled Prophet's Ball, had a glorious evening.[13]

Within a week, Peter was in Memphis to give a reading of "The Old Forest" in Overton Park, the setting of the story. To a reporter he mentioned that girls on whom he modeled his characters had lived on Kenilworth, the street bordering the park. No names were supplied, but he was referring to Mimi Bennett and Gertrude Fulton. The Entity was much in his thoughts that night, and other friends from the Southwestern days, Tom White and Ward Archer, were in the audience.[14]

After months of a schedule that might tax a much younger man in perfect health, Peter once back in Charlottesville was ready to return to a story he had worked on intermittently for the last year. In the spring he had called the office of the Virginia writing program to secure another typist, or "amanuensis," his preferred usage. As it happened, standing in the office at the moment was a willing young man who had entered the program the preceding fall. It was Brian Griffin, the student Peter had encouraged at Memphis State six years before. On his first visit to Wayside Place, Griffin was dismayed at the change in the revered figure. Soon Griffin was coming to the house every day, and Peter said that just having a typist in the room with him cheered him. Peter Taylor spoke often of the necessity of a "second inspiration." What he meant was that after a story was finished, or almost finished, he needed a new vision in order to make it a great work. He depended upon these dual visions. In the case of some pieces, like "Heads of Houses," he would tear the original version up and completely reconceive the story. In other instances, he would see other sides of issues and rewrite, including all the cross lights that struck him. The process gave much of his fiction the kind of dialectic quality that became his hallmark. Peter had written "The Witch of Owl Mountain Springs" originally in the third person. Now as he worked with Brian Griffin, he was recasting it in first person.[15]

Years before, in the tribute to Jean Stafford delivered at the Institute, Peter spoke of the many roles she had played—"a *grande dame*, a plain-spoken old maid, a country girl from the West, a spoiled rich woman—her diction always changing to fit the role." She also played the part of the writer, he commented, but noted, "Actually, what she was like when she sat down to write her wondrous novels and stories may be something beyond the comprehension of any of us." The same of course is true of Peter Taylor. But we do have a privileged glimpse of the writing of this one story. According to Brian Griffin, Peter would spend mornings on a sofa writing in a notebook with a pencil in what he called "the unintelligible scrawl of a desperate man." (The manuscripts reveal the aptness of his description.) When Griffin arrived in early afternoon, Peter would begin dictating from the notebook, though increasingly in this Owl Mountain story there were no scribbles to be read. Peter simply composed extempore. "I recall looking at him occasionally as he spoke," Griffin has written,

> and I remember especially his eyes. Sometimes as he spoke his eyes were bright and alive, focused not on the page or even on me, but rather on the blank wall beyond me. And he would speak the story to me in a slow, measured, formal way, as though the narrator of the story had actually left the realm of ink and paper and had somehow taken possession of his body. I recall, too, that at certain junctures in the narrative (particularly at points in which the narrator may have said something that was clearly a self-delusion), Peter would laugh sharply and turn to me with a look of utter joy on his face, clearly delighting in the fictional narrator's struggle with his own delusional musings—delighting, too, in my re-action to his narrator's plight.

Peter was of course fully aware that he had come now to the method of composition chosen by "the master" at the end of his career. Somehow, though, one doubts that Henry James made the process itself finally so social.[16]

The story was something new for Peter Taylor, fitting squarely in the American strain of gothic traceable to Hawthorne and Poe. Like Hawthorne, Peter leaves some matters essentially mysterious; like Poe, he uses a deranged narrator, himself the perpetrator of many of the misdeeds he describes. The treatment of the whole tale is so broad that it verges on farce, though with decidedly macabre moments, especially a scene in which corpses are viewed. Startlingly, it also contains the one moment of sexual coupling in all Peter Taylor's work.

In addition to typing, Brian Griffin performed other duties. He took Peter to give readings close by, and once he drove him down to Norwood for an overnight stay. The Taylor's second house in Norwood had now been sold. According to Peter, it had been used merely to store the "Theodore Roosevelt furniture" he had inherited, and those pieces had to be put either in Eleanor's house across the street or in a van rented to take furniture to Sewanee, where the Taylors had just purchased a house. That dwelling was Father Luke's Chapel, and both Taylors were overjoyed to have it back, Eleanor later speaking of it as "my favorite house in the whole world." When asked why he had purchased it again, Peter replied with great delight, "Just to keep up the habit." No matter how much Peter was still enjoying his real estate dealings, and accepting the resultant shifting of possessions, the trip back to Charlottesville was made only very slowly because Peter had to stop frequently to rest.[17]

Fortunately "The Witch of Owl Mountain Springs" was finished by the end of September, when Peter experienced a second debilitating episode of diabetic neuropathy. This was much more intense than the first attack, in the summer of 1982. For over a month, he lived with electrodes attached to his lower leg and a monitor hanging from his neck. When Bill Broadway visited him on the twenty-second of October, Peter, sitting on the library sofa in his pajamas, explained that the device was to divert the pain, but that he had codeine secretly stashed away, which he took at night. "I want to get back to my novel," he said, "but I don't know that I ever will." He had been forced to cancel all his engagements and all other plans, and had begun going to a pain clinic.[18]

In the midst of this terrible episode, Peter had Brian Griffin ready the Owl Mountain manuscript and send it off to the *New Yorker*. On November 16, Pat Strachan composed a generous, supportive letter of rejection. "It's a splendid story," she wrote, "and I deeply regret that it hasn't proved right for the magazine. Our loss." On a rainy, cold, blustery evening a few days later, Peter opened the door to Brian Griffin, who had come to get letters to be mailed. "This young editor," Peter said, "simply has no interest in these silly ghost stories of mine." He was more dejected than Griffin had ever seen him, and he vowed never to send the *New Yorker* another story.[19]

As the year 1989 came to an end, Peter was still suffering awful pain. For a time, he didn't even want to talk to people on the telephone. But he responded with enthusiasm when John Casey called to say that his novel *Spartina* had won the National Book Award. A few days later in an interview with the Boston *Globe*, Casey credited Peter's statement to him at Harvard ("Don't be a lawyer. Be a writer") as being the single most important event in his creative life. Casey had been telephoning regularly during the months of illness, and now in his big moment he was publicly expressing his gratitude and affection.[20]

By Peter's seventy-third birthday, on January 8, 1990, the pain had subsided, and he was driving the car for short trips and writing very slowly, laboriously typing about half a page a day. "At least it makes you feel alive," he told Bill Broadway. He was pleased that "Cousin Aubrey" was coming out in the next issue of *Kenyon Review* and that the journal had also taken "The Witch of Owl Mountain Springs." At the end of the month, he felt strong enough to make the trip to Florida, and this time Lawrence Reynolds had volunteered to transport them. "Peter is frail now," Lawrence wrote in his diary, "but carries on." Driving back, he found himself wondering how Eleanor would do when Peter died and concluded that she would manage well: "She is a quiet, strong, and remarkable woman." Now for the first time, other friends too began to wonder how much longer Peter could hang on.[21]

But once in Florida, Peter seemed to bounce back. Though he simply could not get back into the novel, he began a story set at Stoneleigh Court, the Washington apartment building where Aunt Katty had lived. As he thought about her dabbling in spiritualism, he began making notes and writing passages. Within the first two weeks, he had also accepted reading engagements. In late April, Ward Scott, a former student of Andrew Lytle, drove Peter up to Savannah for a reading sponsored by the Poetry Society of Georgia at Telfair Academy of Arts and Sciences. Peter did a creditable job and enjoyed himself tremendously.[22]

On June 10, the Taylors took possession of Father Luke's Chapel, and ten days later Brian Griffin drove a van down with furniture from Norwood. Two weeks later, when my wife and I visited the Taylors, they seemed very much at home. It was always remarkable how quickly they could settle in and how thoroughly they could make a place their own. In mid-July, Peter read "The Witch of Owl Mountain Springs" at the first Sewanee Writers Conference. Though both he and Eleanor would speak to friends of his periods of depression, his public persona was as sunny as ever. Social life, however, always stimulated him and got him out of himself. Over the phone on August 30, he told me that this was one of the best summers of his life. The next day, however, he had a series of outbursts, one concerned with his parents' lack of appreciation for his calling, ranging back to his father's refusal to allow him to go to Columbia. Within a few hours, he was back to normal, and the Taylors' friend John Reishman would later express his pleasure at their company that summer and "the wonderful conversations that you always generate."[23]

Peter had told me during that last telephone call that, so great was his restlessness now, he didn't like to stay anywhere longer than three months. In early September Ross flew down to drive his parents back to Charlottesville. Then in mid-December he drove them to Gainesville. By the time of Peter's birthday, he could report that he had had four good days in a row after weeks of depression. He was back at work on the Washington story. Six weeks earlier he had complained that he could not even rake the yard anymore; Eleanor was having to do it, as she was having to do everything now. Many people remarked upon the wonderful care that Eleanor gave Peter. Marnie Polk Ross had witnessed the incredible soothing and sustaining power of Eleanor's mere presence at her brother James' bedside, and during these years of Peter's decline, Eleanor virtually made life possible for her husband. At the same time remarkably enough, she was producing poetry, enough for another volume. Peter was particularly proud of a poem that the *New Yorker* had recently accepted, and he urged me to watch for it. He called it "Knives and Forks," but the actual title is "Kitchen Fable":

> The fork lived with the knife
>   and found it hard—for years
> took nicks and scratches,
>   not to mention cuts.
>
> She took tedium by the ears:
>   non-forthcoming pickles,
> defiant stretched-out lettuce,
>   sauce-gooed particles.
>
> He who came down whack.
> His conversation, even, edged.
>
> Lying beside him in the drawer
>   she formed a crazed patina.
> The seasons stacked—
>   melons, succeeded by cured pork.
>
> He dulled; he was a dull knife,
>   while she was, after all, a fork.

His pride reveals both the complexity of this literary marriage, and Peter's respect, above all things, for the making of art from the materials of life.[24]

By spring Peter would say that he had been able to get a lot of writing done because Gainesville had been so dull. But his health had also greatly improved. He was assembling a table of contents for a new volume of stories and looking forward to the Peter Taylor Symposium in Baltimore in late April. Before going back to Charlottesville, however, something occurred for which he was totally unprepared. He had agreed to do a reading in Jacksonville. The friend who drove him up made two terrible mistakes. After taking a wrong turn off the Jacksonville expressway into a bad part of town, he discovered that the car was out of fuel. As Peter waited in the locked car for his companion to return with gasoline, two black men with revolvers approached the car demanding that Peter get out. As he sat frozen with terror, his friend appeared in a truck from a service station, and the robbers disappeared into the night. Peter was badly shaken. It seemed a scene out of his poem "The Megalopolitans," a work of the imagination written fifteen years before. Life was imitating art.[25]

The Baltimore symposium proved not only a celebration of Peter's achievement but a great reunion ground for friends old and new. Felder Heflin was on hand and the writer-kinsman Robert Taylor. The keynote address was given by Elizabeth Hardwick, and on the program was Albert Griffith, who had brought out in 1990 a revised edition of his book on Peter in the Twayne series—as well as Gaetano Prampolini, Steve Ross, and I. There was a panel of Peter's students: Steve Goodwin, Susan Richards Shreve, Bob Wilson, and David Lynn. Two new devotees also contributed to the sessions: Christopher Metress, who was writing a Taylor dissertation at Vanderbilt, and Madison Smartt Bell, the novelist and short story writer, who five years before in *Harper's* had called Peter Taylor "arguably the best American short story writer of all time." Peter found the weekend exhilarating but exhausting.[26]

Two months later, within the same week two pieces of good fortune came Peter Taylor's way. Christopher Metress had lunch with him in Charlottesville and told him of finding three unpublished stories amid the papers Peter had sold to Stuart Wright, who in turn had sold them to Vanderbilt. The three stories provided, as Peter expressed it, "just the salt and pepper I need for this new collection." (It is obvious that he remembered well Knopf's response to the manuscript he had sent some years earlier that contained only two previously uncollected stories). A few days later, Peter received a letter from Mark Trainer, a graduate of the Virginia writing program and friend of Brian Griffin, asking whether Peter needed a typist. Trainer would be a much valued assistant for the rest of Peter Taylor's life.[27]

Peter and Eleanor spent July and August in Sewanee. They loved being on the mountain, and John Casey seeing them in that setting felt that they were "breathing new air." They had a body of academic friends—the Willie Cockes, the Monroe Spearses, the John Reishmans, the Dale Richardsons (Leslie Richardson being a daughter of Annie Rose and Les Buchman of Memphis), the

Wyatt Pruntys. Wyatt was now director of the Sewanee Writers Conference, which was another attraction, bringing the Taylors in contact with old friends and with young writers that they may not have known otherwise. Peter might complain that the constant social life was taxing, but it was exactly what he needed and most enjoyed. Monteagle friends would also come over, and various Taylor kin visited that summer, Uncle Alf's grandson who taught in Murphreesboro and Aunt Louise's stepdaughter from Knoxville. Tom and Sarah White came up on their way to an over-seventy tennis tournament in Knoxville. Later, in the midst of a match, Tom's doubles partner and Peter's old friend Ward Archer dropped dead on the court. "You can't dwell on it," Peter said, "because it's happening all around us." Before the return to Charlottesville, however, the Taylors had made the decision to be buried in the Sewanee cemetery.[28]

Back in Charlottesville, Peter was working with Mark Trainer steadily on the Washington story (the title had been changed from "The Fortuneteller at Stoneleigh Court" to the "The Oracle at Stoneleigh Court") and on putting together the new collection. Lawrence Reynolds had offered to drive Peter and Eleanor down to another symposium, "A Peter Taylor Homecoming," in Greensboro the second weekend in November. When the time came, Peter was suffering with rheumatism. He managed the event gracefully, however, and read well one of the stories from Vanderbilt, "At the Art Theatre." But worried about his health, within two weeks Eleanor had him settled in Florida. Immediately after they arrived in Gainesville, Peter mailed the manuscript of the new collection to Judith Jones, and on December 12, she telephoned her acceptance. It would be months before the manuscript was actually complete and a contract signed, and the role Judith Jones would play in shaping the collection would be far greater than Peter Taylor had ever allowed an editor. Right before Christmas, we received a card from Eleanor and Peter containing notes from both. "Cheers from an old couple in Florida," Peter wrote in a shaky, disjointed, and barely legible script. "His new book of stories has just been accepted and now he is trying to learn to write in longhand again."[29]

The year 1992, his seventy-sixth, amid his infirmities Peter Taylor immersed himself in his writing with a strength of will that is staggering and inspiring to contemplate. In Gainesville, he was employing for the second year a writing student, Jeff Peters, as amanuensis, but much of the material for the new collection Mark Trainer had in Charlottesville. As a result, Knopf was receiving shipments from both places. Both the title and the contents of volume kept changing. The title, first "The Witch of Owl Mountain Springs and Other Stories," became, next, "The End of Play and Other Stories," and finally "The Oracle at Stoneleigh Court and Other Stories," after Judith Jones convinced Peter that the Washington novella was too short for separate publication and belonged in this collection of ghostly pieces. Only a month after the Taylors' return to Charlottesville, on May 6, 1992, was the contract for the volume finally signed, calling for an advance of $50,000.[30]

By that time, Peter was again working steadily with Mark Trainer on the novel. The Gainesville house had been put up for sale. Peter had wanted to sell it for the last several years, but the Gainesville real estate market had been depressed, and the house itself had all sorts of problems. Now Don and Jean Ross Justice were leaving the University of Florida and returning to Iowa, and the Taylors' main link with the city was about to be broken. During the summer at Sewanee, the Gainesville house sold. Eleanor investigated rentals and houses for sale in Key West, but found the market there much too inflated. Finally, the Taylors settled on St. Augustine for the next winter. During the fall in Charlottesville, Peter would sometimes have spells of weakness and pain and have to cancel social engagements, but he remained focused on the novel. During many sleepless nights, he got out of bed and dictated passages into a tape recorder, and he was always ready for the thrice-weekly sessions with Mark.[31]

Trainer recalls Peter's going over and over some passages. Many sessions would begin with the wonderful opening of the novel, which was revised many times: "In the Tennessee country of my forebears it was not uncommon for a man of good character suddenly to disappear. He might be a young man or a middle-aged man or even sometimes a very old man. Whatever the case, few questions were ever asked. Rather it was generally assumed that such a man had very likely felt the urging of some inner compulsion and so could not do otherwise than gather up his chattels and move on to resettle himself elsewhere" (*ITC* 3). It is subtly different from the opening of "Cousin Aubrey," the original beginning of the projected novel "To the Lost State." During the fall Peter was going over the whole manuscript for what he thought would be the last time, spinning out his tale with a new amplitude of vision. In November he mailed off to Judith Jones the novel he was now calling "Cousin Aubrey Redux."[32]

On Peter's birthday in January, the Taylors set out for the Monterey Inn in St. Augustine, planning to remain a month. Both were immediately smitten with the place, and before a month was out, they had bought a house at 98 Markland Place. They got possession on February 22. The Gainesville furniture, which had been transported to Norwood, was soon on its way again to Florida, and the Taylors had moved in by the time the reviews of *The Oracle at Stoneleigh Court and Other Stories* began appearing.[33]

As Peter would later admit, the reviews were "not altogether favorable." The piece in the *New York Times Book Review* by Gail Godwin was graceful homage to "an old master of subtlety and subtext," though it skillfully avoided making judgments about the present stories. As expected, Jonathan Yardley in the *Washington Post Book World,* after ranking the title novella "among Taylor's finest work," concluded that Peter Taylor "is, in his 76th year, the best writer we have." None of the reviews was hostile. In a thoughtful piece in the *New Republic,* Wendy Lesser made perceptive points about the collection. She paid particular attention to the three plays in the volume, judging that "the fact that Taylor wanted to write plays but couldn't has, perhaps, enriched his fiction in very much the way it did James's," and she pointed to the influence of Ibsen "not only in the dramatic structure, but in the repeated idea of the old and dead reaching out beyond the grave to stifle the young and living." But she found the entire volume, "a little less masterful, a little less under his control" than his best work. Similar positions were taken by Joyce Carol Oates in the *Times Literary Supplement* and by Robert Towers in the *New York Review of Books,* Towers finding nothing in the volume on the scale of "The Old Forest" and "In the Miro District."[34]

Peter seemed to take all the reviews in stride, appreciating the praise, remaining unruffled by criticism. After all, at the age of seventy-six, he was receiving a lot of attention, and Viking Penguin had just reissued the *Collected Stories.* He did a telephone interview with the *New York Times Book Review,* and on March 13, the journalist Ben Yagoda flew down to interview him for the *Washington Post Magazine.* The Taylors were impressed with Yagoda, who wrote an excellent piece suggesting parallels between Peter and Senator Taylor in their general bonhomie and capturing Peter's joy in telling tales. The accompanying color photograph, however, revealed the toll Peter's seventy-six years had taken.[35]

Eleanor kept projects going in the yard that pleased and interested him, one day having a thirty-foot palm tree brought in and lowered into place by a crane. The reading aloud that the couple had shared and enjoyed for many years had fallen to Eleanor since Peter's stroke in 1987, which had made the act of reading (of processing unfamiliar written material) often difficult and sometimes impossible for him. For the past six years after meals and in the evening, she had read aloud all sorts of books—including Prescott's *The Conquest of Mexico* and *The Conquest of Peru,* and many volumes of Trollope. At the moment she was in the midst of James' *The Ambassadors.* Peter continued to labor over passages and other matters of substance that Judith Jones had criticized in his novel.[36]

The manuscript that Judith Jones had returned to him in December was covered with notes and questions. He was making changes and offering responses. He agreed to the "recasting of the mother's narrative," but on one matter he was adamant: he would not change anything regarding "the emergence of Brax's [the son's] role in the novel." He concluded a letter in March: "This can only lead me to ask if my withdrawal of the manuscript isn't the only way to resolve the problem. I would hate that, because, as you know, I have very much appreciated all the other suggestions you have made about the manuscript. I am afraid somehow that all of this may sound like the voice of doom, and I don't mean to sound so. But I want to speak frankly and to be willing to face what may be the inevitable consequences. And I count on your being equally frank with me about where we go from here." On April 7, Judith Jones responded, conceding the importance of Brax but insisting that the writing in those sections often seemed "murky, repetitive, and sometimes overworked." She concluded, however: "Take your time with it and do what you can. I would, of course, want to publish the novel no matter what." She had won Peter over, and back in Charlottesville he set to work "de-Jamesing" some of the passages (as he put the matter to Mark Trainer) and strengthening his treatment of the son. On June 9, Peter told me that he might dedicate the novel to "all the boys who typed and, above all, to Judith Jones."[37]

Fully aware that his novel was one of his most ambitious works, Peter Taylor, despite moments of discouragement, was determined to make it what it should be. Over the years he had changed his original conception that the work would center on the senator's funeral train, surrounded by shifts to other time periods. He retained a fascinating historical dimension, from the first pages ranging over the history of Tennessee and the three grand divisions. The senator was put in historical perspective, as were his three sons-in-law, all children of Confederate veterans, imbibing the martial spirit but without any means of testing themselves, and thus given to hollow posturing. Into the family group Peter placed Cousin Aubrey, significantly an *illegitimate* nephew of the senator and a figure much more sensitive than the sons-in-law. He becomes the figure who breaks away from the smothering values of the family, in the narrator's mind the figure representative of the artist that the narrator himself lacks the courage or ability to become. Peter then complicated the plot by giving the narrator a son, Braxton, who does achieve the freedom of the artist.[38]

But there is still another dimension provided by the narrator's mother. On one level, in fact, the novel can be viewed as a companion piece to *A Summons to Memphis*. In that earlier novel, Peter explored the character of his own father and dramatized the necessity of Oedipal resistance. In this novel, Peter engaged his relationship with his mother, coming to terms with the aspects of her that had puzzled and confused him as an adoring son. Binding all together is a joy in the writing, in the spinning out of the tale. It is an amazing performance and his most autobiographical work, drawing as it does on family history and the history of his own early development as an artist. Interestingly, the collection on which he had worked almost simultaneously, *The Oracle of Stoneleigh Court and Other Stories*, stands as a sort of source book for the novel, gathering works that earlier dealt with themes and even events given more extended treatment in the novel.

In May, Peter was disappointed that he could not go to New York for Ann Beattie's induction into the American Academy. He was fond of Ann and respected her work. But he did not feel up to the trip. So he worked hard at the novel, and the Taylors planned a party on June 4 to celebrate their fiftieth anniversary—just a dozen or so old friends. When one of the expected guests died suddenly, the event was postponed for a week. Though another friend was subsequently hospitalized, the Taylors went ahead with the party. Peter told Bill Broadway that all guests arrived on canes or walkers. Shortly before setting out to spend July and August in Sewanee, Peter mailed the revised manuscript to Judith Jones.[39]

Settled in Sewanee, Peter was making notes on a new novel, tentatively titled "Call Me Telemachus," based on his play *A Stand in the Mountains*. But he was also enjoying an extremely active social life. The Sewanee Writers Conference was especially pleasant that summer, bringing in old friends like Bob Giroux and Richard Wilbur and Horton Foote, as well as young intimates, John Casey, Steve Ross, and Mary Flinn, editor of the *New Virginia Review*, to whom Peter had given "The Oracle of Stoneleigh Court." On the last night of the conference, one of the writers led a group to the Sewanee cemetery, where over Allen Tate's grave, he read Tate's "Ode to the Confederate Dead." Some old Sewanee residents were scandalized, but Peter protested that Allen would have loved it, that with his sense of drama "he lived for moments like that."[40]

After the conference was over, I visited the Taylors both before and after a trip to work at Vanderbilt, where the largest collection of Peter's papers are housed. It had been decided for some time now that I would write Peter's biography, though in an unusual Peter Taylor way, we never directly discussed the matter; it was simply understood. The previous spring I had started interviewing systematically, beginning with a session in Memphis with Tom and Sarah White, and Peter had shown great interest in everything I was doing. During these visits at Sewanee, Peter was frailer than ever, having real difficulty rising from a chair and seeming very uncertain once on his feet. On the last day, I had lunch at the Hospitality Center in Sewanee with the Taylors and Susan and Bill Eason of Nashville, friends since the Fort Oglethorpe days. People were constantly coming up to our table to greet Peter and Eleanor, and Peter and Bill kept up a stream of army stories. The Easons left for Nashville, and I felt that I should leave too, not wishing to tire Peter. But he wanted to talk. We sat in his study in Father Luke's Chapel surrounded by pictures of Allen Tate and Andrew Lytle, a colored lithograph depicting Tennessee history, and a snapshot of Peter, Cal, and James Waller at Monteagle taken before the Taylors' marriage. He told me that for the new novel he was using two tapes, one for notes and one for the narrative, but when he spoke into the tape recorder, the sentences were not as good, and he had to go over them later. He wanted to talk about a number of things, and when I finally left for home, we both felt some emotion at the parting.

About the middle of October, Ross flew down and drove his parents back to Charlottesville for a round of consultations with doctors about recent troubles with Peter's vision. By the beginning of October, Peter had learned that he was to be given the PEN Malamud Award for the Short Story, but he realized that he wouldn't know until the last minute whether he'd feel well enough to attend the ceremony in Washington on December 3. Mark Trainer was coming regularly to work on the new novel, which Peter was now calling "The Brothers Taliaferro" (he had again appropriated the old Taylor code name, Tolliver, this time in its pure form, for the Weaver brothers of A Stand in the Mountains). "I've done my serious work," he said. "Now I'll take that play by that other fellow and do whatever I want with it." He had also settled on the title of the novel in press. Since Cousin Aubrey was no longer the primary focus, Judith Jones had suggested *In the Tennessee Country,* the initial phrase of the memorable first sentence. On the first day of November, he had a new conclusion typed to send to Judith.[41]

Before the end of the month, she wrote that *In the Tennessee Country* had gone to the printer. As the time approached for the PEN events in Washington, the Taylors decided that they would take a limousine up to the city and that Peter would remain in his hotel room resting all day before the activities on the evenings of December 2 and 3. The first night, Peter's niece Sally Dobson Danforth and her husband, Senator John Danforth, hosted a cocktail party and dinner in the Senate reception rooms. Admirers and friends from all periods of Peter Taylor's life gathered to pay him tribute. Early in the evening, John Danforth led a tour of the Senate chambers and spoke of Senator Robert Taylor while standing at the desk that had been Taylor's eighty years before. Peter enjoyed all the family associations amid this gathering of friends, and appreciated anew the Federal grandeur of the Capitol. The next evening at the Folger Library, after Peter received the award, Senator Danforth read the story "Two Pilgrims." Afterward people stood in line to have the author sign copies of *The Oracle at Stoneleigh Court* and other of his works. One man was heard to say, "Can this pitiful old man be the same person that wrote this wonderful book?"[42]

Shortly before Christmas, the proofs of *In the Tennessee Country* arrived. Day after day, Peter and Mark Trainer labored over them, making corrections and answering queries. The process was taking so long that the move down to St. Augustine had to be delayed. The middle of January, Peter mailed the corrected proofs to Knopf and included a dedication to "Judith Jones and Mark Trainer without whose patience and persistence and encouragement this book of mine could never, ever have got itself written."[43]

Soon the Taylors were in Florida, taking walks and enjoying St. Augustine more than ever. Peter had told Wyatt Prunty that one attraction of the place was that, knowing no one, as he strolled he could eavesdrop on all sorts of interesting conversations. He described the residents wryly as "all just genteel old couples." He was continuing to dictate into the machine new passages of "The Brothers Taliaferro," though he was always afraid that he would push the wrong button and erase.[44]

In Florida visiting friends, Mark Trainer drove the Taylors back to Charlottesville in the middle of May. On the last day of the month, Peter collapsed from the effects of a stomach ulcer. While in the hospital, he suffered two mild strokes. As he had after Peter's initial stroke in 1986, Dick Crampton advised that Peter have surgery to clear the carotid artery in his neck. By the middle of June, Peter had decided against the surgery, reasoning that it was "better to have a few months than to go out next Tuesday." The beginning of July, he was moved to the Blue Ridge Rehabilitation Center. His right leg was still completely useless and his right hand could not control a pencil. On August 5, he came home. Eleanor had had the downstairs bathroom enlarged and turned the library into a bedroom. During the long period of hospitalization, she had read aloud to him all four volumes of *Phineas Finn*.[45]

Eleanor still had Mark Trainer come to the house regularly as much to give Peter something to occupy himself with as anything. Judith Jones had now responded to the manuscript of "The Brothers Taliaferro." It was, as Mark had felt, not really ready. Had Peter been in better health, he would have worked on it more before sending it out. "Novels are for rambling old men," he would sigh to Mark, but he still wanted to work on the manuscript. "All I can do anymore is write," he told Bob Wilson over the telephone, his voice, as Wilson characterized it, "a mixture of wonderment and woe."[46]

Knopf released *In the Tennessee Country* the first week in August. The "writing appears to be produced without any struggle and is so graceful and lucid one has the impression that it just *happened,* dropping from the heavens onto the page," wrote novelist Mary Flanagan in the *New York Times Book Review*. Then she qualified her praise: "My only quarrel with such mellowness, such flawless elegance, is that it is too beautiful and therefore, in places, a little dull." Such qualified response was also evidenced by Martha Duffy in *Time* and by the *Christian Science Monitor,* the review there headed "A Languid Narrator Spins a Southern Tale." Jonathan Yardley offered his usual appreciative reading in the pages of the *Washington Post Book World*, but perhaps the most positive and certainly the most sensitive review appeared in the Cleveland *Plain Dealer*. "Whatever your response to the book," Alicia Metcalf Miller wrote, "it is impossible not to feel strongly about it, because under an extravagantly bland exterior, it seethes with anger, failure, and pain." She concluded: "It is impossible to believe that anyone writing today except Taylor could so skillfully draw the willing reader into a story like this, in which decorum smothers tragedy, tragedy obliterates passion and cultivated blindness cancels, finally, even regret." Peter Taylor's response to the bundle of reviews was uncharacteristically mild. "I've been lucky not to have anybody scalp me," he said. "In my condition, I couldn't take it."[47]

He was failing. The middle of September, in response to my nervous, awkward query, "How are you?" over the phone, he answered in a measured way, "I'm still existing as a person, but that's about all I can say." But two weeks later he rallied as we talked, and soon he warmed to the tale of Mercer Taylor, his cousin who had vanished from Gibson County in 1921, a memory that he had treated first in his story "Demons." Friends were calling and coming from a distance for visits, people whose lives he had made richer. Eleanor and the therapist said that he was making progress, but he felt doubtful. Within two weeks, he had another stroke. His right side was completely paralyzed, and though he could hear, he could not speak. In a space of days, he went into a coma. On the night of November 2, 1994, Peter Taylor died.[48]

Three days later, a small group gathered on the Cumberland Plateau for the funeral service at All Saints' Chapel at Sewanee. Many friends lived far away, and even those in Nashville did not learn of the ceremony. But Tom White and Tommy Mitchell were there, and Steve Ross, and David Lynn had flown down to represent Kenyon. After the service, the group followed the priest carrying the ashes as he made his way to the Sewanee cemetery. We passed the grave of Allen Tate and the plot of the ninety-year-old Andrew Lytle, whose remains would lie there soon. A shovel was passed among the party with the family, and we each added a spade of dirt to the mound of the grave. As we left the place, I was remembering Peter's childish vision as he perched in the tree, looking down upon the little village he had just made and thinking of his grandfather recently dead and perhaps ascending to heaven. I knew that this was the perfect resting place for Peter Taylor. Like his grandfather, from this spot on the mountain of which he was so fond, he might survey "the whole of his beloved state of Tennessee."

Appendix: Genealogical Charts

The West Tennessee Taylors

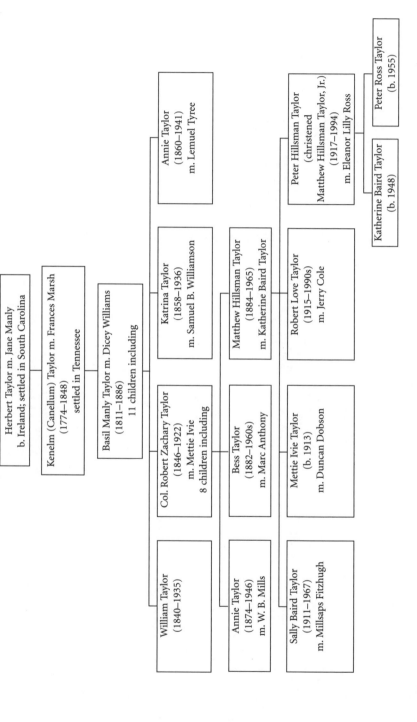

Herbert Taylor m. Jane Manly
b. Ireland; settled in South Carolina

Kenelm (Canellum) Taylor m. Frances Marsh
(1774–1848)
settled in Tennessee

Basil Manly Taylor m. Dicey Williams
(1811–1886)
11 children including

William Taylor
(1840–1935)

Col. Robert Zachary Taylor
(1846–1922)
m. Mettie Ivie
8 children including

Katrina Taylor
(1858–1936)
m. Samuel B. Williamson

Annie Taylor
(1860–1941)
m. Lemuel Tyree

Annie Taylor
(1874–1946)
m. W. B. Mills

Bess Taylor
(1882–1960s)
m. Marc Anthony

Matthew Hillsman Taylor
(1884–1965)
m. Katherine Baird Taylor

Sally Baird Taylor
(1911–1967)
m. Millsaps Fitzhugh

Mettie Ivie Taylor
(b. 1913)
m. Duncan Dobson

Robert Love Taylor
(1915–1990s)
m. Jerry Cole

Peter Hillsman Taylor
(christened
Matthew Hillsman Taylor, Jr.)
(1917–1994)
m. Eleanor Lilly Ross

Katherine Baird Taylor
(b. 1948)

Peter Ross Taylor
(b. 1955)

THE EAST TENNESSEE TAYLORS

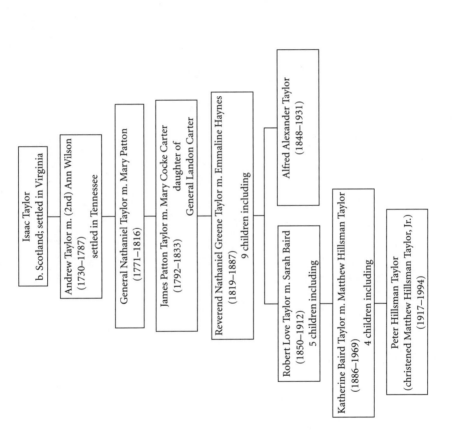

Isaac Taylor
b. Scotland; settled in Virginia

Andrew Taylor m. (2nd) Ann Wilson
(1730–1787)
settled in Tennessee

General Nathaniel Taylor m. Mary Patton
(1771–1816)

James Patton Taylor m. Mary Cocke Carter
(1792–1833)
daughter of
General Landon Carter

Reverend Nathaniel Greene Taylor m. Emmaline Haynes
(1819–1887)
9 children including

Alfred Alexander Taylor
(1848–1931)

Robert Love Taylor m. Sarah Baird
(1850–1912)
5 children including

Katherine Baird Taylor m. Matthew Hillsman Taylor
(1886–1969)
4 children including

Peter Hillsman Taylor
(christened Matthew Hillsman Taylor, Jr.)
(1917–1994)

Notes

ABBREVIATIONS USED

Books by Peter Taylor

ASTM   *A Summons to Memphis.* New York: Alfred A. Knopf, 1986.
CS   *The Collected Stories of Peter Taylor.* New York: Farrar, Straus and Giroux, 1969.
HF   *Happy Families Are All Alike.* New York: McDowell, Obolensky, 1959.
IMD   *In the Miro District and Other Stories.* New York: Alfred A. Knopf, 1977.
ITC   *In the Tennessee Country.* New York: Alfred A. Knopf, 1994.
LF   *A Long Fourth and Other Stories.* New York: Harcourt, Brace, 1948.
ML   *Miss Leonora When Last Seen and Fifteen Other Stories.* New York: Ivan Obolensky, 1964.
OF   *The Old Forest and Other Stories.* New York: Dial, 1985.
OSC   *The Oracle at Stoneleigh Court: Stories.* New York: Alfred A. Knopf, 1993.
Pres   *Presences: Seven Dramatic Places.* Boston: Houghton Mifflin, 1973.
SITM   *A Stand in the Mountains.* New York: Frederic C. Beil, 1985.
TDSL   *Tennessee Day in St. Louis.* New York: Random House, 1957.
WOM   *A Woman of Means.* New York: Harcourt, Brace, 1950.
WOT   *The Widows of Thornton.* New York: Harcourt, Brace, 1954.

Other Works Frequently Cited

CEOPT *Critical Essays on Peter Taylor,* ed. Hubert H. McAlexander. New York: G. K. Hall, 1993.

COPT *The Craft of Peter Taylor,* ed. C. Ralph Stephens and Lynda B. Salamon. Tuscaloosa: University of Alabama Press, 1995.

CWPT *Conversations with Peter Taylor,* ed. Hubert H. McAlexander. Jackson: University Press of Mississippi, 1987.

"Garland" "A Garland for Peter Taylor on His Sixtieth Birthday," *Shenandoah* 27 (winter 1977): 5–85.

Persons Frequently Cited

AT	Allen Tate
BT	Barbara Thompson
EH	Elizabeth Hardwick
ERT	Eleanor Ross Taylor
HHM	Hubert H. McAlexander
HT	Hillsman Taylor
JCR	John Crowe Ransom
JS	Jean Stafford
JT	John Thompson
JWB	J. William Broadway
KBT	Katherine Baird Taylor
KTT	Katherine Taylor Taylor
KW	Katharine White
MJ	Mary Jarrell
PT	Peter Taylor
RJ	Randall Jarrell
RL	Robert Lowell
RM	Robie Macauley
RPW	Robert Penn Warren
RT	Ross Taylor
SW	Stuart Wright
TW	Thomas J. White

CITATION OF INTERVIEWS AND LETTERS

Interviews are cited by name of the person interviewed and date: PT, 3 Sept. 1993.

Letters are cited by writer, recipient, date, and present location: RM to PT, 15 Mar. 1946, ERT.

Chapter 1: The Taylors

1. *Nashville Tennessean,* 9 Jan. 1908, p. 5; PT, "Tennessee Caravan," *Tennessee: A Homecoming* (Nashville: Third National, 1985), 63.

2. PT, 8 Aug. 1993; genealogical collection of Mrs. Frank Sanders, Johnson City, Tenn.; Samuel C. Williams, "Brigadier-General Nathaniel Taylor," *East Tennessee Historical Society Publications* 12 (1940): 28–44.

3. Williams, 42.

4. Zella Armstrong, *Notable Southern Families* (Baltimore: Genealogical Publishing, 1974), 2, 61–70.

5. *Sketches of Prominent Tennesseans* (1888; repr. Easley, S.C.: Southern Historical Press, 1978), 212–13, 564–65; John Trotwood Moore, ed., *Tennessee: The Volunteer State* (Chicago: S. J. Clarke, 1923), 2:147–48, 232–33.

6. *New York Times,* 1 Apr. 1912, p. 7.

7. *Life and Career of Senator Robert Love Taylor (Our Bob) by His Three Surviving Brothers* (Nashville: Bob Taylor Publishing, 1913), 104.

8. Dumas Malone, ed., *Dictionary of American Biography* (New York: Charles Scribner's Sons, 1936), 18:341–43.

9. Mrs. Frank Sanders, 20 June 1994.

10. *Life and Career,* 180–200.

11. *New York Times,* 1 Apr. 1912, p. 7; *Nashville Tennessean and Nashville American,* 2–6 Apr. 1912.

12. PT, 1 Sept. 1987; Mrs. Sanders, 20 June 1994; ERT, 11 Sept. 1995; PT, dedication to *CS.*

13. "Paul Flowers' Greenhouse," *Memphis Commercial Appeal,* 16 May 1963, p. 4.

14. PT, "Tennessee Caravan," 61–62.

15. PT, 13 Sept. 1994; Mrs. Evelyn Wade Harwood, 16 Aug. 1994; Mettie Taylor Dobson, 2 Aug. 1995.

16. Taylor genealogy, compiled by Jane Cobb circa 1985, copy in possession of Mrs. Merle Prunty, Athens, Ga.

17. W. P. Greene, ed., *Gibson County, Tennessee: A Series of Pen and Picture Sketches* (Nashville: Press of Gospel Advocate Publishing Co., 1901), 25–26; PT, "Tennessee Caravan," 60.

18. Forrest Hill Tyree, *A Tyree Genealogy* (Nashville: privately published, 1983), 105; obituary of Samuel B. Williamson, *Trenton Herald-Democrat,* 23 May 1902, p. 3; Mrs. Prunty, 6 July 1994; PT, 11 Sept. 1991.

19. Mrs. Harwood, 16 Aug. 1994; Mrs. Dobson, 7 Sept. 1995; Conrad Frederick Smith, "Our Home Town," *Trenton Herald-Register,* 18 May 1961, p. 5; Mrs. Evelyn Elder Sawyer, 29 Sept. 1994.

20. BT, "Interview with Peter Taylor," *CWPT,* 151–52.

21. Mrs. Dobson, 13 Sept. 1995.

22. PT to Mr. and Mrs. TW, [28 Jan. 1948], TW; BT, 141; ERT, 15 July 1996.

23. Smith, 5.

24. Obituary of Col. R. Z. Taylor, *Trenton Herald-Democrat,* 10 June 1922, p. 4; Hillsman Taylor, "The Night Riders of West Tennessee," *West Tennessee Historical Society Papers* 6 (1952): 77–86; PT, "Tennessee Caravan," 63–64.

25. Mrs. Dobson, 2 Aug. 1995; obituary of Col. R. Z. Taylor; PT, "Tennessee Caravan," 62; PT to Mr. and Mrs. TW, 28 Jan. 1948, TW.

26. Obituary of Hillsman Taylor, *Memphis Press-Scimitar,* 13 Nov. 1965, p. 12; "Paul Flowers' Greenhouse"; PT, "Tennessee Caravan," 62.

27. PT, 15 July 1993; PT, "Tennessee Caravan," 64–65.

Chapter 2: Nashville and St. Louis

1. Don H. Doyle, *Nashville in the New South, 1880–1930* (Knoxville: University of Tennessee Press, 1985), 212, 223–26.

2. PT, "Tennessee Caravan," *Tennessee: A Homecoming* (Nashville: Third National, 1985), 66.

3. PT, 6 May 1985; Mettie Taylor Dobson, 2 Aug. 1995.

4. PT to RM [Oct. 1941], Vanderbilt; Colonel Hensley Williams, 2 Oct. 1994.

5. PT to RPW, 9 Dec. [1947].

6. Grace Benedict Paine, 16 Oct. 1996; Maxwell Williams, 29 Nov. 1994.

7. Mrs. Dobson, 2 Aug. 1995; ERT 11 Nov. 1996.

8. Mrs. Dobson, 2 Aug. 1995; PT, *ASTM,* 44–45.

9. ERT, 11 Nov. 1996; John Berry McFerrin, *Caldwell and Company* (Nashville: Vanderbilt University Press, 1939, repr. 1967), 27. PT's most extensive treatment of his father's relationship with Caldwell is in *ASTM,* 158–69.

10. *New York Times,* 14 Jan. 1926, p. 34; PT, "Tennessee Caravan," 64.

11. McFerrin, 49–50.

12. Mrs. Dobson, 11 Aug. 1995; Julius K. Hunter, *Westmoreland and Portland Places: The History and Architecture of America's Premier Private Streets, 1888–1988* (Columbia: University of Missouri Press, 1988), 64–67.

13. Hunter, 71–72; "Society News," *St. Louis Post-Dispatch,* 12 Oct. 1930 and 20 Sept. 1931.

14. Mary Bartley, *St. Louis Lost* (St. Louis: Virginia Publishing Co., 1994), 143–44; Mrs. Dobson, 12 Nov. 1996.

15. PT, "Tennessee Caravan," 66; Mrs. Dobson, 13 Sept. 1995.

16. PT, 11 Aug. 1994.

17. PT, "Tennessee Caravan," 64–65; PT, 19 Oct. 1992.

18. Mrs. Dobson, 13 Sept. 1995.

19. PT, interview with BT, 11 Dec. 1981; Mrs. Dobson, 13 Sept. 1995; ERT, 11 Nov. 1996; PT, 2 Nov. 1993.

20. PT, 2 Nov. 1993; Mrs. Dobson, 2 Aug. 1995; BT, "Interview with Peter Taylor," *CWPT*, 140–41.

21. PT, 19 Oct. 1992, 2 Nov. 1993.

22. Hunter, 66; PT, 2 Nov. 1993.

23. PT, interview with JWB, 22 Oct. 1989; John Gunter, 5 Apr. 1995; Ashley Gray, 14 Nov. 1996.

24. Jackson Johnson Shinkle, 13 Nov. 1966; Mrs. Dobson, 13 Sept. 1995.

25. BT, "Interview with PT," 139–41.

26. John Gunter, 5 Apr. 1995; Ashley Gray, 14 Nov. 1996; Maxwell Williams, 29 Nov. 1994; Mrs. Dobson, 13 Sept. 1995; ERT, 7 Sept. 1995.

27. Doyle, 227; "Caldwell's Life Built Legend," *Nashville Tennessean,* 10 Oct. 1968, p. l; McFerrin, 134–36, 120; Maxwell Williams, 29 Nov. 1994.

28. *St. Louis Post-Dispatch,* 6–12 Oct. 1930.

29. Doyle, 220; McFerrin, 179–86, 239.

30. "Missouri State Life Voting Trust Sought," *St. Louis Post-Dispatch,* 9 Nov. 1931, p. 7A; ERT, 11 Nov. 1996.

31. "Taylor Will Leave Missouri State Life," *New York Times,* 2 Dec. 1931, p. 37. PT treats the Caldwell betrayal fictionally in both "Dean of Men" and *ASTM.*

32. PT, 5 May 1985.

33. PT, 6 Aug. 1993.

Chapter 3: Memphis

1. Mettie Taylor Dobson, 13 Sept. 1995; PT, "Tennessee Caravan," 62.

2. PT, 3 Apr. 1993; *Memphis 1937 Social Directory.*

3. PT, 10 Aug. and 3 Apr. 1993.

4. Felder Heflin, 2 Dec. 1993.

5. ERT, 4 Aug. 1995; *Memphis Commercial Appeal,* 18 Apr. 1933.

6. PT, 3 Apr. 1993; ERT to Linda Wertheim, 11 Mar. 1995, ERT.

7. Bruce Fulton, 24 Oct. 1995.

8. *Central High (Memphis, Tenn.) Warrior,* 21 Sept., 5 Oct., 29 Nov. 1933; Felder Heflin, 6 Oct. 1995.

9. Felder Heflin, 2 Dec. 1993; Bruce Fulton, 24 Oct. 1995; Heflin, 5 Oct. 1995.

10. *Memphis Commercial Appeal,* 15 Oct. 1933; Ann Watkins Boatner Grove, 3 Sept. 1993; PT, 14 Nov. 1992.

11. PT, 8 Aug. and 3 Apr. 1993; ERT, 8 Sept. 1995.

12. TW, 22 Oct. 1996; *Warrior,* 2 Nov. 1933.

13. PT, interview with JWB, 13 Aug. 1987.

14. PT, Travel Diary, 29 May to 18 July 1935, ERT; PT, interview by JWB.

15. PT, 8 Aug. 1993; ERT to HHM, 30 Sept. 1994, HHM.

16. PT, 3 July 1992.

17. HHM, "A Composite Conversation with PT," *CWPT,* 116.

18. PT, 3 July 1992; AT, "Peter Taylor," "Garland," 10; PT, "Reminiscences," *The Fugitives, the Agrarians, and Other Twentieth Century Southern Writers* (Charlottesville: Alderman Library, 1985), 17.

19. Ann Waldron, *Close Connections: Caroline Gordon and the Southern Renaissance* (New York: G. P. Putnam's Sons, 1987), 158.

20. PT to RPW, 9 Dec.[1947], Yale; PT, 3 July 1992.

21. Stephen Goodwin, "An Interview with Peter Taylor," *CWPT,* 7.

22. The story appeared in *River* 1 (Mar. 1937): 4–8.

23. *River* 1 (Apr. 1937): 50–54.

24. PT to RPW, 9 Dec. [1947], Yale; PT, "Reminiscences," 17–18.

Chapter 4: Vanderbilt and the Return Home

1. PT, "Reminiscences," *The Fugitives, the Agrarians and Other Twentieth Century Southern Writers* (Charlottesville: Alderman Library, University of Virginia, 1985), 18.

2. HHM, "A Composite Conversation with PT," *CWPT,* 125; AT, *Memoirs and Opinions* (Chicago: Swallow Press, 1975), 40; PT, "Reminiscences," 18.

3. Opie Craig Handly, 3 Dec. 1994; ERT, 6 Dec. 1994.

4. ERT, 6 Dec. 1995; Caroline Bartholomew, "Artist's Influence Shown in Nashvillian's Works," undated clipping from *Nashville Banner.*

5. Felder Heflin, 2 Dec. 1993; PT, 5 Sept. 1989.

6. Jane Bagley Alexander, 18 Oct. 1994; Felder Heflin, 2 Dec. 1993.

7. PT, "Randall Jarrell," in *Randall Jarrell, 1914–1965,* ed. Robert Lowell, Peter Taylor, and Robert Penn Warren (New York: Farrar, Straus and Giroux, 1967), 242; ERT, 3 July 1997; JCR, in *RJ,* 155; RL, in *RJ,* 101–102; PT, in *RJ,* 242; Felder Heflin, 6 Oct. 1995.

8. RPW to PT, 21 Sept. 1936, ERT; PT, 16 Feb. 1988.

9. Thomas Daniel Young, *Gentleman in a Dustcoat: A Biography of John Crowe Ransom* (Baton Rouge: Louisiana State University Press, 1976), 272–87.

10. PT, 5 Sept. 1989.

11. Mrs. Frank Sanders, 20 June 1994; ERT, 15 Sept. 1995.

12. Mrs. R. L. Taylor of Knoxville, 21 June 1994.

13. Louise St. John Taylor, 20 June 1994.

14. Undated clipping [spring 1936] in Robert D. McCallum file at University of Memphis; Virginia Jett McCallum, 23 Oct. 1995; TW to PT, 8 Jan. 1943, ERT; McCallum, 3 Aug. 1995; Katherine Farnsworth Cavender, 25 Oct. 1995.

15. Gertrude Smith Fulton, 7 Sept. 1995.

16. ERT, 20 June 1995; Tommy Mitchell, 17 July 1995; Gertrude Smith Fulton, 24 Oct. 1995.

17. PT, 5 Sept. 1989 and 6 Oct. 1993.

18. Gertrude Smith Fulton, 7 Sept. 1995; Tommy Mitchell, 17 July 1995.

19. Annie Rose Wallace Buchman, 3 Sept. 1993; ERT, 8 Sept. 1995; PT to TW, 7 July 1945 and 4 Nov. 1949, TW.

20. BT, "Interview with PT," *CWPT*, 150.

21. Bruce and Gertrude Smith Fulton, 24 Oct. 1995; Tommy Mitchell, 17 July 1995.

22. Alex A. Sternberter to PT, 6 Oct. 1986, ERT; Felder Heflin, 2 Dec. 1993; Gertrude Smith Fulton, 27 Oct. 1995.

23. Tommy Mitchell, 17 July 1995; JCR to PT, 2 May and 13 May 1938, Vanderbilt; David McDowell, "A Year without Peter," "Garland," 36.

24. BT, "Interview with PT," 148; JWB, "A Conversation with PT," *CWPT*, 79.

25. Maureen Andrews, "A Psychoanalytic Appreciation of Peter Taylor's 'A Spinster's Tale' " and Roland Sodowsky and Gargi Roysircar Sodowsky, "Determined Failure, Self-Styled Success: Two Views of Betsy in Peter Taylor's 'Spinster's Tale,' " both repr. in *CEOPT*.

26. Virginia Jett McCallum, 3 Aug. 1995.

Chapter 5: Kenyon

1. JT, 16 Nov. 1994; Thomas E. Mitchell, 17 July 1995; RM, 17 June 1993.

2. Ian Hamilton, in *Robert Lowell: A Biography* (New York: Random House, 1982), drew much of his treatment of Douglass House from interviews with PT.

3. See Hamilton, 44–56; Paul Mariani, *Lost Puritan: A Life of Robert Lowell* (New York: W. W. Norton, 1994), 60–76; Helen Ransom Forman, 4 Sept. 1996.

4. JT, 16 Nov. 1994; Hamilton, 28–29; Frank Parker, 16 June 1993.

5. Elizabeth Hardwick, 19 Nov. 1994; Robert Wilson, "Peter Taylor Remembers Robert Lowell," in *CWPT*, 39; Mieke H. Bomann, "Once More, with Feeling: Peter Taylor Summons Up That Southern Mystique," *Kenyon College Alumni Bulletin*, Sept. 1987, p. 18; Mariani, 74; PT, "Robert Lowell," unfinished and undated manuscript, Vanderbilt; JT, quoted in Hamilton, 56.

6. Hamilton, 54–55; PT, "1939," *CS*, 335; Hamilton, 56.

7. Virginia Jett McCallum, 3 Aug. and 23 Oct. 1995; PT, 22 May 1985.

8. The exchange between Charlotte Lowell and Merrill Moore is preserved in six

documents in the RL Papers, Harry B. Ransom Humanities Research Center, University of Texas.

9. PT, 22 May 1985; RM, "Kenyon in the Age of Ransom," Honors Day Address, 15 Apr. 1986, Kenyon Library; JT, 16 Nov. 1994.

10. William H. Pritchard, *Randall Jarrell: A Literary Life* (New York: Farrar, Straus and Giroux, 1990), 50–52; Hamilton, 58; Mariani, 69; PT, "Randall Jarrell," in *Randall Jarrell, 1914–1965,* ed. RL, PT, and RPW (New York, Farrar, Straus and Giroux, 1967), 245–46.

11. JT, 16 Nov. 1994; Helen Ransom Forman, 4 Sept. 1996.

12. PT, "Reminiscences," *The Fugitives, the Agrarians and Other Twentieth Century Southern Writers* (Charlottesville: Alderman Library, University of Virginia, 1985), 18–20; RM, quoted in Bomann, 16; RM, "Kenyon in the Age of Ransom," 5; RL, "John Ransom's Conversation," *Sewanee Review* 55 (July–Sept. 1948): 375.

13. BT, "Interview with PT," *CWPT*, 147; PT to RPW, 9 Dec. [1947], Yale.

14. PT contributed to twelve of the sixteen issues of *Hika* published while he was at Kenyon. J. William Broadway has graciously allowed me access to the complete run for these years, a part of his Peter Taylor collection. Stuart Wright's *PT: A Descriptive Bibliography, 1934–87* (Charlottesville: University Press of Virginia, 1988) contains complete bibliographical information on the *Hika* contributions.

15. This poem is found in the PT Papers, Vanderbilt.

16. *Kenyon Review* 1, no. 3 (summer 1939): 308.

17. PT, 20 June 1987.

18. PT to RM, 27 June 1939, Vanderbilt.

19. PT to RM, 27 June 1939, Vanderbilt; Ann Waldron, *Close Connections: Caroline Gordon and the Southern Renaissance* (New York: G. P. Putnam's Sons, 1987), 185.

20. PT to RM, undated [summer 1939], Vanderbilt.

21. PT to RM, 15 Aug. and 16 Aug. 1939, Vanderbilt.

22. JT, 16 Nov. 1994; Hamilton, 62–73; David Roberts, *Jean Stafford: A Biography* (Boston: Little, Brown, 1988), 173–74.

23. AT to PT, 8 Dec. 1939, Vanderbilt; ERT, 4 Dec. 1995.

24. ERT, 11 Nov. 1996; BT, "Interview with PT," 149; Stephen Goodwin, "An Interview with PT," *CWPT*, 9.

25. ERT, 11 Nov. 1996; Roberts, 186; PT, "For the School Boys," *Hika* 6 (Feb. 1940): 10.

Chapter 6: Limbo

1. PT to Nadine Lenti Parker, 4 June 1940, University of Memphis.

2. PT, quoted in Ian Hamilton, *Robert Lowell: A Biography* (New York: Random

House, 1982), 74; PT, "Robert Trail [*sic*] Spence Lowell, 1917–1977," *Ploughshares* 5 (1979): 79–81; Henry Adams, *The Education of Henry Adams* (Boston: Houghton Mifflin, 1961), 57.

3. Eileen Simpson, *Poets in Their Youth* (Boston: Little, Brown, 1988), 120; Robert Wilson, "Peter Taylor Remembers Robert Lowell," *CWPT*, 36; Bruce Fulton, 24 Oct. 1995.

4. Mary Jane Peeples Ray, 27 Mar. 1993; Virginia Jett McCallum, 23 Oct. 1995.

5. PT to Nadine Lenti Parker, 2 Aug. 1940, University of Memphis; PT to RM [Aug. 1940], Vanderbilt; Felder Heflin, 2 Dec. 1993; Gertrude Smith Fulton, 27 Oct. 1995.

6. PT to RM, 9 Dec. [1940], Vanderbilt; Sarah Booth White, 27 Mar. 1993; ERT, 2 Nov. 1995.

7. PT to RM [Aug. 1940], Vanderbilt; Stephen Goodwin, "An Interview with Peter Taylor," *CWPT*, 11; RM to PT, 2 May 1941, Vanderbilt.

8. PT to RM [Aug. 1940]; John Nerber to PT, 30 July 1940—both Vanderbilt.

9. PT to RM [Sept. 1940], Vanderbilt.

10. Robert Bechtold Heilman, *The Southern Connection* (Baton Rouge: Louisiana State University Press, 1991), 1–12; Cleanth Brooks, 28 May 1993; Thomas W. Cutrer, *Parnassus on the Mississippi* (Baton Rouge: Louisiana State University Press, 1984), 239–40; Katherine Anne Porter to Albert Erskine, 27 Oct. 1940, University of Maryland.

11. PT, "Reminiscences," *The Fugitives, the Agrarians and Other Twentieth Century Southern Writers* (Charlottesville: Alderman Library, University of Virginia, 1985), 20–21.

12. RL to RM, n.d., quoted in Hamilton, 76; Joseph Blotner, *Robert Penn Warren: A Biography* (New York: Random House, 1997), 157; John Palmer, quoted in Blotner, 157.

13. PT to RM, 9 Dec. [1940], Vanderbilt; PT, quoted in David Roberts, *Jean Stafford: A Biography* (Boston: Little, Brown, 1988), 191.

14. PT to RPW, 9 Dec. [1947], Yale; ERT, 6 Nov. 1997.

15. JS to James Robert Hightower, 21 June 1940, quoted in Ann Hulbert, *The Interior Castle: The Art and Life of Jean Stafford* (New York: Alfred A. Knopf, 1992), 112; PT to Nadine Lenti Parker, 25 Oct. 1940, University of Memphis; PT to RM, 13 Nov. [1940], Vanderbilt.

16. PT to RPW, 12 Mar. 1969, Yale; RPW, "Two Peters: Memory and Opinion," "Garland," 8; PT to RM, 9 Dec. 1940 and [Jan. 1941], Vanderbilt.

17. PT to RM, 13 Nov. [1940], Vanderbilt.

18. PT to AT, 26 Jan. 1941, Princeton; PT, quoted in Roberts, 194; ERT, 6 Nov. 1997; JS to James Robert Hightower, 31 Oct. 1940, quoted in Hulbert, 115; JT, 16 Nov. 1994.

19. PT to Nadine Lenti Parker, 22 Mar. [1941], University of Memphis; PT to RM, [Mar. 1941] and 8 Apr. 1941, Vanderbilt.

20. PT to AT 26 Jan. 1941, Princeton; PT to Nadine Lenti Parker, 14 Feb. 1941, University of Memphis.

21. JCR to PT, 22 Mar. 1941; AT to PT, 9 Jan. 1941; RPW to PT, 4 Mar. 1941 and undated; Bud Southard to PT, 30 Apr. [1941]—all Vanderbilt; PT to Nadine Lenti Parker, 22 Mar. 1941, University of Memphis.

22. RPW, "Two Peters," 9; PT to RM, 8 Apr. 1941, Vanderbilt.

23. PT to RM, 8 Apr. 1941, and undated [mid-May 1941]; Nadine Lenti Parker to PT, 3 July 1945—all Vanderbilt.

24. PT to Nadine Lenti Parker, 10 June 1941, University of Memphis; PT to JS, Sunday night [Sept. 1941], Colorado; PT to HT and KTT, 6 June 1941, Vanderbilt.

25. PT to RM, 18 July 1941, Vanderbilt.

26. PT to JS, 18 Aug. [1941], Colorado; PT to RM, 14 Sept. 1941, Vanderbilt.

27. PT to RM, 14 Sept. 1941, Vanderbilt; Katherine Farnsworth Cavender, 25 Oct. 1995; PT to RM, 11 Aug. 1941, 8 Oct. 1941, and 26 Nov. 1941, Vanderbilt.

28. PT to RM, 26 Nov. 1941, Vanderbilt; PT to JS, 7 Dec. 1941, Colorado.

29. PT to JS, 18 Dec. [1941], Colorado.

30. PT to JS, [Feb. 1942], Colorado; PT to HT, Thursday [Mar. 1942], Vanderbilt; Susan Thompson Peschka to PT, 18 Feb. 1943, Vanderbilt; unsigned letter from the *New Yorker* to PT, 18 Dec. 1941, *New Yorker* Records, New York Public Library.

31. PT to RM, 31 Mar. 1942, Vanderbilt.

32. PT to Nadine Lenti Parker, 29 July 1942, University of Memphis.

33. PT to RM, 22 Apr. [1942], Vanderbilt; PT to JS, Thursday [Aug. 1942], Colorado.

34. PT to JS, 28 June 1942, Colorado; TW to PT, 12 Mar. and 31 Mar. 1943, ERT; PT to TW, 3 Mar. 1943, TW.

35. Unsigned letter from *New Yorker* to PT, 1 Apr. 1942; PT to William Maxwell, 20 Apr. [1943]; unsigned letter from the *New Yorker* to PT, 30 Apr. 1943—all New York Public Library. PT to RM [early fall 1942], Vanderbilt.

36. PT to Nadine Lenti Parker, 27 Apr. 1942, University of Memphis; PT to RM, 22 Apr. [1942], and [fall 1942], Vanderbilt.

37. Roberts, 206–207; PT to TW, 7 Apr. 1943, TW.

38. AT to ER, 23 Dec. 1939, and CG to ERT [Aug. 1942], Vanderbilt.

39. ER to Mrs. Fred Ross, 1 Jan. 1943, ERT.

Chapter 7: Marriage and War

1. ER to Mrs. Fred Ross, 30 Apr. 1943, ERT; Mrs. Frank Donelson, 18 July 1995.

2. ERT, 6 Dec. 1995.

3. PT to JS, 20 May 1943, Colorado; JS to PT, undated [May 1943], Vanderbilt.

4. PT to JS, 24 May 1943, Colorado; PT to KTT, 26 May 1943 and to HT, 26 May 1943, both Vanderbilt; ERT, 4 Aug. 1995.

5. RL to PT 28 May 1943; AT to ERT, 28 May 1943; JS to ERT, 28 May 1943; CG to ERT, undated; PT to KTT, 30 May 1943—all Vanderbilt; ERT to JS, 30 May 1943, Colorado.

6. Gideon Pillow Fryer, 3 Apr. 1998; "Sergt. Peter H. Taylor Weds Eleanor Ross at Monteagle," *Memphis Commercial Appeal,* 8 June 1943; Dannye Romine Powell, "An Interview with Peter and Eleanor Ross Taylor," *Mississippi Review* 20 (1991): 42.

7. PT to KTT, 7 June 1943, Vanderbilt; Powell, 42; ERT, "Love Knows," *New and Selected Poems* (Winston-Salem: Stuart Wright, 1983), 17.

8. PT to KTT, 7 June and 17 June 1943, Vanderbilt.

9. PT to TW, 16 June 1943, TW; ERT to JS, 8 June 1943, Colorado.

10. *OF,* 242–43.

11. PT to JS, 25 July 1943, Colorado; ERT to Jean Ross, 15 July 1943, ERT; PT to TW, 5 Aug. 1943, TW.

12. Caroline Gordon to ERT, Vanderbilt; PT to JS, 6 Sept. [1943], Colorado; JS to ERT and PT [Aug. 1943], Vanderbilt; Ian Hamilton, *Robert Lowell: A Biography* (New York: Random House, 1982), 86–91; PT to JS, 7 Oct. 1942, Colorado.

13. PT to Sarah Booth White, 17 Nov. [1943] and PT to TW, 4 Nov. [1949], both TW.

14. ERT to KTT, 28 Oct. 1943, Vanderbilt; PT to JS, 30 Nov. [1943] and 21 Dec. 1943, Colorado; ERT, unpublished mss, ERT; PT to HT and KTT, 9 Jan. [1944], Vanderbilt; PT to JS, undated, Colorado.

15. PT to KTT, 21 Jan. 1944, Vanderbilt; Gideon Pillow Fryer, 3 Apr. 1998; PT to JS, 18 Feb. 1944, Colorado; PT to Nadine Lenti Parker, 9 Feb. 1944, University of Memphis.

16. PT to JS, 17 Feb. [1944], Colorado; ERT mss, 2.

17. ERT to KTT, 25 Feb. 1944, Vanderbilt; ERT mss, 1; ERT to KTT, 22 Mar. 1944, Vanderbilt.

18. Richard Hill to ERT, 16 Dec. 1994, ERT; ERT to HHM, 1 May 1998.

19. PT to JS, 26 Mar. 1944 and 23 May 1944, Colorado; ERT to KTT, 9 May [1944], Vanderbilt; PT, 10 Aug. 1993.

20. PT to JS, 23 May 1944, Colorado; PT to ERT, 3 Apr. 1944, ERT.

21. Elizabeth Hardwick, "Locations within Locations," *COPT,* 25.

22. PT to JS, 23 May 1944, Colorado.

23. PT to ERT, 8 Apr. 1944 and 17 May 1944, ERT; PT, 10 Aug. 1993.

24. PT to ERT, 21 May and 13 June 1944, ERT.

25. PT to HT and KTT, 6 June and 15 July, 1944; ERT to HT and KTT, 23 June 1944—all Vanderbilt.

26. ERT to KTT, 8 July 1944, Vanderbilt; PT to Nadine Lenti Parker, 22 June 1944, University of Memphis; PT to TW, 22 June 1944, TW; PT to JS, 29 Aug. 1944, Colorado.

27. ERT to KTT, 9 Oct. 1944, PT to HT and KTT, 28 Sept. 1944, Vanderbilt; PT to ERT, 18 Nov. and 17 Dec. 1944, ERT.

28. PT to KTT, 3 Jan. 194[5], Vanderbilt; William Eason, 21 Oct. 1994; ERT, 20 May 1998; PT to ERT, 31 Dec. 1944, ERT.

29. PT to JS, 9 Feb. 1944 and ERT to JS, n.d. [Jan. 1945], both Colorado.

30. PT to HT, 10 May 1945, Vanderbilt; PT to Nadine Lenti Parker, 11 June 1945, University of Memphis; PT to ERT, 30 Aug. 1945, ERT.

31. *OF,* 180; PT to TW, 22 June 1944, TW.

32. PT to JS, 21 May 1945, Colorado.

33. PT to HT, 8 Aug. [1945], and PT to RM, 15 Aug. [1945], both Vanderbilt. For an Agrarian reading of Taylor's work, see Walter Sullivan, "The Last Agrarian: Peter Taylor Early and Late," *Sewanee Review* 99 (spring 1987): 308–17; for a Spenglerian reading of "A Long Fourth," see Albert J. Griffith, *Peter Taylor,* rev. ed. (Boston: Twyane Publishers, 1990), 31–35.

34. PT to JS, 4 June [1944], Colorado; *OF,* 209.

35. PT to KTT, 21 Jan. and 23 Mar. 1944, Vanderbilt.

36. PT to HT and KTT, 31 Aug. [1944]; PT to HT 23 Nov. [1944]; HT to PT, 10 June 1945—all Vanderbilt.

37. ERT to KTT, 15 Apr. 1945, and PT to HT, 2 Aug. 1945, Vanderbilt.

38. PT to ERT, 30 Aug. 1945, ERT.

39. PT to ERT, 17 Sept. and 18 Sept. 1945, ERT; PT to Nadine and Rogers Parker, 24 Sept. [1945], University of Memphis; PT to JS, 10 Oct. 1945, Colorado.

40. PT to KTT, 6 Oct. 1945, and PT to RM, 19 Oct. 1945, Vanderbilt.

41. AT to PT, 23 July 1945, Vanderbilt; ERT to JS, 15 Aug. [1945], Colorado; PT to HT, 3 Aug. [1945], Vanderbilt; PT to ERT, 1 Dec. 1945, ERT.

Chapter 8: Starting Out in the Forties

1. ERT, 4 June 1998; PT to RL and JS, 28 Dec. [1945], Colorado.

2. KBT, 1 May 1998; PT to JS, 5 Feb. 1946, Colorado.

3. PT to RL and JS, 28 Dec. [1945] and to JS, 5 Feb. 1946, both Colorado; ERT, 4 June 1998.

4. PT, 28 June 1986; Ann Waldron, *Close Connections: Caroline Gordon and the Southern Renaissance* (New York: G. P. Putnam's Sons, 1987), 238–48.

5. PT to JS, 8 Mar. 1946, Colorado; PT to RPW, 2 Apr. 1946, Yale.

6. PT to JS, 7 Apr. 1946, Colorado; PT to Caroline Gordon, 14 Apr. 1946, Princeton.

7. ERT, 4 June 1998 and 28 Aug. 1996.

8. PT, "Randall Jarrell," in *Randall Jarrell, 1914–1965,* ed. Robert Lowell, Peter Taylor, and Robert Penn Warren (New York: Farrar, Straus and Giroux, 1967), 246; JT, 16 Nov. 1994.

9. JT, 16 Nov. 1994.

10. ERT, 28 Aug. 1996, ERT to HHM, 15 July 1997; JT, 16 Nov. 1994.

11. PT to RPW, 1 July 1946, Yale; ERT to JS, undated, Colorado.

12. PT to HT, 3 Sept. 1945, Vanderbilt; PT to JS, 23 Apr. 1946, Colorado.

13. RT to RM, 17 July [1946], Virginia; PT to JS, 30 July [1946], Colorado; RL to PT, 16 Aug. 1946 and 19 Aug. 1946, Vanderbilt.

14. JS to PT and ERT, 6 Nov. 1946, and RL to PT, 18 Nov. 1946, both Vanderbilt; PT to RL, 23 Dec. [1946], Harvard; RL to PT, 7 Dec. 1946 and 27 Dec. 1946, Vanderbilt; PT to RL, 2 Jan. 1947, Harvard.

15. PT to RL, 9 Oct. [1946], Harvard; PT to RPW, 26 Oct. [1946], Yale; PT to JS, 23 Dec. [1946], Colorado; HT to PT, 19 Dec. 1946, ERT; PT to RL, 15 Jan. [1947], Harvard.

16. PT to JS, 2 Feb. [1947], Colorado.

17. PT to RM, 13 Feb. 1947, Virginia; RJ to PT and ERT, 20 Mar. 1947, Vanderbilt; Robert Giroux, 13 Oct. 1994.

18. PT to RM, 18 Apr. 1947, Virginia.

19. PT to JS, 22 Apr. [1947], Colorado; Robert Giroux to PT, 8 May and 14 May 1947, ERT; PT to RL, Saturday [June 1947], Harvard.

20. PT to RL, 12 May [1947], Harvard.

21. PT to JS, 9 June [1947], Colorado; HT to PT, 30 June 1947, Vanderbilt; PT to JS, 27 July [1947], Colorado; John Thompson to PT, 6 Sept. 1947, Vanderbilt; PT to JS, 18 Sept. [1947], Colorado.

22. PT to TW, 20 Dec. [1947], TW; ERT, 5 Dec. 1995 and 9 July 1998; ERT, "Greensboro Days," *Randall Jarrell, 1914–1965,* ed. Robert Lowell, Peter Taylor, and Robert Penn Warren (New York: Farrar, Straus and Giroux, 1967), 234–37.

23. AT to PT, 28 Oct. 1946 and PT to AT, 3 Nov. [1947], both Princeton; AT to PT, 24 Nov. 1947, Vanderbilt.

24. RM, 17 June 1993; PT to TW, 20 Dec. 1947, TW; PT to JS, 2 Jan. [1948], Colorado.

25. PT to TW, 28 Jan. 1948, TW.

26. PT to TW, 6 Nov. 1947, TW; HT to PT, 10 Mar. 1948, ERT.

27. PT to RM, 11 Dec. 1947, Virginia; PT to JS, 20 Dec. [1947], Colorado; RPW, "Introduction to *A Long Fourth and Other Stories,* rep. in *CEOPT,* 73–76.

28. *New York Times,* 4 Mar. 1948, p. 6; *New Yorker,* 3 Mar. 1948, p. 124; *New Republic,* 8 Mar. 1948, p. 26; *New York Herald Tribune Books,* 14 Mar. 1948, p. 5; *Common-*

weal, 25 July 1948, p. 262; *New York Times Book Review,* 21 Mar. 1948, p. 6; *Saturday Review,* 27 Mar. 1948, pp. 17–18; HT to PT, 3 Mar. 1948, ERT.

29. PT to RL, 28 June [1948], Harvard; Elizabeth Hardwick, "Fiction Chronicle," *Partisan Review,* June 1948, p. 705.

30. PT to JS, 12 Nov. 1947, Colorado; PT to RL, 17 Dec. [1947] and 28 Feb. [1948], Harvard; PT to TW, 20 Apr. 1948, TW; PT to JS, 15 Apr. [1948] and 24 Mar. [1948], Colorado; PT to RL, Sunday night [May 1948], Harvard.

31. PT to JS, 17 June [1948], Colorado; Donald Justice to PT, 29 Aug. 1994, ERT; TW, 25 Oct. 1995; TW to PT, 3 Aug. 1948, TW; PT to RPW, 23 July [1948], Yale; PT to RL, 10 Aug. [1948], Harvard.

32. KW to PT, 2 Apr. 1948; Robert Giroux to KW, 24 June 1948; KW to Robert Giroux, 2 July 1948; PT to KW to 15 July 1948; KW to PT, 4 Aug. 1948—all *New Yorker* Records, New York Public Library.

33. KW to PT, 23 Aug. 1948, New York Public Library; PT to JS, 27 Aug. [1948], Colorado.

Chapter 9: Bloomington and Hillsborough

1. PT to Mrs. John Kirby-Smith, 29 Mar. 1967, in her possession.

2. PT to RL, Sunday night [Sept. 1948], Saturday night [Jan. 1948], 29 Aug. [1948], all Harvard.

3. PT to RL, 25 Sept. [1948], Harvard; PT to JS, 3 Oct. [1948], Colorado.

4. PT to RM, 6 Nov. [1948], Vanderbilt; Marc Friedlaender to PT, 24 Nov. 1948, Virginia.

5. RJ to PT, 18 Apr. 1949, Vanderbilt; PT to JS, 14 Jan. [1949], Colorado; PT to TW, 14 Feb. 1949, TW.

6. PT to RL, 18 Oct. [1948] and 1 Jan. 1949, Harvard; Ian Hamilton, *Robert Lowell: A Biography* (New York: Random House, 1982), 138–55; JT to PT, 29 Mar. 1949, ERT.

7. BT, "Interview with PT," in *CWPT,* 152–53.

8. Quoted in Hamilton, 156, 158.

9. ERT, 20 June 1995; JT to PT, 9 Apr. 1949, ERT; AT to PT, 10 Apr. 1949, Vanderbilt; PT to RL, 20 Apr. 1949, Harvard.

10. PT to RL, 30 June 1949, Harvard; PT to JS, 18 July [1949], Colorado; PT to Russell Noyes, 9 Aug. 1949, ERT.

11. PT to JS, Monday [fall 1949], Colorado; PT to RL, 11 Oct. [1948] and 14 Sept. [1949], Harvard; JT to PT, 15 Sept. 1949, Vanderbilt.

12. PT to JS, 14 Sept. [1949] and Tuesday [Oct. 1949], Colorado; PT to RL, 14 Sept. [1949], Harvard.

13. ERT, 20 June 1995; AT to PT, 18 Jan. 1946, Vanderbilt; Robert Giroux to PT,

20 Apr. 1948, ERT; PT to KW, 18 Jan. 1949, *New Yorker* Records, New York Public Library.

14. Robert Giroux to PT, 5 Aug. 1949, Virginia; Robert Giroux to PT, 4 Nov. 1949, ERT.

15. Evelyn Eaton, "Stepmomism," *Saturday Review*, 27 Mar. 1948, pp. 17–18; anonymous review in *New Yorker*, 20 May 1950, p. 13; Coleman Rosenberger, "Family in Flux," *New York Herald Tribune Books*, 21 May 1950, p. 10; "As a Boy Grows Older," *Time*, 15 May 1950, p. 111; James Stern, "The Power of Charm," *New Republic*, 26 June 1950, p. 20; Robert Kee, *New Statesman and Nation*, 2 Dec. 1950, p. 566; George Miles, *Commonweal*, 23 June 1950, p. 276.

16. RPW, "Father and Son," *New York Times Book Review*, 11 June 1950, p. 8; Thomas Wilcox, "A Novelist of Means," *Sewanee Review* 59 (winter 1951): 152.

17. PT to JS, 18 Apr. [1947], Colorado.

18. PT to JS, 24 Mar. [1948] and 13 Nov. [1948], Colorado; RPW, "Two Peters: Memory and Opinion," "Garland," 8. Only in two later letters does Peter Taylor specify which works of anthropology he has read—Margaret Mead's *Male and Female* (PT to JT, 19 Feb. 1950, JT) and A. L. Kroeber's basic text *Anthropology*, published in 1923, which he no doubt read in the 1948 revision (PT to JT, 30 Nov. 1950, JT).

19. PT to KW, 5 July 1949, *New Yorker* Records, New York Public Library.

20. Simone Vauthier, "PT's 'Porte Cochère': The Geometry of Generation," in *CEOPT*, 162–79.

21. KW to PT, 13 Sept. 1949 and 21 Oct. 1949, New York Public; PT, 5 May 1985.

22. PT to TW, 4 Nov. 1949, TW.

23. JWB, "A Conversation with PT," in *CWPT*, 79; BT, "Interview with PT," 156; PT, 11 Sept. 1991; PT to RL, 30 Apr. [1950], Harvard.

24. PT to JS, 5 Mar. [1950], Colorado; PT to RL, 20 Mar. [1950] and 20 Apr. [1950], Harvard; ERT to HT and KTT, 21 Apr. [1950], Vanderbilt.

25. TW to PT, 23 Mar. 1950 and 19 July [1950], ERT; JT to PT, 7 June 1950, Vanderbilt.

26. PT to RL and EH, 29 Dec. 1950, Harvard; ERT, 20 June 1995.

27. PT to RM, 13 Jan. 1951, Vanderbilt; PT to RL, 2 May 1951, Harvard; ERT, 5 Dec. 1997; PT, 8 Apr. 1985 and 10 July 1993; PT to RL, 30 Apr. [1950], Harvard.

28. PT to JS, 15 Oct. [1950], Colorado; KW to PT, 7 Dec. 1950 and 15 Oct. 1950, New York Public Library.

29. PT to KW, 15 Oct. 1950, New York Public Library; PT to RL and EH, 29 Dec. [1950], and RM to RL and EH, 3 Jan. 1951, Harvard.

30. "Part of Memphis May Come Alive in Next Novel by Peter Taylor," *Memphis Press-Scimitar*, 20 Oct. 1950, p. 18.

31. PT to RL, undated [Feb. 1951], Harvard.

32. PT to RL, undated [Feb. 1951], Harvard.

33. ERT to HT and KTT, 29 Mar. 1951, Vanderbilt; PT to RL, undated [Feb. 1951], Harvard.

34. PT to RL and EH, undated [May 1951], Harvard; RJ to Mary Von Schrader, [Aug. 1951], in *Randall Jarrell's Letters: An Autobiographical and Literary Selection*, ed. Mary Jarrell (Boston: Houghton Mifflin, 1985), 257–58.

35. PT to RL, 21 Oct. [1951] and 13 Dec. [1951], Harvard; PT to KW, 25 June 1951 and 18 July 1951, New York Public Library.

36. PT to JS, 27 Dec. [1951], Colorado.

37. PT to RL and EH, 28 Jan. 1952, Harvard; RM, 17 June 1993; PT to RL and EH, 2 Apr. [1952], Harvard.

38. PT to RL and EH, 2 Apr. [1952], and PT to RL, 1 May 1952, both Harvard.

39. PT to RL, 1 May 1952, Harvard; drafts of PT to Gordon Chalmers, 15 Apr. 1952, and PT to Dean Hurley, 14 May 1952, both ERT.

40. PT to ERT, Friday [21 June 1952], ERT.

41. RL to PT, undated [Aug. 1952], Vanderbilt; PT to RL, 13 July [1952], Harvard.

42. PT file for 1951, *New Yorker* Records, New York Public Library; PT to RL, 13 July [1952], Harvard.

Chapter 10: The Idyll

1. PT, 3 Apr. 1993.

2. Barbara Kreutz, 28 Aug. 1996; Monique Transue, 29 Aug. 1996; ERT, 30 Aug. 1996.

3. ERT, 30 Aug. 1996; Robb Forman Dew, "Summer's End," *Mississippi Quarterly* 30 (winter 1976–77): 144–46; Monique Transue, 29 Aug. 1996; Helen Ransom Forman, 4 Sept. 1996; HHM, "A Composite Conversation with PT," in *CWPT*, 125.

4. Thomas B. Greenslade, "Presenting 100 Years of Theatre," *Kenyon College Alumni Bulletin* (winter 1987–88): 12–15; James Michael, 29 Aug. 1996.

5. Gordon Chalmers to PT, 17 Dec. 1952, ERT; PT to KW, 23 Dec. [1952], *New Yorker* Records, New York Public Library.

6. Jane Bagley Alexander, 18 Oct. 1994; Ann Watkins Boatner Grove, 3 Sept. 1993; PT to RM, 13 Feb. [1953], Vanderbilt.

7. PT to RM, 23 Feb. [1953] and 2 May [1953]; RJ to PT, 13 Apr. 1953—all Vanderbilt.

8. RJ to PT, 13 Apr. 1953 and 15 May 1953, Vanderbilt; PT to RL and EH, 14 July [1953], Harvard; JT, 16 Nov. 1994; KW to PT, 4 Mar. 1953, PT to KW, 9 Apr. 1953 and 10 Sept. 1953—all *New Yorker* Records, New York Public Library.

9. KW to PT, 21 Sept. 1953, *New Yorker* Records, New York Public Library; PT to RL and EH, undated [late November 1953], Harvard; PT to JT, 13 Dec. 1953, JT; PT, "The Dark Walk," *WOT*, 304.

10. PT to RL and EH, undated [Nov. 1953], Harvard; PT to JT, 13 Dec. 1953, JT; PT to KW, 10 Sept. 1953, *New Yorker* Records, New York Public Library; PT to RL and EH, undated [Oct. 1953], Harvard.

11. PT to KW, 14 Jan. 1954, *New Yorker* Records, New York Public Library; RL to PT, 11 Mar. [1954], Vanderbilt; JT to PT, 26 Apr. 1954, ERT.

12. Dan Wickenden, "A Fine Novel [*sic*] of the South," *New York Herald Tribune*, 2 May 1954, p. 4; Paul Engle, "Finely Poised Stories of Southern Family Life, *Chicago Sunday Tribune Magazine of Books*, 30 May 1954, p. 4; Frank H. Lyell, "The Universal Longings," *New York Times Book Review*, 2 May 1954, p. 5; Mack Morriss, "South in the Sun," *Saturday Review*, 8 May 1954, p. 14.

13. PT to RL, undated [May 1954], Harvard; PT to JS, undated [Mar. 1954], Colorado.

14. ERT to Mr. and Mrs. Fred Ross, 2 July 1954, ERT.

15. Paul Engle to PT, 30 June 1954, and ERT to Mr. and Mrs. Fred Ross, 28 July 1954—both ERT; PT to RL, 18 June [1954], Harvard; ERT to JS, 13 Aug. 1954, Colorado.

16. ERT to Mr. and Mrs. Fred Ross, 11 Oct. 1954 and 9 Sept. 1954, ERT; KW to PT, 28 July 1954 and 13 Oct. 1954, *New Yorker* Records, New York Public Library.

17. HHM, "A Composite Conversation with PT," 120; PT to JS, 24 Dec. [1954], Colorado; PT to KW, 15 Nov. 1954 and undated [Dec. 1954], *New Yorker* Records, New York Public Library.

18. ERT to Mrs. Fred Ross, 4 Jan. 1955, ERT; Monique Transue, 29 Aug. 1996.

19. ERT to Mr. and Mrs. Fred Ross, 2 July 1954, ERT; ERT to JS, 13 Aug. 1954, Colorado; PT to Mr. and Mrs. Fred Ross, 15 Feb. 1954, ERT; PT to RL and EH, 28 Feb. [1955], Harvard.

20. RL to PT, 27 May 1951, Vanderbilt; PT to RL, 1 May [1955], Harvard; RL to PT, 11 Apr. 1955, Vanderbilt.

21. PT Fulbright file, 1955–56, ERT; Eudora Welty to PT, undated [Apr. 1955], Vanderbilt; PT, 5 Aug. 1984.

22. ERT to Mrs. Fred Ross, 9 June 1955, ERT; PT, 15 July 1991 and 5 Aug. 1984; Biddy Abbot to PT, 21 Aug. 1955, Virginia.

23. PT to KW, 1 Aug. 1955, *New Yorker* Records, New York Public Library; Monique Transue, 29 Aug. 1996.

24. PT to TW, 31 Dec. 1955, TW; PT to JCR, 8 Dec. [1955], Kenyon; PT to RL and EH, 24 Nov. 1955, Harvard; PT to JS, 30 Oct. 1955, Colorado.

25. PT to RL and EH, 12 Jan. 1956, Harvard; PT Random House Correspondence, Virginia; PT literary contracts file, ERT.

26. PT to JS, 24 Feb. 1956, Colorado.

27. PT Random House file, ERT; KW to PT, 11 Apr. 1956, *New Yorker* Records, New York Public Library; RL to PT and ERT, 18 June 1956, Vanderbilt; PT to Gordon Chalmers, 17 Apr. 1956, and Gordon Chalmers to PT, 24 Apr. 1956, both ERT; PT to RM, 25 Apr. [1956], Vanderbilt.

28. KW to PT, 6 June 1956, and PT to KW, 16 Aug. 1956, *New Yorker* Records, New York Public Library; PT to RL and EH, 15 Aug. [1956], Harvard; PT to TW, 31 Dec. 1955, TW; PT to RL and EH, 21 Sept. [1956], Harvard.

29. PT to RL and EH, 21 Sept. [1956], Harvard.

30. RL to PT, 7 Mar. 1957, Vanderbilt; PT to RL and EH, 17 Mar. [1957], Harvard; RJ to PT, 23 Mar. 1957; PT to KW, 28 Feb. 1957, and Robert Henderson to PT, 6 Mar. 1957, both *New Yorker* Records, New York Public Library.

31. PT to RL and EH, 14 Mar. 1957, Harvard; Monique Transue, 29 Aug. 1996; RJ to PT, 1 Feb. 1955, Vanderbilt; Andrew Lytle, "The Displaced Family," *Sewanee Review* 66 (winter 1958): 115–20.

32. RL to PT and ERT, 17 Apr. 1957, Vanderbilt; David McDowell to PT and ERT, 24 June 1957, Virginia.

33. Frank E. Bailey to PT, 5 Nov. 1956 and 14 Jan. 1957, and PT to Frank E. Bailey, 28 May and 12 June, 1957—all ERT; PT to RL, Tuesday, Harvard; RL to PT, 21 June 1957, Vanderbilt. Peter Taylor presents the general outlines of the situation in "Dean of Men."

34. Robert M. Estrich to PT, 23 Jan. 1957, and PT undated draft of a letter to Estrich—both ERT; PT to KW, 15 Aug. 1957, *New Yorker* Records, New York Public Library.

Chapter 11: The Middle Years

1. PT, 11 Sept. 1985; ERT, 23 June 1995; KBT, 1 May 1998.

2. PT Payroll Pedigree Card, Ohio State University.

3. PT to HT, 2 Aug. 1945, Vanderbilt; Roy Harvey Pearce, 25 Aug. 1996; Andrew Wright, 28 Aug. 1996; ERT, 20 June 1995.

4. PT to Albert Erskine, undated draft; Albert Erskine to PT 18 Sept. 1957; PT to David McDowell, 5 Jan. 1958—all Virginia.

5. PT to KW, 30 Sept. 1957, and William Maxwell to PT, 2 Oct. 1957—both *New Yorker* Records, New York Public Library.

6. KW to PT, 4 Sept. 1957, and PT to KW, 11 Sept. 1957—both *New Yorker* Records, New York Public Library.

7. William Maxwell to PT, 2 Oct. 1957, and PT to William Maxwell, 7 Oct. 1957—both *New Yorker* Records, New York Public Library.

8. JCR to PT, 25 Sept. 1957 and 2 Nov. [1957], both Vanderbilt.

9. Alice Hunt Seelye, 19 June 1995; HHM, "A Composite Conversation with PT," *CWPT*, 122–23.

10. PT to RL and EH, Monday [Nov. 1957], Harvard; Jane Farrar Seymour to HHM, 9 Sept. 1996; ERT, 20 June 1995.

11. PT to RL and EH, Monday [Nov. 1957], Harvard; PT to RJ, Friday [Nov. 1957], Berg Collection, New York Public Library.

12. JCR to PT, 2 Nov. [1957], Vanderbilt; JCR to AT, 2 Oct. 1957, 25 Oct. 1957, and 5 Nov. 1957—all Princeton; Ian Hamilton, *Robert Lowell: A Biography* (New York: Random House, 1982), 238–53; RL to PT, 15 Mar. 1958, Vanderbilt.

13. PT to RL, 7 Apr. 1958, Harvard; undated clipping, ERT; Edwin Howard, "When Peter Taylor Is Home," *CWPT*, 5.

14. PT to William Maxwell, 12 May 1957, *New Yorker* Records, New York Public Library; PT to RJ and MJ, 18 Jan. [1958], Berg Collection, New York Public Library.

15. PT, 15 Aug. 1984.

16. *Randall Jarrell Letters: An Autobiographical and Literary Selection*, ed. MJ (Boston: Houghton Mifflin, 1985), 257; MJ, "Peter and Randall," "Garland," 33.

17. ERT, "Greensboro Days," *Randall Jarrell: 1914–1965* (New York: Farrar, Straus and Giroux), 239–40; MJ, "Peter and Randall," 31; KBT, 1 May 1998.

18. JWB, "A Conversation with PT," *CWPT*, 110; Stephen Goodwin, "An Interview with PT," *CWPT*, 13; PT to William Maxwell, 3 Aug. 1958 and 14 Aug. 1958, *New Yorker* Records, New York Public Library.

19. PT, 15 Aug. 1984; Susan Otis Thompson, 19 Nov. 1995; Sally Fitzgerald, 19 Apr. 1995; Sally Fitzgerald to ERT and PT, 27 Sept. 1958, Vanderbilt; JT, 16 Nov. 1994.

20. PT to Jarrell Family, 8 Sept. [1958], Berg Collection, New York Public Library; RJ to PT and ERT, 1 Nov. [1958], Vanderbilt; RPW to RL, 10 Mar. 1958, Harvard; PT to William Maxwell, 14 Nov. 1958, *New Yorker* Records, New York Public Library.

21. PT to William Maxwell, 3 Aug. 1958, 5 Aug. 1958, 14 Aug. 1958, 16 Sept. 1958—all *New Yorker* Records, New York Public Library; Doubleday and Company, Inc., Publishers, to JCR, 2 Sept. 1958, Kenyon; PT to William Maxwell, 14 Nov. 1958, 25 Nov. 1958, 29 Nov. 1958, and Robert Henderson to PT, 2 Dec. 1958, and William Maxwell to PT, 10 Dec. 1958—all *New Yorker* Records, New York Public Library.

22. Harold Rosenberg to PT, 8 Jan. 1959; correspondence with Row, Peterson, and Company and with Kinseido Ltd., Publishers, Tokyo; "Memphian Winner of O. Henry Award," *Memphis Commercial Appeal*, 7 Mar. 1959, clipping; Elizabeth Farnsworth Hanna to PT, 11 Apr. 1959; Tom White to PT, 26 Apr. 1959—all ERT.

23. PT to David McDowell, 25 Nov. 1958, Virginia; RL to PT and ERT, 20 Mar. 1959, Vanderbilt; PT to RL, 14 Apr. 1959, Harvard.

24. BT, "Interview with PT," *CWPT*, 143–44.

25. PT to RM, 6 Feb. [1959], Vanderbilt; PT to RJ and MJ, 25 Aug. 1959, and ERT to RJ and MJ, 22 July [1959]—both Berg Collection, New York Public Library; PT to JT, Tuesday, JT.

26. PT to RJ and MJ, 10 Dec. [1959], Berg Collection; PT to RM, 19 Nov. 1959, Kenyon.

27. William Maxwell to PT, 25 Nov. 1959; PT to William Maxwell, Sunday [Dec. 1959], and 6 Mar. [1960]—all *New Yorker* Records, New York Public Library.

28. Gene Baro, "A True Short-Story Artist," *New York Herald Tribune Books,* 6 Dec. 1959, p. 9; William Du Bois, "Books of the Times," *New York Times,* 12 Jan. 1960, p. 45; Ruth Blackman, "Complex Stories of Family and Community," *Christian Science Monitor,* 24 Dec. 1959, p. 11.

29. RPW to PT, 9 Apr. 1960, and RL to PT, 10 Dec. 1959 and 2 Feb. 1960—all Vanderbilt; PT to RJ and MJ, 10 Dec. [1959], Berg Collection; Martha Murphy to PT, 6 Jan. 1960, Virginia.

30. W. McNeil Lowry to PT, 3 Aug. 1959, ERT; PT to RL, 10 Feb. 1960, Harvard; RL to PT, 31 Oct. 1958, Vanderbilt; PT to AT 11 Dec. [1959], Princeton; PT to RL, 3 Apr. [1960], Harvard; HHM, "A Composite Conversation with PT," 124.

31. PT to RL, 10 Feb. 1960, and 3 Apr. [1960], both Harvard; Peyton M. Rhodes to PT, 19 Mar. 1960, ERT; RL to PT, 27 June 1960, Vanderbilt.

32. PT to William Maxwell, 9 July [1960] and 5 Mar. [1960], *New Yorker* Records, New York Public; Andrew Lytle to AT, 15 Nov. 1960, Princeton; PT to JT, Sunday [June 1960], JT.

Chapter 12: London and Ohio State

1. PT to RL, 3 Apr. [1960], Harvard.

2. PT to William Maxwell, 16 Aug. 1960 and 22 Sept. 1960, *New Yorker* Records; PT to RJ and MJ, 22 Oct. [1960], Berg Collection, New York Public Library.

3. John Holmes, review of *Wilderness of Ladies,* by ERT, *New York Herald Tribune Book Review,* 4 Sept. 1960, p. 6; RL to PT, 17 Dec. 1960, and RJ to PT and ERT, 13 Dec. 1960—both Vanderbilt; BT, "Interview with PT," *CWPT,* 155; Stephen Goodwin, "An Interview with PT," *CWPT,* 12; Roger Angell to PT, 17 Jan. 1961, *New Yorker* Records, New York Public Library.

4. Eric Solomon, 16 July 1996; Monique Transue, 29 Aug. 1996; ERT to MJ and RJ, 9 Jan. [1961], Berg Collection, New York Public Library; Andrew Wright, 28 Aug. 1996; PT to RL, 19 Mar. 1961, Harvard; ERT, 30 Aug. 1996.

5. PT to JS, 3 Apr. 1961, Colorado; PT to RL, 19 Mar. 1961, Harvard.

6. PT to RJ and MJ, 3 Apr. [1961], Berg Collection, and PT to Roger Angell, 19 Apr. 1961, *New Yorker* Records—both New York Public Library.

7. PT to RJ and MJ, Tuesday [21 June 1961] and Sunday [26 June 1961], Berg Collection, New York Public Library.

8. William Maxwell to PT, 12 Dec. 1960; PT to Roger Angell, 17 Aug. 1961 and 13 Sept. 1961; Roger Angell to PT, 7 Sept. 1961—all *New Yorker* Records, New York Public Library; PT, "There," in *CS*, 367.

9. PT to RJ and MJ, 11 Oct. 1961, Berg Collection.

10. Anna May Franklin, the Theatre Guild, to PT, 17 May 1961, ERT; PT to Roger Angell, 13 Sept. 1961, *New Yorker* Records, New York Public Library. See the discussion of both story and television adaptation in Richard L. Kurtz, "Freud Checks In: The 'Oedipus' in Peter Taylor's 'Reservations: A Love Story,' " *North Carolina Literary Review*, no. 5 (1996): 55–57.

11. PT to RL, 16 Dec. 1961, Harvard; Roger Angell to PT, 14 Nov. 1961, *New Yorker* Records, New York Public Library; PT to RJ and MJ, Sunday night [Dec. 1961], Berg Collection, New York Public Library.

12. PT to Mr. and Mrs. T. J. White, Jr., 28 Jan. 1948. "Demons" was most recently collected in *OSC* (1993).

13. PT, "At the Drugstore," in *CS*, 138.

14. Roger Angell to PT, 20 Feb. 1962, and PT to Roger Angell, 13 Jan. 1962—*New Yorker* Records, New York Public Library.

15. PT to RL, 16 Dec. 1961, Harvard; PT to JS, Saturday [Jan. 1962], Colorado.

16. PT to JS, Saturday [Jan. 1962], Colorado; Andrew Wright, 28 Aug. 1996.

17. ERT to Mr. and Mrs. Fred E. Ross, 1 May 1962, and 9 September 1962—both ERT; ERT, 23 June 1995 and 30 Aug. 1996; PT, 11 Sept. 1991; PT to JT, Sunday, JT; Eric Solomon, "Free Speech at Ohio State," *Atlantic Monthly*, Nov. 1965, pp. 119–23; Eric Solomon, 16 July 1996.

18. JWB, "A Conversation with PT," in *CWPT*, 105; Frank C. Waldrop, ed., *Mountain Voices: The Centennial History of Monteagle Sunday School Assembly* (Nashville: Parthenon Press, 1982), 9; PT to RL, 16 Dec. 1961, Harvard.

19. JWB, "A Conversation with PT," 98; PT to AT, 18 Aug. [1961], Princeton; Mary Polk Kirby-Smith, 10 Aug. 1995; Jane Bagley Alexander, 18 Oct. 1994; ERT, 4 Aug. 1995.

20. ERT, 4 Aug. 1995; ERT to Mr. and Mrs. Fred E. Ross, 24 June 1962, ERT; Grace Benedict Paine, 28 Nov. 1995; PT to Roger Angell, 3 July 1962, *New Yorker* Records, New York Public Library.

21. PT to Roger Angell, 1 Oct., 15 Nov., and 28 Nov. 1962; and Roger Angell to PT, 21 Jan. 1963—all *New Yorker* Records, New York Public Library; PT to RJ and MJ, 18 Nov. [1962], Berg Collection, New York Public Library; Christopher P. Metress, "An Oracle of Mystery: A Conversation with PT," in *COPT*, 145.

22. ERT to Mr. and Mrs. Fred E. Ross, 15 Oct. 1962 and 4 Nov. 1962—both ERT; PT to EH and RL, 1 Jan. 1963, Harvard.

23. Caroline G. Mercer to PT, 20 Jan. 1963; PT to Mercer, 18 Mar. 1963; ERT to Mr. and Mrs. Fred E. Ross, 15 Oct. 1962 and 4 Nov. 1962—all ERT. ERT, "Recipe for a Carolina Christmas," *Greensboro Daily News,* 20 Dec. 1962, p. 8; ERT to MJ, 10 Feb. 1963, Berg Collection, New York Public Library.

24. PT to Louis Rubin, 13 Apr. 1963, ERT; PT to RJ and MJ, 15 Apr. 1963 and 6 May 1963, Berg Collection, New York Public Library; PT to RPW, 26 June 1963, Yale; PT to RL, undated [fall 1963], Harvard.

Chapter 13: Greensboro

1. PT to RM, 5 Oct. [1963], Vanderbilt; PT to RL, undated [fall 1963], Harvard.

2. PT–Ivan Obolensky, Inc., Correspondence, 1963–64, Virginia.

3. *Time,* 13 Mar. 1964, pp. 107–108; Glendy Culligan, "Struggling to Swim Clear of the Undertow," *Bookweek,* 8 Mar. 1964, p. 11; Richard Sullivan, review of *Miss Leonora When Last Seen,* by PT, *Chicago Sunday Tribune Books Today,* 5 Apr. 1964, p. 4; Gene Baro, "How Time Changes Things," *New York Times Book Review,* 29 Mar. 1964, p. 4; John Thompson, "The Stories of Peter Taylor," *New York Review of Books,* 11 June 1964, p. 11; T. A. Hanzo, "The Two Faces of Matt Donelson," *Sewanee Review* 73 (winter 1965): 106–11.

4. William H. Chafe, *Civilities and Civil Rights: Greensboro, North Carolina, and the Black Struggle for Freedom* (New York: Oxford, 1980), 5; PT to John Gerber, 11 Dec. 1963, ERT.

5. *Randall Jarrell's Letters: An Autobiographical and Literary Selection,* ed. MJ (Boston: Houghton Mifflin, 1985), 486–91; Ian Hamilton, *Robert Lowell: A Biography* (New York: Random House, 1982), 306.

6. PT to RL, 10 Mar. 1964, Harvard; Fred Chappell, "Peter Taylor: The Genial Mentor," *North Carolina Literary Review,* no. 5 (1996): 49.

7. PT to RM, 20 Feb. [1964], Vanderbilt; David Roberts, *Jean Stafford: A Biography* (Boston: Little, Brown, 1988), 345–48; PT to ERT, 12 Apr. 1964, ERT.

8. PT to JS, 22 May 1964, Colorado; ERT to Mr. and Mrs. Fred Ross, 19 June 1964, ERT; PT to RJ and MJ, 18 June 1964, Berg Collection, New York Public Library.

9. Lisa Reynolds, 20 Oct. 1985; Lucy Roberts, 5 June 1998; RM to PT, 4 Nov. 1963, and Robert Weston to PT, 18 Feb. 1964, both ERT; PT file 1964, *New Yorker* Records, New York Public Library.

10. ERT to Mr. and Mrs. Fred Ross, 2 Aug. 1964, and PT to ERT, 30 Sept. 1964—both ERT; ERT, 31 Mar. 1999.

11. PT to ERT, 15 June 1963, and 26 Sept., 27 Sept., and 30 Sept. 1964—ERT.

12. James Thackara, 15 Apr. 1999.

13. PT to ERT, 30 Sept. 1964 and 4 Oct. 1964, ERT; William Alfred, 15 Sept. 1994; PT to ERT, 15 Oct., 20 Oct., 2 Nov. 1964—ERT.

14. PT to ERT, 17 Oct., 2 Nov., 28 Oct., 16 Nov. 1964—ERT; Sally Fitzgerald, 19 Apr. 1995; PT, 3 Aug. 1993.

15. EH, 19 Nov. 1994; Esther Brooks, 26 Sept. 1994; Helen Ransom Forman, 4 Sept. 1996.

16. PT to ERT, 10 Dec. 1964, ERT; PT to Roger Angell, 20 Dec. 1964, *New Yorker* Records, New York Public Library; John Casey, "Peter Taylor as Merlin and Mr. O'Malley," "Garland," 75.

17. Thackara, 15 Apr. 1999.

18. PT to ERT, 20 Dec. 1964, ERT; *Randall Jarrell's Letters*, 497.

19. PT to ERT, 6 Jan., 13 Jan. 1965—ERT; PT to RL, 21 Jan. [1965], Harvard; Adrienne Rich to PT, Monday evening [Dec. 1964], Vanderbilt.

20. PT to RL, 21 Jan. 1965, Harvard; PT to JS, 14 Mar. [1965] and Tuesday [Apr. 1965], Colorado; *Randall Jarrell's Letters*, 509, 516.

21. Ivan Obolensky to PT, 19 Sept. 1964, and PT to Ivan Obolensky, 4 June 1965, Virginia; RL to PT, 12 Oct. 1960, Vanderbilt; PT–Farrar, Straus and Giroux contract, 1 July 1965, ERT.

22. PT to Roger Angell, 24 Oct. 1965, *New Yorker* Records, New York Public Library.

23. "Professor Granted $13,500," *Greensboro Daily News*, 9 Oct. 1965; PT to AT, 7 Dec. 1965, Princeton; William H. Pritchard, *Randall Jarrell: A Literary Life* (New York: Farrar, Straus and Giroux, 1990), 294–95; KBT, 1 May 1998.

24. "Noted Poet Randall Jarrell Killed by Car at Chapel Hill," *Greensboro Daily News*, 15 Oct. 1965; RL to ERT, 6 Oct. 1965, Vanderbilt; PT drafts to Adrienne Rich, undated, and to Robert Fitzgerald, 3 Nov., ERT; PT to AT, 7 Dec. 1965, Princeton; PT draft to RL, undated, Vanderbilt.

25. PT draft to Robert Fitzgerald, 3 Nov., ERT; PT to JS, 19 Nov., Colorado; PT to MJ, 25 Nov. 1965, Berg Collection, New York Public Library.

26. RPW to PT, 19 Oct. 1965 and 19 Dec. 1965, Vanderbilt; PT to Robert Haugh, 20 Dec. 1965, Michigan.

27. PT drafts to Robert Fitzgerald, 3 Nov., to Adrienne Rich, undated, to RL, undated, to Roger Straus, undated—ERT.

28. PT to JS, 19 Nov. 1965, Colorado; PT to AT, 7 Dec. 1965, Princeton.

29. MJ, "Peter and Randall," "Garland," 28, 33; PT to RPW, 1 Jan. 1966, Yale.

30. PT to RPW, 1 Feb. 1966, Yale; Ann Watkins Boatner Grove, 3 Sept. 1993. See PT, "Randall Jarrell," in *Randall Jarrell: 1914–1965*, ed. RL, PT, and RPW (New York: Farrar, Straus and Giroux, 1967), 241–52; and PT, "That Cloistered Jazz," *Michigan Quarterly Review* 5 (fall 1966): 237–45.

31. "17 Students Given Duke Scholarship," *Greensboro Daily News*, 25 Mar. 1966; PT to AT, 17 Jan. [1966], Princeton; Kathleen Mather Bulgin, 29 Mar. 1995.

32. PT to AT, 17 Jan. [1966], and ERT to AT, 27 Mar. [1966]—Princeton; Chappell, "Peter Taylor: The Genial Mentor," 47–48, 51; Fred Chappell, 30 Mar. 1995.

33. Randolph Bulgin, 29 Mar. 1995; Chappell, 30 Mar. 1995; MJ, "Peter and Randall," 29.

34. MJ, 25 Sept. 1998; MJ, "Peter and Randall," 29; Jonathan Yardley, "The Remarkable Peter Taylor," *Washington Post*, 7 Nov. 1994, p. D2; Randolph Bulgin, 29 Mar. 1995.

35. PT to Mr. and Mrs. Radcliffe Squires, 17 Apr. 1966, Washington University Library; Eudora Welty to PT and ERT, 7 Apr. 1966, Vanderbilt.

36. PT to AT, 27 May 1966 and 14 July [1966], Princeton; PT to Sally Fitzhugh, 19 June 1966, ERT.

37. PT to Roger Angell, 17 Jan. 1966 and 10 Aug. 1966; Roger Angell to PT, 22 Aug. 1966; PT to Roger Angell, 29 Aug. 1966—all *New Yorker* Records, New York Public Library.

38. PT draft to Bob [?], undated [1965], ERT; PT, 20 Apr. 1985; PT to AT, 17 Jan. [1966], Princeton; PT to Andrew Lytle, 12 Mar. 196[6], and PT draft to Andrew Lytle, undated [Aug. 1967], ERT.

39. PT to Robert Giroux, 3 Sept. 1966, Farrar, Straus and Giroux Papers, New York Public Library; "Taylor Given UNC-G Alumni Professorship," *Greensboro Daily News*, 13 Nov. 1966; PT to Roger Angell, 30 Nov. 1966, *New Yorker* Records, New York Public Library; "Fiction Writers Get Tips at Georgetown Parley," *Washington Star*, 2 Aug. 1966; Roger Angell to PT, 13 Dec. 1966, *New Yorker* Records; PT to RL, 13 Dec. 1966, Harvard.

40. PT to George Lanning, 10 Mar. 1967, Kenyon; PT to AT, 10 Mar. 1967, Princeton; ERT, 17 Sept. 1995.

41. PT to Mary Polk Kirby-Smith, 29 Mar. 1967, in her possession; PT to RL, 2 June 1967, Harvard.

42. PT to RL, 2 June 1967, Harvard; PT to Radcliffe Squires, 29 Sept. 1967, Washington University Library.

Chapter 14: Charlottesville

1. PT to George Lanning, 10 Mar. 1967, Kenyon; Shelby Coffey III, "Meet Albemarle's Landed Gentry," *Potomac* (*Washington Post* magazine section), 23 Apr. 1967, pp. 23–29; Felicia W. Rogan, "Albemarle's Ambassadors," *Albemarle Monthly*, Feb.–Mar. 1979, pp. 24–33.

2. Joseph Blotner, *Faulkner: A Biography* (New York: Random House, 1974), 2:1641, 1706, 1748–49; ERT, 19 June 1995; Barbara Yalden-Thompson, 2 July 1999; PT, 5 May 1985.

3. Barbara Yalden-Thompson, 2 July 1999; ERT, 16 June 1999; Tony Winner, 14 June 1999; Henderson Heyward, 30 June 1999; PT, 5 May 1985.

4. HT to PT, 20 Feb. 1951, ERT; PT, 5 May 1985.

5. PT to Roger Angell, 6 Jan. 1967 and 24 Sept. 1967, *New Yorker* Records, New York Public Library.

6. PT to Robert Giroux, 5 May 1967 and 3 Sept. 1966, Farrar, Straus, and Giroux Papers, New York Public Library; PT to Robert Giroux, 25 July 1967 (draft), and PT to Albert J. Griffith, 14 Mar. 1968—both Vanderbilt.

7. PT to George Lanning, 28 June 1967, Kenyon; PT to AT, 1 Nov. 1967, Princeton. Citations are from the 1985 edition of the play (New York: Frederic C. Beil).

8. PT to RL, 5 Feb. 1968, Harvard; Adrienne Rich to PT, 9 Sept. 1968, Vanderbilt.

9. "Fitzhugh Estate: Mother Given Life Income—Others to Share," *Memphis Commercial Appeal,* 28 Mar. 1967; PT, 1 Sept. 1987; PT to RL, 5 Feb. 1968, Harvard.

10. PT to RL, 5 Feb. 1968, Harvard; PT to George Lanning, 6 Dec. 1967, 11 Jan. 1968, 2 Feb. [1968]—all Kenyon; Sarah Booth White, 27 Mar. 1993; PT, 3 Apr. 1993.

11. "To Pay a Poet Honor," *Life,* 10 May 1968, pp. 109–110; PT to George Lanning, 12 May 1968, Kenyon; Judith Jones, 18 Nov. 1994.

12. PT, 1 Sept. 1987; PT to George Lanning, 12 May 1968, Kenyon; PT to RL, 16 Mar. 1968, Harvard; PT to Lawrence Reynolds, 11 Nov. 1968, in his possession; PT to Kathleen Mather Bulgin, 6 Oct. 1968, in her possession.

13. PT to George Lanning, 12 May 1968, Kenyon; Roger Angell to PT, 26 July 1968, *New Yorker* Records, New York Public Library.

14. Contract dated 9 Sept. 1968, SW; PT to RL, 5 Nov. 1968, Harvard; PT to Lawrence Reynolds, 11 Nov. 1968, in his possession; Shelby Coffey III, "Sophisticated Fugitive," *Potomac,* 24 Nov. 1968, pp. 28–29.

15. Postcards from PT to Lawrence Reynolds, 1968 and 1969, and Lawrence Reynolds, unpublished manuscript on Peter Taylor—both in his possession.

16. Stephen Goodwin, 1 July 1999; Stephen Goodwin, "Like Nothing Else in Tennessee," "Garland," 54; PT to RPW, 12 Mar. 1969, Yale.

17. Goodwin, "Like Nothing Else in Tennessee," 55.

18. 1968 PT file, *New Yorker* Records, New York Public Library, correspondence of 14 Nov., 21 Nov., 7 Dec. and 16 Dec.

19. PT to Lawrence Reynolds, 19 Jan. 1969, in his possession; PT to RPW, 15 Jan. 196[9], Yale; RPW to PT, 9 Jan. 1969, and 8 Feb. 1969—both Vanderbilt.

20. PT to JT, 2 Apr. 1969, JT; Stephen Goodwin, 1 July 1999.

21. PT to RL and EH, Sunday [May 1969], Harvard; Mettie Taylor Dobson, 13 Sept. 1995; PT interview with JWB, 2 Oct. 1987; PT, 8 Aug. 1993.

22. Stephen Goodwin, 1 July 1999; Adrienne Rich to PT, 4 Aug. 1969, Vanderbilt; PT to JS, 27 June 1969, Colorado; PT to Robert Giroux, 27 Aug. 1969, Farrar, Straus,

and Giroux Papers, New York Public Library; PT to Lawrence Reynolds, 8 Aug. 1969 and 19 Jan. 1969—both in his possession.

23. RPW to Robert Giroux, 18 Oct. 1969, Farrar, Straus, and Giroux Papers, New York Public Library.

24. R. V. Cassill, "The Departure of Proserpine," *Chicago Tribune Book World,* 12 Oct. 1969, p. 12; Richard Howard, "Twenty-one Holding Actions by a Modest American Master," *New York Times Book Review,* 19 Oct. 1969, pp. 4, 26; Geoffrey Wolff, "Master of Hidden Drama," *Newsweek,* 20 Oct. 1969, p. 120; Barbara Raskin, "Southern Fried," *New Republic,* 18 October 1969, pp. 29–30; Jonathan Yardley, letter in "Correspondence," *New Republic,* 22 Nov. 1969, pp. 27–29; Roger Sale, Review of *The Collected Stories of Peter Taylor, Hudson Review* 22 (winter 1969): 710; Christopher Ricks, "The Unignorable Real," *New York Review of Books,* 12 Feb. 1970, p. 22.

25. JT, Review of *The Collected Stories of Peter Taylor, Harper's* 239 (Nov. 1969): 134; Stephen Goodwin, "Life Studies," *Shenandoah* 21 (winter 1970): 100–102; Joyce Carol Oates, "Realism of Distance, Realism of Immediacy," *Southern Review* 7 (winter 1971): 302.

26. Thomas Lask, "Brief Lives," *New York Times,* 11 Oct. 1969, p. 35; Robert Phillips, Review of *The Collected Stories of Peter Taylor, Studies in Short Fiction* 8 (summer 1971): 489; PT to RPW, 17 Nov. 1969, Yale.

27. PT to Robert Fitzgerald, 3 Nov. [1965], draft, Vanderbilt; PT to Roger Angell, 6 Dec. 1969, and Roger Angell to PT, 12 Dec. 1969 and 17 Dec. 1969—all *New Yorker* Records, New York Public Library.

28. Katherine Anne Porter to PT and ERT, 10 Dec. 1969, Vanderbilt; Joan Givner, *Katherine Anne Porter: A Life,* revised edition (Athens: University of Georgia Press, 1991) 482–88; BT, interview with PT, 21 May 1981.

29. TW to PT, 16 Feb. 1970, and 28 Mar. 1970—both ERT; PT to Lawrence Reynolds, 5 July 1970, in his possession.

30. AT to PT and ERT, 10 June 1970, Vanderbilt; PT to Lawrence Reynolds, 5 July 1970, in his possession.

31. Anne Hobson Freeman, 13 June 1999.

32. Anne Hobson Freeman, 13 June 1999.

33. Anne Hobson Freeman, 13 June 1999; PT to AT, 23 Feb. 1969, Princeton; John Casey, 15 June 1999.

34. PT to RL, 31 Oct. 1970, University of Texas; PT to Lawrence Reynolds, 5 July 1970, in his possession; RL to PT, 1 Nov. 1970, Vanderbilt; JT to PT, 26 Dec. 1970, ERT.

35. ERT, 16 June 1999; PT to JS, 1 Dec./2 Dec. [1970], Colorado; PT to RM, 30 Mar. 197[1], Vanderbilt.

36. PT to RM, 30 Mar. 197[1], Vanderbilt.

37. PT to RPW, 23 Feb. 1971, Yale; Lawrence Reynolds, 12 June 1999.

38. PT to JS, 1 Dec. [1970], Colorado; "Mr. T Meets Mr. P: A Play is Produced," Charlottesville *Daily Progress*, 30 June 1971, 1-B; PT to Michael Norell, 18 Apr. 1971, and 1 Apr. 1971—both Vanderbilt.

39. PT, 8 Aug. 1993; Mrs. Robert L. Taylor of Knoxville, 21 June 1994.

40. Felder Heflin, 2 Dec. 1993; Tony Winner, 14 June 1999; Lawrence Reynolds, 12 June 1999; and Stephen Goodwin, 1 July 1999.

41. Kenyon 1971 commencement file, Kenyon; PT to Robert Giroux, 8 June 1971, Farrar, Straus and Giroux Papers, New York Public Library.

42. PT to TW, 22 June 1971, TW; PT to Robert Giroux, 8 June 1971 and 2 Dec. 1971, Farrar, Straus and Giroux Papers, New York Public Library.

Chapter 15: An Extension of Time

1. PT to Robert Giroux, draft of 12 Jan. 1972, ERT; PT file, Jan.–Mar. 1972, Farrar, Straus and Giroux Papers, New York Public Library; PT contract with Houghton Mifflin Company, 29 Mar. 1972, SW.

2. PT to AT, 25 Feb. 1972, Princeton; PT to RL, 24 Mar. 1972, Texas; PT to Lawrence Reynolds, 23 Mar. 1972, in his possession; PT to Robert Giroux, 23 Apr. 1972, Farrar, Straus and Giroux Papers, New York Public Library; PT to JS, 6 May 1972, Colorado; ERT to RL and Caroline Blackwood, 21 May [1972], Texas.

3. PT to RL and Caroline Blackwood, 9 June 1972, Texas; PT, interview with JWB, 15 Feb. 1985.

4. Stephen Goodwin, 1 July 1999; PT to RPW, 12 Jan. 1972, Yale; PT, interview with JWB, 15 Feb. 1985; ERT, 19 June 1999; Reynolds Price, "James Dickey, Size XL," *New York Times Book Review*, 23 Mar. 1997, p. 31.

5. PT to RPW, 12 June 1972, Yale; RL to PT and ERT, 28 June 1972, Adrienne Rich to PT, 30 July 1970, and RL to PT, 24 June 1971—all Vanderbilt; Adrienne Rich, Review of *Welcome Eumenides, New York Times Book Review*, 2 July 1972, p. 3; Adrienne Rich to ERT, 15 May 1972—ERT.

6. PT to Robert Giroux, 7 Aug. 1972, Farrar, Straus and Giroux Papers, New York Public Library; PT to JS, 7 Aug. 1972, Colorado; PT to Lawrence Reynolds, 29 July 1972, in his possession; PT to RL, 8 Aug. [1972], Texas.

7. PT, "Literature, Sewanee, and the World," Founders' Day Address 1972, p. 4.

8. AT to PT, 13 Jan. 1971 and 10 Apr. 1971—both Vanderbilt; PT to RL, 16 Sept. 1971, Texas; ERT diary entries for 13 Nov. and 14 Nov. 1972, ERT; PT interview with JWB, 15 Feb. 1985.

9. AT to PT, 30 Nov. 1972, Vanderbilt; PT to AT, 8 Dec. 1972, Princeton; PT to RL, 14 Nov. [1972], Texas; PT, 20 Aug. 1984.

10. RL to PT, 6 Nov. 1972, Vanderbilt; PT to RL, R. E. Lee Day [19 Jan. 1973], Texas.

11. PT to RL, 14 Nov. [1972], 18 Dec. 1972, R. E. Lee Day [19 Jan. 1973]—all Texas; RL to PT, 17 Feb. 1973, Vanderbilt.

12. Paul Theroux, "Old-Family Vapors," *Washington Post Book World,* 25 Feb. 1973, p. 13; Richard D. Olson, Review of *Presences,* by PT, *Library Journal,* 1 Jan. 1973, p. 83; "Notes on Current Books," *Virginia Quarterly Review* 49 (spring 1973): cxii; Richard Howard, "Urgent Need and Unbearable Fear," *Shenandoah* 24 (winter 1973): 47, 45; Richard Howard, 13 Aug. 1998; PT to RPW, 11 Apr. 1973, Yale.

13. Stephen Goodwin to PT, 6 Nov. 1972, Virginia; Stephen Goodwin, "An Interview with PT," in *CWPT,* 21.

14. PT to RL, 10 Mar. 1973, Texas; RL to PT, 18 Mar. 1973, Vanderbilt.

15. John Casey, 15 June 1999.

16. John Casey, 15 June 1999; Jane Barnes, 11 Jan. 1995; Alan Williamson, 10 May 1995.

17. Alan Williamson, 10 May 1995; Richard Howard, 13 Aug. 1998.

18. Lawrence Reynolds, 12 June 1999.

19. "An Evening with the Arts," *Charlottesville Daily Progress,* 6 May 1973, p. E2; PT, 5 May 1985.

20. PT to RL, 5 Aug. 1973, Texas; Opie Craig Handly, 3 Dec. 1994.

21. ERT to JS, 26 Jan. [1974], Colorado; ERT, 25 Aug. 1999; Ian Hamilton, *Robert Lowell: A Biography* (New York: Random House, 1982), 444; Paul Mariani, *Lost Puritan: A Life of Robert Lowell* (New York: Norton, 1994), 424; Elizabeth Bishop to RJ, 7 Oct. 1956, and to Ashley Brown, 17 Sept. 1973—both in *One Art: The Letters of Elizabeth Bishop,* ed. Robert Giroux (New York: Farrar, Straus and Giroux, 1994), 326, 581; PT, 15 July 1991 and 8 Aug. 1993.

22. ERT to RL and Caroline Blackwood, 21 Jan. [1974], Texas; ERT to JS, 26 Jan. [1974], Colorado; PT to Alan Heimert, 25 Jan. 1974, ERT.

23. ERT to JS, 26 Jan. [1974], Colorado; John Casey, 15 June 1999; Alan Williamson, 10 May 1995.

24. PT to RL, 4 Feb. [1974] and 10 Mar. [1974], Texas; Goodwin, "An Interview with PT," 16.

25. PT to RL, 10 Mar. [1974], and James Seay to RL, 15 Feb. 1974—both Texas; PT to Dr. and Mrs. Thomas Paine, 1 Apr. 1974, in her possession; Opie Craig Handly, 3 Dec. 1994; Tom Molyneux to PT, 19 July 1974, Virginia; ERT, 14 Oct. 1993.

26. PT, 5 May 1985; PT to RL, 6 July 1974, Texas; JT to PT, 29 May 1974, Virginia.

27. PT to TW, 22 June, 1971, TW; PT to RL, 6 July 1974, Texas.

28. PT to RL, 6 July 1974, Texas; PT 1974 Harvard University file, ERT; PT to RPW, 8 Aug. 1974 and 30 Aug. 1974, Yale.

29. RL to PT, 22 Feb. 1974 and 5 Sept. 1974, Vanderbilt; Gordon Lish to PT, 13 Aug. 1974, enclosed in PT to JS, 20 Aug. [1974], Colorado; RPW to PT, 17 Aug. 1974, Vanderbilt; PT to RPW, 30 Aug. 1974, Yale.

30. PT to Radcliffe Squires, 6 Sept. 1974, Washington University Library; PT to RPW, 30 Aug. 1974, Yale; PT to RL, 27 Aug. 1974, with poems enclosed, Texas.

31. PT to AT, 24 Oct. [1974], Princeton; PT to RL, Thanksgiving Day [1974], Texas; Karen Cook, "Regarding Harriet: Louise Fitzhugh Comes in from the Cold," *Village Voice Literary Supplement,* April 1995, pp. 12–14; Joan Williams, 15 July 1995; PT, 11 Sept. 1991.

32. RL to PT, 12 Dec. 1974, Vanderbilt; PT to RL, Thanksgiving Day [1974] and 18 Dec. 1974—both Texas.

33. PT to RL, 21 Jan. 1975, Texas; PT, 8 Aug. 1993; PT to Lawrence Reynolds, 8 Mar. 1975, in his possession; Elizabeth Bishop to James Merrill, 28 Mar. 1975, in Bishop, *One Art,* 595; PT to AT, 7 May 1975, Princeton; ERT to Lawrence and Margie Reynolds, 9 Apr. 1975, in their possession; PT to JT, 6 May 1975, JT; PT to JS, 5 May 1975, Colorado.

34. PT to AT, 6 July 1975, Princeton; PT to RL, 1 Aug. 1975 and 26 Aug. 1975— both Texas; PT to William Maxwell, 6 Sept. 1975, and Roger Angell to PT, 16 Sept. 1975—both *New Yorker* Records, New York Public Library.

35. PT to RL, 30 Sept. 1975 and 30 Nov. 1975—both Texas; PT diary, 30 Dec. 1975–12 Jan. 1976, Vanderbilt; PT to AT, 3 Feb. 1976, Princeton; James and Davina Thackara to PT, undated [Feb. 1976], Virginia; James Thackara, 16 Apr. 1999.

36. Craig Claiborne to PT, 14 Jan. 1975, Vanderbilt; Irvin Ehrenpreis to PT, 12 Jan. 1976, Virginia.

37. Tom Molyneux to PT, 30 Jan. [1976], and Willie Cocke to PT, 2 Mar. 1976— both Virginia; PT to RL and Caroline Blackwood, 27 Feb. 1976, 27 Apr. 1976, and 6 May 1976—all Texas; "UNC-G to Award 4 Honorary Doctorates," *Greensboro Daily News,* 5 May 1976, p. B2; ERT to Randolph and Kathleen Mather Bulgin, 22 May [1976], in her possession; Jonathan Coleman to PT, 17 Feb. 1976, ERT; Jonathan Coleman, "Becoming Peter's Editor," *Charlottesville Weekly,* 20–26 Dec. 1994, pp. 10–11; Daphne A. Ehrlich to PT, 28 Apr. 1976 and 9 June 1976, and PT contract with Alfred A. Knopf, 7 June 1976—ERT.

38. PT to RL, 15 June 1976, 4 July 1976, and 7 Aug. 1976—all Virginia; PT file 1976, *New Yorker* Records, New York Public Library.

39. PT to RL, 15 June 1976 and 7 Aug. 1976—both Texas; PT to AT, 14 Oct. 1976, Princeton; deed to 1207 Pine Street, Key West, 20 Dec. 1976, ERT; PT and ERT to Radcliffe Squires, undated [Christmas 1976], Washington University Library; PT, 1 Sept. 1987.

Chapter 16: Fruition

1. PT to Kathleen Mather Bulgin, 1 Mar. 1977, in her possession; James Boatwright to PT and ERT, 4 Feb. 1977, Vanderbilt.

2. ERT, 19 Sept. 1995; PT to Lawrence and Margie Reynolds, undated [Apr. 1977], in their possession; KBT to JS, 30 Nov. 1976, Colorado; PT to Dr. and Mrs. Thomas Paine, 1 Mar. 1977, in her possession; John C. Danforth to PT, 11 Nov. 1976, Virginia.

3. Anatole Broyard, Review of *In the Miro District,* by PT, *New York Times Book Review,* 3 Apr. 1977, p. 14; Jonathan Yardley, "Discovering an American Master," *Washington Post Book World,* 10 Apr. 1977, p. E7; Doris Grumbach, "Short Stories to Long Remember," *Los Angeles Times Book Review,* 24 Apr. 1977, p. 14; Margaret Manning, "Peter Taylor, An Original," *Boston Globe,* 10 Apr. 1977, p. E1; Larry Swindell, "Stories As Stories Should Be," *Philadelphia Inquirer,* 10 Apr. 1977, p. D3; AT to PT, 14 Apr. 1974, Virginia.

4. Alfred A. Knopf memo to PT, 18 Apr. 1977, Knopf files; AT to PT, 2 Mar. 1976, Vanderbilt; PT to Dr. and Mrs. Thomas Paine, 10 May 1977, in her possession; PT to AT, 24 May 1977, Princeton; Lawrence Reynolds, Molyneux memoir, in his possession.

5. PT to AT, 24 May 1977, Princeton; Lawrence Reynolds, Molyneux memoir; PT to Mr. and Mrs. Molyneux, 30 May 1977, copy in the possession of Jacob Molyneux.

6. PT to AT, 24 May 1977, Princeton.

7. PT to Lawrence Reynolds, 10 May 1977, in his possession; ERT to RL, 1 July 1977, Texas.

8. PT to JT, 30 July 1977, JT.

9. RL to PT and ERT, 4 Sept. 1976, Vanderbilt.

10. ERT, 2 Apr. 1998; PT, 1 Sept. 1987; PT to W. H. Bond, 26 Sept. 1976, ERT; David Lynn, "Peter Taylor and the Kenyon Connection," in *COPT,* 130–31.

11. Richard F. Shepard, "Majestic Service Marks Farewell to Robert Lowell," *New York Times,* 11 Sept. 1977, p. 25; JT to PT, 9 Oct. 1977, Vanderbilt.

12. Ruth Dean, "Peter Taylor: A Private World of Southern Writing," in *CWPT,* 28–29.

13. Robert Wilson, "A Smiling Sixty-Year-Old Public Man," in "Garland," 83; ERT, 20 June 1995; JT to PT, 9 Oct. 1977, Vanderbilt.

14. PT, "Robert Lowell," draft, Vanderbilt; PT, "Robert Traill Spence Lowell," *Proceedings of the American Academy and Institute of Arts and Letters,* 2d ser., no. 28 (1978), 71–79; PT to JT, 19 Nov. 1977, JT.

15. PT to Dr. and Mrs. Thomas Paine, 4 Jan. 1978, in her possession; PT to AT, 24 May 1977, Princeton; "Acceptance by PT," *Proceedings of the American Academy and Institute of Arts and Letters,* 2nd ser., no. 29 (1979), 31–32.

16. Lawrence Reynolds, 12 June 1999.

17. ERT, 4 June 1998; PT to RPW, 11 June 1978, Yale; McPherson letters to PT, Vanderbilt; John Casey, 15 June 1999.

18. Jane Barnes, 11 Jan. 1995.

19. The Jane Barnes Casey and Alan Williamson essays are collected in *CEOPT*—see pp. 124–35 and 136–47, respectively.

20. PT to RPW, 11 June 1978, Yale; Don Keck DuPree, "An Interview with PT," *CWPT,* 58, 56; BT, "Interview with PT," *CWPT,* 142; PT to Frances Kiernan, 1 Aug. 1978, *New Yorker* Records, New York Public Library; PT to Frances Kiernan, 12 Aug. 1978, in her possession.

21. PT to RPW, 11 June 1978, Yale; ERT to TW and Sarah Booth White, 14 Oct. 1995, TW; PT to Grace Benedict Paine, 29 Oct. 1978, in her possession; PT to JS, Monday, Colorado.

22. PT to Frances Kiernan, 3 Jan. 1979, in her possession; Jonathan Yardley, "Who's Peter Taylor? The Best Unknown Writer Around," *Miami Herald,* 10 Apr. 1977, p. E1; Richard Wilbur, 5 Oct. 1994; Robert and Martha Wilson, 12 Sept. 1999.

23. Stephen Goodwin to PT, 6 Feb. 1979, Vanderbilt; Alison Lurie, 13 Sept. 1999; Richard Wilbur, 5 Oct. 1994; Elizabeth Hardwick, 19 Nov. 1994.

24. Yardley, 7E; Richard Wilbur, 5 Oct. 1994.

25. Liz Lear, 15 Sept. 1995; Alison Lurie, 13 Sept. 1999; Richard Wilbur, 5 Oct. 1994.

26. PT to AT, 24 May 1977 and 24 Oct. [1974]—both Princeton; JT, 16 Nov. 1994; David Roberts, *Jean Stafford: A Biography* (Boston: Little, Brown, 1988), 413.

27. Breece Pancake to PT and ERT, 7 Mar. 1977 and 9 Jan. 1978, and James Alan McPherson to PT, 30 May 1979—all Vanderbilt; John Casey, 15 June 1999.

28. Frances Kiernan to PT, 4 June 1979, and ERT to PT, 9 Aug. 1979—both Vanderbilt.

29. Daniel O'Neill, 15 June 1999.

30. PT records, University of Virginia Medical Center, 1978–80, TW; James Merrill to PT, 17 June 1980, Vanderbilt; ERT, 14 Sept. 1999.

31. Malcolm Jones, "Mr. Peter Taylor When Last Seen," *Greensboro Daily News/ Record,* 27 July 1980, p. C5; ERT, Sewanee real estate notes; *Yaddo Annual Report 1980,* p. 7; RPW to PT, 5 Aug. 1980, Vanderbilt.

32. PT to Frances Kiernan, 7 Sept. 1980 and 23 Feb. 1981, both in her possession; Frances Kiernan, 14 June 1993.

33. Jean Strouse, "Cream of the Crop," and Walter Clemons, "Songs of the South," *Time,* 3 Nov. 1980, pp. 86, 85; PT, "Eudora Welty," in *Eudora Welty: A Tribute* (Printed for Stuart Wright: 1984), 31–32; Robert Wilson, 12 Sept. 1999.

34. Robert and Betty Watson, 29 Mar. 1995; PT, interview with BT, 11 Dec. 1981; TW, 25 Oct. 1995; Alan Williamson, 10 May 1995; PT, 11 Sept. 1991.

35. James Merrill to PT, 16 Aug. 1981, Vanderbilt; BT, 14 June 1993.

36. Duane Whelan to PT, 6 Apr. 1981, Vanderbilt; Daniel O'Neill, 15 June 1999.

37. BT, 14 June 1993; Daniel O'Neill, 15 June 1999; James Alan McPherson to PT, 7 June 1981, Vanderbilt.

38. PT to AT, 24 May 1977, Princeton; Daniel O'Neill, 15 June 1999.

39. SW, 24 Sept. 1998; Stephen J. Ross, 20 Oct. 1995; Jerusha Northrop, "Homecoming for Filmmaker Ross," *Bridgeport Post,* 7 Apr. 1985, p. C1.

40. PT, interview with BT, 10 Dec. 1981.

Chapter 17: Turning Points

1. PT to SW, 27 Jan. 1982, SW; BT, 14 June 1993; deeds to 1207 Pine Street, ERT; ERT, 21 Sept. 1999.

2. BT, 14 June 1993; BT, "Interview with PT," in *CWPT,* 169.

3. PT to Judith Jones, 1 Aug. 1982, Knopf files.

4. PT contract with Alfred A. Knopf, 20 Aug. 1980, and Judith Jones to PT, 18 Oct. [1982], and Judith Jones to Tim Seldes, 19 Nov. 1982—all Knopf files; Judith Jones, 18 Nov. 1994.

5. Robert Jennings, "Taylors' Real Home Now Movie Home," *Memphis Commercial Appeal,* 8 Dec. 1982, p. D4; "Academy of Arts and Letters—U. Va.'s Taylor Elected," *Charlottesville Observer,* Dec. 9–15, 1982, pp. 1, 25; PT, 21 July 1986.

6. PT to Dale Richardson, undated draft [fall 1982], Vanderbilt; ERT, 14 June 1999.

7. Stephen Goodwin to PT, 23 May 1983, Vanderbilt; Richard Howard, "Eat Some, Drink Some, Bury Some," *Kenyon Review* 44 (fall 1992): 184–89; Alan Williamson, "Between Two Worlds: The Poetry of Eleanor Ross Taylor," in *Eloquence and Mere Life: Essays on the Art of Poetry* (Ann Arbor: University of Michigan Press, 1994), 56–64; Frederic C. Beil contract, 2 May 1983, Vanderbilt; ERT, 21 Sept. 1999.

8. Robert Taylor to PT, 5 Mar. 1983, ERT; Wyatt Prunty, 1 Dec. 1994.

9. Stephen J. Ross, 18 Sept. 1999; Mimi Bennett Mitchell to PT, 23 Aug. 1972, ERT; Thomas E. Mitchell, 17 July 1995; JWB, "A Conversation with PT," in *CWPT,* 91.

10. Brian Griffin, 23 Sept. 1999; Brian Griffin, "A Conversation Continues: Some Memories of Peter Taylor," *New Millennium* 2 (winter 1997–98), 146.

11. Timothy Seldes to PT, 12 Aug. 1976, ERT; Daniel O'Neill, 15 June 1999; Doubleday contract, 23 Sept. 1983, and Allen H. Peacock to PT, 23 Oct. 1983—both ERT.

12. Allen H. Peacock to PT, 15 Feb. 1984, ERT; Jean Ross Justice, 24 Sept. 1999; ERT, 14 Sept. 1999.

13. PT to James Thackara, 6 May 1984, in his possession; Tom Jenks, "In the Works," *Esquire,* August 1984, p. 116.

14. RPW to PT, 6 Dec. 1984, and PT to RPW, undated draft [spring 1985]—both Vanderbilt.

15. Frances McCullough to PT, 4 Sept. 1984, ERT; Review of *The Old Forest,* by PT, *Publishers Weekly,* 21 Dec. 1984, p. 81; Wendy Smith, "PW Interviews: Peter Taylor," *Publishers Weekly,* 18 Jan. 1985, pp. 77–78; Stephen J. Ross, 20 Oct. 1995.

16. Anne Tyler, "Peter Taylor: The Lessons of the Master," *USA Today,* 26 Jan. 1985, p. 3D; Walter Clemons, "Southern Comfort," *Newsweek,* 11 Mar. 1985, p. 74; Jonathan Yardley, "Peter Taylor: The Quiet Virtuoso," *Washington Post Book World,* 27 Jan. 1985, p. 3; Robert Towers, "A Master of the Miniature Novel," *New York Times Book Review,* 17 Feb. 1985, pp. F1, F26; Paul Gray, "Codes of Honor," *Time,* 4 Feb. 1985, p. 74.

17. PT, 26 Feb. 1985; JWB to HHM, 28 Sept. 1994; transcription of JWB interview with PT, 15 Feb. 1985, JWB.

18. PT to RPW, undated draft [Mar. 1985], Vanderbilt; Deaderick C. Montague to PT, 22 Mar. 1985, Vanderbilt; SW, *Peter Taylor: A Descriptive Bibliography, 1934–87* (Charlottesville: University Press of Virginia, 1988), 52; J. D. McClatchy, Review of *The Old Forest and Other Stories,* by PT, *Saturday Review of Literature,* May–June 1985, pp. 73–74.

19. ERT to Patricia and Hubert McAlexander, 23 July 1985, HHM; PT Russell and Volkening file for 1985, ERT; JWB, Broadway Journal: Peter Taylor Conversations, 22 Sept. 1985–19 Sept. 1994, 1 Dec. 1985, JWB; Robert Giroux to PT, 4 Sept. 1985, ERT.

20. PT to TW, 25 Nov. 1985, TW; PT files, 1985 and 1986, Alfred A. Knopf.

21. PT, 5 Jan. 1986; Stephen Goodwin, 27 Sept. 1999.

22. PT, 27 May 1986; Elizabeth Kastor, "The Author Side of the Story," *Washington Post,* 12 May 1986, p. B1; Stephen Goodwin, 27 Sept. 1999; PT to James Thackara, 27 June 1986, in his possession.

23. PT, 20 July 1986; ERT, 27 July 1986.

24. PT, 30 Aug. 1986; Broadway Journal, 3 Sept. 1986; Eudora Welty to PT, Sunday night [17 Sept. 1986], and Elizabeth Hardwick to PT, 11 Aug. 1986—both Vanderbilt.

25. "Esquire's Guide to the Literary Universe," *Esquire,* Aug. 1987, p. 56; Paul Gray, "Codes of Honor," *Time,* 4 Feb. 1985, p. 74; HHM, "A Composite Conversation with PT," in *CWPT,* 127.

26. Review of *A Summons to Memphis,* by PT, *Publishers Weekly,* 1 Aug. 1986, p. 68; Jonathan Yardley, "Peter Taylor's Novel of Fathers and Sons," *Washington Post Book World,* 14 Sept. 1986, p. 3; Paul Gray, "Civil Wars in the Upper South," *Time,* 29 Sept. 1986, p. 71; Walter Clemons, "You Can't Go Home Again," *Newsweek,* 29 Sept. 1986, p. 64; Robert Wilson, "Peter Taylor's Perfect Puzzle," *USA Today,* 3 Oct. 1986, p. 4D: Michiko Kakutani, "Books of The Times," *New York Times,* 24 Sept. 1986, p. 24; Robert Towers, "Way Down South," *New York Review of Books,* 25 Sept. 1986, p. 57.

27. John Updike, "Summons, Indictments, Extenuating Circumstances," *New Yorker,* 3 Nov. 1986, pp. 158–65. Michael Gorra notes the conspicuous omission of

Peter Taylor in *The Best American Short Stories of the Century,* a volume co-edited by Updike in 1999. See "Supreme Fictions," *New York Times Book Review,* 9 May 1999, p. 8.

28. Marilynne Robinson, "The Family Game Was Revenge," *New York Times Book Review,* 19 Oct. 1986, p. 1; Ann Hulbert, "Back to the Future," *New Republic,* 24 Nov. 1986, pp. 37–40.

29. PT, 29 Oct. 1986; Charles Trueheart, "Awards to Doctorow, Lopez: Much Attention Is Focused on Peter Taylor's Protest," *Washington Post,* 18 Nov. 1986, p. D1.

30. PT to Judith Jones, 21 Nov. 1986, Knopf files; Broadway Journal, 26 Dec. 1986 and 11 Mar. 1987; PT 1987 appointment calendar, ERT; Robert Wilson, 10 Oct. 1999.

31. PT, 17 Apr. 1987; Robert Wilson, 10 Oct. 1999.

32. William Thomas, "Pulitzer, Champagne 'Wonderful,' " *Memphis Commercial Appeal,* 17 Apr. 1987, p. 2; Mary Polk Kirby-Smith, 10 Aug. 1995; Jonathan Yardley, "Peter Taylor's Long-Overdue Pulitzer," *Washington Post,* 20 Apr. 1987, p. B2; HHM, "A Composite Conversation with PT," 124; Eudora Welty to PT, 16 Apr. 1987, Vanderbilt.

Chapter 18: Art and Life

1. Stephen Goodwin, 27 Sept. 1999; Mieke H. Bomann, "Once More, with Feeling: Peter Taylor Summons Up That Southern Mystique," *Kenyon College Alumni Bulletin,* Sept. 1987, p. 18; PT, JWB interview, 20 June 1987.

2. BT, 14 June 1993; Bomann, 16.

3. JWB, Broadway Journal, 13 Aug. 1987; PT to SW, 3 July 1987, SW; James Alan McPherson to PT, 30 Aug. 1987, Vanderbilt; Donald La Badie, "Pulitzer Prize–Winning Author Is Summoned to Memphis," *Memphis Commercial Appeal,* 14 Sept. 1987, pp. C1–2.

4. PT, 30 Aug. 1987; JWB, Broadway Journal, 2 Oct. 1987; Bess Gore to PT, 1 Nov. 1987, Vanderbilt.

5. PT, 3 Sept. 1987 and 14 Dec. 1987.

6. JWB, Broadway Journal, 2 Oct. 1987 and 17 Nov. 1987.

7. JWB, Broadway Journal, 1 Feb. 1988; PT, 16 Feb. 1988. This piece appeared first as "Something in Her Instep High" in *Key West Review* 1 (fall 1988): 7–18.

8. PT to RPW, 12 Feb. 1988, Vanderbilt; Alison Lurie, 13 Sept. 1999; James Thackara, 27 Aug. 1998 and 4 Oct. 1999; James Thackara to PT, 16 Mar. 1988, Vanderbilt.

9. Thomas E. Mitchell, 17 July 1995.

10. Cleanth Brooks to PT, 2 June 1988, Vanderbilt; JWB, Broadway Journal, 11 Aug. 1988; PT, 29 Sept. 1988.

11. Frances Kiernan to PT, 15 Dec. [1987], and Pat Strachan to PT, 7 Apr. 1988 and 31 Aug. 1988—all Vanderbilt.

12. PT, 13 Nov. and 23 Oct. 1988; JWB, Broadway Journal, 7 Dec. 1988; PT, 2 Apr. 1989.

13. Thomas E. Mitchell, 17 July 1995; Thomas E. Mitchell to PT, 14 Mar. 1988, Vanderbilt.

14. Donald La Badie, "Taylor Still Hooked on Overton Park," *Memphis Commercial Appeal,* 18 June 1989, pp. G1–2; PT, 24 Apr. 1989.

15. Brian Griffin, 16 Sept. 1999; Stephen Goodwin, "An Interview with PT," in *CWPT,* 9; BT, "Interview with PT," in *CWPT,* 142–43.

16. PT, "Jean Stafford, 1915–1979," *Proceedings of the American Academy and Institute of Arts and Letters,* 2nd series, no. 30 (1980): 82–83; Brian Griffin, "The Conversation Continues: Some Memories of Peter Taylor," *New Millennium Writings* 2, no. 2 (winter 1997–98): 147–48.

17. Brian Griffin, 16 Sept. 1999; PT to HHM, 1 Aug. 1989, HHM; ERT, 20 July 1999; JWB, Broadway Journal, 7 Jan. 1990.

18. JWB, Broadway Journal, 22 Oct. 1989; PT, 24 Oct. 1989.

19. Pat Strachan to PT, 16 Nov. 1989, Vanderbilt; Brian Griffin to HHM, 23 Sept. 1999, HHM.

20. Charles E. Claffey, "John Casey Writes 'Words I Couldn't Say," *Boston Globe,* 22 Dec. 1989, pp. 43, 55; PT, 15 Jan. 1990.

21. JWB, Broadway Journal, 7 Jan. 1990; PT, 15 Jan. 1990; Lawrence Reynolds diary, 28 Jan. 1990.

22. PT, 18 Feb. and 14 Apr. 1990, JWB, Broadway Journal, 6 Mar. 1990; Patricia J. McAlexander, 22 Apr. 1990.

23. PT, 30 May 1990 and 30 Aug. 1990; ERT to HHM, 30 Sept. 1996, HHM; John Reishman to PT and ERT, 12 Sept. 1990, Vanderbilt.

24. PT, 30 Aug. 1990 and 6 Jan. 1991; JWB, Broadway Journal, 30 Nov. 1990; Marnie Polk Ross, 30 Mar. 1995; PT, 2 Apr. 1991; *New Yorker,* 11 Mar. 1991, p. 34.

25. PT, 2 Apr. 1991 and 16 July 1991; "The Megalopolitans," *Ploughshares* 2, no. 4 (1975): 141–50.

26. Madison Smartt Bell, "Less Is Less: The Dwindling American Short Story," *Harper's* 272 (Apr. 1986): 69.

27. PT, 24 June 1991 and 5 Nov. 1991; Mark Trainer to PT, 26 June 1999, Vanderbilt.

28. John Casey, 15 June 1999; PT, 16 July 1991 and 11 Aug. 1991.

29. PT, 11 Sept. 1991; PT to Lawrence Reynolds, undated [late Nov. 1991], in his possession; PT to Judith Jones, 20 Nov. 1991, Knopf files; JWB, Broadway Journal, 13 Dec. 1991; PT and ERT to Hubert and Patricia McAlexander, 20 Dec. 1991, HHM.

30. Knopf PT files, 1992; contract for *The Oracle at Stoneleigh Court,* ERT.

31. PT, 3 May 1992 and 19 Oct. 1992; Jean Ross Justice, 24 Sept. 1999; ERT to

Sarah Booth White, 21 Oct. [1992], in her possession; Mark Trainer, "Notes from a Typist," *Charlottesville Weekly,* 20–26 Dec. 1994, p. 11.

32. Mark Trainer, 29 Oct. 1999; Judith Jones to PT, 18 Dec. 1992, Vanderbilt.

33. PT and ERT to Hubert and Patricia McAlexander, 22 Dec. 1992, HHM; PT, 14 Feb. and 23 Mar. 1993.

34. Christopher Metress, "An Oracle of Mystery: A Conversation with Peter Taylor," in *COPT,* 146; Gail Godwin, "The Things That Haunt Them," *New York Times Book Review,* 21 Feb. 1993, pp. 13–15; Jonathan Yardley, "Peter Taylor: A Late Flowering," *Washington Post Book World,* 21 Feb. 1993, p. 3; Wendy Lesser, "Free Spirits," *New Republic,* 8 Mar. 1993, pp. 40–41; Joyce Carol Oates, "In Familiar Haunts," *Times Literary Supplement,* 19 Feb. 1993, p. 21; Robert Towers, "Out of the Blue," *New York Review of Books,* 25 Mar. 1993, pp. 43–45.

35. Kathryn Court to PT, 23 Sept. 1992, ERT; Ben Yagoda, "The Oracle of the South," *Washington Post Magazine,* 9 May 1993, pp. 11–13, 29–30; PT, 23 Mar. 1993.

36. PT, 3 Apr. 1993; RT, 30 Oct. 1999; PT to Judith Jones, 3 Mar. 1993, and Judith Jones to PT, 7 Apr. 1993—both Knopf files.

37. PT to Judith Jones, 3 Mar. 1993, and Judith Jones to PT, 7 Apr. 1993—both Knopf files; Mark Trainer, 29 Oct. 1999; PT, 9 June 1993.

38. Peter Taylor discussed his original conception of the novel and then his changing vision in three interviews—one on 9 Sept. 1987 with James Curry Robison, published in his book *Peter Taylor: A Study of the Short Fiction* (Boston: G. K. Hall, 1988), 141; the second in Feb. 1991, with Dannye Romine Powell, published as "An Interview with Peter and Eleanor Ross Taylor," *Mississippi Review* 20 (1991): 46; and the third with Christopher Metress on 11 Aug. 1993, published as "An Oracle of Mystery," in *COPT,* 143–56.

39. PT, 9 June 1993; JWB, Broadway Journal, 12 June 1993; PT to Judith Jones, 2 June 1993, Knopf files.

40. PT to Judith Jones, 16 July and 30 Aug. 1993; PT, 5 Aug. 1993; Metress, 144.

41. PT, 6 Oct., 14 Oct., 2 Nov. 1993.

42. PT, 28 Nov., 18 Nov., 11 Dec. 1993.

43. Judith Jones to PT, 22 Dec. 1993 and 14 January 1994, Knopf files; PT, 11 Jan. and 22 Feb. 1994.

44. ERT to Grace Benedict Paine, 5 Feb. 1994, in her possession; Wyatt Prunty, 1 Dec. 1994; PT, 22 Feb. 1994.

45. Mark Trainer, 29 Oct. 1999; ERT, 9 June, 17 June, 4 July 1993; PT, 5 Aug., 11 Aug. 1994.

46. PT, 11 Aug. 1993; Mark Trainer, 28 July 1995 and 29 Oct. 1999; Robert Wilson, "Peter Taylor: All He Could Do Anymore Was Write," *Atlanta Journal Constitution,* 13 Nov. 1994, p. D11.

47. Mary Flanagan, "In the Land of Lost Men," *New York Times Book Review,* 28 Aug. 1994, p. 6; Martha Duffy, "Odd Cousin, Far Removed," *Time,* 22 Aug. 1994, p. 84; Sam Walker, "A Languid Narrator Spins a Southern Tale," *Christian Science Monitor,* 26 Aug. 1994, p. 13; Jonathan Yardley, "Precious Memory Is All," *Washington Post Book World,* 21 Aug. 1994, p. 3; Alicia Metcalf Miller, "Blinking Back Lifelong Reality," *Cleveland Plain Dealer,* 7 Aug. 1994, p. C1; PT, 13 Sept. 1994.

48. PT, 13 Sept. and 30 Sept. 1994; ERT, 26 Oct. and 3 Nov. 1994.

Index